D1590255

"OUR CONNECTION WITH SAVANNAH"

Major Arthur Shaaf (Courtesy of the Maryland Historical Society)

"OUR CONNECTION WITH SAVANNAH"

History of the First Battalion
Georgia Sharpshooters
1862-1865

Russell K. Brown

Mercer University Press
Macon, Georgia
25th Anniversary

ISBN 0-86554-916-8
MUP/H673

© 2004 Mercer University Press
1400 Coleman Avenue
Macon, Georgia 31207

First Edition.

∞The paper used in this publication meets the minimum requirements
of American National Standard for Information
Sciences—Permanence of Paper for Printed Library Materials, ANSI
Z39.48-1992.

Library of Congress Cataloging-in-Publication Data

Brown, Russell K.
"Our connection with Savannah" : history of the First Battalion
Georgia
Sharpshooters, 1862-1865 / Russell K. Brown.-- 1st Edition.
    p. cm.
Includes bibliographical references and index.
ISBN 0-86554-916-8 (hardcover : alk. paper)
1. Confederate States of America. Army. Georgia Sharpshooters, 1st
Battalion. 2. Georgia—History--Civil War, 1861-1865—Regimental
histories. 3. United States—History—Civil War, 1861-1865—
Regimental histories. I. Title.
E559.9.B76 2004
973.7'458—dc22

2004020510

For my own squad of sharpshooters,
Andy, Pam and Suzanne,
Evelyn and Margaret,
Jim and Steve:
A Father's Love

CONTENTS

The Publication of this book is due in part to a generous gift from the Watson-Brown Foundation.

PREFACE

More than a dozen years ago, while working on the biography of General W.H.T. Walker, I became acquainted with the First Battalion Georgia Sharpshooters and their combat commander, Major Arthur Shaaff. Some six years later I began a biographic sketch of Shaaff for a possible magazine article but soon gave up for lack of material. In December 2001 I stumbled across Kevin Thurman's web page devoted to the 1st Georgia Sharpshooters. That was catalyst enough to renew my interest in Arthur Shaaff and to expand the scope of my project to write a full history of the unit while highlighting Shaaff's role in its activities. Soon afterward I opened a correspondence with Kevin and this is the result.

Kevin's interest in our topic, his generosity in sharing sources and contacts, his unflagging enthusiasm in forging ahead when my own energy or interest waned, and his knowledgeable reading and constructive criticism of passages of my writing have all contributed greatly to completion of this book. It would be fair to say that this work would never have been completed without his participation. In addition to gaining a research collaborator, in meeting Kevin I also found a friend and associate with common interests and common outlook, despite our differences in age and origins.

Many other persons contributed to the making of this story and I want to list some of them here. I am indebted to Brenda Kepley, especially, and to Jill Abraham, Charles Johnson and Trevor Plant of the Old Military and Civil Records Branch, National Archives, Washington, D.C., for response to telephone, email and postal requests for information, and for assistance in finding source material when I was at the Archives. John and Ruth Coski, at the Eleanor S. Brockenbrough Library, Museum of the Confederacy, Richmond, Va., rendered valuable assistance by mail and during my visit to their facility. Andy Phrydas and Carl Andersen, Georgia Department of Archives and History, formerly in Atlanta and now in Morrow, Georgia., and Joanna McDonald, U.S. Army Military History Institute, Carlisle, Pennsylvania., helped me penetrate the intricacies of their archival collections to find the material I wanted. In like manner, Jewell Anderson Dalrymple, Research Coordinator at the library of the Georgia Historical Society, Savannah, provided assistance in ferreting out and copying useful information. Howard M. Madaus, Curator, National Civil War Museum, Harrisburg, Pennsylvania, and Greg Biggs, Clarksville, Tennessee, especially the latter, both authorities on Confederate battle flags, lent me some of their expertise. Wanda McGahee, McCollum Public Library, Wrens, Georgia, adjusted her work schedule to allow me more time to use materials in her library. Archivists and research assistants at other institutions deserve thanks for responding to my letters, emails and phone calls seeking documents, photographs, copies, or clarification of details of information. I did not always find what I wanted, but help and courtesy were universally available.

Two individuals deserve recognition in their own categories. One is Paulette Pack, interlibrary loan coordinator at Woodworth Library, Fort Gordon, Georgia. Mrs. Pack patiently sorted through my seemingly endless stream of requests for books and microfilm and never once let me down in finding what I asked for, no matter how esoteric. The other is my daughter, Pamela Brown Robinson, an accomplished reference librarian, whose skill in discovering electronic sources of information in the new world of cyberspace was both a revelation and a help to me. My heartfelt thanks to Paulette Pack and Pam Robinson.

Special mention should be made of Rhonda Watson, Director, and the volunteer staff at the Latter Day Saints Family History Center in Evans, Georgia. Without their help, my ability to access and use National Archives microfilm records would have been severely restricted, if not impossible. I thank them all, individually and as a group, for their cheerful and patient assistance. Also, I wish to thank Fay Verburg, Director of Reference Services, Reese Library, Augusta State University, Augusta, Georgia., and Charles "Rick" Sulzycki of her staff for assistance with their collections and for help in copying images of sharpshooters.

I gratefully acknowledge the assistance of Richard A. Baumgartner of Acorn Press, Huntington, W.Va., and William S. Smedlund, Sharpsburg, Georgia, themselves established historians and authors, who shared with me some sharpshooter research material they had collected and tried to help me find more. Dr. Keith Bohannon, State University of West Georgia, Carrollton, Georgia, provided useful information. Maps and drawings in this book were prepared by the expert hand of Bill Blackard, Appling, Georgia. When it appeared that I might be stranded without a mapmaker, Bill stepped into the breach and made readable maps of my awkward sketches. Any errors or omissions in these maps are mine and not Bill's.

Another kind of assistance was given by descendants of the sharpshooters, direct or collateral. Among them were Lt. Gen. Ranald T. Adams, Jr., Alexandria, Virginia; Betty Fitzgerald Brown and her son, Royal Fitzgerald Brown, Rochelle, Georgia; Horace D. Brown, Miami, Florida; Barbra Crites,

Tampa, Fla.; Edward John Derst, III, Savannah, Georgia; Fred Gleaton, Atlanta, Georgia; Betty Bennett Joiner, Gainesville, Georgia, with whom I communicated through Kevin Thurman; Eileen King, Rockville, Maryland; Edwin R. MacKethan, III, Grosse Pointe Farms, Michigan; Father James Thornton, Garden Grove, California; Joe D. Parrott, Decatur, Alabama; Thomas A. Valentine, Roswell, Georgia, and Linda L. Valentine, Ellijay, Georgia; and Cindy Forehand Watts, Conyers, Georgia. Besides learning colorful details about the lives of the soldiers, I found people who were willing, even eager to share some of the stored oral and written history of their ancestors. I am grateful to Betty and Royal Brown for providing a trove of wartime letters and a photograph of their ancestor with permission to publish them. Ranald Adams and Tom Valentine provided photographs of their ancestors, with permission to publish, Horace D. Brown gave permission to quote from his memoir of his grandfather, and Eileen King granted permission to quote from her copy of a wartime journal.

Other than those mentioned above, permission to quote from published or manuscript sources or to use photographic images has been granted by the following: Honorable Richard B. Abell, Alexandria, Va.: *Sojourns of a Patriot: The Field and Prison Papers of an Unreconstructed Confederate*; Broadfoot Publishing Co., Wilmington, North Carolina: James H. Wilson Journal and photographic image of Thomas S. Wayne; Robert B. Woodruff Library, Emory University, Atlanta, Georgia: James McCord Letter, Civil War Miscellany Collection; Georgia Department of Archives and History, Morrow, Georgia: C.M. Hardy Letters 1861-1864, Mrs. O.E. Lancaster Collection; Georgia Department of Natural Resources, Parks and Historic Sites Division, Hofwyl-Broadfield Plantation State Historic Site, Brunswick, Georgia: photograph of George Columbus Dent; Georgia Historical Society, Savannah, Georgia: George A. Mercer Diary; *The Memoirs of Charles Olmstead*; C.C. Wilson Letters; Nathaniel C. Hughes, Jr., Chattanooga, Tenn.: *General William J. Hardee, "Old Reliable;"* Eugene W. Jones, Jr., Goose Creek, South Carolina: *Enlisted for the War: The Struggles of the Gallant 24th Regiment, South Carolina Volunteers, Infantry, 1861-1865*; Maryland Historical Society, Baltimore, Maryland: image of Arthur Shaaff; Eleanor S. Brockenbrough Library, Museum of the Confederacy, Richmond, Virginia: Department of South Carolina and Georgia Collection; Dr. Benjamin C. Rountree, Amherst, Massachusetts: Letters of Angus McDermid; Tennessee State Library and Archives, Nashville, Tennessee: B.F. Cheatham Papers; Georgia Division, United Daughters of the Confederacy, Atlanta: *Confederate Reminiscences and Letters, 1861-1865*, Vol. 6; University of Georgia Press, Athens, Georgia: *Confederate Letters of John W. Hagan*; Hargrett Rare Book and Manuscript Library, University of Georgia Libraries, Athens: Hamilton Branch Letters, Margaret Branch Sexton Collection; Southern Historical Collection, University of North Carolina, Chapel Hill, North Carolina: Thomas Butler King Family Papers, William Whann Mackall Papers, William Moody Letters; South Caroliniana Library, University of South Carolina, Columbia, South Carolina: Clement H. Stevens Papers, Williams-Chesnut-Manning Family Papers; Western Reserve Historical Society, Cleveland, Ohio: William P. Palmer Collection of Braxton Bragg Papers.

It is with considerable regret that I acknowledge two failures in my research efforts, namely, my inability to obtain permission to use some historic images from Savannah that I wanted, the colors of the DeKalb Rifles and a portrait of "Captain" John Derst.

Few books, no matter how absorbing or informative, can reach the public without the assistance of editor and publisher. It was my good luck to be steered to Mercer University Press by several friends and colleagues, and to find there Dr. Marc Jolley. Accomplished in the skills of his profession, and familiar with the foibles and wiles of writers, Marc has been a joy to work with and has become a trusted adviser, not only for publication, but also for historiography. I owe much to his patient counsel and insightful interpretation of my intentions. My thanks also to the members of his staff.

I cannot omit to express gratitude to my wife, Jin Brown. For almost three years she has forsworn interesting vacations for research field trips, spent evenings and weekends alone in the house while I was huddled over the computer keyboard, reheated meals gone cold, shared with me my shouts of glee over facts discovered or groans of dismay over files lost, and otherwise served as a sounding board for ideas and opinions about events and persons long since past. Not a murmur of complaint has passed her lips; in fact, she gives me only love and encouragement.

It should be said that despite the generous and valuable input of all the individuals and organizations named here, this unit history is wholly my own creation. Any real or perceived errors in fact, interpretation, opinion, or conclusion rest fully with me. I hope that readers will enjoy reading it as much as I have enjoyed creating it. I take credit for all of its good qualities and accept blame for all of its shortcomings.

Russell K. Brown
Grovetown, Georgia
August 1, 2004

PHOTOGRAPHS, ILLUSTRATIONS, AND MAPS

BRIG. GEN. ROBERT H. ANDERSON.

Robert H. Anderson
Organizer of the Sharpshooters
(*Roll of Officers and Members
of the Georgia Hussars*)

ALFRED BRYAN.

Alfred Bryan
(*Roll of Officers and
Members of the Georgia
Hussars*)

George C. Dent as a young
man (Courtesy of the
Georgia Department of
Natural Resources,
Hofwyl-Broadfield State
Historic Site)

Richard Cuyler King (Courtesy of Lt. Gen. Ranald T. Adams Jr.)

John Isom Royal (Courtesy of Betty and Royal F. Brown)

Green L. Sheppherd
(Courtesy of Richard A. Baumgartner)

William Lewis Valentine
(Courtesy of Thomas A. Valentine)

Thomas S. Wayne (Courtesy of
Broadfoot Publishing)

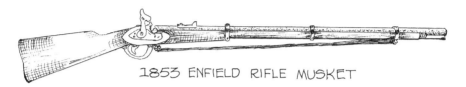

1853 Enfield Rifle Musket
(By Bill Blackard)

Sharpshooters on the Skirmish Line.
(By Bill Blackard)

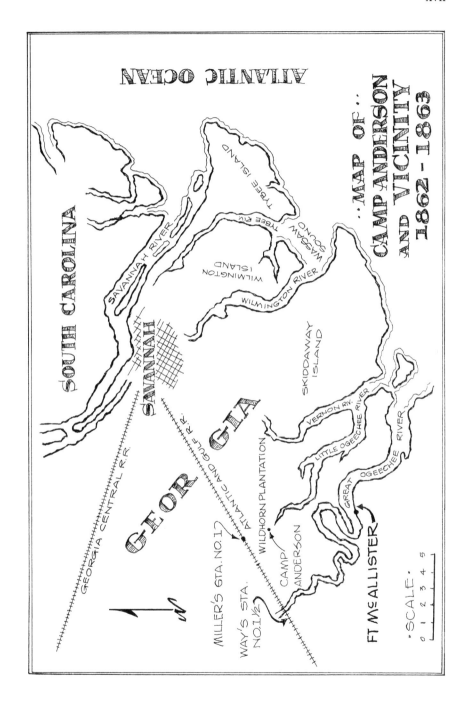

McPHERSON

SOUTHERN RR OF MISS.

WALKER
EARLY AM

NEW ORLEANS, JACKSON & GREAT NORTHERN RR

TO CANTON

FORTIFICATIONS

N
W — E
S

0.0   0.5
SCALE IN MILES

UNION
CONFEDERATE

RETREAT
2:30 PM

DEPOT

JACKSON

DEPOT

LYNCH CREEK

THOMPSON
3 KY.

TUTTLE
2 PM

FORTIFICATIONS

SHERMAN

TUTTLE
11 AM

1 GA. 55
MARTIN'S
GA. BTTY.

STEELE
4 PM

PEARL RIVER

BATTLE OF JACKSON
MAY 14, 1863

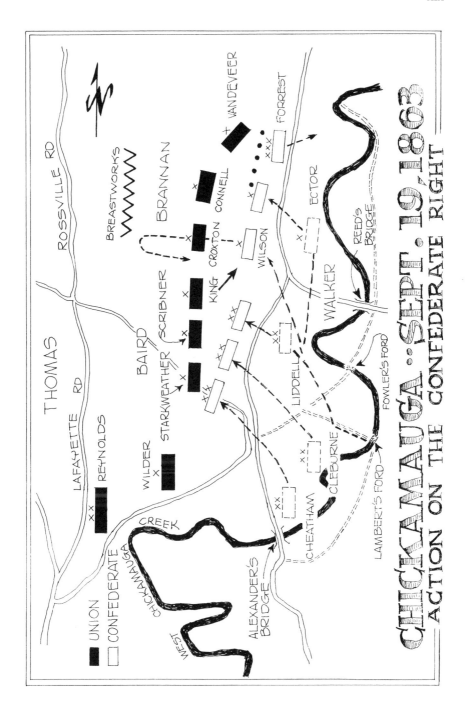

CHICKAMAUGA · SEPT. 19 1863
ACTION ON THE CONFEDERATE RIGHT

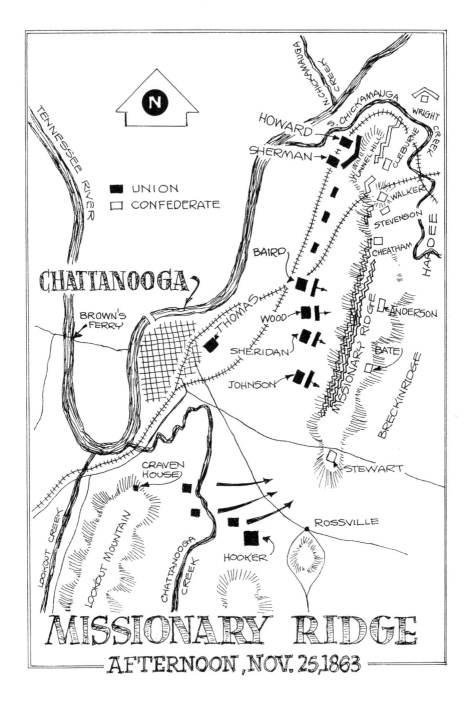

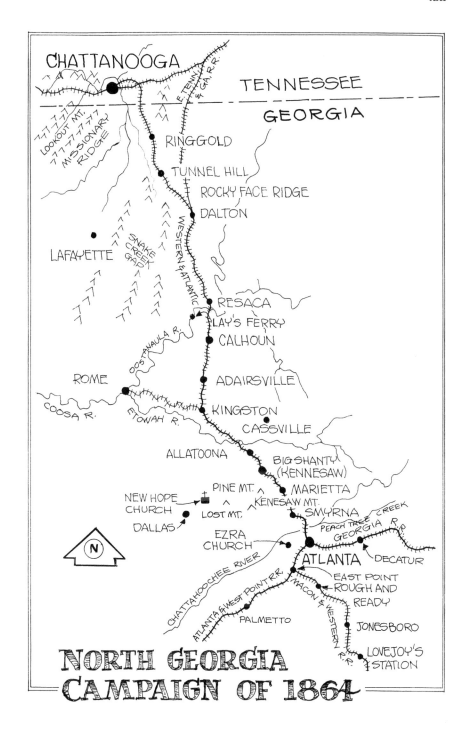

NORTH GEORGIA
CAMPAIGN OF 1864

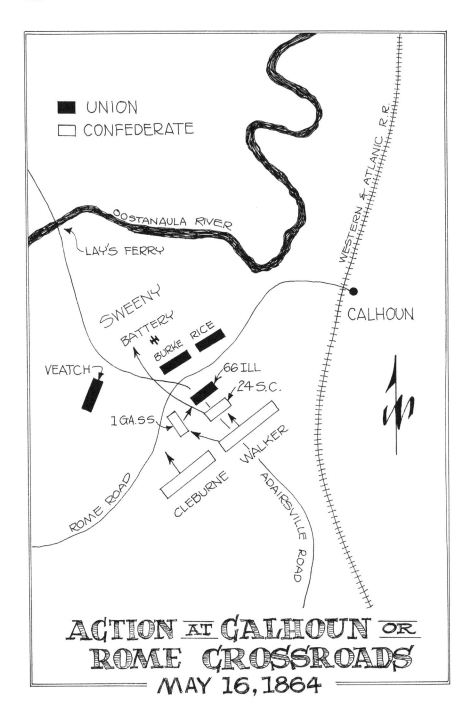

ACTION AT CALHOUN OR ROME CROSSROADS
MAY 16, 1864

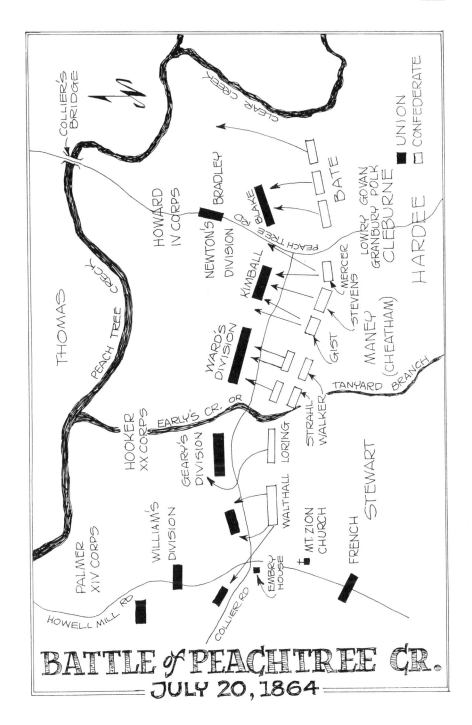

BATTLE of PEACHTREE CR.
JULY 20, 1864

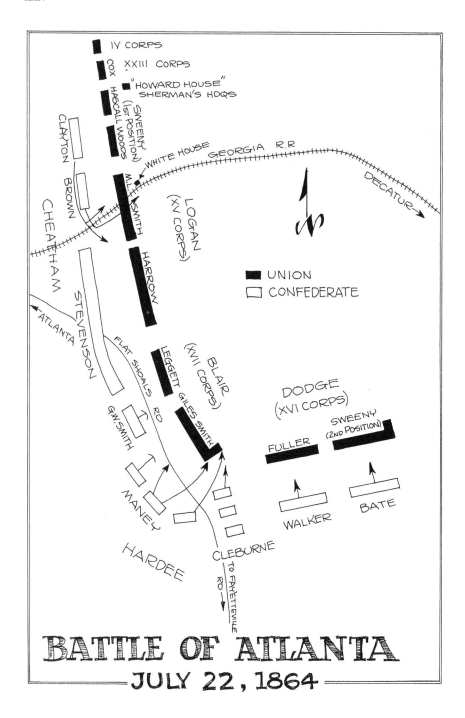

IV CORPS
XXIII CORPS
COX
"HOWARD HOUSE" SHERMAN'S HDQS
SWEENY (1ST POSITION)
HASCALL WOODS
CLAYTON
BROWN
M.L. SMITH
WHITE HOUSE
GEORGIA R.R
DECATUR →
CHEATHAM
LOGAN (XV CORPS)
HARROW
UNION
CONFEDERATE
STEVENSON
ATLANTA →
FLAT SHOALS RD
BLAIR (XVII CORPS)
LEGGETT GILES SMITH
DODGE (XVI CORPS)
G.W. SMITH
SWEENY (2ND POSITION)
FULLER
MANEY
WALKER
BATE
HARDEE
CLEBURNE
TO FAYETTEVILLE RD →

BATTLE OF ATLANTA
JULY 22, 1864

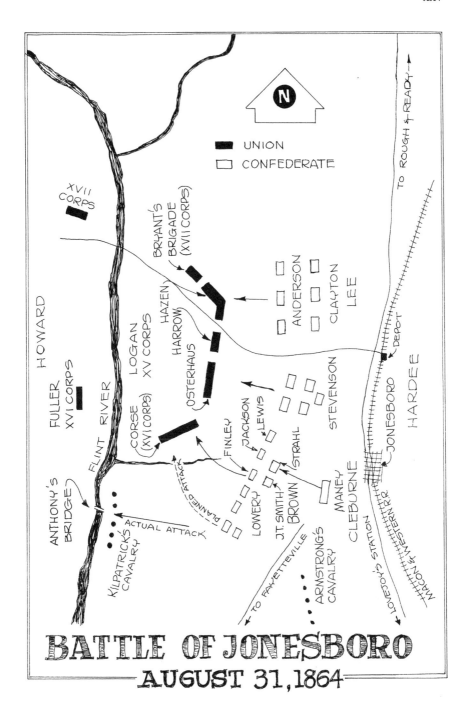

BATTLE OF JONESBORO
AUGUST 31, 1864

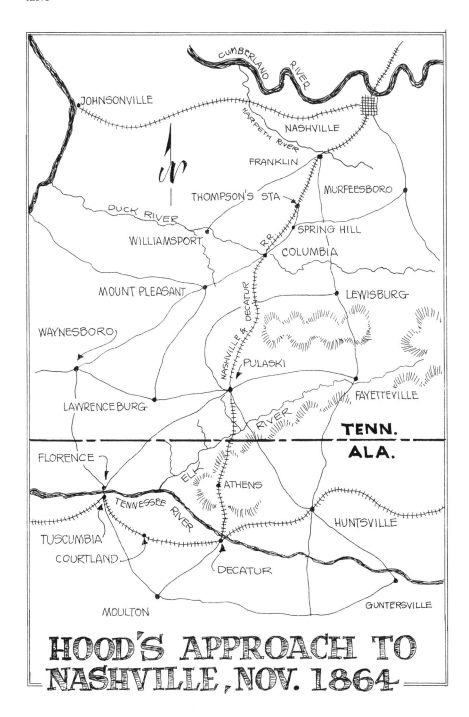

HOOD'S APPROACH TO NASHVILLE, NOV. 1864

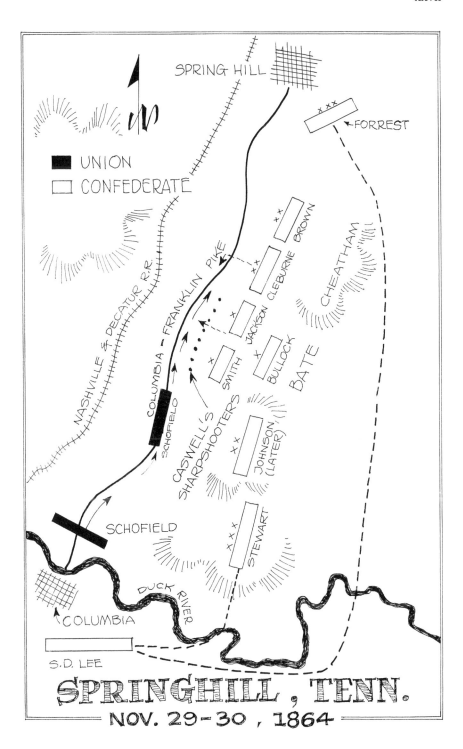

SPRINGHILL, TENN.
NOV. 29-30, 1864

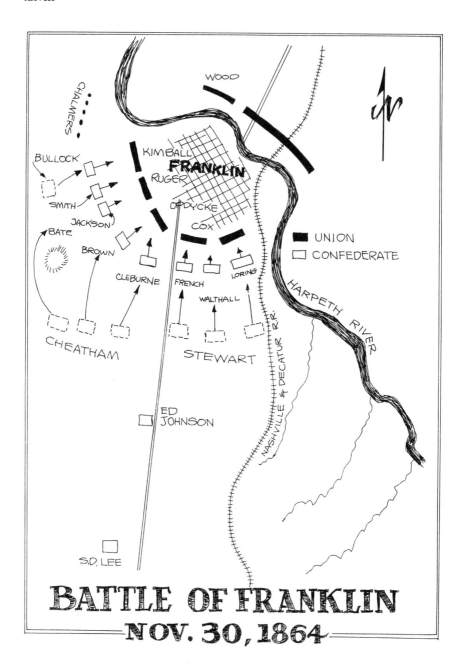

UNION
CONFEDERATE

BATTLE OF FRANKLIN
NOV. 30, 1864

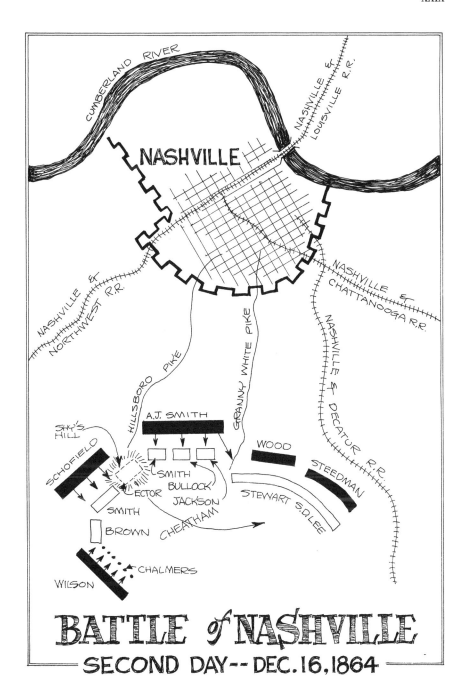

BATTLE of NASHVILLE
SECOND DAY -- DEC. 16, 1864

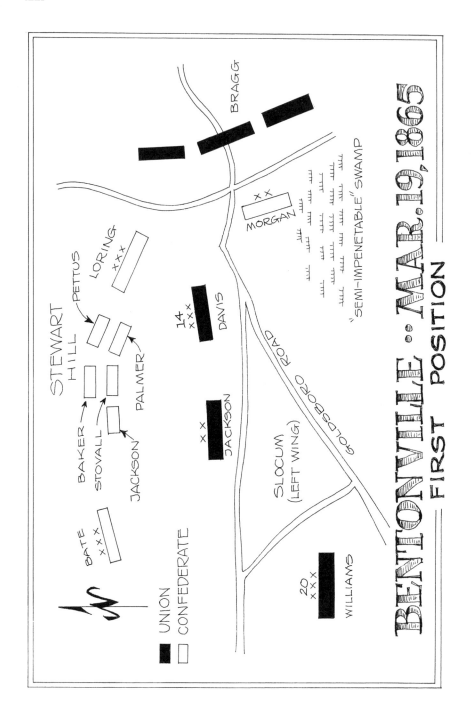

BENTONVILLE · MAR.19,1865

FIRST POSITION

INTRODUCTION

The formation of the 1st Georgia Sharpshooter Battalion in 1862 was an experiment at once noble and harmful. Georgia organized four such battalions. Besides the 1st, described in these pages, a 2nd Battalion was formed at Corinth, Mississippi, in June 1862 from three excess companies of the 5th Georgia Volunteers and one or two Alabama companies. They were called "Cox's Wildcats," after their first commander, Major Jesse J. Cox, an Alabamian. The 3rd Georgia Sharpshooters, a battalion of six companies, was organized in late April or early May 1863 from the regiments of General William T. Wofford's brigade in the Army of Northern Virginia. Their first commander, Lieutenant Colonel A. H. Patton, was killed at Chancellorsville before the battalion had a number and before his name could appear on any muster roll. The 4th Battalion of three companies came from the Georgia troops in east Tennessee in spring 1863. It was led by Major Theodore D. Caswell of Augusta, Georgia, and served in the Georgia-Tennessee brigade of General William B. Bate and his successors. Other states had sharpshooters as well, some earlier than Georgia.[1]

Who first suggested the idea of sharpshooter battalions is not known. Recruiting for a battalion of sharpshooters was conducted in Georgia in summer 1862 by Lieutenant Colonel John A. Jones of the 20th Georgia Volunteers. His authority was a general order from the "commander-in-chief" of the Confederate "Army of the Potomac." James H. Ogden, National Park historian at Chickamauga, has suggested the theory that General P. G. T. Beauregard may have been the first to present a plan for sharpshooters. Certainly, he was with the Army of the Potomac (forerunner of the Army of Northern Virginia) shortly before the enabling legislation was enacted, and sharpshooter battalions appeared in the Southern army in Mississippi within months after he arrived there.[2]

The concept of taking the best men in an army and uniting them in elite units is as old as armies themselves. Caesar's Praetorians, Napoleon's Guards, the British army's light infantry and grenadiers, modern commandos and special forces, are all of the same genre. In American history, Anthony Wayne did it with his light infantry brigade, hand-picked and specially trained, at Stony Point in 1777, and Winfield Scott attempted the same thing with his storming parties at Molino del Rey in 1847, but with disastrous results. While the commander of the special force has a hand-picked group of men to mold and operate, the commanders of the ordinary units are never happy to lose their most reliable men, those who can be counted on to hold the unit together in adversity, to serve to rally the less intelligent or the faint of heart. In fact, the average commander will normally send on special detail the men he can most easily spare, his laggards and shirkers. Major Robert Anderson had just such reservations about the men he was receiving in 1862, while General Hugh Mercer worried about losing his best men to Anderson's command.

From the outset, the 1st Georgia Battalion had problems. Much of the trouble lay in the organization of Civil War regiments and companies. Very few were the companies in the early years of the war that were not made up almost exclusively of men from the same town or county. Later, of course, conscription and the need for replacements diluted the homogeneity of the companies. The concept of the sharpshooters was alien to this hometown tradition. Men were asked to leave the comfortable companionship of their neighbors and friends and go into a unit with people they had never met before. Today, such association is the norm for military life although, even now, National Guard and Reserve units use a hometown basis for their constituency. But in the 1860s such an idea was alien to the average volunteer soldier.

Former regular army officers such as Robert Anderson and Arthur Shaaff were used to dealing with men from diverse backgrounds and perhaps were not aware of the enormity of what they were asking these volunteers to do. However, the company officers in their original regiments understood the men and it is no surprise that some resisted change; indeed, it is surprising that so few resisted. So it was that Anderson, who had such high hopes to start with, found himself having to accept men being drafted from other regiments into his battalion, and even taking conscripts to fill up his ranks.

Despite this poor beginning, the battalion was turned into a small but fine unit by the skill and energy of its officers and non-commissioned officers. Its officers were from the aristocracy of coastal Georgia and they and their men were proud of their association with Savannah, the mother city of the state. The sharpshooters early won the praise of Generals Beauregard and Mercer and of its inspecting and mustering officers. The battalion won good comment for its drill demonstrations and for its conduct on its numerous calls to aid in the defense of Fort McAllister. When need required, it was available for deployment to another theater of war. True, some of the soldiers who thought they had signed up only for the defense of Georgia balked at going to Mississippi, but most of the men were loyal to their oath and went to the defense of Vicksburg.

The 1st Sharpshooters served as part of the Walker-Wilson-Stevens-Jackson Georgia brigade from May 1863 to the end of the war. Under General

W. H. T. Walker, the battalion got its first taste of real combat operations at Jackson in May 1863 and it was there that the probable brigade tactic was evolved. No written record exists to authenticate this supposition, but it seems that the standard role of the sharpshooter battalion was to act as skirmishers to protect the brigade while line of battle was formed from column of march. Normally, skirmish lines were formed by detachments from the units in a brigade under the major of one of the regiments. This policy often resulted in troops and commanders being strangers to one another. The first employment of a single regiment acting as skirmishers in Virginia was in May 1862 and the first employment of an ad hoc sharpshooter battalion was at Fredericksburg in December.

Frederick L. Ray has suggested that sharpshooters could be pickets on the defense, skirmishers in the advance or on the defense, and flank guards in action or on the march. An officer of the 3rd Georgia Sharpshooter Battalion in the Army of Northern Virginia gave this description of his unit in action: "We are always in front of the Brigade, about 300 to 400 yds., to clear out the way..." When the skirmish line was recalled, the battalion would fall in on, and become, the left of the line.[3]

In all accounts that have survived, the Walker-Wilson-Stevens-Jackson brigade line usually consisted of the 29th and 30th Georgia Regiments on the right, the 25th Georgia in the center, and the sharpshooters on the left. At Chickamauga the 25th Georgia held the right but after its strength was badly reduced it shifted to the center. In the early days of the brigade's existence, the 4th Louisiana Battalion was next on the right of the sharpshooters. Later, the newer regiments in the brigade, 66th Georgia and 1st Confederate, were designated for that position in the line-up. Writing in 1867, former Sergeant Theodore Winn of the 25th Georgia made this abbreviated but informative comment on the sharpshooters in battle: "Schoup [sic], with his fine battalion, [was] ever in the van on a skirmish or where the danger was thickest..."[4]

Like most Civil War units, the sharpshooter battalion had difficulty in maintaining its strength. Weakened by sickness and desertion, the unit always struggled to maximize the number of effective soldiers it could put in the field and was far from successful. By the author's count, no more than 360 officers and men served actively in its ranks, and its maximum strength may have been the 270 present for duty it carried to Mississippi in May 1863. Beginning with the battle of Chickamauga, serious combat casualties added to the toll of losses. By late fall 1863, the battalion could muster barely one company equivalent in strength, and by the beginning of the spring 1864 campaign it was the equivalent of about two large companies of infantry. Thereafter, there was no recouping the steady wastage of men. The battalion was no more than company strength during Hood's Tennessee campaign and after Nashville was little more than an ineffective corporal's guard.

Sometime between April 1864 and April 1865 the battalion lost that élan that had marked its early life. Perhaps it was the wear of two-and-a-half years of constant defeat, loss of territory, loss of comrades, poor food, poor equipment, and no pay. Perhaps it was the lack of confidence in superiors, the unwillingness to charge breastworks again and again. No doubt it was a combination of all of these factors, and the draining away of company officers and non-commissioned officers did not help the men's morale. Without the example set by their lieutenants and sergeants, the riflemen who had charged into enemy fire willingly and with a yell at Chickamauga and Peachtree Creek and Atlanta broke "causelessly" at Kinston in March 1865. As Nathaniel C. Hughes observed, "The rank and file had been palsied by the successive defeats under Hood." This observation applied not only to Shaaff's battalion.[5]

Although the men of the sharpshooter battalion came from all over Georgia, the unit came to call Savannah its home city. It was organized there in 1862 and most of its officers and senior non-commissioned officers were residents there. Throughout the war, names of casualties and other events in Shaaff's battalion were reported in the Savannah newspapers. In fact, when the news of the men's reenlistment for the war in 1864 was sent in by Adjutant George H. Johnston, he wrote "we proudly cherish our connection with Savannah...." Other counties with large representations in the battalion were Appling, Bryan, Clayton, Dooly, Fayette, Screven, and Thomas.[6]

Precise figures on casualties suffered by the sharpshooters are difficult to compute because of inaccuracies, inconsistencies, and gaps in the records. Based on his own review of compiled service records and published casualty lists, this writer has arrived at the following numbers.

Killed in action or died of wounds:	22
Died of natural causes:	60
Wounded in action, not mortal:	105
Captured or missing:	92

Two more men may have been killed in action but the record is contradictory.

There is a variety of permutations of these numbers. Two of the killed had previously received non-fatal wounds. Eight of those wounded were hit on two different occasions; one was wounded three times. Eight of those wounded were also captured. Five of the prisoners of war were paroled and six were exchanged;

one of each category was captured a second time. Nine of those who died of natural causes were prisoners of war at the time of death. One soldier was captured, paroled, and died.

The number of soldiers who deserted is almost impossible to determine. In 1862 and 1863 the battalion advertised publicly for thirty-five different deserters. Some of them returned voluntarily, some were captured. Some of the men who were missing from the unit in 1863 and 1864 were deserters rather than captives but records are difficult to sort out. What is clear is that at least twelve prisoners of war or detainees took the oath of allegiance to the US government before the end of the war, some as soon as a few days after being apprehended, and at least sixteen others enlisted in US service, half of them immediately after apprehension.

In the course of their existence, Shaaff's sharpshooters took part in several major campaigns and a number of battles. In early 1863, General P. G. T. Beauregard authorized them to display honors for Fort McAllister 1 February and 3 March 1863 on their colors. Other honors for which they might have been eligible but for which no documentation of award has been found include: Jackson, Mississippi, 14 May and 10–16 July 1863; Chickamauga, Georgia, 19 and 20 September 1863; Missionary Ridge, 25 November 1863; North Georgia Campaign, 6 May–9 July 1864; Resaca, Georgia, 14 May 1864; Calhoun, Georgia, 16 May 1864; Siege of Atlanta, Georgia, 10 July–2 September 1864; Peachtree Creek, Georgia, 20 July 1864; Battle of Atlanta, 22 July 1864; Utoy Creek, Georgia, 6 August 1864; Jonesboro, Georgia, 31 August–1 September 1864; Hood's Tennessee Campaign, 10 October–25 December 1864; Decatur. Alabama, 28 October 1864; Franklin, Tennessee, 30 November 1864; Nashville, Tennessee, 15 and 16 December 1864; Carolina Campaign, February–26 April 1865; Kinston, North Carolina, 10 March 1865; Bentonville, North Carolina, 19 March 1865.

As for sharpshooter identification, Michael L. Ray's article in *America's Civil War* discusses a badge designed by a battalion commander in the Army of Northern Virginia in 1863 and depicts another, apparently different, badge. Whether or not the Georgia sharpshooters, or any others in the Western armies, wore a special badge is a question that has been asked but for which this author has no answer.[7]

Notwithstanding its poor performance in the last months of its existence, Shaaff's battalion had a high reputation that was well deserved. In late 1864, Henry R. Jackson referred to them as "the Battn. of Sharpshooters, distinguished in many previous conflicts for its firmness and gallantry." It was a reputation that the soldiers were proud of and that the veterans cherished always.

Captain George C. Dent's obituary called the battalion "that splendid command," and that of R. Cuyler King referred to its "enviable record." Joseph T. Derry, author of the Georgia volume of *Confederate Military History*, called the sharpshooters "one of the best drilled and most efficient battalions in the service." The battalion may not have always lived up to the expectations of its organizers and commanders, but it was not for want of valor or exertion of effort on the part of the enlisted soldiers, NCOs, and junior officers of the unit. Rather were they failed by the senior commanders to whom they looked for inspiration and direction and by the government for which they fought.[8]

PRELUDE

MAJOR ARTHUR SHAAFF

One officer in the Confederate Army of Tennessee at Dalton, Georgia, in winter 1864 had more reason to be despondent than most others. Major Arthur Shaaff had longer regular army experience than any other officer in the Georgia division of the army except Major General William H. T. Walker, the division commander. But after three years of service, he was still a major commanding the 1st Battalion of Georgia Sharpshooters and recent events had conspired to keep him in that position and at that rank.

Born in the District of Columbia to a Maryland family in 1831, Arthur Shaaff was well connected in the Confederacy on his mother's side. His father was Arthur Shaaff of Georgetown and Annapolis but his mother was Mary Athenia, the daughter of former Georgia governor, senator, and United States secretary of state John Forsyth, who had "objected vigorously" to her marriage in 1825. The major's maternal uncle was John Forsyth, Jr., former minister to Mexico, newspaper editor and mayor of Mobile in the war years. His mother's sister was the second wife of Senator Alfred Iverson, Sr., of Columbus, Georgia, and the senator's sons were Confederate Brigadier General Alfred Iverson, Jr., and Lieutenant Colonel John Forsyth Iverson of the 5th Georgia, making them Arthur's first cousins.[1]

Arthur Shaaff's maternal great-grandfather, Robert Forsyth, father of the governor, was a man of distinction in his own right. A Revolutionary War veteran, he was the first US Marshal for the District of Georgia, appointed by President George Washington in 1789. In 1794 Robert Forsyth became the first Federal law enforcement officer in the United States to be killed in the line of duty, shot by a man in Augusta, Georgia, upon whom he was trying to serve papers in a civil suit. His assailant was apprehended and jailed, but escaped and was never found. Robert Forsyth was forty years old when he died and left a widow and two sons.[2]

Just as the Forsyths were prominent in Georgia, so too were the Shaaffs in Maryland. Major Shaaff's father, Arthur, was the son of Dr. John Thomas Shaaff. The doctor's father, Casper Shaaff, married Alice, the daughter of Arthur and Elenor Charlton, in All Saints' Parish in Frederick in 1759. Their children included John Thomas, born in 1763, and Arthur, born 1765. The elder Arthur Shaaff, the doctor's brother, was a prominent lawyer and a member of the Maryland House of Delegates for several years before his death in 1817. His portrait (ca. 1800) is in the collection of the Maryland Historical Society.

Dr. John Thomas Shaaff married first Mary Sydebotham; she died in 1810. Their children were Arthur, Anne, Mary, Margaret Jane, and Charles. Dr. Shaaff's second wife was Mary Stewart, whom he wed in Anne Arundel County in 1812. Among his children, Margaret Jane became the wife of Reverend John Johns, future president of William and Mary College and Episcopal bishop of Virginia. Daughter Mary's husband was Andrew Stevenson, Speaker of the US House of Representatives and minister to Great Britain. When Dr. Shaaff died in 1819, the executors of his will were Roger B. Taney and William Marbury; one of the witnesses to his signature was Francis Scott Key.

After his marriage to Mary Forsyth, the second Arthur Shaaff (the doctor's son) practiced law for a time in Augusta, was secretary of the executive department of Georgia when John Forsyth was governor, and was employed for several years as clerk to the secretaries of state in the administration of President Andrew Jackson, including his father-in-law. Shaaff died in 1834 at the approximate age of thirty, leaving his widow with four or five small children.[3]

All three of Arthur's sons served as Confederate officers during the War Between the States. John Thomas was a graduate of West Point, class of 1851; he later became a Confederate commissary officer in charge of depots in Macon, Nashville, and other locations and died in New York in 1877 at the age of forty-seven. He was probably the same John T. Shaaff who was captain in the 1st Louisiana Heavy Artillery early in the war. Another was Captain Francis Scott Key Shaaff, who served with and commanded the 15th Alabama Volunteers in the Army of Northern Virginia. He was a private in the US Regular Army and may have been private in the Confederate 1st Kentucky Infantry.

Of the two daughters, Mary and Julia Frances, Mary married Alexander A. Lowther, later colonel of the 15th Alabama Volunteers, and moved to Columbus, Georgia. Julia Frances married Richard Tilghman Brice of Anne Arundel County. Brice died in 1851 at the age of thirty-nine, leaving Julia with a son, Arthur Tilghman Brice. Julia's picture is also in the image collection of the Maryland Historical Society.[4]

Frank Shaaff's enlistment in the US Army in New York City in September 1860 gives us a glimpse of the physical appearance of an adult male member of the family. He was twenty-seven years old, a native of Georgetown, DC, and a clerk by occupation. He stood 5 feet, 9 1/2 inches tall, and had hazel eyes, brown hair, and a ruddy complexion. His enlistment was short-lived: in

May 1861 he was discharged at Carlisle Barracks, Pennsylvania, "by order of the secretary of war."[5]

The 1850 US census found twenty-year-old Arthur employed in Baltimore, Maryland, as a clerk. In 1855, while he was living in St. Louis, where John T. Shaaff was assigned at Jefferson Barracks, Arthur applied for and received a commission as second lieutenant in the 4th US Infantry. His contemporaries as lieutenant in that regiment included such future luminaries as Phil Sheridan and George Crook. Shaaff served for five years with his regiment in Washington Territory. In late 1860 he was transferred to Fort Mojave in the southern California desert and was there when war started. He resigned from the army effective 10 July 1861.

Shaaff was one of the group of Southern officers and civilians who accompanied Albert Sidney Johnston on his trek from California to Texas that summer. The party left Los Angeles by horse about 22 June 1861, crossed the Colorado River at Yuma on 4 July, and arrived at Mesilla, New Mexico, recently taken by Confederate forces, on 28 July. From there they traveled by stage to San Antonio.

When Shaaff arrived in Texas, he found waiting for him a commission as a second lieutenant in the Confederate States regular army. He had already been commissioned lieutenant and captain in the regiments organized by Georgia after secession, probably on the recommendation of his uncle, Senator Iverson, but he may have been unaware of the appointment. Instead, Shaaff was assigned to Confederate service in Arkansas with William J. Hardee in fall 1861, served briefly as ordnance officer in Sibley's Texas brigade of mounted volunteers at San Antonio, and then was ordered east to Savannah, arriving in December 1861. He was put to work as a member of an examining board, presumably to improve the city's defenses, but possibly to pass on the qualifications of soldiers enlisting for service. Within a few months he was to find other, more congenial duty.[6]

1

SAVANNAH

In April 1862 the Confederate Congress authorized the formation of battalions of sharpshooters, one battalion for each brigade or similar organization, and each battalion to consist of from four to six companies. The men were to be selected from the other regiments in the brigade and the officers to be appointed by the government. Further, "for the purpose of arming the said battalion, the long range muskets and rifles in the hands of the troops" could be taken from them to arm the new unit, if no other comparable weapons were available.[1]

The enactment of the legislation was followed on 3 May by issuance of War Department General Order No. 34, which spelled out regulations for the formations of the battalions. Important stipulations were that commanding generals could take men from existing regiments as long as the strength of the unit was not drawn below the minimum number required by law and that long-range muskets and rifles could be taken from existing units to arm the sharpshooters until requisitions for such weapons could be filled by the Ordnance Department.[2]

Georgia organized four such battalions. On 1 June 1862 Major Robert Houston Anderson, a Georgia native serving as inspector general at the headquarters of the Department of South Carolina and Georgia in Charleston, wrote a letter to Major General John C. Pemberton, the department commander, asking permission to organize a battalion of four companies of sharpshooters from the regiments in the brigade of Brigadier General William Duncan Smith in the District of Georgia at Savannah. Anderson asked also to be allowed to go to Savannah for that purpose, to select his own officers, and to send them throughout Georgia on a recruiting mission. Pemberton gave his approval in an endorsement to the letter but restricted Anderson to nominating officers, whose names would be forwarded to the Secretary of War for approval.[3]

The same day, 1 June, Pemberton issued Special Order No. 262 from his department headquarters, giving essentially the same authority and conditions he had laid out in the endorsement. Two weeks later, on 14 June, Brigadier General Hugh W. Mercer, the new commander of the District of Georgia at Savannah, issued his own General Order No. 3: "The Brigadier General Commanding, having been called upon to organize for this District a Select Battalion of 'Sharpshooters,' Commanders of Regiments, Battalions and Independent Companies of Infantry will call upon their respective commands for volunteers for this Battalion and will with as little delay as practicable send to these Head Qrs. the names of said volunteers." Thus was the battalion of sharpshooters formed.[4]

Over the several days following the issuance of Pemberton's order there was a flurry of correspondence as individual gentlemen wrote asking for appointments as officers in the new battalion. On 6 June, Anderson wrote again from Savannah asking that General Alexander R. Lawton, the former district commander, be directed to turn over the men who had already volunteered. Anderson called them "splendid materiel, fine rifle shots and...anxious to join my Battalion." He feared that if they were not transferred immediately they would be whisked away for it was rumored that the regiments they belonged to were intended for Virginia.[5]

The departure of General W. D. Smith from the District of Georgia a few days later prompted Anderson to ask for a change in the parameters of his task. From Charleston, he wrote yet again to J. R. Waddy to request that his authority for raising a battalion of sharpshooters be extended to the whole district and not limited to Smith's brigade. In the same letter, Anderson presented his slate of officer nominations. He listed the names and their current status:

For Captains
1. Arthur Shaaf   1st Lieut CSA
2. William Ross   not now in service
3. Alfred Hartridge   Capt De Kalb Riflemen
4. G. C. Dent   not now in service

For 1st Lieutenants
1. Cuyler King   not now in service
2. D. Allcott   not now in service
3. J. Holcombe   not now in service
4. S. W. Lawrence   not now in service

For Second Lieutenants
1. Horace Crane   Private Co. B, 8th Ga. Regt.
2. Bayard Saddler   Private, Chatham Artillery
3. Alfred Bryan   Private, 2d Battn. Ga. Cavalry
4. M. Molina   Private, Chatham Artillery

For Bvt. 2d Lieuts.
John Terrill   Private, Capt. Anderson's Ind. Co.
E. J. Oliveros   Private, Major Screven's Battalion
G. W. Moore   not now in service

George H. Johnston   Private, Chatham Artillery[6]

On 20 June, Pemberton wrote to Adjutant and Inspector General Samuel Cooper in Richmond nominating Anderson to be major of the battalion with Arthur Shaaff, William Ross, George C. Dent, and Alfred L. Hartridge to be captains of companies. Pemberton told Cooper that seniority had been determined by an impartial drawing of lots by the four men concerned. He followed that letter with another on 11 July nominating for commissions as lieutenants the men whose names Anderson has submitted to him on 11 June.[7]

Meanwhile, recruiting was not going well. By 8 July only seventy-three men had volunteered despite General Mercer's General Order No. 3. Anderson fretted that it was taking too long and that the men were being deterred by their officers. He was also concerned that although the first volunteers were of high quality and good shots, those who came in under Mercer's order might not be suitable material and the units they belonged to were allowing them to leave to get rid of them. He felt the solution would be an order detailing the best men to be selected from each existing company.

Now Anderson wanted to be able to select men in good physical condition and give them marksmanship training. He proposed that he and a surgeon be allowed to select four men from each infantry company in the district that had at least its minimum strength. He hoped to make up four companies of 64 men each for a battalion strength of 256 enlisted men.[8]

The effort to complete Anderson's battalion was complicated by competing claims for the attention of the marksmen of Georgia. Throughout early summer 1862 advertisements appeared in Georgia newspapers asking for 750 men to be organized into a battalion of sharpshooters for service in Virginia. The originator of the notices was Lieutenant John A. Jones of the 20th Georgia Volunteers who left the brigade of General Robert Toombs in late June on a recruiting campaign. He must have been unsuccessful because no Georgia battalion of sharpshooters appeared in Virginia until May 1863 and then in a different brigade.[9]

Anderson's plea of 8 July seemingly bore fruit. By departmental Special Order No. 116, dated 23 July 1862, A Company, 1st Georgia (Olmstead's) Volunteers, was transferred and redesignated as B Company of the 1st Georgia Sharpshooter Battalion, subject to the approval of the War Department. The company was known as the "DeKalb Rifles" or "DeKalb Riflemen," formed as a volunteer unit in Savannah in 1850 by city residents of German descent. They had been mustered into service in early summer 1861 by Captain Augustus Peter Wetter who resigned his command in October 1861 and was replaced by Captain Alfred L. Hartridge.

Although nominally a rifle company, the men had been serving as artillerymen for over a year and seem an odd choice for the nucleus of a battalion of sharpshooters. The company had been on duty at Genesis Point on the Great Ogeechee River just above Ossabaw Sound since June 1861. There they began the construction of Fort McAllister, the great earthen rampart built to protect Savannah's western approaches, under the direction of a military engineer and with the assistance of slave labor. Returns from the District of Savannah for September and October 1861 show two officers and forty to fifty men present for duty manning a battery of four or five heavy guns at Genesis Point. By June 1862 the company was manning a battery of one 42-pounder gun and five 32-pounder guns at the fort. Captain Hartridge and his company fired their first shot in anger at a Union vessel on 1 July 1862 shooting with "considerable accuracy" and causing the enemy ship to withdraw. On 29 July they successfully fought off a reconnaissance by four Union vessels, again firing accurately. Hartridge relinquished control of the post to another company and joined the new battalion at the end of August.[10]

An explanation should be given here for the reader unfamiliar with the numbering of Georgia Civil War regiments. Georgia had an abundance of regiments bearing the number "1." At least three of these entered Confederate service: 1st Georgia Regulars, 1st Georgia Volunteers (Ramsey's), and 1st Georgia Volunteers (Olmstead's). The 1st Regulars was that group of men raised in two regiments in winter 1861 to be the army of the "Republic of Georgia" and in which Arthur Shaaff was first offered a commission. As soon as Georgia became a part of the Confederacy, the recruits already collected were combined into a single regiment and tendered to the Richmond government for service as the 1st Regulars. They retained that designation throughout the war.

A regiment of twelve months volunteers was assembled at Macon in March 1861 and sent to Pensacola, Florida, in response to a call from Richmond for troops at that point. Their colonel was James Ramsey, so they were the 1st (Ramsey's) Georgia Volunteers. In March 1862 the regiment was disbanded and the men were discharged. Most of them immediately enlisted in new units.

Another 1st Georgia Regiment was based in Savannah and was composed of pre-war volunteer companies from that city. Its first colonel was Alexander R. Lawton who led it to the capture of Fort Pulaski from its lone US Army caretaker on 3 January 1861. Lawton was succeeded as colonel by Hugh W. Mercer, and he, in turn, by Charles H. Olmstead, who took command in December 1861 and retained his position until the end of the war. Even while Olmstead was a Yankee prisoner for several months in 1862, his unit was known as 1st

(Olmstead's) Georgia Volunteers. It was from his regiment, and while he was a prisoner, that the DeKalb Rifles were detached.

Some of the men Anderson had recommended to be officers in his new battalion were already in service in other units in enlisted status. General Pemberton acted on 15 July to bring them under Anderson's command so they could be commissioned as requested. Bayard Sadler, Alfred Bryan, M. Molina, John Terrill, E. J. Oliveros, and George Johnston were ordered to "report at once to [Major Anderson] for duty." All of them eventually assumed leadership positions in the sharpshooters except Terrill. Why he did not is unknown.[11]

By Special Order No. 259, District of Georgia, dated 30 July 1862, men were chosen from the regiments manning the defenses of the city to fill up the other companies of the new battalion. A Company was composed of men taken from the 1st, 25th, and 47th Regiments of Georgia Volunteers; C Company from the 32nd and 54th Georgia Regiments and the Savannah Volunteer Guard Battalion; and D Company from the 29th, 30th, and 47th Georgia Regiments and the 8th Georgia Battalion. A few men from the 13th Georgia Battalion also went to D Company. Additional small increments of transfers were made during August. Not all the men in the battalion were volunteers. Some forty men conscripted at Camp Randolph in Gordon County in late July and early August were transferred into B Company, making it the largest in the battalion.[12]

One small group of soldiers from the 25th Georgia had a background different than most. Six new sharpshooters from E Company of that regiment were from Henry County, Alabama, and their old company was called the Irwin Invincibles, after the man who had organized the unit in August 1861, or the Henry Light Infantry. The company served in an independent status in western Virginia from September to December 1861. Following transfer to Savannah, they were integrated as a unit of the 25th Georgia in January 1862.[13]

Major Anderson informed department headquarters on 29 July that General Mercer had issued an order for the organization of the new battalion on 1 August. He asked that he and Captains Shaaff and Hartridge be relieved from court-martial duty so they could attend the organization and begin troop instruction because there was only one unnamed captain available for duty without the three serving on the court. On 13 August he wrote again, complaining that only one of the men he had nominated to be lieutenants, Horace Crane, had as yet received his commission. He noted that all the others were on duty and needed their positions regularized. He was particularly desirous of receiving an appointment for Robert Footman, who was filling the duties of quartermaster and was "an excellent officer in every respect qualified for the position." Never backward, Anderson also asked if his own commission as major could be upgraded to lieutenant colonel. That aspiration went unfulfilled for the moment. He appended his new list of recommendations:

For First Lieutenants
  1. Benjamin Hardee
  2. H. D. Twyman
  3. Joseph [sic] Holcombe
  4. S. W. Lawrence
For Second Lieutenants

Sr. 2d Lieuts.	Jr. 2d Lieuts
1. Henry Hermann	1. Robert Wayne
2. M. Molina	2. Cuyler King
3. Bayard Saddler	3. Alfred Bryan
4. [blank]	4. George Johnston

R. H. Footman, Capt. & A. Q. M.[14]

Some of the new sharpshooters had been in service with the Georgia State Troops since fall 1861. When Governor Joseph Brown decided that the Confederacy was not providing adequately for coast defense in his state, he organized a division of state troops for six months service in and around Savannah. Their expiration of service occurred in April 1862. By that time, the Confederate Congress had passed its conscription act making all Southern men between the ages of 18 and 35 liable for service. Large numbers of the state troops quickly volunteered to enter new Confederate regiments, thereby making up, for example, the 32nd and 54th Georgia Regiments. The older regiments had been in service since at least summer 1861 except the 47th Georgia which had its nucleus formed in March 1862.[15]

At least some of the "volunteers" for the new battalion were not happy to be separated from their home companies. Captain George A. Mercer, son of and adjutant to General Mercer, commanding the District of Georgia, wrote that there was "great opposition" among the officers of the regiments in the Savannah garrison when the men were taken from them. In particular, the commanders of two companies of the 54th Georgia, B and K, refused to parade so that sharpshooters could be selected from their ranks.

General Mercer wrote to department headquarters on 16 August notifying them that he would be forwarding court martial results concerning "open and mutinous disobedience" to orders dealing with formation of the sharpshooter battalion. He asked that the commanding general render his decisions on the cases as quickly as possible to "produce an excellent effect and add to the efficiency of the service" by making examples of the offenders.

Eventually, Captain George W. Eason and Lieutenants John J. Roberson and Richard Bennett were charged with disobedience of orders and other offenses and court-martialed. Eason and Roberson were found guilty, Bennett not guilty. Roberson was cashiered and Eason was dismissed from the service. The results were published in departmental General Order No. 82, 21 October 1862.

What General Mercer saw as "mutinous disobedience" was viewed more leniently by a Savannah newspaper. A story about the incident in camp related that all of the men in the two accused companies were sick and unable to perform duty and their officers, therefore, did not order them on parade. On a subsequent visit staff officers collected their arms and placed the officers under arrest but the paper was "happy to report" that there was no mutiny."[16]

In his letter of 16 August Mercer complained that Major Anderson wanted to take his new battalion to Virginia. Mercer assured General Pemberton that such a move would never meet his own approval. His understanding of the legislation authorizing sharpshooter battalions was that they should be part of the "brigade" from which they had been formed, and he suggested he would never have consented to such an undertaking if he thought the best troops in his command were to be taken away from him.[17]

Despite the "mutiny" in the 54th Georgia, some men were quite pleased to be in the new unit. Corporal William Moody of Appling County, formerly in Company K, 54th Georgia, and before that a sergeant in the Georgia State Troops, was now a member of Company C in the sharpshooters. He wrote his wife from camp: "Dear wife, you did not want me to join the Sharpshooters but if you noed the difference Between the Batallion and the old Regt. you would be verry glad that I joined it. I could not be hierd to go Back in the Regt."[18]

The battalion was gradually formed during July and early August, and by the nineteenth of that month was complete. Some of the soldiers had not yet been paid their bounty money and some did not have complete uniforms, which had not yet been received from Messrs. Henry Lathrop & Co., of Savannah, a pre-war dry goods merchant who contracted with the quartermaster bureau to manufacture military clothing. Nevertheless, on 21 August, the new unit marched from their rendezvous point at Camp Pemberton near Savannah to set up their own Camp Anderson, named for the battalion's commander. Their first muster was conducted at 4:00 P.M. on 31 August, with Major Anderson serving as inspector and mustering officer. By regulation, the Articles of War were read to the assembled men. At about the same time, a minister of the gospel was engaged to conduct Sunday services for the battalion. When General Pierre G. T. Beauregard, the new department commander, came from Charleston to review the Savannah garrison in October 1862, the sharpshooter battalion attracted his particular attention. Captain Mercer thought their superiority to the line regiments was easily explained: their officers were appointed by the government, not elected by the men.[19]

Camp Anderson was situated on Wildhorn Plantation, 12 miles below Savannah on the west bank of the Grove or Little Ogeechee River and near the line of the Savannah, Albany, and Gulf Railroad. Co-located with the sharp-shooters was a Georgia field battery, the Columbus Artillery. William Moody described the camp to his wife thus, "We are camped about 1 1/2 miles from [Number] 1 station and in 1/4 mile from the little Ogechee River on a very high pleasant place tho I exspect it is a sickly place. The sand flies is very bad."[20]

The battalion's first commander, as mentioned, was Major Robert H. Anderson. The captains of the four companies were Arthur Shaaff, commander of Company A; Alfred Lamar Hartridge, Company B; William Henry Ross, Company C; and George Columbus Dent, Company D. The battalion staff consisted of an adjutant, a quartermaster and an assistant surgeon, all commissioned officers, and a sergeant major, quartermaster sergeant, and ordnance sergeant as non-commissioned staff.

Major Anderson was the Savannah-born, twenty-six-years-old son of businessman John Wayne Anderson and a graduate of West Point in the class of 1857. He resigned his US Army commission in 1861 while in the Washington Territory, where he probably knew Arthur Shaaff, and was made lieutenant of artillery in the Confederate army. His mother was a Wayne and the brothers Robert and Thomas Wayne were his cousins, as was Mrs. Alfred Hartridge. His first assignment was as aide-de-camp to General William H. T. Walker at Pensacola, Florida. When Walker transferred to Virginia in July 1861, Anderson went with him, but when Walker resigned from the army in October 1861, Anderson remained in Confederate service and was promoted to major. He returned to Florida for another six months service on the staff of Brigadier General James H. Trapier and then was assigned to the department staff in Charleston.[21]

Besides Shaaff, all the company commanders had at least a year's active duty experience and some had formal military training. Alfred Lamar Hartridge, a twenty-five-year-old former bank clerk, had already been at Genesis Point for a year. Hartridge had been a cadet at the Georgia Military Institute in Marietta until he dropped out to marry in 1854. Alfred's older brother was Julian Hartridge, a local lawyer and politician who was soon to be Confederate congressman from the 1st District of Georgia. William Henry Ross, a twenty-five-year-old Macon businessman, had been a captain in the 2nd Georgia Battalion and a former commander of his own battalion of Georgia State Troops for six months. Like Hartridge, Ross had the additional advantage of training at the Georgia Military Institute.[22] A pre-war lieutenant of volunteers, as early as 27 December 1860, Ross had offered his company, the Floyd Rifles, to South Carolina Governor Francis Pickens to aid in the defense of Charleston.

George C. Dent, a forty-year-old native of South Carolina, was a Glynn County farmer. His occupation disguised Dent's fine family background and schooling. Born in Walterboro or Charleston in 1822, he was the son of deceased Navy Commodore John Herbert Dent of Maryland. Commodore Dent as a young officer had fought the Barbary pirates and had for a time commanded the USS *Constitution*. George's mother was a member of the Horry family of Colleton District. After her husband died, she moved to an estate near Darien, Georgia. As a youth, George was educated at an experimental agricultural school in Switzerland and traveled in Europe. He married Ophelia Troup, niece of former governor George Troup, in 1847. Dent's "farm," named Hofwyl after his Swiss school, was a sprawling rice plantation on the Altamaha River that his wife had inherited from her father. The couple moved there from Dent's mother's house in 1856. Ophelia's brother, James Robert Troup, was the Dents' near neighbor in Glynn County. He later served on the staff of General William H. T. Walker. George Dent's fourth cousin was Julia, the wife of a Union army officer named Ulysses Grant.

Dent had commanded the Glynn Guards, a company organized in August 1861. He styled his company "dismounted rifles" and they served on the south Georgia coast in the 13th Georgia, most of the time manning a battery of artillery on St. Simon's Island. In early 1862 they were detached from the regiment, now numbered the 26th, and went to Savannah as artillery. By April 1862 the company was mounted and was patrolling the coast line south of Brunswick. In May the men reenlisted for the war in a company that became part of the 4th Georgia Cavalry. Dent was out of a job until he was accepted into Major Anderson's battalion.[23]

The battalion adjutant was Second Lieutenant Robert Pooler Wayne, a twenty-one-year-old former clerk from Savannah. Wayne's older sister, Julia, was the wife of Captain Alfred Hartridge. His father, Thomas Smythe Wayne, a native of Screven County, was a Savannah commission merchant and nephew of James Moore Wayne, justice of the US Supreme Court. At different times Thomas Wayne served as city marshal, responsible for tax collection, and member of the board of health. Justice Wayne's son was Henry C. Wayne, Adjutant General of Georgia. Robert Wayne had something of a temper. A few months before the war it was reported that in a drunken brawl Wayne had cut another young man on the face. No witness to the incident came forward but the alleged victim was seen wearing a bandage on his head.

Wayne had enlisted in the Brooks Guard Volunteers of Kershaw's 2nd South Carolina Volunteers (2nd Palmetto Regiment) at Charleston in May 1861 and was a veteran of the First Battle of Bull Run. When the DeKalb Rifles of Chatham County elected their company officers in fall 1861, Robert Wayne was selected in absentia to be junior second lieutenant. He was discharged as a sergeant from the Carolina regiment, joined his new unit in Savannah, and transferred with them into the sharpshooters. At first Wayne was an officer of B Company who acted as adjutant. At the request of Major Anderson, on 17 November he was formally appointed to the position and promoted to first lieutenant from 18 October 1862.[24]

The battalion quartermaster was Captain Robert Habersham Footman, a native of Florida, a twenty-nine-year-old former insurance broker, and an officer in a Savannah volunteer company since he was 18 years old. Footman was appointed 11 August 1862 to rank from 16 July. The assistant surgeon was John Theodore McFarland, a twenty-five-year-old resident of Savannah, a graduate of the medical school there, and another former cadet at the Georgia Military Institute in Marietta. He had already seen varied service, having been with the 8th Georgia at Manassas and captured with the 1st Georgia at Fort Pulaski in April 1862. After a brief imprisonment in New York, he benefited from the unconditional exchange of medical officers in July 1862 and joined the sharpshooter battalion in early August.[25]

While Major Anderson was engaged in selecting and recommending officers of good quality for his battalion, the bureaucratic machinery of the adjutant general's department in Richmond seemed at times to be working at cross-purposes to his objective. As late as November 1862, more than two months after the first muster of the sharpshooters, Anderson wrote to General Thomas Jordan, chief of staff of the Department of South Carolina and Georgia, asking for his assistance in obtaining commissions for eleven of the battalion's officers. At that late date the four first lieutenants and seven of the eight second lieutenants were still serving without commission, causing, said Anderson with fine understatement, "a great deal of annoyance."[26]

In addition to the commissioned staff, by special order Sergeant Major Esidro J. Oliveros, Quartermaster Sergeant Mortimer L. Faries, and Ordnance Sergeant Nathaniel T. Brunner were transferred from the Savannah Guard Battalion to the 1st Sharpshooters. Oliveros was a medical doctor by profession and had come to Georgia from St. Augustine, Florida. He was of Corsican descent, about twenty-four years old in 1860, and the son of Bartolo or

Bartolomeo Oliveros, a gunsmith. Family legend held that an earlier Oliveros had attended school with the young Napoleon Bonaparte. Faries was a native of Savannah and twenty-eight years old. He was superintendent of a grist mill and married with a child when the war started in 1861. Brunner, a native of Beaufort, South Carolina, may have been the son of Isaac Brunner, a Virginia-born plasterer who had come to Savannah by way of Beaufort and was active in civic affairs as well as in business. Nathaniel was about thirty years old and a native of Carolina. His pre-war occupation is unknown but after the war he was a railroad engineer.[27]

Of great importance to the discipline and drill of the command were the first sergeants, or orderly sergeants as they were also known then, of the four companies. These were Charles S. Pattillo for A Company, Dominique or Dominick Brown in B Company, Peter Derst in C Company, and Charles L. Schlatter in D Company. Brown and Derst were both German born immigrants to Savannah. Brown (probably Braun in his homeland) was thirty-eight years old, a native of Baden, and a shoemaker. He had enlisted in the DeKalb Rifles in June 1861, had been the first sergeant of that company, and had transferred with that rank into the battalion of sharpshooters. Pattillo and Schlatter were native-born Americans and had come to the sharpshooters from the Savannah Volunteer Guard Battalion.

Peter Derst (Durst) was fourteen years old when he was enumerated in the 1850 census of Savannah with his father and two brothers. All four were identified as shoemakers. Peter's name cannot be found in the 1860 census but the Savannah City Directory of 1860 shows him operating a shaving saloon. He had been married in Savannah in 1855. Local lore has it that he, his father, and two brothers came to Savannah from Germany before 1850. His father was said to be a shoemaker at the old Planter's Hotel. Derst and his brother John had enlisted in Captain Wetter's company at the same time as Dominique Brown. Peter Derst transferred to the sharpshooters with B Company as a private but on 18 August was promoted to 1st Sergeant of C Company.[28]

At its first muster on 31 August, the battalion had present for duty 16 officers and 213 men, one officer and 67 men present but not available for duty (sick, in arrest, or on extra duty), and one officer and 63 men absent (sick, detached, on leave, or absent without leave). The battalion aggregate strength present and absent was 18 officers and 343 men for a total of 361. A month later, the return showed figures of 12 officers and 186 men present for duty, one officer and 75 men present but not available for duty, and 6 officers and 67 men absent. The aggregate strength was 347. Losses included three men who had died and nine deserters. Battalion strength continued to decline slightly in

October. On 13 October there were 211 present for duty, 283 total present, and 344 present and absent. A week later, on 20 October, the sharpshooters had 203 present for duty, 279 total present, and 336 men on the rolls, present and absent.[29]

Officers of the battalion traveled back and forth from the camp to Savannah on official or personal business, as did some of the enlisted men. On 30 November, two officers who happened to be in town were engaged in an incident that earned them noteworthy mention. Early that morning a fire broke out in several stores in a block of buildings, possibly a case of arson. The city fire brigade responded along with soldiers of the 4th Louisiana Battalion and many volunteers. Among them were Lieutenants S. W. Lawrence and Bayard Sadler of the sharpshooters, both of whom were commended in a newspaper article. The next day the Louisianians received a letter of thanks from the chief of police.[30]

Throughout fall 1862 the battalion watched the Georgia coast with other Confederate troops for signs of a Yankee invasion fleet. Hilton Head and Beaufort, South Carolina, had already been occupied by Federal troops and an attack on Savannah was presumed imminent. Alarms were constant. On 2 November Union vessels appeared off Genesis Point and shelled an officer who was offshore in a small boat. When barges from the squadron attempted to capture the boat, fire was returned from the fort. On 19 November three US vessels again approached Fort McAllister and opened fire. More than an hour passed before the fort responded, but a well-aimed first shot struck the USS *Wissahickon* below the water line, causing all three vessels to withdraw. William Moody told his wife about the Sharpshooters' involvement in the exchange, "Last Wednesday they had a fight down at Genesis Point and we had to march down there on Thursday and we came back yesterday But we had no fight. We are all werred [sic] from the march."[31]

Life in camp and the rudimentary medical practices of the day had taken their toll on the battalion almost from the day of its organization. Private Anson Asbeal died of a bowel disorder and Private Alsa Bodie of typhoid in September, both of C Company and both at Camp Anderson. Private Daniel Vanzant of B Company, twenty years old, died of typhoid in Savannah on 10 September, just over six weeks after being conscripted at Camp Randolph in Gordon County on 27 July . He was buried in Laurel Grove Cemetery the same day. In October Privates James A. Reed and W. H. Thompson, D Company, died of typhoid fever; Nathan Smith, B Company, died of congestion at Camp Anderson; and John Reddick, C Company, a resident of Sardis in Burke County, of chronic diarrhea in hospital at Guyton. Frederick Fischer, a private in B Company, died of dysentery in Savannah in November, and Private A. J. Newmans, C Company, of Reidsville, Georgia, succumbed to typhoid pneumonia at Camp Anderson in December.

James Reed's brother Joseph was also a sharpshooter; they had enlisted at Camp Black the same day in October 1861. Their widowed mother, Elizabeth Read of Dawson County, claimed James's accumulated pay in May 1863. John Reddick's father, Nicholas, a planter, claimed his twenty-four-year-old son's pay in November 1862.[32]

Not all sicknesses and injuries proved fatal. On 7 December, William Moody wrote to his wife from Camp Anderson, "Timothy Thornton got hurt very bad this morning by some mules running away with a waggon throwed him out on his head and shoulder But I think he is a little better."[33]

Timothy did survive and served on in the battalion until at least fall 1864. He was one of six Thorntons from Appling and Wayne counties who had enlisted in the 54th Georgia in April 1862 after service in the state troops; four of them transferred to C Company of the sharpshooters. Besides Timothy, the other three were James, Jonathan, and William. All four of them were grandsons of Isaac Thornton, a farmer who had settled in Appling County before 1830. Timothy and Jonathan were brothers, ages nineteen and twenty-one, respectively, in the 1860 census, and the sons of George W. Thornton, also a farmer. Of the other two, James was twenty-three years old and William sixteen in 1860. The four must have shown soldierly ability because all of them were non-commissioned officers, sergeants or corporals, during some part of their military careers. James was so badly wounded at Chickamauga that he was retired to the Invalid Corps in April 1864. Timothy and William were captured at Jonesboro in August 1864 and exchanged. James and William were paroled in 1865; Jonathan and Timothy were last accounted for in September 1864.[34]

Another family group in the battalion were the Boggs brothers of Talbot County. James, Barney, and Samuel were the sons of Joseph Boggs, a farmer. They were, respectively, twenty, eighteen, and seventeen years old in the 1860 census and at that time, James and Barney were still attending school. In October 1861 all three enlisted in the Georgia State Troops. Barney and Samuel served until mustered out in April 1862; James was discharged for disability in January 1862. Subsequently, they enlisted in B Company, 32nd Georgia Volunteers, in Savannah and then transferred to the sharpshooter battalion in July. A fourth brother, Joseph, fifteen in 1860, enlisted in the 32nd Georgia in 1862 and served with that regiment until he was wounded in the head and lost an eye at Charleston in 1864.[35]

Although the sharpshooter battalion was composed of selected men with hand-picked officers, it was not immune to that other scourge of Civil War armies, desertion. By the end of 1862, some twenty-nine of its men had left permanently without authorization and were counted as deserters. Some, especially men of the DeKalb Rifles, had never reported to the unit at all in August. In early November and mid-December the battalion adjutant, Lieutenant Robert P. Wayne, issued orders to be printed in Georgia newspapers offering $25.00 rewards for the return of any deserter. Five men were listed in the first order and ten in the second. The orders were as follows:

Headq'rs
1st Battalion Georgia Sharpshooters
Camp Anderson
November 5, 1862

Special Order No. 58

A reward of $25 will be paid for delivery at this Camp, or $15 for the delivery in any Jail in the State of Georgia, of each of the following named men, deserters from Co. A of this Battalion:

Thomas Coleman is 23 years of age, 6 feet 1 inch in height, ruddy complexion, dark hair, born in Ireland, and by occupation a laborer. Deserted October 11, 1862.

John Burke is 22 years of age, 5 feet 7 inches high, ruddy complexion, blue eyes, auburn hair, born in Ireland. Deserted October 11, 1862.

L. Beacher is 17 years of age, dark complexion, blue eyes, dark hair, born in Appling county, Ga.

W. A. Kent is 19 years of age, 5 feet 3 inches high, fair complexion, blue eyes, light hair, born in Effingham county, Ga., but living in Savannah. Deserted October 23, 1862.

Isiah Tanner, light complexion, gray eyes, light hair, born in Appling county, Ga. Deserted August 2, 1862.

Headq'rs
1st Battalion Georgia Sharpshooters
Camp Anderson
December 16, 1862

Special Order No. 71

A reward of $25 will be paid for delivery at this Camp, or $25 for the delivery in any Jail in the State of Georgia, of each of the following named men, deserters from this Battalion:

1. James Anson, 24 years old, 5 feet 9 inches high, light complexion, blue eyes, brown hair, born in Dinwiddie, Va. Enlisted November 18, 1862, at Camp Anderson, Ga.; deserted 15th December 1862

2. D. Barrentine, 47 years old, 6 feet high, dark complexion, grey eyes, light hair. Enlisted at Somersville, Ga., 26th March, 1862. Supposed to be in Appling County, Ga. Deserted 6th December 1862.

3. W. E. Baxter, 16 years old, 5 feet 2 inches high, light complexion, light hair, blue eyes, born in Mobile, Ala. Enlisted 27th July, 1861 by Major Dunwoody, at the Camp of Instruction, Calhoun county, Ga.

4. Charles Draeser [sic], 32 years old, 5 feet 5 inches high, dark complexion, brown hair, grey eyes, born in Haddin, Germany. Enlisted 7th August, 1862, deserted 9th Dec. 1862.

5. Joseph Isaacson, 37 years old, 5 feet 7 inches high, light complexion, dark eyes, brown hair, born in Germany, by occupation a painter. Enlisted 25th August, 1862 at Savannah; lives in Randolph county, Ga.; deserted from this camp 2nd September, 1862. Supposed to be in Florence, Ga., on the Chattahoochee river.

6. W. T. Lightfoot, 31 years old, 6 feet high, dark complexion, grey eyes, dark hair. Enlisted 4th March, 1862 at Reddsville [sic], Ga.; deserted 6th December 1862. Supposed to be in Tattnall county, Ga.

7. J. A. Mullins, 26 years old, 5 feet 8 inches high, dark complexion, black eyes, dark hair, born in Monroe County, Ga. Enlisted 4th March, 1862 at Randolph county, Ga. Deserted 6th December, 1862. Supposed to be in Randolph County.

8. Alexander R. McCook, aged 24 years, 6 feet high, light complexion, grey eyes, dark hair, born in Randolph county, Ga. Enlisted 8th May, 1862 at Savannah; deserted from Camp Anderson 27th September 1862.

9. James M. Peacock, 36 years old, 5 feet 9 inches high, dark complexion, black eyes, born in Liberty county, Ga. Enlisted 27th September, 1862, in Bryan county, Ga.

10. William Spears, 31 years old, 5 feet 10 inches high, light complexion, dark hair, dark eyes, born in Henry County, Ala. Enlisted 16th April, 1862 at Savannah; deserted from this battalion at Camp Anderson, 27th September, 1862; lives in Randolph county, Ga.

Both orders were signed by R. Wayne, 1st Lieut. and Adj't., 1st Battalion Georgia Sharpshooters, by order of Major R. H. Anderson.[36]

Most of these men were never recovered by the sharpshooters. William Kent, Isaiah Tanner and Doctor Barrentine returned voluntarily. Kent was captured by the enemy in Mississippi in July 1863 and enlisted in the Union army. Tanner deserted in Savannah when the battalion moved to Mississippi in May 1863. Barrentine was convicted by court-martial, punished, and then served two more years in the army. Charles Draeger was arrested 1 March 1863, but he deserted again in May before the sharpshooters went to Mississippi. A man of similar name was captured by the enemy at Atlanta in 1864 while serving with a home guard unit.

J. A. Mullins was probably Jonathan A. Mullins, a married farmer of Randolph County and a native of Monroe County. His service record does not show when he returned but it does indicate that he transferred from the battalion to the 13th Georgia in December 1863, possibly to be with his kinsmen, Joseph C. and Martin V. Mullins of Randolph County. The transfer was possibly an exchange for another young man from Randolph, H. J. Odum, also a married farmer. Odum never made it to the sharpshooters: he died in hospital in Virginia on 23 December 1863, before reporting for duty with Shaaff's battalion. J. A. Mullins surrendered with the 13th Georgia at Appomattox in April 1865.[37]

Besides deaths and desertions, losses from the battalion also occurred from transfers or improper recruiting. Between organization and the end of 1862, twenty-one men left the rolls for administrative reasons. Five were under age and one was over age; two were found to be Navy deserters and one was found to be a deserter from another unit; all three were returned. Seven men were released due to physical disability. Two men left the service under order of civil authority, one by order of the court, and one by order of the District of Georgia. Of those with physical disabilities, one was blind in both eyes, one had two paralyzed legs, and one was judged to have such a serious nervous disorder as to be unfit for service. The enlistment of these men at all reflected the desperation and callousness of recruiting and enlisting officers in meeting their quotas and filling the ranks.[38]

Almost from the time of the battalion's organization, Major Anderson had been concerned about its low strength, a concern only heightened by the above losses. In early October 1862 Anderson wrote to Adjutant and Inspector General Cooper in Richmond asking that 204 conscripts from the camp of instruction at Macon be ordered to his unit. The cryptic War Department endorsement on Anderson's letter says that it was "answered by telegraph to General Mercer," the district commander. Later in the month, Anderson tried again. This time he wrote to General Beuaregard, the new department commander, asking that the battalion be increased to six companies, the maximum allowed by law. Beauregard forwarded the request to Richmond with his endorsement of approval. The War Department endorsement read, "The battalion may be increased as requested."

By War Department Special Order No. 262, 8 November 1862, an increase of two companies was authorized. However, a month later, General Jordan, Beauregard's chief of staff, wrote to General Mercer, "Under recent decisions of the War Department, companies cannot be enrolled to be added to battalions. However, the application will be forwarded. Possibly, Major Anderson might raise the companies from volunteers already in the service and fill their places with conscripts. This course is recommended." The increase in companies never took place; as will be seen, Anderson soon lost interest in the sharpshooters.[39]

One positive result of the correspondence was the evidence of high regard in which the battalion was held by its superiors. On the letter of 28 October, General Mercer wrote, the battalion "is in a high state of discipline and is under the command of select and very efficient officers." To this, Beauregard added, the battalion is "remarkable for its discipline and for its soldier like appearance."[40]

The inspection report completed by Captain William S. Basinger, the mustering officer for 31 October 1862, gives a marvelous glimpse into the battalion's condition at that time. Basinger rated the sharpshooters as follows.

Kinds of arms and accoutrements:	Long Enfield Rifles; accoutrements to match
Condition:	Excellent
No. of rounds ammunition:	21,587 cartridges
Amount and kind of baggage:	None superfluous
Wagon and teams servicable:	2 four horse wagons 4 two horse wagons
" " " unservicable:	1 ambulance
Number of horses & mules:	18
Condition of horses:	Good

All four companies were rated "excellent" in military appearance, drill and discipline.

Company:	A	B	C	D

No. officers present: 4   4   4   4
(on parade)
No. enlisted present: 42   77   46   50
(on parade)
Field & staff: 3 officers and 3 enlisted
Aggregate: 19 officers and 218 enlisted
General Remarks:

The battalion requires a four horse ordnance wagon.

The ration is of good quality.

The police is excellent; sinks are provided.

The Articles of War have been read; Genl. Orders are regularly published to the command.[41]

Yet again, in January 1863, Beauregard issued a general order citing an inspection report that has not been found. In the order he wrote:

It is the agreeable duty of the commanding general to make known to the forces the following extracts from a special report of an Assistant Inspector General of the Staff of these Headquarters.

"The First Battalion, Georgia Sharp-shooters, Major R. H. Anderson, and the Chatham Light Artillery, Captain J. F. Wheaton, are distinguished for discipline, drill, and soldierly appearance. The drill and instruction of the Sharp-shooters and Chatham Artillery will bear a rigid scrutiny—in all three the army regulations are fairly observed, the sick well cared for, battalion and company books well kept, and a most commendable regard paid to the preservation and proper issue of public property. The camp of the Sharp-shooters might be a model to the Confederate army for general neatness and the ventilation of the tents."[42]

These reports reflect the pride Anderson and his officers took in their battalion; they also reflect the regular army influence of Anderson and Shaaff on the other officers and their men.

The "long" Enfield rifle with which the battalion was armed was the Model 1853 muzzle-loaded Enfield rifled musket. It was a British import and the most popular weapon in the Southern armies. Perhaps as many as 400,000 of them were brought into the Confederacy by blockade runners. The rifle was 55 inches long, weighed more than 9 pounds, and could fire the British .577 caliber bullet or the .58 caliber Confederate round. In the hands of a good marksman it could be accurate at a range of up to 1,000 yards.[43]

Since Robert Wayne's promotion and appointment as adjutant there had been a vacancy for a second lieutenant in B Company. On 13 December, Major Anderson wrote to General Cooper in Richmond again, asking for the appointment of First Sergeant Charles S. Pattillo of A Company to fill the position. The request was approved by Generals Mercer and Beauregard and eventually made its way to the desk of Secretary of War James A. Seddon where it languished. Captain Alfred Hartridge, commanding B Company, wrote another letter to Cooper on 16 February 1863, urging that Pattillo be promoted. Still nothing happened. Seddon finally approved the appointment on 30 May 1863 and Pattillo was advanced, as will be seen.

Two young men, C. S. and R. M. Pattillo, had enlisted in the Savannah Volunteer Guard Battalion at Fort Boggs near Savannah in May 1862. While no conclusive evidence has been found, they were probably the sons of James Pattillo, a merchant tailor in Marietta in Cobb County. James had two sons named Charles and Robert, ages nine and seven in 1850; in the 1860 census James had a sixteen-year-old male in his household named R. M.; an eighteen-year-old clerk named C. S. Pattillo was enumerated separately in Marietta that year.

A Robert M. Pattillo was a soldier in Company D, 7th Georgia Volunteers, a Cobb County unit, from August to November 1861, and in February 1862 a cadet at the Georgia Military Institute named C. S. Pattillo wrote to Governor Brown asking for an opinion on the status of cadets in regard to the new conscription law. These two were probably the same men. Whatever his antecedents, Charles Pattillo must have been a good soldier because he was made first sergeant of the sharpshooter company on 1 August 1862 after transferring from the Savannah battalion on 19 July.[44]

On Christmas Day 1862, by District of Georgia special order, Sergeant Major Oliveros left the battalion to accept a position as assistant surgeon in the 57th Georgia Volunteers. Prior to Christmas he had already been acting assistant surgeon on special service for about two weeks. His vacancy was filled by the appointment of First Sergeant Charles L. Schlatter, Jr., of D Company. Oliveros soon left the 57th to take on the duty as chief of a board of surgeons at a conscript camp near Orangeburg, South Carolina, a post he still held in December 1864. He was married there in June 1864.[45]

In January 1863 Major Anderson was promoted to be colonel of the 5th Georgia Cavalry, a regiment formed from various mounted details in Georgia, fulfilling his ambition for advancement and rendering moot the issue of expansion of the sharpshooter battalion. He was given command of the important garrison at Fort McAllister. The sharpshooters remained under his control with Captain Shaaff as acting battalion commander.[46]

On 26 January the battalion was called once again to go to Genesis Point, marching there from Camp Anderson, a road distance of 17 miles. On 27 January and 1 February 1863 the sharpshooters were at Fort McAllister when the installation was attacked by vessels from the Yankee blockading squadron led by Commander John L. Worden. In the first attempt, the fort and the vessels exchanged fire for four-and-a-half hours, doing minor damage on both sides. The gunners inside McAllister tried to shoot into the open gun ports on the ironclad monitor, USS *Montauk*, and came very near doing so. Worden withdrew when his supply of shell ammunition began to run low.[47]

In the attack on 1 February the fort was bombarded by the *Montauk*, three wooden gunboats, and one mortar boat. The armament of the monitor was one 15-inch and one 11-inch gun. Before the enemy's boats came within range, Colonel Anderson ordered Captain Shaaff to line the river bank with his battalion of sharpshooters with his right about a quarter of a mile in rear of and west of the battery. As soon as Anderson satisfied himself that the enemy had no intention of landing troops on his right flank, he ordered Shaaff to deploy his battalion farther to his right at ten-pace intervals, which enabled him to cover the bank of the river for over a mile with his sharpshooters. The riflemen of the battalion had excellent cover and would have provided heavy small arms fire against the Yankee vessels if they had succeeded in passing upstream.[48]

The firing commenced at 7:45 A.M., lasted until 12:15 P.M., and was lively and accurate on both sides. In addition to the fort's regular battery, Captain Robert Martin was in charge of a 10-inch mortar that fired on the *Montauk*. Martin reported that his aim was faulty at first but improved as the mist cleared and eventually he saw several of his shells burst over the *Montauk*. Colonel Anderson and other observers reported numerous hits on the ironclad; they thought the vessel had been damaged because they could hear hammering on the turret which had ceased to rotate. The *Montauk* succeeded in taking out one of Fort McAllister's guns and destroying the sand embrasures; fifty-six-year-old, Scottish born Major John Gallie, commander of McAllister's artillery battery and formerly a Savannah merchant, was killed and seven men were injured, none in the sharpshooter battalion. The wooden gunboats stayed out of range during the engagement.[49]

Commander Worden reported that *Montauk* had been hit forty-eight times: sixteen hits on the turret, fifteen hits on the side and deck armor, seven on the smokestack, three on the pilot house, and a few on other objects. In some places the armor plates were cracked or split. The greatest hazard to the crew was in the pilot house where screws were sprung from the plates and whizzed across the inside of the house. The problem in operating the turret was attributed to a malfunctioning engine and not to Rebel shells. Fire from Fort McAllister at other ships of the Yankee squadron was negligible.[50]

Colonel Anderson requested that the units of the garrison be allowed to inscribe "Fort McAllister" on their standards and General Beauregard approved by general order. Anderson cited First Lieutenant Robert P. Wayne, the adjutant of the sharpshooter battalion, who was his acting assistant adjutant general at Fort McAllister, for exemplary conduct. Major Henry Bryan, assistant inspector general, and older brother of Alfred Bryan, who arrived at the fort just after the firing had ceased, recommended that Captain Hartridge, commanding B Company of the sharpshooters, be promoted to replace the dead Major Gallie, based on his command of the fort the previous summer.[51]

A week after the attack the battalion suffered its first casualty, although accidental, on 11 February when Sergeant Joseph B. Smith of D Company was killed at the fort by the explosion of a shell. Smith and two other soldiers had found and were examining an unexploded shell which was being used as a campfire andiron. Smith foolishly poked a burning piece of kindling into the fusehole and the shell exploded. He died within an hour; both his companions were injured, one with a serious leg wound. The newspaper noted, "Men must be tired of life when they risk it on such carelessness as this." Smith was a mason from Lincoln County in civilian life. He was twenty-two years old when he enlisted in the 30th Georgia in May 1862 in Savannah and then transferred to the Sharpshooters.

One of the injured may have been Private William D. Warren, also of D Company, a resident of Quitman County and formerly a member of the 29th Georgia. Warren was transferred from Savannah to Macon with a fractured fibula on 28 February. However, he must have recovered sufficiently to rejoin his company because he was sick in a hospital in Mississippi in June.[52]

Sickness and disease continued to take their toll. On 2 January 1863, Private Solomon Herrnstadt of B Company died in hospital in Savannah of unknown cause; on the same day, Private Robert Roberts, also of B Company, suffered a fatal heart attack at Camp Anderson. The next day, Private Thomas J. Murdock of A Company died of typhoid pneumonia in hospital in Savannah. From 1 January to the end of April 1863, nine men died and ten deserted. Of the dead, one was accidental, one self-inflicted, and one by execution. Among the deserters, three later returned. Three others were substitutes as mentioned below.[53]

Losses from deaths and desertions had further depleted the ranks of the sharpshooter battalion during the winter and several efforts were made to fill up the deficiency. During February, Second Lieutenant George H. Johnston, Jr., of C Company, was dispatched to Dooly County on a recruiting campaign. Why that county was selected or how Johnston came to have the duty are unknown, but his efforts met with some success. From 6 to 20 February he engaged thirteen or more men for three year enlistments in his company, most of them in a single day. Among them was John Isom Royal (John J. Ryalls in the muster rolls), a farmer who was native of North Carolina and thirty-six years old in February 1863. Royal and his wife, Mary Jane, had six children. [54]

Another soldier recruited at this time was Sparkman Godwin (Sparknin Goodman in the muster rolls), Mary Jane Royal's brother. Godwin was living with an older married sister in Randolph County in 1850 but was married in Dooly County in 1851. By 1860 he was living in Jackson County, Florida, with his wife, Sarah Frances Culpepper, and one child, born in Alabama. Godwin was thirty-five years old when he enlisted. His service record shows that was sick in hospital in Yazoo City, Mississippi, in June 1863; there is no later record of his service. A Corporal Sparkman Godwin was killed carrying the flag of the 64th Georgia at the Battle of the Crater, Petersburg, Virginia, on 30 July 1864. He had enlisted in April 1863. No one by that name can be found in the 1870 or 1880 censuses, but a Sarah Godwin with Alabama-born children was enumerated in that state both times. She was identified as a widow in 1880. Perhaps Godwin never went to Mississippi, or never even enlisted in the sharpshooters, but joined the 64th Georgia instead. [55]

Other new recruits from Dooly County were David Culpepper, John W. Edwards, John H. Finn (Fenn in the 1860 census), William W. Gamble, Wesley Ivey, Cornelius Patrick, Benjamin Peyton, Green Sheppard, Henry J. Stancel, Edward Stokes, and Jasper N. Sutton. These men were almost all farmers or farm workers. In April John Finn and Cornelius Patrick provided Thomas Campbell and Edward Stiles as substitutes, thereby escaping duty themselves. Stiles was probably the Savannah dry-goods salesman of that name; he deserted soon after his enlistment. His service record shows that he had enlisted himself in February 1863 and was not a substitute, but perhaps the date refers to Patrick's original enlistment. There is no record of Campbell's service; perhaps he never joined the battalion.

The ultimate success of Johnston's recruiting may be assessed from the service records of the men involved. David Culpepper, a thirty-nine-year-old farmer, was married and had six children. Culpepper served for a year and a half before going home on sick furlough in August 1864 and apparently never returning. John Edwards, about thirty-three years old when he signed up, was frequently sick but served until he was captured at Nashville in December 1864.

He died of pneumonia at Camp Chase, Ohio, a Federal prison, in January 1865. William Gamble, twenty-five, served until wounded in the thigh at Jonesboro in August 1864. Wesley Ivey was discharged from the army at age thirty-four in January 1864, possibly due to sickness or wound.

Benjamin Peyton or Paton, twenty-two, was sick for much of his service but was still on the muster roll in August 1864 and surrendered with the remnants of the battalion in April 1865. Green L. Sheppard was thirty-six years old in the 1860 census. Georgia born, he was a farmer with a wife and four children at that time. Sheppard died in a field hospital at Chickamauga in September 1863, possibly of pneumonia, although family history says he had been wounded in the battle. However, his name does not appear in a list of wounded there.

Henry J. Stancel, was sick for much of his service and was marked absent on every surviving muster roll from December 1863 to August 1864. He was forty years old when he enlisted and probably not fit for field duty. Edward Stokes, thirty-seven, served until being wounded at Jonesboro in August 1864. Jasper Sutton, thirty-two, was wounded at Chickamauga; he was frequently sick and died in Dooly County in January 1864.[56]

After the affair at Fort McAllister, the sharpshooters returned to Camp Anderson on 14 February and the next day changed base to Camp Jordan in Savannah. That same month, the two newly organized regiments of the Georgia State Line were assigned to the defenses of Savannah. Always on the lookout to increase battalion strength, Shaaff thought he had found another source of recruits to fill his ranks. However, when he wrote to the state adjutant general, Henry C. Wayne, asking for permission to transfer men from the 1st State Line Regiment to his battalion, he learned that the units had been raised for state duty only and were exempt from service in the Confederate army.[57]

A week after moving to Savannah, the battalion had an opportunity on 20 February to show off their tactical skills. General Beauregard was in Savannah on one of his periodic visits and General Mercer arranged a review of the infantry and cavalry units forming the garrison, to be followed by a supper and ball hosted by the ladies of the city. The review, on the city common, last two hours and was attended by the generals, their staffs, and a throng of civilian spectators. It concluded with a skirmish drill by the sharpshooters, followed by a cavalry charge, both of which were praised by the audience. Said the newspaper, "The [sharpshooter drill], especially, was excellent. Every movement was executed with the greatest promptness and precision, showing remarkable proficiency in that peculiar and important branch of the service." Anderson's and Shaaff's men had learned their lessons well.[58]

New recruit John I. Royal was settling into army life with the sharpshooters. Despite some mild sickness, he assured his wife that "I am as well satisfide hear as I would be any whear [sic] but I had rather be at home." He asked for news from home and the prayers of well-wishers, and commented favorably on his rations. About the review of 20 February Royal wrote that he had seen Generals Beauregard and Mercer and the "most people I ever saw."[59]

Commander Worden and the *Montauk* returned to the Ogeechee River on 28 February and succeeded in destroying the *Nashville*, despite heavy fire from Fort McAllister and damage to his ship from an underwater torpedo (mine). On 3 March another US squadron under Captain Percival Drayton, composed of three ironclads, three gunboats and a number of mortar boats, made an attack on McAllister. They bombarded the fort for seven hours in daylight and the mortar boats kept up the fire until 6:00 A.M. on 4 March. The damage was minimal. Most of the mortar rounds went completely over the fort. Of the 224 shells that were fired, only 50 struck the fort; of those, only 27 fell in the batteries; and of those, only 12 exploded. The major result was that McAllister's 8-inch gun was thrown off its mounting, but it was repaired during the night. Captain Robert Martin's 10-inch mortar landed one sand-filled shell squarely on USS *Passaic*, crushing the deck plating and planking, but doing no other damage. The Yankee squadron withdrew on 4 March.[60]

As soon as the new attack on McAllister commenced, the 1st Sharp-shooters marched there from Camp Jordan, a distance of 18 miles. Part of the battalion was placed in the fort while other remained outside as a reserve in case of a Yankee landing. Those inside worked during the night of 3 March to repair the fort's damage and remount the guns, supervised by their own officers and the fort's engineers. It was Shaaff's men who mounted the fort's 8-inch gun on its new carriage. One man, Private James J. Mims, of Thomas County and formerly in the 29th Georgia, had his leg and ankle crushed while working and was carried to Savannah for treatment. His injury was not permanently disabling because he returned to duty, but he was absent sick for much of the balance of his service. Some of the sharpshooters who were friends of the gun captain were allowed to assist in serving the 32-pounder cannon during the bombardment. Privates William Burns and William Muller, both former members of the Savannah Volunteer Guards, and an unnamed corporal were mentioned. On 8 March, after insuring that the crisis was over, the sharpshooters marched back to Camp Jordan.[61]

Private John Royal gave his own account of the action. In his version, the distance covered by the battalion was 30 miles, 20 of which they traveled by railroad. If he was correct, no doubt they rode from Savannah to Way's Station in Bryan County, then marched on foot from there to the fort. Royal was among the party that went into the fort to repair damage. He wrote to his wife about the Yankee shells: "They look dangus [sic] when they coming at us[.] I was friten [sic] a little at first but soon got used to it[.]"[62]

General Mercer issued a congratulatory order to the troops of Fort McAllister on 9 March, mentioning all the units concerned and promising to recommend to General Beauregard that they be allowed to inscribe "Fort McAllister, March 3, 1863," on their flags. Beauregard replied with his own general order on 18 March, also commending the troops and approving the inscription requested by Mercer. In May 1863 the formal thanks of the Confederate Congress was extended to the McAllister garrison. The 1st Georgia Sharpshooters henceforth carried on their flag honors for Fort McAllister for both 1 February and 3 March 1863.[63]

At the end of March 1863 General Beauregard was obliged to address the issue of the relative dates of rank of Captains Shaaff and Hartridge. Shaaff was the senior officer in the battalion and was acting commander after Robert Anderson's departure, but it will be recalled that Hartridge had been a captain and company commander and Shaaff had been a lieutenant before the battalion was organized. Anderson had based his seniority list of captains on an impartial drawing of lots the previous July. Apparently, after Shaaff took command of the battalion Hartridge asserted a claim to seniority. The correspondence has not been found, but a letter of 1 March from the adjutant general's office in Richmond pronounced Hartridge the senior, giving him a claim on battalion command. Beauregard remonstrated with Samuel Cooper, noting that a letter from his office on 20 November 1862, (not found, but possibly the answer to Anderson's plea of 9 November, mentioned above) had recognized Shaaff's seniority, and that Hartridge had accepted the list of June 1862, when the commissions were first requested. Beauregard felt certain that the original list would withstand any scrutiny and asked Cooper to reconsider the decision of 1 March.[64]

During the winter, a tragic incident had occurred when a soldier, Michael Kiener, deserted his sentry post at Cheves Landing by going off in a boat on the night of 21 January and then attempted to shoot Major Anderson and another officer on 22 January. He was charged with desertion and conduct highly prejudicial to good order and discipline. A court-martial in February, presided over by Colonel Olmstead, found him guilty of all charges and specifications and sentenced him to be shot to death.

In a letter to General Beauregard on 11 March asking for a delay in his execution to arrange his personal affairs, Kiener claimed that an evil spirit had come over him. He and Private Charles Gleichman were in a boat with their weapons cocked. When Gleichman shot and killed himself, Kiener jumped up in shock and his rifle discharged accidentally, so he said. Major Anderson must have been close by, perhaps in the act of apprehending the deserters. Kiener told the general that he was a native of France and had lived in America for only a year before the incident. He claimed to be innocent of deliberate wrong-doing and to have only respect for Major Anderson as an officer and a gentleman.[65]

Kiener's execution on 10 April 1863 was an elaborate rite, expected to instill better respect for authority in the whole garrison in Savannah. A firing squad of twelve men was drawn by lot from the battalion. Then an officer to command the squad was chosen, also by drawing lots. The dubious honor fell to Lieutenant Alfred Bryan. A twelve-man squad to escort the condemned to the place of execution was drawn, and a non-commissioned officer, Sergeant Cornelius M. Hardy of C Company, drew the responsibility of leading the escort.

At the appointed hour all the regiments around Savannah were assembled. The escort, whose duty it was to complete the execution if the firing squad botched it, brought Kiener out. The squad lined up six paces from the victim and, on Bryan's command, fired. There was no need for the back-up squad: four of the balls struck Kiener squarely in the chest. As Hardy wrote, "He was killed so dead he hardly moved." William Moody witnessed Kiener's execution and wrote to his wife, "We shot one of our men last friday, the one that deserted his post and tried to get to the garsters [quarters?] and Shot the Major. His name was Keiner. It was an awful looking sight, tho it was a satisfaction. We have three more to be shot But I don't no when we will shoot them." Private John Isom Royal, the new recruit from Dooly County, also wrote home about the execution. He expressed relief that he had not been one of those who drew a lot to be in the firing squad but that the man next to him had been selected.[66]

It was reported in the newspaper that Kiener's real name was Michael LaVol [Laval?], that he was a native of Alsace, a laborer, and 23 years old. When he and Gleichman deserted, they became lost in the marsh and were discovered only by accident. It was then that Gleichman killed himself rather than be apprehended. Kiener's musket discharged accidentally, according to the report. His execution took place on the city common and he was attended by a Catholic priest.[67]

Moody's reference to others to be shot brings up the tales of a number of other deserters who were court-martialed in winter 1863. They were James F. Butler, Frank Englehart, Robert D. Garrison, Zachariah Green, Miles McDaniel, and Doctor Barrentine. The first five deserted from Camp Anderson in a group and were apprehended near enemy lines and while on their way to St. Augustine, Florida. At the same court that tried Kiener they were all found guilty. Garrison, Green, and McDaniel were sentenced to be shot and must have been the three to whom Moody referred. Butler and Englehart were sentenced to one year in ball and chain, because of their youth and previous good character and because it was believed that each of the two men had been persuaded or compelled to desert by the others. Barrentine was tried in April 1863 by a separate court. He had been away a little over a month and had returned voluntarily. The charge of desertion was dropped; he was found guilty of absence without leave and sentenced to forfeiture of one month's pay.

Obviously the military hierarchy thought better of the death sentences issued by the Olmstead court. First, in February 1863, the sentences were delayed for twenty-one days. Then, on 30 March, they were suspended. When the battalion shipped out for Mississippi on 5 May the five offenders remained behind in Chatham County jail, three still under suspended death sentences. But in August 1863 President Jefferson Davis declared a general amnesty and pardon for all accused or convicted deserters. Major Alfred Hartridge, still serving in the defenses of Savannah, had not forgotten his former sharpshooter subordinates. On 7 August he wrote a letter asking that the men be released under the terms of the amnesty; they were and they returned to duty with the battalion.[68]

Private Royal had bee wanting to get a home leave and hoped that his company commander, Captain Ross, would let him go if he could recruit one of his neighbors to come back with him to join the sharpshooters. However, Ross would only consent to send the prospective recruit a pre-paid one-way ticket to Savannah so that he could come in on his own. Royal's wife was also interested in finding and paying a substitute for her husband. Royal approached Ross again but the answer was an emphatic no. Another recent recruit, Donald B. Pearson, had enlisted in C Company in Macon on 1 January, then supplied John Fadden as a substitute in April. Fadden ran off within days. Ross told Royal he would be taking no more substitutes for the time being.

Instead of going home, Royal had his picture taken for his wife. He wrote her on 18 April, "I have had my ambrotype taken today with my uniform and gun and all my harness on as I thought you would like to know how I look in the army...."[69]

In March, Brigadier General William H. T. Walker, newly restored to Confederate service, was assigned to the District of Georgia and given command of a brigade made up of the 25th, 29th, and 30th Georgia Infantry Regiments and Captain Robert Martin's Georgia Battery. His brigade went to the defense of Charleston, in April 1863 but the sharpshooter battalion did not accompany them. At the end of April, Arthur Shaaff was promoted to major, with his rank back-dated to 20 January, and given formal command of the battalion. At the same time, Captain Hartridge was promoted to major also and transferred to the artillery, probably assuaging his feelings about serving under Shaaff and removing any further controversy concerning battalion command.[70]

In Company A, 1st Lieutenant Horace D. Twyman was advanced to replace Shaaff as captain. Twyman was twenty-three years old, a native of Virginia, and a former cadet at West Point, from where he had resigned in early winter 1861. He had been a Confederate staff officer on ordnance duty in Savannah before the formation of the sharpshooter battalion.[71]

The new first lieutenant of A Company was Horace A. Crane, a twenty-year-old native of Camden County and a former clerk in his father's commission house in Savannah. His father was Herman A. Crane who had come to Georgia from Connecticut in the 1830s and established himself as a wholesale grocer. At different times he was associated in business with Thomas Holcombe and George H. Johnston, whose sons also were officers in Shaaff's battalion. Horace Crane and his older brother William had served in the 8th Georgia Infantry at the First Battle of Manassas in 1861 where William was killed. Colonel Charles L. Olmstead, who worked with Crane before the war, described him as "a handsome young fellow with rosy cheeks and dark eyes. He had then the same equable, pleasant temperament that [he had later]; he has been a much beloved man all his life… There are few better men or more worthy citizens."[72]

The second lieutenants in the company were Alfred Bryan and Charles L. Schlatter, Jr. Bryan, Savannah-born, was twenty-four years old and a former clerk in a commission house. His father was Joseph Bryan, a slave trader, a former naval officer, and one-time chief of police in Savannah. Alfred Bryan's grandfather, also Joseph, had been a US congressman from Georgia in the early years of the century. Newly commissioned in September 1862, Bryan had been junior second lieutenant until Crane's promotion.

Schlatter had begun his military career in May 1861 as third corporal of the Brunswick Rifles. He transferred into George Dent's Glynn Guards when that company was formed and followed its fortunes until May 1862. He served for two months in the 4th Georgia Cavalry, one day in the Savannah Volunteer Guards Battalion, and became the original first sergeant of D Company of the sharpshooters on 2 August 1862. He replaced E. J. Oliveros as battalion sergeant major on 1 January 1863. Incredibly, he was only twenty or twenty-one years old, so he must have been a model soldier. Recommended for promotion by Major Shaaff on 4 May 1863, he assumed his position the same day. His paperwork flowed smoothly to and from Richmond and he was formally promoted on 30 May with date of rank of 2 May. Schlatter was a civil engineer by training and a native of Pennsylvania. His father, Colonel Charles L. Schlatter, was president of the Brunswick and Florida Railroad. In 1839–1840 the elder Schlatter had been the surveyor of the trans-Alleghany route of the Pennsylvania Railroad between Harrisburg and Pittsburgh.[73]

First Lieutenant Benjamin Hopkins Hardee was the new captain of B Company. He was a twenty-nine-year-old native of Camden County and had been a commission merchant in Savannah before the war. His father was the older brother of General William J. Hardee, and his own older brother was the better known Charles Seton Hardee. Second Lieutenant Henry Herrmann, age thirty-four, a Prussian-born grocer from Savannah, was advanced to first lieutenant, and Second Sergeant Thomas Smythe Wayne, younger brother of Lieutenant Robert P. Wayne, was commissioned junior second lieutenant and transferred from Company A to Company B. Hardee and Herrmann had both been officers of the DeKalb Rifles since the company was formed in 1861. The younger Wayne had enlisted in the 1st Georgia Volunteers in 1861 when he was sixteen years old. His commission was also approved 30 May to rank from 2 May.[74]

Previously, on 5 April, First Sergeant Charles S. Pattillo of A Company had been transferred to B Company as second lieutenant by battalion special order. It will be recalled that his recommendation for promotion had been pending at the War Department since December. It was finally approved 30 May, giving him date of rank from 2 May. Hermann's promotion made Pattillo the senior second lieutenant with Thomas Wayne his junior. It should be recalled that these late May appointments did not reach the battalion until after its departure from Savannah.[75]

In the battalion staff, Captain Robert Footman, the quartermaster, trans-ferred to the 5th Georgia Cavalry, Colonel Anderson's regiment, at the end of March. His appointment was disallowed by the quartermaster general in June and he wound up in the 18th Georgia Battalion, formerly the Savannah Volun-teer Guard Battalion. Later still, he was quartermaster of the famous Stonewall Brigade, defending the Richmond and Danville Railroad, and in 1865 he came full circle, being transferred to Robert H. Anderson's cavalry brigade in Wheel-er's corps. Footman was paroled at Hillsboro, North Carolina in May 1865.[76]

One of Footman's final official acts as sharpshooter quartermaster was to requisition food supplies for the last two weeks in March. The "Abstract of Provisions" in his file provides an opportunity to confirm battalion strength as well as examine the diet of the Civil War soldier. For the week beginning 15 March Footman drew rations for 278 enlisted men, and for the week beginning 22 March the number was 280.

The items of food included bacon, corn meal or bread, sugar, vinegar, molasses, salt, and soap. A note indicates that in lieu of coffee, not often available in the Confederacy, additional meal would be issued at a ratio of 8 pounds of meal per 100 men. The bread ration was six-sevenths corn meal and one-seventh rice one week and nine-tenths corn and one-tenth rice the next. The daily ration was seven ounces of bacon and a half a gill of molasses per man. The monotony of the diet and the lack of greens is self-evident. In his comments on rations in February, John Royal had told his wife that some of the staples of his diet were bacon, beets, and rice. Rice as a substitute for corn meal was acceptable to the soldiers from the coastal counties, perhaps less so for those whose homes were inland.[77]

Footman was replaced in the sharpshooter battalion by Captain Willis or Willie G. Gray at the end of April on the recommendation of General Mercer. Gray was a native of Edinburgh, Scotland, about twenty-eight years old, and a businessman in Savannah for several years. He had been a private in the 1st Georgia Volunteers in the early days of the war. The duties of quartermaster were performed by Robert Wayne during the interval between Footman's departure and Gray's arrival. In fact, Alfred Hartridge recommended Wayne for promotion and permanent assignment as quartermaster but Mercer overruled him.

Footman's departure was preceded by that of Dr. John T. McFarland, the battalion medical officer, who left to join the 5th Cavalry at the end of February. McFarland became surgeon of Beverly H. Robertson's cavalry brigade in December 1864, was promoted to Major Surgeon in June 1864, became commander of Walker Hospital in Columbus, Georgia, in January 1865, and was reunited with Footman and Robert Anderson in the latter's brigade in April 1865. He, too, was paroled at Hillsboro in May 1865.[78]

McFarland was succeeded by Assistant Surgeon John Marshall Dent, a man about twenty-eight years old, who had been commissioned in September 1862, and was second cousin to Captain George Dent. Dr. Dent's father, Dr. John Dent, had been an early trustee of the Medical College of Georgia. Dent joined the Oglethorpe Light Infantry of Augusta in April 1862 as a private. That company had been a part Ramsey's 1st Georgia Regiment in 1861 and served at Pensacola and in western Virginia. Many of the members of the Oglethorpes and three other companies banded together in 1862 to become the 12th Georgia Artillery Battalion at Augusta and later Savannah. Dent must have left the ranks in September 1862, accepted a commission as assistant surgeon, and evidently became medical officer of the 12th Battalion until his transfer to the sharpshooters in February 1863.[79] Thus constituted and commanded, the 1st Battalion Georgia Sharpshooters was prepared to enter on new fields of conflict.

2

JACKSON

General William H. T. Walker's brigade, including the sharpshooter battalion, was ordered to Mississippi on 5 May 1863. Their mission was to join the army being formed by General Joseph E. Johnston to prevent the Union capture of Vicksburg. Confederate forces there under General John Pemberton were besieged by the Union army under General U. S. Grant. Walker's brigade was composed of the same three regiments it had before plus the 4th Louisiana Battalion, 1st Battalion Georgia Sharpshooters, and Captain Martin's Georgia battery of six guns. Brigade strength was about 2,500 men. The Georgia-South Carolina brigade of General States Rights Gist was also sent to Mississippi; Gist was the senior of the two brigadiers and was in charge of both brigades.[1]

John I. Royal captured the flavor of the way the order was received in the sharpshooter battalion. "All is hustle and confusion. Some pleased some mad some laughing some cursing But as for my part I don't want to go for I had rather stay closer home than to go away of[f] in that far off country." Then he added stoically, "I am in my country's Service and She has the Right to Call for my services anywhere and I will go as cheerful as I possibly can...." Royal added that he was sending some things home because the men were limited to taking with them only what they could carry in a knapsack.[2]

Amid the preparations for departure, Augustus P. Adamson, a private in the 30th Georgia, noted in a letter home on 7 May that "[my] regiment has not yet left but will leave, in all probability, this evening at 3 o'clock. The 25th regiment left yesterday evening, the 4th battalion and 1st battalion Georgia Sharpshooters have also left. They are now moving the baggage to Savannah. Everything is in a bustle."[3]

The size of the sharpshooter battalion at the time of the movement is not precisely known but an approximation can be made. On 8 May, Major Shaaff signed a voucher at Selma, Alabama, for a consignment of firewood to be used as fuel. The voucher listed one major, 5 captains, 13 lieutenants, and 250 non-commissioned officers and privates with the battalion. Whether this figure was the authorized strength or actual number of men present is not evident. It appears that Assistant Surgeon Dent was not present with the battalion at this time. He had been granted thirty days furlough beginning 4 April and had not returned in time for the troop movement. A report of 3 May 1863 showed that he was absent from his unit.[4]

Unfortunately, Dent was not the only member of the unit left behind. Not all soldiers shared John Royal's sense of patriotism and the records show that seventeen men deserted from the battalion on the eve of departing for Mississippi. More than half of them were from B Company, the former DeKalb Rifles of Bryan and Chatham counties. To those men, the concept of service "for the war" obviously meant only service close to home. Of the others, several caught up with the battalion in Mississippi and some returned later in the year in north Georgia. Besides the men left in Savannah, three men deserted while in transit, one of them a sergeant. He also came back before year's end. One of the other two caught up to the battalion in Jackson but deserted again in June 1864.

Besides those unauthorized departures, an additional slight loss of manpower occurred when General Mercer allowed, on 1 May, an exchange of men between the sharpshooters and the Navy. As a result of the exchange, seven sailors became infantrymen while nine soldiers "went to sea" for a net loss of two to the battalion. Two other men, left behind in hospital in Savannah, died in early May. Private B. Kersey died of typhoid fever on 6 May and Private W. H. T. Conway died on 10 May of an unstated cause. Both were buried in Laruel Grove Cemetery. B. Kersey was possibly Bannister Kersey, the younger brother of Corporal William Kersey of A Company. If so, he was eighteen years old at the time of his enlistment in his brother's company at Camp Jordan in March 1863. He survived army life less than two months.[5]

Two of the new men from the Navy were the Withrow brothers, John and Joshua, twenty-six and twenty-one years old, respectively. They were North Carolina-born and the sons of James Withrow, a farmer in Fannin County. In all likelihood they were conscripts because they had entered service at the camp of instruction at Decatur in February 1863. Service in the sharpshooters was no more to their liking than service in the Navy: by December 1863 they were absent without leave and by February 1864 they were listed as deserters. Possibly they were Union sympathizers; Fannin County was in that part of the state known for its dissatisfaction with secession.[6]

The sharpshooters left Savannah 5 May and arrived at Jackson, Mississippi, on the tenth or eleventh. The route was by way of Macon and Columbus, Georgia; Montgomery, Selma and Demopolis, Alabama; and thence to Jackson. In some places where the rail lines did not connect, the troops marched between points or were ferried by boat. The turnout of the civilian populace was overwhelming, with men and officers of both brigades feted and feasted at every stop. Colonel Claudius C. Wilson, commanding the 25th Georgia, devoted a large part of a letter to his wife to a description of the excursion, as in this sample, "At Fort Valley & many other stations between Macon & Columbus the ladies sent out eatables, milk, and bouquets in any quantity. I got a fresh one at almost every place we stopped and gave it away to the prettiest girl I could find at the next."[7]

Claudius Wilson was a respected lawyer from Savannah. A native of Effingham County, he was twenty-nine years old, a graduate of Emory College, and a former solicitor-general of the Eastern District of Georgia when he was mustered into Confederate service as captain of the Bryan Guards from Chatham County in August 1861. In September he was elected colonel of the 25th Georgia Volunteers and served with his regiment on coast defense duty from Savannah to Wilmington, North Carolina. From time to time he acted as commander of a brigade of two or three regiments, including his own. Wilson's wife, with whom he corresponded regularly, was the former Katherine Morrison of Augusta. On his father's side Wilson had a three-year-old cousin named Theodore Roosevelt, future president of the United States.[8]

The men of Walker's brigade traveled for six days in open rail cars and were subjected to all the hazards of the ramshackle Southern rail system: flying soot and hot embers from the engine, sudden accidents on the poorly-maintained road, and even low bridges. Private Angus McDermid of the 29th Georgia wrote on 13 May to his father at home, "Father, we had a bad luck last Saturday. We was nearly all of us up on top of the train a riding and it run under too bridges and kiled 2 of our men. I was rite side of the one that got kiled. He was a standing up and I was a seting down."[9]

The natural desire of the men to visit their families before leaving Georgia and Carolina, with or without official permission, led to very bad straggling. General Thomas Jordan, Beauregard's chief of staff in Charleston, reported to the Confederate War Department that straggling was "disgraceful" and one regiment had left 500 men behind. George Mercer in his diary also commented on the straggling, saying, "Our troops behaved badly when ordered to the West. They were taken by surprise and unwilling to leave without bidding farewell to their families." One may suppose that some men of the 1st Sharpshooter Battalion participated in this mass absence.[10]

The day after arrival in Jackson, 12 May, Walker was sent out from the town with the 1st Battalion Georgia Sharpshooters, 25th Georgia Regiment, 4th Louisiana Battalion, and Martin's Georgia Battery to support General John Gregg's forces facing the Yankee advance from Port Gibson. Walker and Gregg met as the latter was withdrawing from his encounter with the advancing Union troops under General James B. McPherson, and the combined force spent the night of 12 May at Mississippi Springs. The next day, 13 May, they remained in line of battle to repel a further Union advance but no action took place.[11]

According to Sergeant Isaac Hermann of Martin's Battery, who had been with the crew that served the mortar at Fort McAllister, that day General Walker personally placed one of the battery guns at a bend in the road where they would surprise an unsuspecting advancing column. Hermann claims there was no infantry in the immediate vicinity of his battery and he asked the general where his support was. "Support, Hell," answered the general, "If they charge you, fight them with the hand spikes. Don't you never leave this post," after which Walker left. While it makes a good story and presents a fair appraisal of the general's fire-eating character, this anecdote omits the likely presence of the infantry elements of Walker's brigade.[12]

General Johnston decided to evacuate Jackson and to give him time to carry away the stores he had accumulated, he ordered Gregg to use all available forces to hold off McPherson's advance. Besides his own brigade, Gregg now had for defense of the city most of Walker's brigade and the advance party of Gist's brigade under Colonel Percy Colquitt of the 46th Georgia.

Early in the morning of 14 May, Gregg deployed his small force, about 6,000 men with 3 batteries, to check the advance of John B. McPherson's XVII Corps and William T. Sherman's XV Corps. In his center, on the Clinton road, Gregg posted Colquitt with the 900 men of Gist's brigade, which was made up of the 24th South Carolina, some companies of the 46th Georgia, a battalion of the 14th Mississippi, and a Mississippi battery. Walker, with the 25th and 30th Georgia Regiments and the 4th Louisiana Battalion, was placed in Colquitt's support. Gregg's own brigade was on the Livingston road about 2 1/2 miles to Colquitt's right. On the Mississippi Springs or Raymond road, on Colquitt's left, at a bridge over Lynch Creek, southwest of Jackson, Gregg placed the 3rd Kentucky Mounted Infantry, the 1st Battalion Georgia Sharpshooters, and Martin's Georgia battery, the last two detached from Walker's brigade, all under Colonel Albert Thompson of the Kentucky regiment.[13]

At 9:00 A.M. McPherson's column came up the Clinton road and Sherman's force showed itself on the Raymond road soon thereafter. For five hours amid a heavy rainstorm, the two forces clashed with skirmishers and dueling batteries.

Thompson's men had barely taken their positions when the Yankees came in sight and Captain Robert Martin gave the order to fire. The battery began dropping shells among Sherman's advancing men. After a quick reconnaissance of the position, Sherman ordered General James M. Tuttle to form his division for an attack. At 11:00 A.M., after the heavy rains had subsided, Sherman's force, four times larger than Thompson's, advanced on the position with twelve guns covering deployment. For a brief time Thompson was able to hold the bridge but eventually fell back to a woodline fronting the rifle pits on the west side of Jackson, but without destroying the bridge over the creek. Isaac Hermann described the scene from his artillery viewpoint: "The ground on which we stood was a gradual incline, while that of the enemy was about on a level with us, leaving a sort of basin or valley between both lines. It was a novel sight to see our skirmishers contending every inch of the ground before an overwhelming force, to see them load and fire, and gradually falling back, facing the advancing foe."[14]

Tuttle's division was redeployed on a two-brigade front and charged Thompson's position in the woodline. In the face of such strength, the little command withdrew into the Jackson defenses. Without doubt, the skirmishers on that front must have been the sharpshooters. Meanwhile, on the right, Colquitt's brigade, astride the Clinton Road, had met and been driven in by Crocker's division of McPherson's corps after a sharp artillery barrage. By 2:00 P.M., word had been received from Jackson that General Johnston had successfully removed most of the stores, and Colquitt retired to Jackson.[15]

Gregg admitted to a loss of 200 men, and Colquitt also reported 200 casualties, more than half of them in the 24th South Carolina. Walker refused to make a report after the battle. A telegram was received in Savannah on 28 May that said, "Sharpshooters all right; nobody hurt," but the records show one man wounded and one man captured in A Company. English-born Private Daniel Brannon, 30 years old, was wounded in the right hand necessitating the amputation of two fingers. He was a former resident of Savannah and had served in the 29th Georgia before coming to the sharpshooters. His name appeared as Daniel Branwood on a list of Georgians in hospitals in Meridian, Mississippi, on 26 May. He was shifted from hospital to hospital over the next year and was finally retired for disability in October 1864. Sergeant James A. Thornton of C Company wrote four weeks afterward that the battle had been fought "before I got up with them" and that the battalion had only one man wounded. His comment suggests that the whole battalion may not have arrived in Jackson by 14 May.

No losses were recorded on the muster rolls of the other three companies but the service records of Privates James Comaskey, A Company; Abraham Ehrlish, B Company; Patrick Gately, C Company; and Stephen Chitwood, D Company, all show that they were captured on 14 May and paroled at Demopolis, Alabama, on 5 June. According to Colonel Wilson, some sick men of his brigade were captured in hospital in Jackson before they could be evacuated. Sherman gave orders to parole Confederate prisoners on 15 May but individual records show they were held until 5 June.[16]

Lieutenant Colonel James Harrison Wilson, inspector general and chief topographical engineer on Grant's staff, recorded in his journal for 14 May: "A prisoner captured this morning says he belongs to 1st Georgia Battalion (Shaaff's), brigade of Walker; left Savannah on May 5 by [railroad] cars; arrived at Jackson on Sunday morning last." Grant and his senior staff may have been aware reinforcements were on the way to Pemberton but this was the first notice of who they were and where they were from.[17]

Gregg's miscellaneous commands retreated into Jackson and then out the north side of the city toward Canton in a driving rain. While the withdrawal from the battlefield had been orderly, the retreat out of Jackson was precipitous. Major Shaaff of the sharpshooter battalion was so rushed that he left behind the horse he had stabled in the city that morning in anticipation of the combat. The men also lost most of their baggage. Colonel Wilson with the 25th Georgia, 1st Sharpshooters and Martin's Battery held a position in the city until the rest of the army had withdrawn, then acted as rear guard for the column. They marched in the rain and mud for 7 miles before camping for the night.

Sherman withdrew from Jackson on the fifteenth after destroying rail and industrial facilities. Johnston's army reoccupied the city on the sixteenth and were joined there by Samuel Maxey's brigade and the rest of Gist's, the balance of the 46th Georgia and the 16th South Carolina; and the 29th Georgia, the final component of Walker's brigade. These units had been warned not to enter Jackson when its fall seemed imminent and had withdrawn to Forest.[18]

General Johnston regrouped his forces and on 23 May received approval from Richmond to promote W. H. T. Walker to major general. Walker was given command of a division composed of his own brigade plus those of States Rights Gist, Matthew Ector, John Gregg, and Evander McNair, the cavalry brigade of John Adams, and some miscellaneous troops. After Walker's promotion, senior regimental commander Colonel Claudius C. Wilson of the 25th Georgia took charge of Walker's brigade.

Because Walker had taken all of his brigade staff officers to form the staff of the new division, Wilson was left to fend for himself in forming a new brigade staff. He solved his problem by taking officers from the units of the brigade and giving them acting staff rank. Captains A. M. Bryan of the 25th Georgia and John D. Cameron of the 29th acted at different times as brigade quartermaster.

Similarly, First Lieutenants Josiah Law Holcombe and Robert P. Wayne of the 1st Sharpshooter Battalion served variously as brigade adjutant, inspector, and ordnance officer. Wayne was normally adjutant of the battalion, while Holcombe was an officer in Company C. Holcombe had the advantage of having had professional training at the Georgia Military Institute and had been a sergeant in the 8th Georgia in the first year of the war. Like Wayne, Holcombe, now twenty-five years old and a native of Savannah, had been a clerk in the US Customs House. His father, Thomas Holcombe, a merchant, had been elected mayor of Savannah for a one year term in October 1862.

With Robert P. Wayne now acting as brigade adjutant, Major Shaaff appointed 2nd Lieutenant George Houston Johnston, Jr., as acting battalion adjutant. Johnston was a bookkeeper and the son of a bank officer in Savannah. He was a twenty-two-year-old native of Chatham County in 1860. In 1861 he enlisted in a volunteer company in Savannah and joined the Sharpshooters in October 1862 as junior second lieutenant of C Company with date of rank of 19 August 1862. It will be remembered that Johnston had been the recruiting officer for his company in Dooly County in February.[19]

In March 1863 General Beauregard, commanding the Department of South Carolina, Georgia, and Florida, had ordered new battle flags for each regiment, battalion, and battery under his command. These flags must have been distributed in April or May. The regiments of Walker's and Gist's brigades may not have received theirs until after arrival in Mississippi. A comment in Robert Wayne's service record shows that on 27 May 1863, at Clinton, he turned in five battle flags to Major N. O. Tilton, the division quartermaster. These were probably the old flags of the brigade's five regiments and battalions being turned in for the new ones, but there is no corresponding record for the replacement colors. If they did receive a new flag, the battalion would carry it for another year.

The Beauregard flags have been described as similar to those of the Army of Northern Virginia but with the field surrounded on all four sides by a white bunting border. The flag was attached to the staff by a red or dark blue bunting sleeve sewn to the white border. Some of the flags may have carried their unit designations painted in black numerals on cotton strips sewn to the flag.[20]

In Shaaff's battalion, after Josiah Holcombe went to brigade staff and George Johnston became acting battalion adjutant, Captain William Ross had only one full time junior officer remaining in C Company to share duty with him, Second Lieutenant Nicholas Bayard Sadler of Jacksonville, Florida. The junior officer, about twenty-five years old, was a former cadet at the Georgia Military Institute in Marietta, and a physician, having graduated from the Medical College of Virginia. After his attempts to obtain a commission in early

1861 failed, Sadler enlisted as a private in the 2nd Florida Volunteers and went to Yorktown, Virginia, with his regiment. At the request of the governor, he was returned to Florida, given a state commission as lieutenant, and made a drill master. It was probably while on this duty that he met Robert H. Anderson. In 1862, perhaps at Anderson's urging, he became a private in the Chatham Artillery in Savannah and then transferred to the sharpshooters.[21]

Nicholas's brother, Houston, was a member of the Savannah Volunteer Guard Battalion. The brothers were the sons of Henry Robinson Sadler, a businessman with wide-ranging interests along the coast of Georgia and Florida. The elder Sadler had died in Jacksonville in 1854 and his widow, Catherine Ann, had moved to Marietta where she kept up an active social life. On his mother's side Nicholas came from two distinguished families. Mrs. Sadler was a McIntosh, a prominent Georgia family. Her collateral ancestor, Lachlan McIntosh, had been an American general in the Revolutionary War, and succeeding generations had provided other men to the country's armed forces. Mrs. Sadler's mother was Elizabeth Bayard, whose family name in New York dated back to the days of New Amsterdam, when Nicholas Bayard, of French Huegenot blood, had been Pieter Stuyvesant's brother-in-law and confidant. Later generations of men in the same family had amassed considerable wealth and prestige in municipal affairs.[22]

As medical officer after their arrival in Mississippi, it appears that Assistant Surgeon Thomas R. Cosby was assigned to the sharpshooters in the absence of Dr. John M. Dent, left behind in Savannah. Cosby's record shows that he was from Virginia and was with a New Orleans artillery battery in November 1861. By November, 1862, he was on duty in Jackson, Mississippi, and must have been there when the sharpshooters arrived. He was issued forage by the battalion quartermaster for June 1863 and was still on the muster roll in February 1864. Not much else is known about him.[23]

Reference has already been made to notification of promotions reaching the sharpshooters after their arrival in Mississippi. By a three-page letter of 26 May from Vaughn's Station, Mississippi, Major Shaaff acknowledged to the War Department receipt of his own promotion to major and those of the other officers in the battalion. However, he took exception to the dates of rank and to the placement of officers within the companies. As he put it, "As promotion is now made by company and as the Dept. have clearly fallen into the error that Lieuts. Hardie [sic] and Hermann were both in 'A' Company, from which I was promoted, I respectfully request that I may be authorized to alter the names in the appts. of Hardie & Hermann to those of Capt. H. D. Twyman and 1st Lieut. Horace Crane." Shaaff's request was approved but his letter set off a reaction that reached to Charleston as well as Richmond. Because of the manner in which it had been organized, the War Department looked on the sharpshooter battalion as an integrated unit in which all officers served on a single seniority list unlike volunteer regiments in which seniority was within companies and then within the regiment. Shaaff maintained that the battalion should be treated the same as the volunteer regiments. General Beauregard, who felt that Walker's and Gist's brigades still belonged to his department, more politely questioned the War Department's decision. An endorsement by Secretary of War James A. Seddon sided with Shaaff and that settled the issue.[24]

Following the battle at Jackson and retreat to Canton, Johnston sent Walker's division northeast of Vicksburg to secure Yazoo City and watch the bridge over Big Black River. The sharpshooter battalion served as town provost guard while the division occupied Yazoo City for two weeks. The division maneuvered in that area during June, changing base from Yazoo City to Vernon while Johnston tried to assemble a force for the relief of Pemberton in Vicksburg. The troops were plagued by the lack of good water. Sickness began to mount, with Colonel Wilson reporting 300 men absent sick from his brigade. In addition, desertions and unauthorized absences were on the increase. Angus McDermid estimated that 250 men had deserted from the brigade.[25]

On leaving Yazoo City the battalion, which had already lost so much in the evacuation of Jackson, was forced to strip itself down to what each man could carry in his pack. "B" (possibly Captain Benjamin H. Hardee) wrote that he was limited to two shirts, two pairs of undergarments, two pairs of socks, and one pair of trousers. Everything else he had was left with a Colonel White who had offered hospitality to the officers and men of the sharpshooters while they were in Yazoo.

Years after the war, Cuyler King received a letter from a Colonel White offering to return to him the remains of the personal belongings left in his attic in June 1863. White lamented the loss of items of clothing to moths and damp, but reminded Cuyler, "The loft where they were deposited leaked from the many bullet holes the raiders made in the roof of the house (you know we had two severe battles in Yazoo City after you left)." The writer went on to say that "yourself and Lt. Twyman" were the only two who had not responded to his initial request for instructions on how to dispose of the property. Twyman's service record contains a request, dated 16 April 1864, for a duplicate of his regular army commission because the original had been captured at Yazoo City in June 1863.[26]

A review of compiled service records shows that only two members of Shaaff's battalion were sick enough to be admitted to hospital in May, but the numbers increased dramatically thereafter. Forty-four men were sent to hospital in June and six of them died. In July twelve men entered hospital, three of them re-admissions. For August twelve men were admitted, two of them readmissions, and three died. One died in Alabama after being evacuated, one died in Mississippi after Walker's division had left him behind, and one was carried to Georgia and died in Marietta in October. Only one sharpshooter, a musician, is known to have deserted in May and none in June.[27]

Morris Harris Allen and Seaborn M. Allen, brothers of Fayette County, enlisted separately in two different units in fall 1861 when they were eighteen and sixteen years old. They were the sons of Coleman A. Allen and Matilda W. Harris, the daughter of Morris Harris, formerly of Warren County, North Carolina. On their mother's side, the young men were distant kin to Confederate Governor Isham Green Harris of Tennessee and Young L. Harris, the benefactor of the north Georgia college that bears his name.

In August 1862 the brothers transferred into D Company of the sharpshooter battalion. Morris was sent to hospital in Canton, Mississippi, with an unspecified illness on 19 June 1863. He was evacuated to Alabama and died in a hospital in Mobile on 21 August, although he was carried on the company roll as sick in hospital as late as 31 December 1863. Possibly unaware of his brother's fate, Seaborn fought at Chickamauga where he was wounded and was hospitalized for many months. He survived the war and lived until 1893. When he died, he was buried in the Allen family cemetery near Jonesboro.[28]

Private John Asa Oliver Mann of C Company had an unusual occupation for an enlisted soldier: he was a lawyer in civilian life and had lived in Decatur in DeKalb County with his mother and younger brother before the war. A native of Elbert County, he entered service in Atlanta in October 1862, perhaps as a conscript, although the record does not say so, at the approximate age of twenty-nine years and somehow found his way to the sharpshooters. Taken sick in June 1863, he was hospitalized first in Canton, then in Breckinridge's division hospital at Lauderdale Springs. Mann was furloughed in September, then discharged for disability. He died in Decatur on 1 November and his final pay was claimed by his mother, Mrs. Malinda Mann.[29]

An especially poignant loss to the sharpshooters and to their family was the death of the Cobb brothers, William, twenty-five, and Marcus, seventeen, sons of Randolph County farmer Absalom Cobb. They had enlisted in their home county only the previous 23 January and were whisked off to Mississippi within three months of joining up. Possibly both possessed frail constitution or poor health when they entered service. Three weeks of hard marching in the dusty, waterless conditions of summertime Mississippi proved too much for them. William died at Canton on 2 June and Marcus at Yazoo City on 7 June, both of "brain fever" or encephalitis. There is no record to tell if they were buried locally or if the bodies were sent home.[30]

Another of the men who went to hospital in June was First Sergeant Peter Derst's brother, Private John Derst of B Company. Twenty-two years old in 1860, he had come from Hesse-Darmstadt, Germany, in 1855 to join his father and brothers already in Savannah. Later he was a member of the DeKalb Rifles. John had been a baker in Savannah and once his talent became known in the army he was detailed as baker to Walker's division hospital. He continued in that occupation for the rest of the war. At Fair Grounds Hospital in Atlanta in 1864 his bread was judged by the chief surgeon to be the best of any of the fourteen hospitals in the city. After Atlanta fell to Sherman, Derst is supposed to have walked home to Savannah, taking three weeks to make the trip.[31]

While the sharpshooters were marching and fighting in Mississippi, a small drama was playing itself out in Savannah. On Thursday, 26 May, Mena Landgraff, a shopkeeper and the wife of Private Charles A. Landgraff of D Company, disappeared. A woman who was living with her said Mrs. Landgraff had left the house early to go to market, carrying with her about $150 in cash. She was expected home for breakfast but was never seen again, although several people reported seeing her in the marketplace. Her friends suspected she had been kidnapped or murdered. The incident was reported in the newspaper and three weeks later the city council offered a reward of $500 for information about Mrs. Landgraff. No report of her reappearance has been found, nor any record of her burial in a Savannah cemetery.

Charles "Landkraft," her husband, age thirty, a florist born in Germany, was enumerated in the 1860 census, but he appeared to be unmarried at that time. The muster roll shows that Andrew C. Landgraff was sick in camp on 30 June 1863 and sick at a hospital in Alabama on 31 August. If he was told of his wife's disappearance, his reaction went unrecorded.[32]

At Canton during May or June, the 29th Georgia had recovered a man, Ernest J. Chapman, who had deserted months previously and run off to Mississippi. He was picked up by a soldier from the 1st Sharpshooter Battalion, possibly performing provost duty, and returned to his unit, where he was tried by court-martial and eventually executed. Later, at Morton, the sharpshooter battalion was given the unpleasant duty of executing another deserter, this one from the 25th Georgia, who had been discovered by Colonel Wilson serving in a cavalry regiment in Mississippi. He, too, was sentenced to death and, despite repeated appeals to General Johnston for clemency, was shot by Shaaff's men.[33]

Arthur Shaaff had not forgotten the men who had shirked duty by remaining in Savannah when the battalion left in May or deserting since then. On 1 July 1863 a reward of $30 was posted in the city's newspapers for the apprehension of each of twenty men "who have shamefully abandoned their commands when about marching against the marauding foe." The notice was to run for one month. The men were as follows:

From A Company:

Sergeant Stephen B. Rhymes, enlisted in Henry County, Ala., 16th April, 1862, 36 years of age, 5 feet 9 inches high, fair complexion, blue eyes, light hair.

Corporal Hugh Heffernan, enlisted at Savannah, 14th February, 1861, 22 years of age, 5 feet 9 inches high, fair complexion, grey eyes, light hair, deserted at Yazoo, June 8.

Robert A. Beasley, enlisted at Savannah, 8th August, 1861, a blacksmith, 19 years of age, 5 feet 8 1/2 inches high, dark complexion, grey eyes, brown hair, deserted at Yazoo June 8.

T. J. Donnelly, enlisted at Savannah, 14th February, 1862, 25 years of age, 5 feet 8 inches high, fair complexion, blue eyes, dark hair.

Henry W. Jordan, enlisted April 29, 1862, at Causton's Bluff, near Savannah, dark complexion, dark eyes, 5 feet 10 inches high, deserted with Sgt. Rhymes in or near Appling County, Ga., in April 1863.

A. C. Banner, enlisted April 29, 1862, at Causton's Bluff, 28 years of age, 5 feet 10 inches high, dark eyes, dark complexion, dark hair, deserted at Savannah.

G. Banner, enlisted 4th March, 1862, at Homersville, Ga., light complexion, grey eyes, light hair, born in Appling County.

Isaiah Banner, enlisted 4th March, 1862, 25 years of age, 5 feet 11 inches high, light complexion, grey eyes, light hair.

Charles W. Wheeler, from Appling County, Ga., light complexion, light hair, light eyes, 19 years of age, 5 feet 8 inches high, deserted 4th May, 1863.

Benj. F. Wheeler, from Appling County, Ga., 27 years of age, 5 feet 8 inches high, light complexion, light hair, light eyes, deserted 4th March, 1863.

The Banners and Wheelers are supposed to be in Appling County.

From B Company:

Corp. Peter Schaffer, enlisted 5th June, 1861, at Savannah, deserted at Savannah, 5th May, 1863, a native of Germany, a baker by occupation, 19 years of age, 5 feet 6 inches high, light complexion, grey eyes, light hair.

Musician George Eckel, aged 27 years, 5 feet 6 inches high, light complexion, blue eyes, light hair, born in Germany, by occupation a butcher, enlisted in Bryan County, Ga., 18th March, 1862, deserted at Savannah, 5th May, 1863.

John Kessel, aged 27 years, 5 feet 5 inches high, dark complexion, grey eyes, dark hair, born in Prussia, by occupation a gardener, enlisted in Bryan County, 6th March, 1862, deserted at Savannah, 5th May, 1863.

John Deckker, aged 28 years, 5 feet 4 inches high, light complexion, blue eyes, red hair, born in Germany, by occupation a tailor, enlisted 5th June, 1861, deserted 5th May, 1863, at Savannah.

John Blatz, aged 28 years, 5 feet 5 inches high, light complexion, grey eyes, light hair, born in Germany, by occupation a gardener, enlisted in Savannah, June 5, 1861, deserted 5th May, 1863, at Savannah.

Samuel Phillips, aged 31 years, 5 feet 5 inches high, sallow complexion, grey eyes, light hair, born in Bryan County, by occupation a farmer, enlisted in Bryan County, 3rd March, 1862, deserted at Savannah, 5th May, 1863.

Wm. Grauss, 26 years old, 5 feet 11 inches high, dark complexion, grey eyes, dark hair, born in Germany, by occupation a baker, enlisted at Savannah, 5th June, 1861, deserted 5th May, 1863, at Savannah.

Louis Bromm, aged 20 years, 5 feet 6 inches high, light complexion, blue eyes, red hair, born in Germany, by occupation a baker, enlisted at Savannah, 5th June, 1861, deserted 5th May, 1863, at Savannah.

Louis Schnee, aged 35 years, 5 feet 9 inches high, dark complexion, black eyes, black hair, born in France, by occupation a gardener, enlisted in Bryan County, 17 August, 1862, deserted 5th May, 1863.

Jas. M. Thomas, aged 33 years, 5 feet 5 1/2 inches high, light complexion, blue eyes, light hair, born in Ware County, Ga., conscripted August 13th, 1862, deserted 4th May, 1863, at Savannah.[34]

Within a week of Shaaff's announcement a card of protest was posted in the papers. Corporal Hugh Heffernan and Private Robert Beasley wanted it known that they were not deserters but had been taken sick on the march and had absented themselves for six or seven days. They asked that the correction be published for the benefit of their friends in Savannah. Nonetheless, Hefferman, a clerk in Savannah in civilian life, paid a price for his absence: a list of casualties published a month later named him as a private.[35]

Outside Vicksburg, General Johnston unsuccessfully sought a place to penetrate Grant's line north of the railroad. He resolved to move south of the road and make an attack on 7 July, but on 4 July Pemberton surrendered and Johnston retired to Jackson. For the Confederacy to maintain a position in Mississippi he felt it essential to hold that city.

The retrograde march began early on 6 July and continued all through the day. As before, the weather was extremely dry and the roads dusty. Isaac Hermann, perhaps with only slight exaggeration, remembered that men spit out lumps of clay when they coughed. With Sherman pressing in Johnston's rear, the men were allowed only one ten-minute break each hour for twenty-four hours. Walker's division, with Loring's and French's, marched along the Bridgeport road, on the north side of the rail line. A. P. Adamson wrote that the 30th Georgia was given the responsibility of marching in the rear of Wilson's brigade to collect stragglers, the sick and disabled, of whom there were many. Colonel Wilson told his wife that the dust was so thick men were unrecognizable to each other at thirty paces. The 1st Sharpshooter Battalion marched with the rest of the column.[36]

The march continued under the same conditions on 7 July, but by the time the brigade reached Jackson at 11:00 P.M. it was windy and raining. After resting a day and a night, Johnston's army of four infantry divisions filed into the prepared defenses on the west side of Jackson just in time to confront Sherman's advancing forces. Johnston called the position "a very light line of rifle pits…very badly located and constructed" and work soon went into improving the defenses. Sherman, on the outside, assessed the newly-fortified defenses as "enlarged and much strengthened [with] well constructed embrasures of sod and cotton bales."[37]

The second battle or siege of Jackson lasted a week, 10-16 July. For the most part, Sherman, who had three infantry corps present, satisfied himself with artillery bombardment, constant skirmishing, and occasional rushes at the Confederate lines. W. H. T. Walker's division, by now composed of the brigades of Wilson, Gist, Gregg, and Ector, occupied the right center of Johnston's line, facing northwest toward the Deaf and Dumb Asylum, with the divisions of William W. Loring on his right and Samuel G. French on his left. Walker usually kept two or three brigades on line, with at least one in reserve. The four brigades of the division rotated from the line to the reserve, where the men were actually more exposed to enemy fire than those in the line who had the protection of the earthworks.[38]

On 11 July a single Yankee regiment penetrated Loring's picket line on the extreme right of the defenses but its attack was not supported and they had to withdraw. A letter writer reported that "Gen. [sic] Wilson's brave Confederates drove the unprincipled invaders back…our loss was less than ten—we had about thirty wounded." Helm's reserve brigade of Breckinridge's division on Johnston's left was brought to the right in the event Loring needed assistance. An attack on Breckinridge's front on the left on 12 July ended in a repulse with heavy losses for the Union division involved.

Colonel Wilson described the situation at Jackson in a long letter to his wife.

> The enemy commenced entrenching himself at once keeping up a continual fire of artillery & sharp-shooters on our lines. You can not well imagine the anxiety & surprise of those eight days in the trenches… His sharpshooters would pick off every man about the batteries who showed himself above the parapet & the mini balls were flying in every direction. A great many were killed & wounded nearly half a mile to my rear. Gen. Gist brigade & mine were held in reserve & suffered more on that account not having the advantage of earth works. I lost more men than anybody else, 80 killed & wounded. We were supporting the left of Walkers Division & I endeavored to protect my men by placing them in a ravine. My right rested about 60 yards from the trenches & the left about 150 yards the ravine running obliquely to the main line of works. Gen. Ector whose brigade occupied the works & myself made our Hd Quarters together in the ravine on the right of my line.[39]

Sergeant John W. Hagan, whose 29th Georgia was detached from the brigade for part of the time, wrote that "the other Regiments was not in any engagement but suffered from the Shelling." On the last day of the siege, 16 July, the 30th Georgia volunteered to retake a portion of the picket line that had been lost in a forced reconnaissance from the Union IX Corps just as some of Gregg's troops were being relieved by men from Wilson's brigade.

In concert with the 14th Texas of Ector's brigade, and supported by the

25th Georgia, they drove back the Yankees and reestablished the line, thereby winning the written commendation of General Walker. Hagan wrote that the action occurred in the late evening while two Union commanders reported that it happened at 3:00 P.M. Hagan, being a rural Southerner, would call any time after noon "evening." After this action was over, the sharpshooter battalion occupied the position and kept up a hot fire on the enemy line until dark.[40]

Lieutenant Josiah Holcombe of the sharpshooters, acting adjutant for Wilson's brigade, wrote to the newspaper on 24 July to correct what he thought were some misconceptions about the action on the sixteenth. He reported that Ector's and Gregg's brigades were on line with Wilson in support. Ector and Wilson asked General Walker for permission to retake the lost picket line. Walker told them to wait for orders. Later in the day orders were issued for one regiment each from the three brigades to reestablish the lost line. When they advance, they found the enemy too strongly emplaced and the 25th Georgia was sent to their assistance. After several heavy volleys the ground was taken.[41]

By 14 July Johnston learned that a large train load of artillery ammunition had left Vicksburg en route to resupply Sherman at Jackson and that the Union division of General Frank Herron was moving on Yazoo City, which constituted a threat to his right flank. General W. H. Jackson's cavalry division was dispatched to intercept the ammunition train but was unsuccessful. In anticipation of the expected barrage and attack Johnston felt that defense would be futile and he ordered the evacuation of Jackson.[42]

The evacuation was carried out in great secrecy on the night of 16 July. At 9:00 P.M. the field guns were removed and one hour later the infantry, except for skirmishers, evacuated the rifle pits. In Wilson's brigade the 29th Georgia was sent into the line to relieve the regiments that had fought to regain ground that day and was the last unit out. After leaving the line, Walker's division moved through the streets of the city and assembled on the low ground east of the state capitol building. With Walker's division leading, the northern wing of the army crossed the Pearl at Carson's Ferry, while the southern wing crossed lower down, burning the bridges behind them. The army withdrew along two parallel roads toward Brandon, some 4 miles distant to the east.[43]

Johnston had intended to stand at Brandon, but lack of water compelled him to move farther east, and he marched toward Morton in the same terrible conditions as the retreat to Jackson, arriving there, 30 miles east of Jackson, on 20 July. Hundreds of exhausted men were left behind on the roadside. Opinions on the state of the troops varied. "Pitt" wrote that "the men look war-worn and weather-beaten," but "Polk" stated the army was "in fine health and spirits, making their many privations and dangers the subject of jest and merriment."

As Johnston retreated eastward Sherman followed for a few miles and then abandoned the chase. Urged by Grant to harry Johnston, Sherman renewed his effort on 18 July against resistance from Johnston's cavalry. The Union troops advanced no further east than Brandon.[44]

Union losses at Jackson amounted to 1122. Johnston reported a total loss of 600 during the seven-day siege. Sergeant Hagan wrote that "our Regt has Suffered the least of any Regt in our Brigade or division. we only lost 9 in killed & wounded while other Regts lost 3 times that number[.]" On 11 July Captain W. G. Gray, the battalion quartermaster, had telegraphed Savannah, "All our boys are well." On 14 July he signaled again, "Thirteen privates and Captain Dent are slightly wounded. The balance of the battalion well."[45]

Lieutenant Holcombe attached the official brigade casualty list to his letter of 24 July. He reported total losses of nine killed or mortally wounded, including Major John Lamb of the 29th Georgia, seventy-eight wounded and eighteen missing. In the sharpshooters, the losses were as follows:

A Company–Missing: Corpl. L. Burns, Privates H. Hefferman, W. A. Kent.

B. Company–Wounded: Privates A. F. Blakely, severe in chin; L. Brown, slightly in arm; J. R. Hirst, slightly in chin; A. N. Smith, slightly in arm. Missing: Privates F. Ingleheart, H. Heime, W. Krail, A. Metzger, J. Olsen, R. C. Cooper.

C Company–Wounded: Privates Samuel Boggs, through back, severe; Barney Boggs, severely in leg; A. J. Little, severely in shoulder; H. J. Stancell, slightly in shoulder.

D Company–Wounded: Capt. George C. Dent, severely in elbow, compound fracture; Sergt. Phillips, seriously in head; W. F. Cochran, slightly in arm; J. Cooper, slightly in leg; J. C. Winn, slightly in hand.

Total for the battalion was thirteen wounded and nine missing, almost half of the total missing from the brigade.[46]

Individual service records indicate that at least thirteen men of the sharpshooter battalion were captured in or near Jackson after the fall of Vicksburg. One other was listed as a deserter. Some of these may have been stragglers on the march to Jackson. One of those captured is known to have been paroled with the Vicksburg prisoners, but most went to the prison compound at Camp Morton, Indiana, where eight of them enlisted in United States service in August 1863 and one took the oath of allegiance and was discharged. Among those joining the US volunteers was former Corporal Hugh Heffernan, probably still resentful over his demotion.

Captain George C. Dent and Sergeant H. B. Phillips of D Company are shown on the October 1863 muster roll as wounded at Jackson. Dent was shot in the elbow and had two other balls strike but not penetrate his clothing. He was absent for most of the next four months. Corporal Phillips came back to his company while they were at camp in Dalton the next winter. Private J. C. Winn, wounded slightly in the hand at Jackson, apparently survived that wound, but died of typhoid fever in a hospital in Marietta the next October. A post-war biographic sketch of Captain William H. Ross, commanding C Company, mentioned that he had been wounded at Jackson but gave no details.[47]

While Sherman was winding up affairs at Jackson, Grant dispatched the infantry division of General Frank Herron to capture Yazoo City with its Confederate stores and shipping. Herron accomplished his mission against light resistance by 21 June. He reported capturing 300 prisoners among whom must have been the sick of Walker's division left there. One of them was Private William F. Langston of D Company of the sharpshooter battalion who had contracted typhoid fever and was hospitalized in Yazoo City on 13 June. He was left behind when the division moved on and was captured in hospital and paroled, but he died there on 15 July. His final pay was claimed by his father, Edward B. Langston of Jonesboro. William Langston must have towered over his company mates: his parole record shows that he was six feet, six inches tall.[48]

Johnston's army spent more than a month at Morton resting and recuperating. In addition, the paroled men from Vicksburg were gathered at Demopolis, Alabama, to wait until they could be reintegrated into the Confederate army. Many officers took advantage of the hiatus in combat operations to go home on leave. Arthur Shaaff was among them. On 18 August 1863 Shaaff and twenty-year-old Elizabeth L., the daughter of Captain Henry J. Dickerson, a transplanted Baltimore merchant, were married in Savannah by Reverend C. F. McRae, rector of St. John's Church.[49]

Lieutenant George H. Johnston must have accompanied Shaaff on leave. The newspaper of 20 August 1863 and subsequent issues printed a circular, dated 19 August and signed by both officers, calling for all deserters and men absent without leave from the battalion to report to Johnston at his home on Liberty Street in Savannah. An editorial item drew attention to the circular and implored each soldier to "resolve to shoulder his musket at once and repair to his command."[50]

The basis for the appeal was the president's proclamation of pardon on 1 August, followed by General Beauregard's departmental General Order No. 93 to the same effect on 12 August. Shaaff took further advantage of his stay in Savannah to collect the men of his battalion mentioned in chapter 1 whose jail terms had been commuted by the pardon and to outfit them properly before sending them to join the unit in Mississippi.[51]

Another officer who went on leave to Savannah at this time was Second Lieutenant Manuel Molina of D Company, possibly to attend the funeral of his brother-in-law or father-in-law, Thomas Rosis. Molina was a native of the mountainous northwest Asturias region of Spain and about forty years old—above average age for a front line infantry officer—, and a former cigar and tobacco dealer; he had been a resident of Savannah for almost twenty years. He had served a year as a private in the 1st Georgia Volunteers and a few months in an artillery battery before joining the sharpshooters. When one remembers that infantry company officers marched on foot with their men, one appreciates the ability of older men such as George Dent and Manuel Molina to satisfy the physical demands of their positions.[52]

It was the custom for soldiers and officers going on and coming from leave to carry letters and parcels for their compatriots. Molina was no exception. Returning to the battalion at the end of August, he brought with him letters and comfort items for Lieutenant R. Cuyler King, his fellow subaltern in D Company; Cuyler's brother, Mallery P. King, on General Gist's staff; and Colonel Wilson, the brigade commander. In his letter of reply, Cuyler King thanked his sister for the cape, warm shirt and foodstuffs she had sent him.[53]

Many officers who owned slaves brought their personal servants on campaign with them. General Walker had his George and Colonel Wilson his Prince. Lieutenant Cuyler King was served by Neptune, Lieutenant Wayne by Aldo, and Lieutenant Holcombe by Abram. These slaves typically cooked for their masters, tended them when sick or wounded, did laundry, prepared baths, acted as messengers, and oft-times accompanied them into battle. It was not uncommon for the servant to be entrusted with items to be carried home to Georgia, with other items to be brought back. Apparently a slave traveling alone with a master's written permission was not interfered with on the crowded transport system.[54]

The body servants were not the only blacks in camp. The service records of the battalion include those of at least three slaves who were hired to the government by their masters to cook for the army. According to advertisements in the Savannah newspapers in 1862, "colored cooks" were wanted at the monthly rate of $20 for a chief cook and $15 for a cook. One such, John Brown, remained with A Company from August 1862 to February 1864 when Major Shaaff ordered him dropped from the rolls. Two others, Robin and Carolina by name, were cooks for D Company. Carolina was allowed to go home on leave in December 1863 and never came back. Robin was still with the company in August 1864. Judging by their names, some of the musicians on the battalion rolls were either slaves or free blacks. Few of them got as far as Mississippi, and only two musicians were still on the rolls by the time of the Atlanta campaign, both of them enlisted soldiers.[55]

Lieutenant Charles Pattillo took advantage of the lull in fighting at the end of July to address an issue that had been festering with him since late May. It will be recalled that he had been recommended for appointment as second lieutenant to succeed Robert P. Wayne in B Company as early as December 1862. The recommendation had been delayed by the bureaucracy and not finally approved until 30 May, with his date of rank set at 2 May 1863. When the commission was issued, Pattillo was dismayed to find that Second Lieutenant Charles L. Schlatter, who had not been recommended for promotion until April 1863, was given a date of rank the same as his own, and Thomas S. Wayne, also recommended in April, was dated only one day later. True to the tradition of the day, Pattillo took pen in hand at Morton on 22 July to write directly to General Samuel Cooper in Richmond protesting the inequity. His correspondence did little good: before the issue was addressed his own life would end.[56]

3

CHATTANOOGA

On 23 August 1863 Walker's division was ordered to move to join General Braxton Bragg's Army of Tennessee at Chattanooga. The troops began the movement by rail promptly as ordered, with the 29th and 30th Georgia Regiments taking the lead for Wilson's brigade. From Morton they moved across Alabama by train and ferry boat, retracing their trip of almost four months earlier. From Montgomery they traveled to Atlanta, and then to Chickamauga Station in north Georgia, using the Western & Atlantic Railroad or State Road for the last part of the trip.

The 1st Sharpshooter Battalion left Morton on 24 August, passed through Atlanta on the twenty-eighth, and arrived at Chickamauga on the twenty-ninth. Lieutenant King had written to his family for a meeting in Atlanta, but the troops were there for only a few hours before moving on. He later expressed relief that they had not made the attempt because of the short layover.[1]

If Colonel Wilson was relieved to be getting away from Mississippi, he was outraged by the behavior of his men on the return trip to Georgia. Once again, numbers of the men gave themselves permission to leave their units and visit their families. One unit in particular raised the colonel's ire, as he told his wife. "In passing through Georgia, many soldiers deserted their commands & went home. I lost nearly five hundred from my Brigade. The 30 Georgia was raised on the line of Road between West Point & Atlanta & they passed along that route at night. Two hundred & forty of them stopped. I presume they will return after a short furlough, but I was mortified at their conduct." A. P. Adamson of the 30th confirmed the colonel's account and his presumption: "On arriving [at Chickamauga] it was ascertained that a large number of the men had taken 'French leave' by jumping from the cars at East Point and Fairburn to visit their homes for a few days in the surrounding counties. We had left Mississippi with 450 men and arrived at our destination with little more than half that number; but it is due those who went home to say that nearly all of them returned in a few days."[2]

The sharpshooters also lost men on the trip to north Georgia and five of them were reported as deserters, never to return. However, one of the five,

Private M. D. Walker, was also reported as captured on Missionary Ridge the following November, so perhaps he did come back. Besides the losses on the trip, many of the men of the battalion, and of the division, had been left behind in Mississippi, too sick to travel.[3]

By 31 August all of Walker's division had arrived. When he had received the movement order at Morton, Walker had the four brigades of Wilson, Gist, Ector and Gregg under command but Gregg's brigade was removed before arrival, so Walker came to Georgia with only three brigades, about 5,000 men. While General Bragg welcomed the reinforcements, Colonel George W. Brent of his staff was not much impressed with the troops from Mississippi and confided to his journal, "The division of Walker, which has now nearly come up, is poorly equipped. It has many absentees and stragglers. It will give but little help."[4]

The climate in the mountainous area around Chattanooga was far cooler than that of Mississippi and the troops found it refreshing, but they also found themselves inadequately prepared for it. Most had lost their belongings at Jackson and in the subsequent campaign and had no decent clothing or bedding for the bracing night-time air. Colonel Wilson wrote, "The country is exceedingly broken & mountainous & the climate much colder than Mississippi. We are generally pleased with the change," but Cuyler King remarked on the situation to his sister: "The weather since our arrival in this state has been quite cool, last night I found it hard to keep warm even with the assistance of Molina's and Lawrence's bedding, which consisted in an overcoat and buffalo skins." King was referring to 1st Lieutenant Samuel W. Lawrence of D Company. Lawrence was a physician before the war, a native of South Carolina and a resident of Glynn County, Georgia. At age 29 in 1861, he had joined with George C. Dent in forming the Glynn Guards, a short term unit that became A Company of the 26th Georgia. The company later served briefly as artillery and then cavalry. Dent and Lawrence left the company in May 1862, on its reorganization, and joined the sharpshooters in August.[5]

Corporal William Moody was even more emphatic about the cold. He wrote to his wife, "We are faring some better than we did in Miss. tho we have a heap of duty to do and the nites is getting quite cool. We have no blankets yet tho I think we will draw blankets some time shortly. But if they do not furnish me with a Blanket before the wether gets much colder I am going to come home if I can get there." "Polk," a soldier in the 25th Georgia, also wrote about the trip from Mississippi and conditions at Chattanooga. In his opinion, the transit from Morton "was one of real pleasure," rivaling the westward trek from Savannah four months earlier. As for the state of the army and the cooler weather, he said, "Many are barefoot, and at night, having no blanket, have to lie upon the naked ground, so that we naturally dread the approach of frost." He hoped that if the government would not supply blankets the men could capture some from the enemy.[6]

The Confederate situation in southeast Tennessee and north Georgia was almost as difficult as it had been at Vicksburg. In a well-conducted, bloodless summer campaign, Union General William Rosecrans had maneuvered Bragg's small army out of most of eastern Tennessee, leaving him possession of only the city of Chattanooga, a vital north-south rail center. With a new offensive through north Alabama, Rosecrans, whose army numbered 60,000 men in three army corps, was now intent on forcing Bragg out of Tennessee completely. Indeed, Yankee artillery fire was already falling in the city. Thus troops from other locations had been sent to Bragg's army, including Walker's and John C. Breckinridge's divisions from Mississippi. Eventually General James Longstreet led the divisions of John Bell Hood and Lafayette McLaws from the Army of Northern Virginia to Bragg's aid.

A week after Walker and his division arrived, Bragg gave up Chattanooga and retired to Chickamauga, just south of the Tennessee River and east of Missionary Ridge. Here the Army of Tennessee was collected while Bragg and Rosecrans felt each other out and tried to discern the other's intentions.

On 1 September, the day after arrival, Walker's division, including Wilson's brigade and the sharpshooters, was moved to Tyner's Station on the Chattanooga-Knoxville rail line. There Colonel Wilson was hard at work, as he wrote to his wife, "I have been very busy since our arrival endeavoring to organize my trains and get my Brigade in fighting trim." The army was expecting a fight and the troops were confident of success. Angus McDermid wrote his father on 30 August, "The Yanks is a shelling the city now every day but is a cross the river and I think that we can ceepe [keep] them there. They will fite hear [sic] in a short time I think." Cuyler King told his sister, "The armys [sic] of the Confederacy are not by a long ways whiped [sic] nor will they ever be so long as the people at home support them," and "Every body out here feels confident of success in the approching battle."[7]

Walker's division was ordered to Rome on 4 September to face the threat of Rosecrans advancing eastward into Georgia from Alabama, but the next day the order was countermanded and only Gist's brigade went to Rome. Walker was left at Chickamauga with the two brigades of Wilson and Ector, but that same day, 5 September, Bragg created a reserve corps of two small divisions and elevated Walker to its command. General St. John R. Liddell, with his own brigade and Edward C. Walthall's, came under the Reserve Corps in an ad hoc division.[8]

Not all the soldiers were happy with Walker's promotion and the designation of his command. Cuyler King, for one, thought he could foresee the fate of the new Reserve Corps. "So I suppose in a few hours we will again be on the move to support one of the flanks or center, I do not know which. This is why I dislike to be held in reserve for it gives us so much marching and countermarching at all hours both at night and day." In reference to the role of the corps, General Walker himself called it a "shuttlecock concern."

Other onerous duties befell some, if not all, of Wilson's brigade. A. P. Adamson recalled that after marching back to Chickamauga from Tyner's Station, the 30th Georgia spent the whole night loading supplies on rail cars, then marched the next day to Ringgold, and the day after that back to Lafayette, a distance of 26 miles. It was "marching and countermarching at all hours," indeed.[9]

Bragg made two attempts on 10 and 12 September to strike at elements of the Union army debouching into north Georgia from Alabama. On the tenth, Bragg sent two divisions to strike the Union XIV Corps of General George H. Thomas. Walker was in support. One of the Confederate division commanders was slow to act and Thomas withdrew before they could hit him.

Bragg tried again on the twelfth, this time sending the corps of General Leonidas Polk to catch the Union XXI Corps under General Thomas Crittenden. Again Walker's reserve acted in Polk's support. While Polk dithered over whether to attack or not, Crittenden drew his separated divisions together and the opportunity evaporated. Bragg ordered Polk to withdraw.

The Southern troops rightly blamed these unsuccessful ventures on their leaders. A. P. Adamson wrote, "Want of co-operation by the corps commanders caused a failure in both instances." Cuyler King attributed the first failure to "mismanagement." He described the role of the sharpshooters in the attempt on 12 September: "We left here on the evening of the 12th and arrived at Rock Springs the same night, formed a line of battle, our Battalion of course was thrown out about a half mile in front as skirmishers, but as the enemy did not show any any [sic] disposition to attack we remained quiet in this position for thirty six hours. Why the attack contemplated by our General was not carried into effect I do not know."[10]

By 15 September Bragg had finally decided to go on the offensive and take on Rosecrans's army. By 17 September that general had aligned his three corps, finally assembled, along the Chattanooga-LaFayette road and behind Chickamauga Creek. Bragg planned to mount a strong attack on the Union left flank, which was Crittenden's XXI Corps, cut the Federal army off from

Chattanooga, and then drive south along the west bank of the creek, pushing the Yankees before them. The rest of his army, facing the Federal center and right, would then cross the creek and join in the fight. The action was to commence on 18 September. Walker's little Reserve Corps was part of the flanking force together with General Simon B. Buckner's corps and Nathan Bedford Forrest's cavalry.

Bragg's plan was for Walker's corps to cross Chickamauga Creek at Alexander Bridge, but Buckner's troops were ordered to march on the same road and so blocked the route such that Walker did not approach the bridge until near noon. Here, they found their objective protected by a Union battery and Wilder's brigade of cavalry armed with repeating rifles. Walthall's brigade was assigned to drive the enemy off, which they did, but not before sustaining over 100 casualties and not before the bridge was damaged beyond immediate repair. Walker was forced to move downstream to Byram's Ford, cross over, and come back along the creek on the west bank to Alexander's bridge. Colonel Wilson's lucid and detailed report of the battle is the best guide to the action of his brigade and the sharpshooters.[11]

The Georgia brigade did not get across the creek until 1:00 A.M. on 19 September, having been blocked by the supply columns of the units in front of them. The troops were further slowed by the necessity of the wagons to negotiate the ford more slowly than they would have crossed the bridge. Walker's ammunition train not having made it across on the night of 18 September, Wilson was ordered on the morning of 19 September to hold his brigade as a guard until they crossed the ford. He sent the 30th Georgia to help the stalled wagons and also posted two companies on each road leading to the ford to guard against surprise.

By 9:00 A.M. the train was across, and Wilson set out to join the rest of Walker's corps with the 25th Georgia and a section of Martin's battery in the lead and the rest of the brigade following the wagons. They had proceeded about 2 miles in this fashion when a staff officer from Forrest's cavalry arrived with a message from Walker directing Wilson to move to the right to Forrest's aid. The need for assistance stemmed from the dispatch of three brigades from Thomas's corps to advance on the crossings of the Chickamauga. Forrest's dismounted cavalry had run into this stiff infantry advance and were now falling back before it.

Colonel Wilson met with General Forrest and received instructions to form line of battle on Forrest's left. Doing so, Wilson's left almost immediately came under fire and began to advance, "and the line stepped off with the enthusiasm of high hope and patriotic determination, and the precision and accuracy which only disciplined and instructed troops can attain." The brigade line was composed of the 25th and 29th Georgia on the right, the 30th Georgia in the center, and the 4th Louisiana and 1st Sharpshooter Battalions on the left. The sections of Martin's battery were posted in the intervals between regiments and the brigade brought about 1,250 men into battle. The enemy was Croxton's brigade of Baird's division.[12]

Wilson's line had barely begun to move forward when it encountered the enemy skirmishers, who were promptly driven in. The Georgia brigade pressed forward delivering a heavy fire into the enemy first line which broke and fled. The command continued on and met a second line about 400 yards behind the first, which was also overcome after a stubborn fight. Losses on the Confederate side were heavy and Wilson's line wavered, but the men rallied and drove the enemy another 400 yards, all the way to the line of Yankee breastworks.

General Forrest ordered Wilson to go no farther and the Georgians were subjected to a heavy fire from behind the breastworks. Wilson espied King's brigade of US Regulars attempting to turn his left flank and sent for Ector's brigade, in his rear, to move up on his left, but before his messenger could reach Ector, that officer had complied with orders from Forrest to move into action on Wilson's right, replacing the dismounted cavalry.

The Union troops now completed their movement around Wilson's exposed left and poured an enfilading fire along his ranks. The left, composed of the 1st Sharpshooters and 4th Louisiana Battalions, fell back in disarray, carrying the 30th Georgia with them; the 25th and 29th Georgia, on the right, held steady but began to fall back slowly. Wilson rallied the two latter regiments and ordered the 30th Georgia to fall back to the left to serve as a rallying point for the left wing. At this point, matters were taken out of his hands as Ector's brigade entered the line to his right with a rush, carrying the 25th and 29th Georgia forward with them. The two disorganized battalions were reformed behind Liddell's division coming up in relief, were resupplied with ammunition, and took their places in the line. The brigade remained on the battlefield until nightfall.[13]

General Walker recognized the gallant role played by his reserve corps on 19 September when he wrote "The unequal contest of four brigades against such overwhelming odds is unparalleled in this revolution, and the troops deserve immortal honor for the part borne in the action. Only soldiers fighting for all that is dear to free men could attack, be driven, rally and attack again such superior forces."[14]

On 20 September, the second day of the battle, Wilson's brigade, now reduced after the losses the day before to no more than 450 effectives, supported

Gist's brigade when it was thrown into the battle to close a hole that had opened between two brigades in Breckinridge's division. After forty-five minutes of confused fighting, during which Gist's brigade suffered heavily and Wilson lost "some valuable officers and a few men," Walker's troops were withdrawn. They were recommitted in a final charge in the evening but met no enemy and camped that night on the battlefield.[15]

Wilson's losses were horrendous. From his little brigade of 1,100 to 1,200 men, he reported 99 killed, 426 wounded, and 80 missing, for a total loss of 605. The loss in officers was devastating. Of nine field officers present on the morning of 19 September, only two escaped unscathed. Lieutenant Colonel A. J. Williams, commanding the 25th Georgia, was mortally wounded; Colonels William Young and Thomas Mangham of the 29th and 30th Georgia were both so seriously disabled as to have to retire from the army. Major Shaaff was wounded and had his clothing pierced by seven bullets besides. Every officer in the 25th Georgia was killed or wounded except Lieutenant G. R. McRae, who assumed command of the regiment and led its remnants in the attack with Ector's brigade on 19 September. The 4th Louisiana Battalion also ended the battle commanded by a lieutenant. Lieutenant Colonel James S. Boynton listed the names of 111 officers and men killed, wounded, and missing from the 30th Georgia.

In his report, Wilson made special mention of several officers for conspicuous service. Among them was First Lieutenant Robert P. Wayne, adjutant of the sharpshooters, who was wounded in the leg while serving as brigade inspector. Lieutenants Alfred Bryan and Nicholas B. Sadler of the sharpshooters were commended for remaining with their command and discharging their duties though wounded. In a letter to his wife, Wilson reported that he was unharmed himself but his horse had been shot three times and was probably "ruined." Later, he wrote, "I did not even have my clothing pierced with a single ball."[16]

Alfred Bryan's affiliation with the battalion has already been described. Nicholas Bayard Sadler was a second lieutenant in C Company under Captain Ross. Ross was probably absent from the battles of 19 and 20 September, having gone home sick with typhoid fever on 12 September. First Lieutenant Josiah Holcombe of C Company was on detached duty as a staff officer in Wilson's brigade, so only the two second lieutenants, Sadler and George H. Johnston, Jr., were with the troops. No wonder that Sadler felt compelled to remain on duty to rally his men despite having been wounded.[17]

One "valuable" officer who was wounded on September 20 was First Lieutenant Horace A. Crane of A Company. He suffered a gunshot wound above the ankle resulting in a compound fracture of the leg and sending him to hospital in Savannah. As late as July 1864 he was found to be unhealed and unfit for service. He never returned to the sharpshooters and in October 1864 was retired to the Invalid Corps, after which he volunteered for service as adjutant at Fort McAllister. Crane was captured there when the fort fell to Sherman's army in December 1864, sent to the infamous prison at Fort Delaware, and finally released in June 1865.[18]

Captain Gray, the sharpshooter quartermaster, telegraphed Savannah on 22 September, reporting that Major Shaaff, Captain Twyman, and Lieutenants Robert Wayne, Bryan, Crane, and Schlatter had been wounded slightly. On 25 September Lieutenants Wayne and Schlatter and First Sergeant Stephen P. Norris arrived in Savannah, the first of the battalion's wounded to come home. Norris was interviewed by a correspondent of the Savannah *Daily Morning News* and gave a report of the wounded that he knew about. Subsequent issues of the newspapers reported several members of the battalion in hospital in Atlanta.[19]

The first list of casualties was published on 28 September. It was unsigned but appeared to be official.[20]

List of killed and wounded in 1st Battalion Georgia Sharpshooters, at Chickamauga, on 19th and 20th inst[ant]:

Company A—Wounded: Capt. H. D. Twyman, flesh wound in shoulder; 1st Lieut. H. A. Crane, in leg; 2d Lieut. A. Bryan, flesh wound in shoulder; 2d Lieut, C, Schlatter, flesh wound in chest; Sergeant Wm. Kersey, in arm; Privates R. Beasley, in shoulder; T. J. Lee, in head (mortally); R. G. Lang; E. G. Melton, in arm; A. Roath, in leg; Swords, in hand; B. Tharp, in leg; W. Wilcox, in thigh.
Company B—Killed: Corpl. Moody. Wounded: Sergt. Leonard, Privates McDaniels, Ehrlich, Mann.
Company C—Killed: Private O'Quinn, color bearer. Wounded: Sergt. Derst, Corp. Thornton, Privates Bennett, Lundy.
Company D—Killed: Color Sergt. Keith, Private Stewart. Wounded: Sergt. S. P. Norris, Privates Allen, Bryant, Crow, Elkins, Grey, Morley, Peace, and Warren.

On 26 October the complete list of casualties was furnished by the battalion commander. The numbers of men in each company shown in the list are probably the numbers of effectives present on the day the report was prepared. It is not clear if the company commanders were those in the battle or at the time of the tally.[21]

> List of casualties in the 1st Battalion, Georgia Sharpshooters in the battle of Chickamauga
>
> Field & Staff—Wounded: Maj. A. Shaaf, arm slightly; Lt. C. L. Schlatter, acting Adjutant, breast, severe.
>
> Company A, 16 men, Capt. Twyman commanding—Wounded: Capt. Twyman, shoulder, slight; Lt. Crane, leg, severe; Lt. Bryan, shoulder, severe; Sgt. W. Kersey, arm, serious; Pvts. Robert Beasley, arm, slight; T. J. Lee, head, mortal; R. G. Long, through the body (since died); E. G. Melton, arm. slight; A. H. Roath, leg, serious; Henry Swords, hand, serious; B. A. Tharp, leg, slight; W. Wilcox, leg, serious.
>
> Company B, 20 men, Capt. B. H. Hardee commanding—Killed: Pvt. Casper Brickman; Wounded: Sgt. James Leonard, leg, slight; Sgt. Henry Lindner, slight bruise on head; Cpl. Henry Smith, in groin, dangerous; Cpl. William Harrer, foot, serious; Pvts. D. O. Avera, arm and body, mortal; John Booth, hand, slight; Currin Becton, shoulder, serious; James Butler, leg, serious; John Dunn, leg, serious (missing); Zack Green, leg, serious (missing); Abram Ehrlish, arm, dangerous; Wiley Knight, head and body, dangerous (mortal); Miles McDaniels, foot, serious; Mark Roberts, neck, serious; G. C. Underwood, leg, slight; John Wasden, leg, serious; J. D. Underwood, leg, serious; Missing: Pvt. Mathias Williams.
>
> Company C, 23 men, Lt. N. B. Sadler commanding—Killed: Cpl. William Moody, Pvt. George O'Quinn; Wounded: Lt. Sadler, in breast, slight; Sgt. P. Derst, leg and hand, serious; Sgt. James Thornton, arm, serious; Cpl. John Thornton, shoulder, serious; Pvts. James Boggs, hip, serious; H. Bennett, knee, slight; J. Sutton, leg, slight; Jesse Crumley, back by shell, slight; Elbert Mathis, chin, slight; R. Mann, chin, slight; Simon Beckwith, leg, slight; Missing: Pvts. W. Burns, Patrick Gately, Shep Foster.
>
> Company D, 23 men, Lt. M. Molina commanding—Killed: Color Sgt. Eli Keith, Pvt. James R. Stewart; Wounded: Sgt. S. Norris, leg, slight; Pvts. S. Allen, leg, slight; E. Bryant, head, serious; J. S. Crowe, bowels, mortal; J. H. Elkins, thigh, serious; G. C. Maddox, H. H. Gray, wounded and missing; J. Morley, both legs

and hand, serious; J. W. Peace, shoulder, serious; J. W. Parrott, head, dangerous.

Recapitulation: Carried into action, 101; killed 5, wounded 53, missing 4.

B. H. Hardee, Capt. commanding 1st Batt., Ga. S. S.

Thomas S. Wayne, Lt. and Acting Adjutant

Corporal William Moody will be recognized by readers as the writer of letters quoted in these pages. Color Sergeant Eli Keith was said to have died while in advance of the troops. A clerk before the war, a native of Marion District, South Carolina, and nineteen years old in 1862, he had enlisted in the 30th Georgia either in Campbell County in September, or Bibb County in December, 1861, before transferring to the sharpshooters. Private William Jasper "Billy" Parrott, listed by Captain Hardee as dangerously wounded in the head was probably shot in the eye. He had enlisted in the Fayette Volunteers in Fayette County in September 1861, later a company of the 30th Georgia. Billy was eighteen years old when he transferred into the sharpshooters. A descriptive roll taken at that time shows him to be a native of Fayette County, and five feet eight inches tall with dark hair, dark eyes and dark complexion. He survived his wound at Chickamauga and returned to duty later in the year.[22]

Not unexpectedly, the killed included color bearer Private George W. O'Quinn, who was probably shot down in the performance of his important duty, and perhaps at the same time as Color Sergeant Keith. He was born in Appling County in 1844, the son of Stephen O'Quinn, a farmer and a native of the Barnwell District in South Carolina. At the 1860 census, O'Quinn was eighteen years old and farming with his father. He had been a soldier since October, 1861, when he enlisted in the Georgia State Troops. He joined Company K, 54th Georgia in April 1862 and transferred to the sharpshooters the next summer.[23]

John Royal enumerated for his wife the effects of the battle on the Dooly County men. "Me and Shepperd [Green L. Sheppard] was in it all the time. Culppers [David Culpepper] was Detail for back at the waggons. Suttens [Jasper Sutton] was in the first fight he got wounded in the leg slighty.... Shepperd got sick and went to the hospital i haven't heard from him yet nor from Gambel [William C. Gamble] he went to the hospital beforwe went in the fight."

Family history has it that Green Sheppard was wounded and went to field hospital where he came down with pneumonia and died on 23 September. Royal's letter makes no mention of a wound nor does Sheppard's name appear in any casualty list.[24]

Another uncertain casualty was Private Patrick Gately, also in C Company. Although Captain Hardee listed him as missing, the December 1863 muster roll said that he had been killed at Chickamauga and he was dropped from the roll. It appears more likely that he was a deserter. A man of that name, thirty-five years old and a native of County Roscommon in Ireland, had been enumerated in the 1860 census in Savannah. Ten years later, in 1870, Patrick Gately, forty-five years old, Irish born and a laborer in a rice mill in Savannah, was enumerated with a wife and young child. It is very likely he was the same man.[25]

The muster roll for D Company for October 1863, signed by Lieutenant Manuel Molina, gives these casualties for that company at Chickamauga: killed: Sergeant Eli Keith on 19 September and Private J. R. Stewart on 20 September; wounded: First Sergeant S. P. Norris, Privates S. Allen, J. H. Crow, J. H. Elkins, H. H. Gray, G. C. Maddox, J. Morley, J. W. Peace, and W. J. Parrott. Total casualties for the company were two killed and nine wounded. Private Elijah Bryant, a resident of Thomas County, was reported wounded by Sgt. Norris in the newspaper and by Captain Hardee in the casualty list, but he signed the muster roll as present on 31 October. However, the 31 December muster roll shows that he died in hospital in November or December.[26]

Another Chickamauga casualty was Corporal Henry Schmidt (Smith) of B Company, who was wounded in the hip or groin on 19 September. A native of Hanover, Germany, about twenty-eight years old, and a tailor by trade, Schmidt had been living in Augusta and Savannah since the mid-1850s. His wound kept him in hospital for more than two months, but early in December 1863 he was released on sick furlough and went to Augusta to recuperate. There his trade stood him in good stead. By order of the secretary of war, Schmidt was assigned to sew uniforms for the quartermaster department in Augusta's burgeoning system of Confederate Army manufactories. He remained there until the end of the war, serving in the Local Troops Regiment of Colonel George W. Rains.[27]

Captain Hardee's report shows eight men captured or missing from Shaaff's battalion at Chickamauga. A review of individual service records shows six men were in enemy hands at the end of the two day battle. They were Zachariah Green, Sheppard Foster, G. C. Maddox, and Mathias Williams, captured on 19 September, and William Burns and John Dunn on 20 September. Dunn, Maddox, and Green were also wounded. Zach Green was one of those released from Chatham County jail to rejoin the sharpshooters only the month before. Hardee also included H. H. Gray as wounded and captured or missing, and Patrick Gately as missing. Gately's service record shows that he deserted on the march from Mississippi but also that he was killed on 19 September. Gray's record shows that he was absent wounded in December 1863 but does not state that he had been captured. Like Abram Ehrlish, Gately had been captured in Mississippi in May 1863 and paroled before becoming a casualty at Chickamauga. Privates Edwin R. Lundy and W. D. Warren, reported wounded in the first casualty list, were not on Hardee's list.[28]

Sheppard A. Foster, one of the captured soldiers, may have seen more varied service than most of the men in the battalion. A native of Monroe County and a member of the Upson Guards from Upson County in 1861, he and his company were mustered into service at Macon as part of the 5th Georgia Volunteers in April 1861. After three months at Pensacola, Florida, Foster was discharged from the Confederate army but enlisted in the 6th Regiment, Georgia State Troops. He served as a corporal six months in that unit, enlisted in the 32nd Georgia Regiment in May 1862, and then transferred to the sharpshooters. Wounded at Chickamauga, he spent several months in a Federal hospital in Nashville before going to Camp Morton, Indiana, prison. Foster was one of the prisoners released in March 1865.[29]

A tabular return for the brigade prepared sometime in October 1863 showed the sharpshooters had seventy-seven men present in camp of whom forty-nine were fit for duty or effective. The muster roll for D Company showed two officers and twenty-seven men present and two officers and thirty-six men absent on 31 October. Effectives included those men who were armed and ready to form line of battle. Writing two months after the battle, Major Shaaff informed the adjutant and inspector general of the Confederate army that his command had been "destroyed."[30]

In the aftermath of the battle, Cuyler King and his brother, Mallery, who served on the staff of General States Rights Gist in Walker's division, both went home on leave. Mallery came back to the army before Cuyler did and wrote his younger brother a description of conditions in the division on his return. The report was especially depressing in regard to Wilson's brigade and the sharpshooters. After advising Cuyler not to attempt to come back too soon, Mallery wrote, "If you could get a regular sick leave it would be better—Bryan, Sadler and Johns[t]on are off in the same way—Schlatter is Act[ing] Q. M. for the Div Ordnance train—a new kind of an appointment—and Twyman an act[ing] Div Insptr. I was told this afternoon that the Battn has been consolidated into a Company—with Dent in comd—Shaaff is in command of all the old Rgts of the Brigade—consolidated. If true tho [sic], this must be but temporary. I will find out and write you all about it." In fact, George C. Dent had returned to the army after being wounded at Jackson the previous July.

However, his tenure must have been short because, as already shown, Lieutenant Molina signed the October muster roll.[31]

Whatever the consequences to Arthur Shaaff and his men, the battle at Chickamauga was an empty victory for the Confederacy. Rather than vigorously pursuing and destroying his enemy, Braxton Bragg allowed Rosecrans to retreat into Chattanooga. While the Union army fortified themselves and began to bring in reinforcements from other areas, Bragg settled into an ineffectual siege of the town from across the Tennessee River. The Confederate high command collapsed into internal squabbling and frittered away its strength in east Tennessee. Subordinate generals chafed at the inaction, but Bragg could not be stirred.

Governor Joseph E. Brown of Georgia visited the army in early October. He toured the Georgia units, escorted by Generals Bragg, McLaws and Walker, and in so doing subjected himself to the irrepressible and irreverent wit of the American soldier. Brown was dressed in civilian finery, including a white shirt, black suit and beaver top hat, that presented a marked contrast to the ragged and barefoot men. As he moved about the camps there were calls of "Come out of them good clothes," and another man wanted somebody to "stop that hat—thar's a man in it, fur I see it a movin' about." Brown appeared to pay no notice or perhaps he was willing to let the soldiers have their fun.[32]

The presence of Longstreet's troops in Georgia may have made it possible for Arthur Shaaff to visit with a family member. Captain F. Key Shaaff, Arthur's brother, was a company commander in the 15th Alabama, Law's brigade, Hood's division. Their ability to visit was especially likely during the time Walker's division was in Longstreet's corps. Although no record exists, it may be assumed the brothers found opportunities to see each other.

While the generals bickered, the soldiers suffered from the weather, from lack of clothing and equipment, and from insufficient provisions. Conscientious commanders were aghast at the conditions in which the troops lived. On 8 October Colonel Wilson wrote to his wife concerning the sharpshooters and the rest of his brigade, "The climate in these parts is very cold & it is all I can do to keep from freezing now. We have frost on the ground every morning. Our poor soldiers are many of them destitute of blankets & those who are best off have but one. I cannot see how they endure the cold. I could not keep warm with several." A few days later, Wilson added:

> I have nearly fifteen hundred in the hospitals. It does seem to me that unless better food, clothing, & medical supplies are furnished our armies will be exhausted by disease. It is impossible for men reduced

as mine were by sickness before they left home, to stand the hardships of such a campaign in the winter season. They have not a change of clothing, are scacely fed, in the poorest _____, & not one in twenty of my command have a single blanket. I am sure I should freeze to death in this mountainous region. Large numbers are now suffering with diesease of the bowels.

On 13 October, as the fall rains continued, he took up the refrain again.

> They have not a tent to the regiment, not a blanket to ten men, no knapsacks & consequently but a small supply of clothing & no overcoats. When it rains, they have to take it & if this only occurred in the daytime or lasted a few hours they could build fires & dry themselves. But when it rains at night & all night & for several nights & days you must know they suffer. It is with difficulty with several blankets and a good tent I can keep from freezing & when the weather is bad I feel for my men & loose the comfort I might otherwise enjoy remembering their discomfort.[33]

As to the military situation, General Walker's reserve corps had been dissolved a few days after the battle and he now commanded his old division in Longstreet's corps. The division was made up of the brigades of Gist, Wilson, and John Gregg, Ector's brigade having been sent back to Mississippi. Walker's position was on the left of the Confederate line, deployed on the lower slope of Lookout Mountain and in the valley between Lookout and Missionary Ridge.

Colonel Wilson wrote to his wife on 8 October, "My Brigade went into position today just at the foot of Lookout Mountain & as I write an artillery duel is going on over our heads between our batteries on the Mountain and the enemy batteries." Three days later, Wilson's men went into the trenches to relieve Gregg's on the front line. They were engaged in clearing timber that obstructed their view and their fields of fire. Each day the brigade posted an advanced picket of 120 men within 200 yards of the Yankee line. The brigade was scheduled for relieve from the line on 14 October, but the rain had swollen Chattanooga Creek so badly that Wilson was cut off from the rest of the division and no one could get to him. Despite the poor conditions, the men who were healthy remained in good spirits.[34]

Wilson himself lived in uncomfortable conditions, sharing a single tent with six other men and suffering from the malady that would shortly take his life. At the end of October, he wrote his wife, "For six weeks I have been troubled with disorder in my bowels which came very near laying me up a part of the time and I am still quite unwell but improving." A little more than two weeks after writing those lines, Wilson was finally promoted to brigadier general. Eleven days later, having been carried away from Missionary Ridge, he died in camp at Ringgold, Georgia, on 27 November 1863. The cause of death was clearly chronic diarrhea or dysentery, but the official cause was "camp fever" or typhoid. He was thirty-two years old.[35]

The strength of the army was a matter of concern to its commanders and a recurring theme of correspondence. Wilson referred to his thin numbers several times in writing to his wife. On 11 October he told her he had only 800 men fit for duty in the three regiments and two battalions of his brigade. Two days later, he remarked that he carried 2,800 men on his brigade rolls, had 900 men present for duty and 1,500 men in hospital. The other 400 men were the dead and missing from Chickamauga and the unaccounted for men spread from Savannah to Yazoo City. A table of organization for the brigade in October showed 2,561 men on the rolls, 951 present, and 683 fit for duty.

Tabular Statement of the Organization of Wilson's Brigade

	Total Effective	Total Present	Present and Absent
25th Georgia	188	291	702
29th Georgia*	98	168	558
30th Georgia*	195	258	651
4th La. Batt.	146	167	375
1st Bn. Ga. SS	49	77	275
Totals	683	951	2,561

*The 29th Georgia had left two companies and the 30th Georgia had left one company in Savannah in May.

Gist's brigade had 1,638 effectives and Gregg's had 1,131, giving Walker only 3,450 combatants in a division that had brought 5,000 men from Mississippi six weeks earlier.[36]

As mentioned earlier, many officers took home leave in October, Lieutenant Richard Cuyler King of D Company among them. Despite his brother's advice, King returned to camp on 25 October just in time to join the division in its support of Longstreet's mismanaged attack on reinforcements coming to the Federal army in Chattanooga through north Alabama.

Union forces had captured a crossing of the Tennessee River at a place called Brown's Ferry, downstream from Lookout Mountain. Men of General Joseph Hooker's XI and XII Corps from the Army of the Potomac were marching to join the army in Chattanooga via Brown's Ferry. Bragg wanted Longstreet to recapture Brown's Ferry, but the latter general struck instead on 28 October at a lone, isolated Union division in a night-time attack by Hood's Confederate division led by General Micah Jenkins. Captain F. Key Shaaff played a leading role in this affair. The result of the action was miscommunication, failure, and recrimination. The only role of Walker's division was to be available to support Jenkins if need be, but their participation was minimal. Lieutenant King described the operations in some detail in a letter to his sister. "We received orders to move at four in the morning...which we did and had a miserable time in the mud and cold rain, were under a little shelling but did not get under musketry. Last night Jenkins made the proposed attack and was succesful so far as driving the enemy from the hill, but as the yankees were heavily reinforced was obliged to fall back. I think it was a great mistake not putting the whole of our Corps in for as it has turned out we gained nothing except killing a few hundred mules and yankees."[37]

Among the bright young men who made up the officer corps of the sharpshooter battalion, Cuyler King did not stand out, but he came from one of the finest families of the Georgia coast. His father was Thomas Butler King, the renowned owner of King's Retreat Plantation on St. Simon's Island in Glynn County, a native of Massachusetts and a former US Congressman. Cuyler was his sixth son; two older brothers were Mallery Page King of General Gist's staff, already mentioned, and John Floyd King, an artillery officer in Virginia. A third brother, Henry Lord Page King, had been killed in 1862, serving on the staff of Lafayette McLaws.

Cuyler, nicknamed Tip or Hack in the family, was about eighteen in 1860 and was soon to go off to school at the University of Virginia when war intervened. He enlisted as a private in the Glynn Guards, the local company raised by George Dent and Samuel Lawrence that for a time was A Company of the 26th Georgia, and in which his brother Mallery was then second lieutenant. When the two aforementioned officers joined the sharpshooters, King joined them as the junior second lieutenant of D Company. He had served faithfully with his company ever since.

Cuyler kept up a steady correspondence with his family throughout the war, but his special correspondent was his sister, Georgia, the widow of General William Duncan Smith of Augusta, Georgia, who had died of yellow fever at Charleston in 1862.[38]

Following the Battle of Chickamauga, part of the fallout of Braxton Bragg's acrimonious relations with his principal subordinates was a rearrangement of the army. Bragg believed, rightly or wrongly, that the Tennessee Division of General Benjamin Franklin Cheatham was a hotbed of resentment against him. To counter their animosity, on 12 November he broke up the division, exchanging its Tennessee brigades for others in the army. As a result, Walker's division gave up John Gregg's brigade and received in exchange the Tennessee brigade of General George Maney. In addition, the 4th Louisiana Battalion was taken away and brigaded with other troops from their home state.[39]

Colonel Claudius Wilson had been reluctant to go on leave in October because he felt there was no one to whom he could trust the command. Now matters were beyond his control. With Wilson deathly ill, command of his brigade passed from hand to hand; whoever in camp was senior at the moment had the responsibility. Lieutenant Colonel Boynton commanded briefly, as did Major Shaaff. The matter was resolved with the arrival between 12 and 22 November of a new regiment and battalion to increase the brigade's strength. Colonel James Cooper Nisbet with the 66th Georgia, and his brother, Major John W. Nisbet, with the 26th Georgia Battalion, brought more than 900 additional men to Wilson's brigade and increased division strength to 4,400. By virtue of his seniority, J. Cooper Nisbet became acting brigade commander, a position he would retain until the new year.[40]

Nisbet, only twenty-four years old but already a veteran of fighting in Virginia, took a liking to the senior officers he found in the brigade. He thought Lt. Col. Boynton a judicious man, but he reserved his warmest praise for Major Arthur "Shoaf," calling him "a West Pointer of the old navy [sic]. The other officers of [his] battalion were educated military men from the Georgia Military Institute or Savannah volunteer companies and the drill and discipline of their companies was that of regulars. Their efficiency was not excelled by any organization of the army. Major Arthur Shoaf [sic] was well qualified to command a brigade and most any of his officers a regiment." Nisbet's memory as to facts was faulty by the time he wrote his memoir but his impressions are more likely reliable. It is no wonder that higher ranking officers trusted Shaaff and the sharpshooters to perform provost duty or to carry out executions.[41]

The living conditions of the battalion improved somewhat in early November but sickness continued to take its toll. John I. Royal wrote to his wife that he was in a good tent secure from the rain but that there was still many men absent sick. On the day of his letter, he wrote, his company (C) had only three men fit for duty and only twenty-five in the whole battalion. Royal, himself, was in fine health. Royal thought there would be no more fighting around Chattanooga, a poor prediction.[42]

General Walker went on home leave on 14 November, leaving General Gist in command of the division. Lieutenant Cuyler King gave his sister a glimpse of affairs in the tiny sharpshooter battalion during this period of watchful waiting. King had been commanding two companies almost since the day he returned from leave in October because there were so few officers on duty with the Sharpshooters. Captain Dent and Lieutenant Lawrence of King's company were both on leave and not expected back before 1 January. Dent had been disabled at the battle at Jackson, Mississippi, the previous July. Shaaff had sent Lieutenant Manuel Molina to Savannah for 15 days to procure blankets and clothing for the men. Lieutenant Charles Schlatter had just returned to A Company from leave. King thought he was looking well but that he had been unwise to return so soon after being wounded at Chickamauga.[43]

Of the other officers in the battalion, Captain Ross of C Company was probably still at home recovering from his bout with typhoid. Lieutenants Bryan, Crane, Sadler, and Wayne had been wounded at Chickamauga and were likely in hospital or at home. With military affairs at an apparent stalemate and conditions so poor in camp, there was no incentive for them to come back. Captain Twyman had recently gone to division staff as acting inspector, Lieutenant Holcombe was still detailed to brigade staff and Lieutenant Johnston was acting battalion adjutant. That left only one captain, Benjamin Hardee, and two lieutenants, King and Schlatter, with the troops. If Schlatter had just returned, then King had probably have commanded C and D companies while Captain Hardee led companies A and B. If Major Shaaff was temporarily in command of the brigade, Hardee would be at the head of the battalion and King and Schlatter might each lead two companies. For the most part, the men would be tended by their non-commissioned officers.[44]

One other officer, not mentioned by King, was absent from camp near Chattanooga. On 18 November Second Lieutenant Charles S. Pattillo died in Marietta, possibly while hospitalized. Major Shaaff wrote that Pattillo died on 20 October, but his service record contains vouchers he signed on 30 October and 10 November. If it is correct that Pattillo's family lived in Marietta, then he may have died at home. Perhaps he succumbed to a wound received at Chickamauga, although he was not named as a casualty; more likely, he died of sickness. He was the first fatality in the battalion's officer corps and his passing left a vacancy to be filled in B Company.[45]

Finally, Dr. John M. Dent, while on Missionary Ridge, applied to resign his commission on 28 September, declaring that he was "incapable of performing duty" and offering a surgeon's certificate attesting to that statement. Captain Hardee, acting battalion commander, endorsed the application favorably and Dent went home. The resignation was effective 19 October. Assistant Surgeon Thomas R. Cosby remained on duty with the sharpshooters.

Dent's decision to resign may have been colored by more than physical disability. The previous June, before Dent reported for duty in Mississippi, Colonel Henry H. Jones of Newton in Baker County had forwarded to President Jefferson Davis a petition signed by many of the county's leading citizens asking for Dent's release from service. Jones pleaded with the president to allow Dent to return to his former patients because he was the only physician available within 10 miles of Newton. Jones also noted that Dent suffered from severe rheumatism, contracted since he had been in service.[46]

Military matters at Chattanooga were about to be transformed. General U. S. Grant had come there himself to take charge in October. The opening of the Tennessee River and the arrival of Hooker and his men from the east and W. T. Sherman and his corps from Mississippi presaged change. Grant relieved Rosecrans from duty and replaced him with General George H. Thomas who had fought so valiantly at Chickamauga. Cuyler King had written to his sister that Thomas "is said to be a hard fighter but not much of a General does not know when he is whiped ." King would find out what kind of a general Thomas was in a few days.[47]

Grant opened the battle of Chattanooga on 24 November, loosing Hooker's men from his right in an attack on Lookout Mountain in the famous Battle Above the Clouds. Bragg had brought Walker's division under Gist from the foot of the mountain to the east end of Missionary Ridge only the day before. Hooker took the mountain in the face of a badly coordinated defense. At the same time, Sherman advanced on Grant's left to a better position before Missionary Ridge. The next day, 25 November, Sherman continued his attack on the Confederate right while Thomas attacked the ridge head-on in the center. Bragg's disposition of his troops was poor and Thomas's men, thirsting for revenge for Chickamauga, pushed up the ridge and into the rifle pits at the top, sweeping all before them. First one gray-clad brigade gave way, then another. A withdrawal became a rout as the Southern soldiers ran from the Yankee attack.

Hardee's corps was on the right on Missionary Ridge, with the divisions of Patrick Cleburne, Gist, Carter Stevenson, and Frank Cheatham, from right to left. The latter two were those that had defended Lookout Mountain the day before. Action on this front had been relatively mild except where Cleburne was defending Tunnel Hill against Sherman. In fact, the men of Wilson's brigade, under Colonel Nisbet, were preparing supper when the breakthrough occurred.

Cheatham changed front with his division to form a new line perpendicular to the old one and facing the Yankee threat. Stevenson reinforced Cheatham's line. Cleburne formed a second line behind Cheatham with his own and Gist's divisions.

The withdrawal of the Army of Tennessee to Chickamauga Station, then to Ringgold, and finally, to Dalton on 28 November, was covered by Cleburne's division with Gist in support. Gist experienced a relatively small number of casualties in the debacle, 14 men killed, 118 wounded, and 190 missing. General Walker, returning from leave, rejoined the division on 27 November, the day of Colonel Wilson's death.[48]

Specifics about casualties in the sharpshooter battalion at Chattanooga are hard to come by. In a telegram to Savannah from Dalton on 30 November, Captain W. W. Spencer, 29th Georgia, wrote "Wilson's brigade was not engaged in the fight on Missionary Ridge." While many men were marked absent, sick, or wounded, on the muster rolls of 31 December 1863, none are shown to have been victims of enemy action at Chattanooga. The only reported instance of a wound was to Private William Lawrence Thomas of Cuyler King's D Company who "in the course of this fierce and bloody action [on Missionary Ridge], received a severe wound in his left foot, but avoided capture."

Thomas was a married, twenty-one-year-old mill hand and former farmer from Griffin in Spalding County. He had enlisted in 1861 in the 30th Georgia and had served in the same company as A. P. Adamson until transferring in August 1862. Despite his wound, Thomas refused to leave the ranks and soldiered on until July 1864, fighting at Kennesaw and elsewhere. When gangrene finally set in, he was forced to turn himself in to hospital just before the battle of Peachtree Creek. He sat out the rest of the war in medical facilities but lived to return to his home and his wife, although he walked with a cane for the rest of his life. He was a grocer in Experiment, Georgia, for many years, fathered thirteen children, and died of pneumonia in 1912, aged seventy.[49]

The 1st Sharpshooters suffered two other recorded losses at Chattanooga. Private Marion D. Walker of D Company was captured on Missionary Ridge or at Ringgold 25 or 27 November, and Private Jasper Loyd of B Company was taken at Ringgold on the twenty-seventh. Both were carried off to Rock Island, Illinois. Walker, from Gordon County, was working on the farm of his father, Lewis G. Walker, and was eighteen years old in 1860. After capture, he volunteered for frontier service in the US Army in October 1864. Loyd, a resident of Fayetteville in Fayette County, stayed on as a prisoner until his release in June 1865.[50]

As mentioned, Lieutenant Manuel Molina had been sent to procure blankets and other necessities for the men and thereby missed the action at Missionary Ridge. Major Shaaff had written that he had been unsuccessful in every effort to obtain materials through official channels and was therefore turning to private charity. Molina arrived in Savannah about 18 November and his appeal was printed in the newspaper. There was an outpouring of help from public and private sources, the results being printed daily in the paper.

By the time Molina left town on 1 December, he was able to acknowledge the receipt of these items: one heavy carpet to be used for a hospital tent, 33 blankets, 73 carpet blankets, 91 quilts, 126 pairs of socks, 22 pairs of pants, 20 shirts, 30 pairs of underdrawers, 5 coats, 8 pairs of gloves, 2 vests, 2 neck scarves, 4 caps, and $3,725 in cash which he used to buy 101 pairs of shoes and 7 blankets. Besides those private donations, the state quartermaster turned over 400 pairs of pants, 100 coats, 100 hats, 50 pairs of socks, and 50 pairs of shoes. The Confederate quartermaster provided 5,000 pairs of underdrawers and 8,000 shirts, probably for the army as a whole. Molina must have had enough material to fill a rail car. Writing from Dalton on 9 December, Shaaff personally thanked the citizens of the city for their generosity and forwarded a resolution of thanks from the men of the battalion drafted by First Sergeants Dominique Brown and John F. Knowles. The sharpshooters were set for the winter.[51]

Worn down by overwork and strain, Cuyler King left the army to go home for rest. He told his sister in a letter from Marietta on 2 December, "I arrived this morning sick and well nigh worn out by the fatigues of the inglorious retreat of our army from the front of Chattanooga." He wrote that he was suffering from rheumatism (at the age of twenty-one), and that his brother, Mallery, had come down with jaundice, another malady associated with lack of rest. Cuyler's service record shows that he was admitted to hospital in Macon with a tubercular-like complaint on 6 December , and he was still in a hospital on 31 December.[52]

By a return of 10 December, Major Shaaff was in command of the combined 25th Georgia and 1st Sharpshooter Battalion with a strength of 202 effectives and 341 total present, fewer than had been present after Chickamauga. Significantly, the 202 men fit for duty had only 151 weapons, meaning some had lost them or thrown them away on the retreat. The Army of Tennessee now sought refuge to heal its wounds.[53]

4

DALTON

General Bragg was relieved from command on 2 December and General Joseph E. Johnston arrived to take over command of the Army of Tennessee on 27 December. On 1 February 1864 Colonel Clement Hoffman Stevens was promoted to brigadier general and given command of Wilson's brigade, relieving Colonel Nisbet. Stevens's date of rank was 20 January. He had commanded the 24th South Carolina in Gist's brigade since 1862 and had been seriously wounded at Chickamauga. He had a reputation as a strict disciplinarian and had acquired the nickname "Rock;" General Gist later referred to him as "iron-nerved." Stevens was a good commander who showed interest in the welfare of the troops and had their admiration.

While Stevens was pleased with his promotion, he was not happy with his new brigade. In a letter to a friend, he wrote, "My present brigade is a very inferior one. First, because it is a very small one and next because two of the commands, the 66th Geo[rgia] Regt. and the 26th Geo[rgia] Batt[alion] are of such inferior physical material that they will melt away before the end of one week's march." One of Stevens's officers later said, "He took our brigade, the meanest in the army, and made it one of the very best."[1]

Colonel Nisbet described Stevens as "a man about sixty years old, of splendid physique, well versed by military education and experience in the art of war. Although a strict disciplinarian, he soon gained the confidence and esteem of his officers and men." To the twenty-four-year-old Nisbet, Stevens, with his bald pate and gray hair possibly did appear ancient, but in fact, the general was only forty-two when Nisbet met him. Nisbet also reported that Stevens instituted night classes for the officers at brigade headquarters, presided over by the general, "a most competent teacher of military duties and the tactics." His views on the material he had to work with no doubt influenced Stevens in setting up the school for officers, but one wonders how Shaaff, the former regular, took to the training.[2]

Some of the soldiers in the ranks had their own opinions of the new brigadier's discipline. Private Angus McDermid of the 29th Georgia wrote to his mother on 26 March 1864: "We have got the titest Jeneral [sic] now out. He ceeps us strait. He had a man Branded yesterday on the left hip with a letter D for deserting and now has put him in stocks every day for thirty days and another is rideing on a wooden horse—some one way and some a nother. Some a hanging by the thumbs." And again, on 17 April, McDermid wrote, "We have got the titest Brigadeer Jineral [sic] in this world. The boys saies [sic] if they ever get in to a fight that they will kill him." This was the worm's eye view of Nisbet's "confidence and esteem."[3]

Corporal A. P. Adamson of the 30th Georgia commented more favorably on his new brigade commander. In a letter to his sister on 20 March, Adamson wrote, "We have to drill now almost every day, division drill at that, which is not an easy job. Old General Stevens is strict but I think is a reasonable old fellow but he will have discipline." And in a letter to a newspaper, a soldier who signed himself "St. Bernard" wrote "Our brigade could not have found a more competent and brave commander in the army. One who will more strongly combine discipline and mercy to his inferiors could not be found than Gen. Stevens."[4]

Whether or not Stevens was well received in his new command, he was not the only candidate for the vacancy. As early as 16 November, even before Wilson's death, Arthur Shaaff wrote directly to Confederate Adjutant General Samuel Cooper. Citing his regular army experience, his wound at Chickamauga, and his current command of Wilson's brigade, Shaaff asked for direct promotion to brigadier general. This proposal was rejected by the department on the grounds that it had not been transmitted through channels.

Shaaff wrote again on 9 January 1864. This time he had all the proper endorsements. In addition, probably on the advice of his superiors, he lowered his sights to promotion to colonel of infantry. General Walker gave this application a favorable recommendation, writing that Shaaff was a "very superior" officer, was brave and efficient, and would make a "capital colonel," probably of the 25th Georgia, Wilson's old regiment. Colonel Nisbet, General Cheatham, and Colonel Brent for General Johnston, all echoed Walker's appraisal of Shaaff's abilities. Alas, it was not to be: Colonel E. W. Palfrey of the adjutant general's department wrote to the secretary of war on 26 January that Shaaff "has no claim to higher rank."[5]

Shaaff had had one other opportunity for advancement. The 1st Georgia Sharpshooters was a four-company battalion and its commander could never have rank higher than major. But Confederate law prescribed that a battalion of six companies or more would be commanded by a lieutenant colonel. Lieutenant Colonel Leroy Napier of the 8th Georgia Battalion, an eight-company battalion in Gist's brigade, was a native of Macon and a graduate of West Point. Napier was sick most of the time Gist's brigade was in Mississippi in summer 1863 but he commanded his battalion at Chickamauga and indeed succeeded to the command of the brigade on 20 September after all his seniors were wounded. Napier was sick again during the Chattanooga campaign and finally retired to his home in Bibb County. Upon being notified of Napier's condition, the War Department in Richmond wired Shaaff offering him command of the 8th Battalion but he never received the telegram. In the absence of a response, Richmond assumed Shaaff was not interested and gave the command and the promotion to the battalion's senior captain, Zach L. Watters.[6]

General Walker resumed his interrupted leave in January and returned to camp on 10 February. He engaged at once in a round of reviews and inspections to reacquaint himself with the condition of his troops. He had personally selected the camp site 3 miles east of Dalton in early December and in his absence General Gist, once again acting division commander, had seen to the orderliness of the camp. When General Johnston inspected the division in January, he and his staff were struck by the good conditions they found. Captain Richard I. Manning of Johnston's staff wrote his mother about Gist's brigade, "Their camp is a beautiful one, very nice, snug houses-wide streets regularly laid off and looking like a village-the men well clothed and shod-in excellent discipline and well drilled." If Walker, Gist and Stevens insisted on uniform living standards among the brigades, we can be confident the 1st Sharpshooter Battalion, whose camp had been held up as a model the year before, was in similar circumstances. Cuyler King made a reference to the "cabins" in camp in one letter to his sister and A. P. Adamson wrote that the troops had "comfortable houses" and were "faring better" than he had expected.[7]

Frank Roberts, a soldier from Augusta, Georgia, serving in the 2nd Georgia Sharpshooter Battalion in General John K. Jackson's brigade, described just how snug the living accommodations were.

> Our cabins were built of split logs, the cracks being "chinked" during the severest weather with red clay, thus making a very comfortable house indeed. An ample chimney was constructed of sticks "chinked" in the same manner as the house; and when the fireplace was piled up with wood and set going, we had as comfortable quarters as to warmth as one could wish. Our bedsteads were four posts with end and side pieces nailed to them, and boards were placed so as to give us room to fill in with straw, and over this our quilts and blankets were spread.[8]

The army General Johnston had inherited was in terrible condition, physically as well as psychologically. When he took command, he set about the business of putting it back on its feet. He began by providing the basic necessities of life. Shelter was already available in huts built by the soldiers themselves, as described. This was fortunate in the unusually harsh winter of 1863–64. Food and clothing were lacking, principally due to the uncertainty of the supply line from Atlanta. Johnston addressed this issue personally and with good results.[9]

Perhaps to assist in food procurement and distribution for Shaaff's battalion, Sergeant William Stephan or Stevens, B Company, was given the additional duty of commissary sergeant while at Dalton. In this capacity he would probably be assisting the battalion quartermaster, Captain W. G. Gray. Stephan may have been the thirty-year-old, New York City-born, Savannah grocer or baker of similar name listed in the 1860 directory and census. He had performed the same duty while a private with the DeKalb Rifles at Fort McAllister in 1862, and may have been commissary sergeant since the battalion was formed, but his record does not show it. Frank Roberts of the 2nd Sharpshooters attested to the availability of food, listing beef, potatoes, corn bread, cane syrup, bacon, and greens among the daily fare. The soldiers provided their own syrup by purchase. Mexican red peppers were used liberally for seasoning. Roberts recalled that when the army passed back through Dalton in October 1864, the grounds of the former encampment were covered with pepper plants sprouting from the fallen seeds.[10]

John I. Royal wrote from Dalton early in December, asking his wife to send him an overcoat, socks, and gloves. He said he had recently received a good blanket, perhaps from the supplies brought from Savannah by Manuel Molina. Royal asked his wife to find soldiers Edward Stokes or David Culpepper, who were both home on leave, and ask one of them to bring him the clothing. The December 1863 muster roll shows that Culpepper and Stokes were both in camp, so either one could have brought the items to Royal. Culpepper went home again sick in January or February and was still absent in August.[11]

Besides food and clothing, Johnston took measures to increase army strength by successfully declaring a general amnesty for deserters and absentees. The returns had already begun to show an increase in December and this trend continued throughout the winter. Walker's division had shown an effective strength of some 3,400 on 10 December 1863. By 20 January 1864, he had almost 3,800 effectives, and by 20 February more than 4,700. For the rest of the winter, the number of effectives in the division never fell below 4,500 and stood at 5,200 by the end of April.[12]

A system of home leaves was begun, officers were allowed to bring their families to camp, and steps were taken to improve arms and equipment. On their own, the soldiers turned to religious revivals, took up hunting to supplement their rations, and engaged in outdoor activities. Discipline was strengthened by constant drilling and officers attended schools of instruction conducted by their seniors, as in the case of General Stevens.[13]

Reenlistments were encouraged with gratifying results. By winter 1864, the three-year enlistments of the men who had joined the ranks in 1861 were near expiration. Johnston's army stood fair to lose its corps of experienced veterans. A majority of those eligible did sign up for another term. In Walker's division, more than 4,400 men reenlisted by 10 March. His present-for-duty strength in enlisted men that day was 4,800, meaning that 90 percent of the men present were reenlisted veterans.[14]

In the 1st Sharpshooter Battalion sixty men reenlisted, most of them on 16 February, representing probably half the present-for-duty enlisted strength of the unit. Prominent among those reenlisting were First Sergeant John F. Knowles of A Company and a number of other non-commissioned officers. Because all of B Company and many of the men in the other companies had initially enlisted for the war, the battalion was guaranteed nearly 100% of its strength in the coming campaign. The battalion was proud of its accomplishment and wanted it properly publicized. Adjutant Johnston wrote to the Savannah newspaper the day after the reenlistments. "As individually, and as an organization, we proudly cherish our connection with Savannah, and feel sure that our many friends in the dear old city will be gratified to know that the 1st Battalion Georgia Sharpshooters has reenlisted for the war—the first Georgia troops in this army to follow the noble example set by the Tennesseans."[15]

New enlistments were not as promising as reenlistments. Only two men seem to have enlisted in the battalion while at Dalton. One was F. M. Coe who joined on 1 December, and the other was Luke B. Williams, who joined A Company, probably on 25 March. Luke was probably the younger brother of Nathan and William S. Williams of Jasper County. His age was fourteen in the 1860 census, so he must have joined as soon as he was 18.[16]

One soldier whose record did not reflect a reenlistment was Private Alfred Roath of A Company. He had been a soldier in the 25th Georgia prior to transferring to the sharpshooters in 1862, and he suffered a serious leg wound at Chickamauga in 1863. Roath's reason for not reenlisting was a good one: he was not in camp because he had been summoned by civil authority to be a witness at a murder trial in Screven County. Roath must have reenlisted later because he continued to serve until he was captured at Nashville in December

1864. His release record from Camp Chase, Ohio, in May 1865 showed that he was thirty years old at that time.[17]

Toward the end of March General Johnston instituted another morale boosting measure when he ordered formation of an "Infirmary Corps." Three men for every 100 effectives in each regiment or battalion were to be detailed to collect the wounded from the battlefield and transport them to the unit aid station for treatment. Wounded men would thus be saved from bleeding to death unattended or being burned alive by the brush fires sometimes ignited by weapons fire. The detailed men would be unarmed but a non-commissioned officer in charge of the detail would carry his weapon. An officer from each brigade was designated to direct the activities of the combined unit Infirmary Corps. These men, in effect, were litter bearers, and we will see that such details were made in Shaaff's battalion in the coming campaign.[18]

The 1st Georgia Sharpshooter Battalion participated in and benefited from all of these programs. While its strength after Chickamauga had sunk to fewer than 80 men present and fewer than 50 effectives, and probably even lower after Chattanooga, even when combined with the 25th Georgia, by the opening of the spring campaign in 1864 the battalion had 129 effectives in the ranks.[19]

Arthur Shaaff was probably one of the officers who had visitors from home. It is possible his mother and sister came to camp during this time. On 5 February 1864, from camp in Dalton, Brigadier General William W. Mackall, another Marylander in Confederate service and chief of staff of the Army of Tennessee, wrote to his wife in Savannah, "Yesterday I dined with some ladies at General Joe's [Joseph E. Johnston]. Among them happened to be a widow lady, formerly Miss Shaaf (Shofe) [sic] from George Town and Jno. Forsyth's sister, so that I got on very well." Mackall may have been writing of Shaaff's mother ("Jno. Forsyth's [mayor of Mobile, Alabama] sister") and sister, Julia Frances Shaaff Brice, whose husband, Richard Tilghman Brice, had died in 1851. Mrs. Brice was living or visiting in Georgia; Florence King had seen her at Indian Springs in August 1863.[20]

The spelling and pronunciation of Arthur Shaaff's family name were as difficult for his contemporaries as they are for us. The name has been spelled with one "a" or two, with one "f" or two, or with a "c" between the "S" and the "h" or not. General Mackall and Colonel Nisbet seem to have pronounced the name as "Shofe" or "Shoaf;" a veteran in an 1867 letter to a newspaper editor wrote it as "Schoup."[21]

Several of the officers remaining with the battalion took advantage of the opportunity to go home. Perhaps all did, but the records show that Lieutenant Alfred Bryan, who had been wounded at Chickamauga, went on leave about 23

March; Captain W. G. Gray, the battalion quartermaster, departed on 4 March; First Lieutenant Josiah Holcombe, on duty with the brigade staff, took leave on 14 April; Lieutenant Samuel W. Lawrence, now commanding D Company, left on 5 March; and Second Lieutenant Charles L. Schlatter, acting commander of A Company, took leave from 29 February, returning about 23 March.[22]

The absence of Captain Horace Twyman from his company during the winter is suggested by the signature of Lieutenant Schlatter as commander on vouchers and muster rolls for the months of December through March. In fact, Twyman was serving on temporary duty as inspector on General Walker's division staff where he joined Captain William H. Ross of C Company.

Lieutenant Lawrence had been in command of D Company most of the time since summer 1863 due to Captain George C. Dent being made invalid after the second battle of Jackson. During winter 1864, Dent, in Savannah on sick leave, found for himself a position as inspector of artillery at that place and received orders to take it up. Despite that, he remained on the rolls as nominal commander of his company, thereby blocking any chance for promotion for his subordinate officers. Cuyler King was chagrined enough to consider a transfer to another unit but, as he told his sister, "I...dislike the idea of leaving my men and the officers of this Battalion with whom I have gone through so many hard marches."[23]

During the winter Major Hartridge reached out again from near Savannah to make his influence felt in the battalion. This time he needed an ordnance sergeant and on 8 February he asked for James M. Leonard. Leonard was by now Second Sergeant of B Company. He was a resident of Savannah, although born in Massachusetts, about twenty-three years old, and a carriage painter in civilian life. He had served under Hartridge in the old DeKalb Rifles and, more recently, had been slightly wounded in the leg at Chickamauga. Hartridge's request was approved on 24 February, and on 2 March Leonard was appointed ordnance sergeant of Rose Dew (or Rose Dhu) Post on the Georgia coast.[24]

Another soldier in the battalion had received a specialty appointment a few months earlier. Private Justus Kraft was also a former DeKalb Rifleman, having enlisted in 1861. Beginning in October 1862 Kraft had been assigned extra duty as a hospital steward. In February 1863 his status was changed from "extra duty" to "detail," and in November 1863 he received a formal warrant as hospital steward, transferring out of B Company and becoming a member of the battalion staff. His name last appears on the muster roll for February 1864, so he may have left for duty in a hospital thereafter.[25]

About 1 April 1864 Major Shaaff recommended that First Sergeant Dominique Brown of B Company be appointed as ensign, the lowest commissioned rank in the Confederate army, the recommendation no doubt due to Brown's exemplary service. It will be recalled that he had been first sergeant since the founding of the battalion and had held the same position in the DeKalb Rifles. The title of ensign stemmed from older times when the standard bearer of a unit carried that rank. In Sergeant Brown's case, the War Department in Richmond turned down the request on 8 June 1864, with the notation that "Ensigns are not authorized by law for Battalions."[26]

Among the changes made by General Johnston to improve morale in the Army of Tennessee after his arrival was the reformation of the Tennessee division of General Benjamin Franklin Cheatham. Braxton Bragg had considered Cheatham's division as one of the hotbeds of unrest in his army in fall 1863. Just before the battle of Chattanooga, Bragg had broken up the division, sending its Tennessee brigades to other divisions and bringing brigades from other states into the division. This was how Maney's Tennessee brigade had found its way into Walker's division in mid-November.

In early February 1864 Johnston brought the Tennessee brigades together again under their revered commander. In making this move, Johnston, either purposely or inadvertently, created a Georgia Division under General Walker when he replaced Maney's Tennesseans with the Georgia-Mississippi brigade of General John K. Jackson, a native of Augusta. Now Walker's division boasted the Georgia brigade of General Clement Stevens, including the sharpshooter battalion; the Georgia-South Carolina brigade of States Rights Gist; and Jackson's brigade consisting of the 47th and 65th Georgia Regiments, the 1st Confederate Georgia Regiment, the 2nd Georgia Sharpshooter Battalion, and the 5th and 8th Mississippi Regiments. The members of Shaaff's battalion gave an especially warm welcome to the 47th Georgia, their former compatriots in the Savannah garrison.[27]

Just before Walker's return from home leave, the prospect of action in the field surfaced once again. Early in February 1864 William T. Sherman, who had returned to Mississippi after the victory at Chattanooga, launched an offensive toward the rail facilities at Meridian. General Leonidas Polk's Confederate army of three divisions was too small to intervene effectively. Cleburne's and Cheatham's divisions from Dalton were moved to Demopolis, Alabama, by rail. Walker was alerted to follow them. The baggage and supplies of his division were loaded on railroad cars in preparation for a movement but the crisis passed when Sherman withdrew and Walker's orders were rescinded.

The possibility of a return to barren and disease-ridden Mississippi was too grim an eventuality for many of the men in Walker's division, especially Stevens's brigade, to contemplate. Angus McDermid wrote his father on 20

February: "There is nearly half of our Brigade that says they will desert before they ever see Miss. again. On the way they will leave us if we start their and I dont blame them for it nother." Soldiers in the sharpshooter battalion must have been counted among that half. As for himself, McDermid would go because, "any thing before Deserting for me."[28]

During this episode, Union General George Thomas with the Army of the Cumberland moved forward in force from Ringgold toward Dalton on the suspicion that Johnston's army had been weakened to support Polk in Mississippi. This time Walker did leave camp in command of his own and Patton Anderson's divisions to protect the Tunnel Hill-Cleveland road. Again the Federals withdrew and the Southern troops returned to Dalton. The sharpshooter battalion moved from their winter camp to the lines with the rest of the division and then marched back to their comfortable huts again.[29]

Another of General Johnston's efforts to rebuild the Army of Tennessee was the introduction of a uniform battle flag for all units. The pattern he chose was modeled after the flag he had introduced in the Eastern armies in 1861. He also instituted a system of headquarters flags based on his Virginia experience. Various factors interfered with the completion of his plan. For one, an insufficient number of battle flags was delivered. As a result, Walker's division did not get new flags and the brigades that had come from Georgia and South Carolina in 1863, Gist's and Stevens's, including Shaaff's battalion, kept the flags issued to them by General Beauregard.

After the new flags were issued, Generals Hardee and Hood, the corps commanders, issued orders that each unit should have inscribed on its flag the number of the regiment and the state from which it came. At about the same time, General Hood directed that sharpshooters and skirmishers should not carry their flags when deployed as such because of the additional risk of capture and to preserve the element of surprise when approaching the enemy. If General Hardee gave a similar order, it would have had a direct bearing on the operations of the Georgia sharpshooters.[30]

Of all the events in Dalton that last hopeful winter of the Confederacy, nothing evoked more comment in the years after than the celebrated snowball battles. Winter 1864 was unusually cold and was accompanied by frequent and enduring snowfall. Early on in the winter, the men, many of whom had never seen more than a dusting of snow, turned to snowball fighting for recreation and for relief from boredom.

Late in March, after a downfall of 5 or 6 inches, snowball fights broke out generally in the army. None of the snow battles excited more interest than that between the Tennessee and Georgia divisions. The two divisions were camped quite close to each other, separated only by a creek bed, probably Mill Creek. Rivalry between the two was fairly intense. Maney's and Jackson's brigades had been exchanged between the divisions only a month before.

After some desultory fighting during the morning, one side or the other issued a challenge which was quickly accepted. Lines possibly a mile long were drawn up on each side. Estimates of the total combatants run to 5,000 men or more. Snow ammunition was stockpiled. The affray began when Cheatham's men charged across the creek and up the hill against the Georgians. Unfortunately, they had not brought enough ammunition with them, and they were driven back. The Georgia Division counterattacked, and charges and counter-charges continued for hours. Finally, with both sides exhausted, the battle came to a temporary halt.

The first combat had been led by enlisted soldiers acting as officers. Now a bona fide field grade officer appeared to lead each side. For the Tennesseans, it was Colonel George W. Gordon of the 11th Tennessee; for the men of Walker's division, an unidentified major. Seizing a makeshift banner, Gordon rode right into the Georgia lines. Following their colonel's lead, the Tennessee men sprang forward and completely routed their opponents, even capturing the Georgia camp and looting it.

When most of the Georgians refused to renew the fight, two of the Tennessee brigades turned on each other and continued for the rest of the afternoon. Not all of the Georgians, however, gave up so easily. The men of John K. Jackson's brigade turned against the Tennesseans of Otho Strahl. It was an ill-conceived movement. Summoning help from other brigades, Strahl's men counterattacked and captured Jackson. In response to a demand from his captors, the general praised their prowess and wished them as much success against the Yankees as they had had against his Georgians. Cheers were given for Georgia and Tennessee and the men retired to their huts. As for the men of the 1st Georgia Sharpshooter Battalion, Cuyler King gave his own description of the fight: "Men and officers enjoyed the snowballing very much. Brigades and Divisions were engaged against each other within regular lines of battle giving a spectator a very good idea (leaving out the noise except the shouting) of how our men fight when engaged with the enemy, first one side and then the other would charge, take prisoners &C, one poor wretch got his eye nocked out which I believe was the only harm done."[31]

The snowball battle was followed within a few weeks by the end of winter. Warmer weather brought back the reality of the impending spring campaign and the different corps of the army spent some of their energy on sham battles. Walker's division was scheduled for one for 1 April but it was canceled, much to the dissatisfaction of the men, who enjoyed such theatrics as long as there was no return fire. The army corps of General John Bell Hood dramatically conducted another such affair later in April and ended the day in high spirits. General Johnston conducted a review of the whole army on 19 April that lasted for several hours and thrilled at least one participant.[32]

While the soldiers in camp at Dalton were being restored, both physically and in spirit, deaths from disease continued to thin the ranks of the sharp-shooters. John I. Royal had complained of being unwell in his letter to his wife in December. Early in the new year, 1864, he was taken to hospital in Atlanta with chronic diarrhea and then to Greensboro, Georgia. He died there on 9 March, leaving his wife in Dooly County with six children and a struggling farm. Mary Jane Royal was summoned to her husband's deathbed by a Greens-boro clergyman who served the spiritual needs of the sick soldiers. After John's death, Mary Jane hired a man with a wagon to bring the body home for burial.[33]

Besides Royal, E. W. Callahan died of dropsy in camp at Dalton, and James McBride of Henry County, Alabama, died of dysentery in Atlanta, both in December; George W. Middleton of Appling County died of pneumonia in Atlanta, and Jasper Sutton, Royal's neighbor in Dooly County, died at home, both in January; James A. Cox, formerly a conscript, died in hospital in Kings-ton, Georgia, not far from his home in Euharlee, in February; and Sergeant J. Irwin Morel of Effingham County died of chronic diarrhea in March.[34]

At the end of April, another Georgia brigade, General Hugh W. Mercer's, was brought from Savannah and added to Walker's division. Although it had only two regiments, the 54th and 63rd Georgia, they were both large and the brigade had 1,400 effective men, a welcome addition to the army. Unfortunately, they had been in garrison for much of their service and were not experienced field troops. Two more regiments, the 1st Georgia Volunteers and the 57th Georgia, came from the coast to join Mercer's brigade before the end of May. There were men still remaining in Shaaff's battalion who had transferred from the 1st and 54th Georgia in summer 1862, and, of course, General Mercer was a familiar figure.[35]

During the first week in May, the army began to bestir itself for active operations. Cuyler King told his sister that "we are under marching orders" and "We have been kept in readiness now for several days." Other signs made future action obvious. General Johnston informed the ladies on 1 May that it was time for them to leave and they were shipped off to Atlanta about 6 May. Soldiers began sending home their excess baggage as Angus McDermid did his favorite coat on 1 May, with a dire warning to his mother, "Dont let nobody ware it."[36]

5

ATLANTA

At the opening of the spring campaign in May 1864 the 1st Sharpshooter Battalion had a strength of 129 effectives and was still in Walker's division in the old Walker/Wilson brigade, now commanded by Brigadier General Clement H. Stevens. Arthur Shaaff continued as battalion commander. His acting adjutant was Second Lieutenant George H. Johnston of C Company and Captain W. G. Gray remained as quartermaster. The company commanders were Captain Horace Twyman in A Company, Captain Benjamin H. Hardee in B Company, Second Lieutenant Nicholas B. Sadler in C Company, and First Lieutenant Samuel W. Lawrence in D Company. Captain William H. Ross of C Company served on division staff and First Lieutenants Robert P. Wayne, the nominal battalion adjutant, and Josiah L. Holcombe of C Company were on the staff of General Stevens.

Still on duty with the troops were Second Lieutenants Alfred Bryan and Charles Schlatter in A Company, First Lieutenant Henry Herrmann and Second Lieutenant Thomas S. Wayne in B Company, and Second Lieutenants Manuel Molina and R. Cuyler King in D Company. King's father, Thomas Butler King, died in Ware County on 10 May, but none of his sons were able to go home for the funeral. Despite letters of notification from his sister, as late as September Cuyler was still sending regards to his father in his letters home.[1]

B Company had a new second lieutenant in the person of Stephen P. Norris, formerly first sergeant of D Company. Norris had been wounded at Chickamauga and had been promoted for conspicuous gallantry in that battle to replace the deceased Charles S. Pattillo. Norris was twenty-two years old, had been an apprentice mechanic before the war, and was the son of an English-born merchant tailor. He was promoted 28 April 1864 to rank from 21 April.

Norris was replaced as first sergeant in D Company by Benjamin F. Walker, who had enlisted in the 8th Georgia Battalion at Camp Black in 1861 and had served continuously as a non-commissioned officer in the sharpshooters since August 1862. John F. Knowles remained as first sergeant of A Company, a position he had held since replacing Pattillo in May 1863. Dominique Brown, the original first sergeant of B Company, was shown to be still in his place. At this time the recommendation for his appointment as ensign was still pending.

First Sergeant Peter Derst of C Company, wounded at Chickamauga, may not yet have returned to duty. If not, his place was probably filled by Second Sergeant Cornelius Marion Hardy, formerly a sergeant in the Jasper Blues, Company A of the 32nd Georgia. He had been in Arkansas at the outbreak of war and served in a local company there in 1861, going to fight in Missouri. Later he came back to Georgia and enlisted in the State Troops in February 1862. Hardy was twenty-six years old when the 1860 census was taken in Jasper County, and one of three men with that name in the county. The other two were his grandfather and his uncle, the former a native of North Carolina. His father, William P. Hardy, was a farmer near Monticello.[2]

The battalion sergeant major was Alfred H. Gordon, whose early military service was in the 1st Georgia Volunteers and the Chatham Artillery. He had risen to the rank of corporal but last appeared on the muster roll of that company in April 1863 when he was present for duty. When he joined the sharpshooters is something of a mystery. Although his name first appears on the muster roll for January-February 1864, he could have been a member of the unit as early as May 1863. The muster rolls for field and staff (battalion headquarters personnel) for June, August, October, and December 1863, are missing, so there is no indication of who, if anyone, was sergeant major during that period. It will be remembered that Lieutenant Charles Schlatter, the previous sergeant major, had been promoted in May. Gordon could have joined the unit from Savannah the same month and accompanied them in Mississippi and at Chickamauga. The February 1864, muster roll shows that he was paid by Captain W. G. Gray, the sharpshooter quartermaster, on 31 October 1863 so he was certainly with the battalion by that time.

On 11 December 1863 Captain J. A. Maxwell had asked for Gordon to be adjutant of his proposed new battalion of artillery near Savannah. Lieutenant Johnston prepared a request for Gordon to be sent on recruiting duty for Maxwell's battalion but Colonel George Brent, assistant adjutant general of the Army of Tennessee, disapproved on the grounds that Gordon's services were indispensable to the sharpshooters. General Cheatham, acting commander of Hardee's corps, also disapproved, writing that Maxwell's request was premature and should be presented after his battalion was formed.

Gordon's service record indicates he had been almost continuously hospitalized from the beginning of December 1863 until well into March 1864. A former clerk, Gordon had been living in a hotel in Savannah with his mother and brother in 1860. The census record shows that all three were natives of Orange County, New York. The 1850 census of Savannah included a couple who were probably Alfred's parents, George Gordon, a Massachusetts-born merchant, and his wife, Louisa. Alfred Gordon was twenty-five years old in 1860. How a corporal from another regiment came to be selected for the important position of sergeant major of Shaaff's battalion is an issue that cannot be resolved from available records.[3]

The battalion had a new medical officer also. Cornelius T. Ford was a combat veteran as well as a physician. He was a native of the Marion District of South Carolina and a graduate of Wake Forest College in North Carolina. He had entered military service in September 1861 at the age of twenty-five as lieutenant of G Company, 10th South Carolina Volunteers, had fought under Braxton Bragg in the western theater, and had been promoted to captain. Sent home on recruiting duty in March 1863, Ford resigned his line commission in May and applied for and received a position as assistant surgeon backdated to April 1863.

Ford's first assignment was to Joseph Johnston's army in Mississippi in May 1863. He remained during the campaign and was one of five surgeons left behind with the sick and wounded when Jackson was evacuated in July. He may or may not have been captured and paroled, but from Jackson he went to Mobile, and then to Dalton and the Army of Tennessee in December when he joined Walker's division. His name first appeared on Shaaff's battalion muster roll on 29 February 1864. Ford's brother was a deputy sheriff in Marion District and the sheriff was his brother-in-law.[4]

According to the records, Ford replaced Dr. John M. Dent who had resigned from service after the battle of Chickamauga. The battalion had had no assigned medical officer since then, although Dr. Thomas R. Cosby's name was still on the February 1864 muster roll. His association with the battalion is murky from the time he joined in June 1863. Cosby transferred to the 45th Mississippi Volunteers in Lowrey's brigade in March 1864.[5]

At the outset of the 1864 campaign Walker's division served much of the time as an army reserve and did some hard marching and counter-marching around Dalton and Resaca as General Johnston tried to determine and thwart the intentions of the enemy. Arthur Shaaff's future brother-in-law, Lieutenant Hamilton Branch of the 54th Georgia in Mercer's brigade, summarized the activity in a sentence when he wrote to his mother in Savannah, "My boys are all well but nearly worn out and we, Walker's Foot Cavalry, have been doing all the strategy for Genl. Johnston and have marched night and day for the last 10 days with very little rest." Shaaff and his men shared the marching and hardship of the first ten days of the Atlanta campaign but saw little real fighting. Sergeant John W. Hagan informed his wife on 16 May that "we have not been in the fight but we have been held in resirve ," and later, "We are wore out a marching."[6]

During the first day of the battle at Resaca, 14 May, the bulk of Walker's division was posted on the south side of the Oostanaula River near Calhoun, watching for Union troops to try to cross the river and outflank the Confederate army on its left. A. P. Adamson of the 30th Georgia wrote that his brigade was in plain view of the battle to the north and came under enemy fire but did not participate in the action. That night, with no sign of a crossing in their sector, the division was summoned back to Resaca, leaving only Stevens' brigade (with Shaaff's battalion) south of the river. Then, Johnston did receive reports of Federal activity along the river bank to his south, and Walker's division was marched right back again in the dark. Although there is no record of an engagement on the part of the 1st Sharpshooters at Resaca, they suffered a few casualties as reported in the *Savannah Republican* of 28 May 1864 (see below).[7]

On 15 May troops of the Federal division of General Thomas Sweeney did successfully cross the river at Lay's Ferry on Walker's front. An attack on their bridgehead by John K. Jackson's brigade failed with serious casualties and Johnston brought his whole army south of the Oostanaula in order to protect his line of communication to Atlanta. The next day, 16 May, the sharpshooter battalion saw its first real action of the campaign.[8]

From their bridgehead on the Oostanaula, Sweeney's division was pushed forward to intercept Johnston's line of retreat at a place south of Calhoun called Rome Crossroads. Before long, Rebel pickets were driven back so far by the Federal brigade of Colonel Patrick E. Burke that the bivouac area of Hardee's corps came under a galling artillery fire. About 2:00 P.M. Hardee ordered Walker to clear away the annoying Yankee force and the Georgian turned to General States Rights Gist. Gist selected the 24th South Carolina of his own brigade under Colonel Ellison Capers and Major Arthur Shaaff's 1st Battalion Georgia Sharpshooters from Stevens's brigade. Earlier in the day Walker's men had been forced by the Federal advance to retire from a hilltop position where they had been posted to observe the bridgehead. When Capers organized his counterattack, Shaaff made it his personal mission to retake the hill.

As senior officer, Capers took command. He planned that Shaaff's men would charge the enemy from the right rear, while the 24th assaulted the front. The sharpshooters reached the assigned position over a trail protected by a stand of woods and shielded by a dense hedgerow and formed a line perpendicular to the South Carolinians. By this time, the Yankee skirmishers, the 66th Illinois, had seized the crossroads and advanced beyond it.

As soon as the sharpshooters were in position, Capers marched the 24th

Regiment into the open. Without hesitation, the Georgians came from the other direction "with a yell." The Carolinians advanced with precision, then on order, also charged, catching the blue-coated skirmishers by surprise in front and flank and nearly capturing their supporting battery. Some of the cannoneers left their knapsacks on the field as they retreated. Because of the swiftness and vigor of the attack, the enemy fired wildly over the heads of the charging Confederates and fell back in disorder. So fast and so far went the advance that Gist feared they would be lost to the whole Federal army and sent a courier to bring them back

Capers wrote in his report that "Both commands behaved in the most admirable order." A private from the 16th South Carolina who witnessed the action wrote "Our skirmishers repulsed the whole Yankee skirmishers." Another observer recalled that "he never saw anything of the kind ever done." Captain William L. Roddey, who commanded a company of the 24th South Carolina during the attack, wrote "It impressed me very broadly as much as any occurrence during that campaign... In a very short time [our] line came forward and all [enemy] firing stopped."[9]

General Grenville Dodge, the Union XVI Corps commander, naturally put a different face on the event. In his version, the 66th Illinois, equipped with Henry repeating rifles, put out such a tremendous volume of fire that Sweeney's two brigades routed the Rebel attack. General John M. Corse, who later succeeded Sweeney in division command, wrote in his report that the 66th Illinois was surprised because they had advanced too far beyond the line prescribed for them. On the Union side, there was a total of about seventy men lost, of whom fifty-two were from Burke's brigade. Colonel Burke, the brigade commander, was wounded in the leg at the head of his troops and died later in Resaca. Captain George A. Taylor, who had led the precipitate advance of the 66th Illinois, was shot in the head and killed while trying to rally his men.[10]

Lieutenant Hamilton Branch provided a description of the activities of the 1st Sharpshooter Battalion to the *Savannah Republican* and repeated much of the information in a letter to his mother.

> At Resaca they, with others, checked the enemy skirmishers and kept them from crossing the river on our left flank, and at Calhoun on the 16th, they were, as usual, again out skirmishing. On the morning of that day, the skirmishers on their flanks retiring from some cause, compelled them to fall back from a strong position on a hill. In the evening, the enemy skirmishers advancing in strong force, the gallant Major Shaaff determined to retake this hill. To do this, he was

compelled to charge the enemy through an open field, which he did, leading his battalion as he always does, with conspicuous gallantry, and his brave command followed him, as they always do, with determined bravery. After driving them from this hill, not satisfied, he again charged them and drove them back 2 miles, but with pretty heavy losses in his small command. Major Shaaff escaped unhurt, although leading his men the whole time, but the brave Captain T[w]yman, than whom no more gallant officer lives, whilst leading and beckoning his men to follow him, received a ball in his right leg breaking it and passing through the fleshy part of his left leg. Lieut. Herman and Sergt. Major Gordon were both of them severely wounded. But with all this, the gallant Major and his brave boys are here ready and anxious to join in the grand whipping which General Johnston is going to give Sherman and his hireling soldiers.[11]

Later, Shaaff's wife "Lizzie" wrote Branch a thank you note for his published description of her husband's valor: "A friend of mine has sent me over the Republican to read a letter from you! How can I thank you sufficiently for thoughts so kindly expressed for my dear Husband! I cannot express my thanks dear Hammie, but pray that God may bless and give you a safe and speedy return home."[12]

The 24th South Carolina lost forty-one killed, wounded, and missing in the action. Two telegrams to Savannah that were printed in the press gave the first news of the sharpshooters' casualties. In the first, it was reported that Captain Twyman, Lieutenant Herrmann, Sergeant Major Gordon, and Corporal Maddox had been wounded and two men killed, names unknown. In the second, Shaaff himself wrote from Adairsville on 17 May that he, Molina, and Johnston were unhurt and Twyman, Herrmann, and Gordon had been wounded.[13]

The full report of losses of the sharpshooter battalion in the battles at Resaca and Calhoun on 14 and 16 May was sent in by Adjutant Johnston on 20 May.

Field & Staff—Wounded: Sergt. Maj. Alfred H. Gordon, dangerously.
Company A—Killed: Private J. W. Love; Wounded: Capt. Horace D. Twyman, severely; Corp. E. G. Melton, slightly; Private L. B. Burton, severely.
Company B—Wounded: Lieut. Henry Hermann, slightly; Privates M. Roberts, slightly; John Booth, severely; J. R. Hurst, severely; C. Larson, slightly.

Company C—Killed: Private C. Stilwell; Wounded: Sergts. R. W. Price, severely; Jonathan Thornton, severely; Privates H. B. Dobson, slightly; N. M. Williams, severely; W. W. Gamble, severely; W. Jones, severely.

Company D—Wounded: Corp. G. W. Layne, slightly; Privates W. D. Warren, slightly; J. E. Cooper, slightly.

Total—Killed, 2 men; wounded, 2 officers and 16 men.

After Gordon's death Major Shaaff wrote that he had been severely wounded in the thigh. Twyman's wounds put him out of action for the next ten months. He went to Atlanta to recuperate and later to his family home in Virginia.[14]

The "Corporal Maddox" identified among the wounded in the telegram published on 19 May does not appear on this list. Private George C. Maddox was wounded and captured at Chickamauga in September 1863. Private William H. Mattox was captured in Campbell County, possibly at home, on 17 July 1864, and soon took the oath of allegiance. He had deserted on the march from Mississippi to Chickamauga and may have never returned to the battalion. He seems an unlikely candidate to have been corporal.[15]

Following the engagement at Calhoun, Hardee's corps, including Walker's division, remained in line of battle until after midnight, providing cover for the rest of the army and the supply trains to safely transit through Calhoun and move on to Adairsville. Johnston's troops bivouacked there the night of 17 May. On the march that day, A. P. Adamson of the 30th Georgia was sick, and with a group of men in similar state straggled behind the column of his division as it moved back. He and the others were apprehended by the advancing Yankees 5 miles south of Calhoun and taken off as prisoners of war to Rock Island, Illinois, where he spent the rest of the war. Corporal Joseph Reed of D Company, whose brother had died at Camp Anderson in 1862, and Private Henry C. Kittles of A Company of the sharpshooters, a resident of Screven County, were captured the same day and possibly under the same circumstances. Like Adamson, Kittles arrived at Rock Island on 27 May and stayed there until June 1865. There is no record of Reed's captivity.[16]

General Walker, the division commander, probably did not know and may not have cared about Private Kittles, but if he had known, he might have recognized the name of an old neighbor. In the pre-war years Walker had owned and operated a plantation, Mobley Pond, in the northeastern part of Screven County known as "Fork of Briar Creek." One of his neighbors there was planter and state legislator John R. Kittles, fifty-four years old. There were three Kittles sons and in summer 1861 two of them, Peter, twenty-four, and Henry, eighteen, went to Savannah to join a company of the 25th Georgia Volunteers, then forming. The brothers transferred to the sharpshooter battalion in 1862. Peter Kittles hired a substitute, Martin Doyle, in March 1863, and went home, but Henry remained in the army to meet his fate on the road outside Adairsville.[17]

The next day, 18 May, Private Joseph B. Lee of A Company was captured at Adairsville. Although Lee had been a member of Shaaff's battalion since August 1862 he had spent most of the intervening time on detached duty as a teamster with the quartermaster and ordnance departments. It is not clear what his status was when he was captured. Perhaps he was a wagon driver who had lingered behind the army. Like Henry Kittles, Lee was a resident of Screven County, but at thirty-five, he was considerably older. He remained a prisoner at Rock Island until June 1865.[18]

Before the capture of Reed, Kittles, and Lee, Private Luke Logan of C Company had been taken at Dalton on 13 May. Logan had been detailed to medical duty during the winter and may have been left in Dalton to care for the sick when the army departed. He remained a prisoner until he was exchanged in March 1865. Logan was an Irish-born former clerk for the Central of Georgia Railroad with a wife and three children; he was forty-five years old in the 1860 census. He was one of the first men to enlist directly into the battalion in August 1862 rather than being transferred from another unit. Logan's co-worker and neighbor in Savannah, Martin Doyle, was also a native of Ireland, and was the man who had enlisted in the battalion as a substitute for Peter Kittles in 1863. Doyle had a wife and two children. The 1860 census gave his age as thirty-three, but when he was discharged as a prisoner of war in 1865, the record showed he was forty-five years old.[19]

Another loss at this time was that of Private George W. Garner of D Company. Born in DeKalb County in 1842, Garner was living in Paulding County when he enlisted at Dallas in B Company, the Littlefield Volunteers, of the 8th Georgia Battalion in October, 1861. After transferring to the sharpshooters in 1862, he served for almost two years. About 17 May he was taken sick. Being close to his home at New Hope, he went there to recuperate but never returned to his command. When the report of losses in the company was made out at the end of June, his absence was attributed to enemy capture, however, there are no records of his imprisonment. An error in the rolls made the loss to be that of John Garner, not George Garner.[20]

General Johnston expected that the terrain would be suitable for making a stand at Adairsville, but he was disappointed at what he found there and fell back farther to Cassville. Hardee's corps with the baggage trains moved south along the railroad to the Rome Spur Junction at Kingston while Johnston moved directly to Cassville. The Confederate commanders hoped that Sherman would think Hardee's corps was the whole Army of Tennessee and follow it, giving Johnston an opportunity to defeat Schofield's corps which was by itself further east.

On the morning of 19 May Johnston positioned Polk's and Hood's corps north of Cassville ready to pounce on Schofield in front and flank. However, when Hood sensed the advance of a small force of Union cavalry in his rear, he changed his position, without notifying Johnston, thereby making the attack on Schofield impracticable. Johnston withdrew his army, including Hardee's corps, now come up, from his first position to a new position along a woody ridge southeast of Cassville. Johnston later said it was the best position he ever held during the war. The stage seemed set for the stroke he had been looking for. Nevertheless, Generals Hood and Polk opposed giving battle there, due, supposedly, to being enfiladed by enemy artillery, so Johnston reluctantly yielded and withdrew.

Johnston's army crossed the Etowah River on 20 May and moved to Allatoona Pass. This position proved to be too strong for Sherman and he attempted a wide swing to the west around the Confederate left flank. Johnston responded by sending Hardee's corps to Dallas and keeping Hood at Allatoona, while placing Polk at Lost Mountain, halfway between the two.

On 24 May, in response to Johnston's orders, Walker's division marched to Dallas and the next day, shifted to its right to a position near New Hope Church. Johnston had now concentrated his three corps and established a strong line from Dallas to New Hope Church. Hardee's corps was at Dallas, Hood's was around New Hope Church, and Polk held the line between them. The Georgia division of Walker supported Stewart's division of Hood's corps. Late in the afternoon of 25 May Hooker threw his three divisions blindly forward in the thick underbrush and Stewart's men, who were well placed to bring heavy fire to bear, slaughtered them.

After a one day lull, fighting resumed at Dallas and Pickett's Mill. Over two days, 26 and 27 May, the Federal army repeatedly attacked Johnston's army to no avail, again suffering heavy losses. Walker's division was in support of Bate's but took no direct part in the action. For the last three days of May Johnston launched his own attacks on Sherman to prevent him from disengaging and returning to the line of the railroad. It was not until 1 June that Sherman finally pulled away. By 7 June the Union army was at Acworth and Big Shanty (now Kennesaw). Sherman's tactical attempt to turn Johnston's left flank had failed but his strategic position was improved because he was south of

Allatoona and closer to Atlanta.

Walker's division had been barely engaged during the Dallas phase of operations. Official casualty figures, which are probably understated, show that the division as a whole lost 15 men killed and 162 wounded, while Bate's and Cleburne's division had losses of more than 400 men each. The losses in Stevens' brigade were two killed and thirty-eight wounded. Understandably, on 5 June Angus McDermid of the 29th Georgia informed his parents, "We hav not [been] in are fight yet only skermishs." Compiled service records of the 1st Sharpshooters reflect no casualties for this time period but the muster rolls for May and June 1864 are missing.[21]

Lieutenant Josiah Holcombe of the sharpshooters, still acting adjutant to General Stevens, sent a casualty list for 7 May to 6 June for the latter's brigade to the *Atlanta Confederacy* on 6 June and it was published a few days later. The list showed these additional casualties in Shaaff's battalion since the publication of the list of 20 May:

A Company—Killed: Isaiah Tanner; Wounded: N. W. Lee, slightly.

B Company—Wounded: W. Smith, severely; G. Knerr, slightly.

C Company—Wounded: Corp. W. S. Williams, severely; J. Stanfield, slightly.

Casualties in D Company were not shown. Some of these losses might have occurred in the first two days at Lost Mountain, as described below, and some in actions since 16 May.[22]

The next phase of operations was on the Lost Mountain line and lasted two weeks, from 4 to 18 June. Hood's Corps was on Johnston's right at Brushy Mountain, Polk held the center, and Hardee was posted to the left of Lost Mountain with Bates division posted forward in a salient on Pine Mountain. The line was stable for ten days until Sherman attacked Bate's position on 14 June. The attacks failed but Johnston feared that Bate might be cut off and pulled him back to the main line. General Leonidas Polk, the "Fighting Bishop," was killed by a cannonball on Pine Mountain on 14 June before the attacks began.

For the first time since the beginning of the campaign, Walker's division held a position in the front line, with Cleburne of Hardee's corps on his left and French of Polk's on his left. For four days, Sherman pushed constantly against the Confederate line. Attacks against Cleburne in the Battle of Gilgal Church on 15 June failed because of the strength of the Southern position. On 16 June the Federals took control of commanding heights on their right, forcing Johnston to shorten his line and retire Hardee behind Mud Creek. Sherman attacked Cleburne again on 17 June with heavy artillery barrages, inflicting serious casualties. A salient had been created at the juncture of Polk's and Hardee's corps when the latter pulled back on 16 June. Sherman pushed three divisions against this exposed point on 18 June, driving back Walker's pickets and bringing enfilading fire on French's division in the action at the Latimer house. In view of French's vulnerability, Johnston withdrew from Lost Mountain on the night of 18 June and fell back to the Kennesaw Mountain line.

In its position between Cleburne and French, Walker's division was involved in all the fighting of 15–18 June and suffered considerably. Sergeant John Hagan summed up the battle of 15 June, "We all had as much to do as we could." He reported six men killed, thirty-two wounded, and four missing in his regiment, the 29th Georgia. Angus McDermid wrote that the fight lasted from 4:00 P.M. until 10:00 P.M. He estimated that he had fired his rifle fifty times during the action but he was uncertain if had hit anyone or not. Captain George A. Mercer, adjutant to his father, General Hugh Mercer, noted in his diary that his brigade had lost 100 men, 70 of them from Olmstead's 1st Georgia Volunteers. In the Mud Creek attack of 18 June, the 63rd Georgia in Mercer's brigade fought for twelve hours and lost twenty-nine men.[23]

Shaaff's sharpshooters shared in the action and in the losses. Confirmed losses include one man killed and five missing, but C Company was especially hard hit. The fatality was Private Burris J. Cochran of D Company, who was killed on 18 June. He had enlisted in Bryan County in March 1863. During the battle of Gilgal Church on 15 June, Lieutenant Nicholas B. Sadler, the acting company commander, and Private Elbert Mathis were captured. On 16 June Sergeant Frank Bierhalter and Private Julius Stackfleth were lost, and on 18 June, during the action around the Latimer house, Private James Lipford was taken. Stackfleth, a thirty-four-year-old, German-born soldier from the DeKalb Rifles, was a well-known figure in Savannah. He had been the clerk at the popular Planters Hotel. His companion in captivity, Sergeant Frank Bierhalter, was a tailor who lived at the Planters.

During this period Private Henry W. Jordan of A Company was shown as a deserter. He had been listed as a deserter on the move to Mississippi in May 1863 but had returned. This time he disappeared permanently on 14 June. Losses in killed and wounded cannot be given specifically by date but were numerous and will be summarized later. Published figures indicate that C Company lost nineteen men in combat from 14 May to 1 July. On 19 June the battalion could muster only thirty men fit for duty. The loss of Bayard Sadler was especially troubling because he was the only officer serving with C

Company. All of the others, it will be remembered, had been detailed to division, brigade, and battalion staff.[24]

Brief items in the *Savannah Republican* attested to the imprisonment of some of the sharpshooters. On 1 August the newspaper published a note that Sadler had written to his brother in Savannah in June giving assurance of his well-being at Johnson's Island, Ohio, prisoner of war camp. Five days later, another item in the paper informed the reading public of the city that a group of men, many of them German-Americans, and some of whom had been reported as deserters, were instead prisoners of war at Camp Morton, Indiana. Among them was Sergeant Frank Bierhalter. However, Bierhalter's service record shows he was sent to Rock Island, Illinois, after capture and that he enlisted in the US Army in October 1864.[25]

A notice of another kind had appeared in the newspaper some days earlier under the lead, "A Flag for the Sharpshooters." It will be recalled that the battalion was still carrying the flag issued under General Beauregard's order of March 1863. That flag had seen service in Mississippi, at Chickamauga and Missionary Ridge, and in the campaign from Dalton thus far.

> We have reason to know that the 1st Georgia Battalion Sharpshooters are almost destitute of a battle flag and that a new one at this time would be most acceptable. The old battle flag has been riddled by bullets and torn by the bushes until it hangs in shreds from the staff. It will do to march home with but answers little or no purpose on the battlefield. We speak with authority and now we turn the whole matter over to the ladies of Savannah who we know will supply their want without delay. When completed, if brought to this office we will see that it is safely delivered to the battalion.

No follow-up article has been found. It may be that a new flag was supplied through army channels and that the ladies never had to sew one. Perhaps the Savannah quartermaster, who had been so forth-coming with clothing after Manuel Molina's appeal appeared in the newspaper in November 1863, responded to this one, too.[26]

General Johnston's men occupied the previously prepared position at Kennesaw Mountain early on 19 June and Sherman caught up with them by ten o'clock that morning. The first Confederate alignment had Hood on the right, Polk's corps, temporarily under Loring, in the center, and Hardee on the left. The line stretched across Kennesaw and Little Kennesaw mountains and Pigeon Hill, and then ran west along an as yet unnamed ridge, later called Cheatham's

Hill. Walker's division was on Hardee's right flank, with French's division of Loring's corps to his right, just as they had been on the Lost Mountain line. Walker had Mercer's, Jackson's and Gist's brigade in line, right to left, and Stevens, including the sharpshooters, in reserve.

A particularly fierce night action developed on Walker's front on 20 June. About four o'clock in the afternoon a Union brigade made a demonstration with a strong line of skirmishers along its whole front. The demonstration turned into a charge against a hill, which they captured, driving in Gist's and Jackson's pickets and making a lodgment in Gist's line. Major C. C. O'Neill of the 16th South Carolina, commanding Gist's picket line, was killed. Gist counter-attacked and drove the attackers out of his position but could not retake the hill. Three subsequent attacks also failed. Losses were heavy in Gist's brigade, especially in the 46th Georgia.

There is no record of participation in this action by the sharpshooters but some of Stevens's brigade was involved. Sergeant Hagan wrote that the 29th Georgia had been heavily engaged in combat on 19 and 20 June, that his regiment was "much deminished," that his captain was leading the regiment and that he was acting company commander. A day later he wrote again that the 29th had lost eighty-three men killed, wounded, and missing since 14 June, and of those only seven were missing. Angus McDermid offered the opinion that the regiment had suffered ninety-two casualties since the beginning of the campaign. He attempted to list all of the killed and wounded for his parents but gave up, "It is not worth while for me to tri to give you all the names for I cant do." McDermid may have confused the actions on 15 and 20 June. Possibly the description given earlier for 15 June belongs here.[27]

As Sherman continued to feel his way around Johnston's left, reaching for the railroad and the Chattahoochee River, the Confederate commander countered by sending Hood's corps from his right flank to his left, extending his lines several miles west, to the Powder Springs Road and Ollie's Creek. Loring's corps on Kennesaw and Little Kennesaw Mountains became the right flank and Hardee held the center. Sherman had Hooker's and Schofield's corps deploy in strong defensive positions opposite Hood. In the battle of Kolb's Farm on 22 June, Hood attacked his enemy without reconnaissance and without consulting Johnston. The result was heavy Confederate losses and complete failure to dislodge the Union forces.

Sherman determined on 25 June to make a frontal assault on Johnston's position. The constant rains had muddied the roads, making flanking movements difficult. Sherman later wrote that he felt the mood of his army was one of impatience and that the men wanted to "have a go" at the enemy. His plan was for a two pronged attack on 27 June, with the main effort against the center of Hardee's corps and a large scale diversion up the slope between Little Kennesaw and Pigeon Hill. The first thrust would take him up against Cheatham's division and the other against the hinge between Walker's division of Hardee's corps and French's of Loring's. If the diversion proved successful in penetrating the Southern defenses, it would be exploited accordingly. Sherman's subordinates had misgivings about his plan but dutifully carried out his orders.

The main attack met with disaster. Cheatham's men slaughtered the advancing blue soldiers from the ridge now know as Cheatham's Hill at a place now notoriously called "Dead Angle." Although the lines halted within yards of each other, the Northern men could advance no further. The commanders of both leading Federal brigades were killed and 3,000 men were shot down in thirty minutes.

The diversion met with initial success. The picket line of Mercer's brigade was comprised of six companies of the 63rd Georgia. Advancing silently, the Union skirmishers appeared suddenly out of the morning mist, surprising and routing the pickets. They threatened to penetrate Mercer's line but heavy artillery fire from French's skillfully placed batteries on Kennesaw held them at bay for the rest of the day.

The role of Stevens's brigade and the sharpshooters in all of this action was minimal. The day before, on 26 June, they had been moved to the left of the line in support of Hindman's division of Hood's corps. They did not return to Walker's command until the night of 27 June or sometime on the twenty-eighth. Private Hines H. Gray and Stephen M. Touchstone of D Company are reported to have been wounded at Kennesaw Mountain on 27 June but the circumstances are unknown. Touchstone's name is included in a list of battalion wounded for the period of action on the Kennesaw line; Gray's is not.[28]

Following the Battle of Kennesaw, the two armies rested for several days. By now, summer heat was added to spring rains to make the soldiers' lives miserable. In the Southern army especially, poor sanitary conditions and poor diet added to the debilitating effects of the weather. Professor Steven Newton has done projections of losses due to wounds and sickness for the Army of Tennessee in the Atlanta campaign. He estimates that 12,300 sick and 2,300 wounded were hospitalized in May and 10,100 sick and 3,500 wounded in June. Of these, only 5,300 were returned to duty in May and 5,000 in June, for a net loss of 18,000 soldiers. Those on duty were sick a good part of the time. Chronic diarrhea from the unhealthy diet was a common malady and officers were as likely to be subject to illness as soldiers.[29]

Among those struck by chronic diarrhea was Second Lieutenant Manuel

Molina of D Company of Shaaff's battalion. He was admitted to Foard Hospital in Atlanta about 24 June and died there on 28 June. His funeral was in Savannah on 30 June; he left a wife and several children. With his death, First Lieutenant Samuel Lawrence and Second Lieutenant Cuyler King remained as the two officers in their company. Besides the loss of Molina, the battalion was saddened by the news of the death of Sergeant Major Alfred Gordon, who had been dangerously wounded in the thigh at Calhoun on 16 May. After lingering for a month, he died in an Atlanta hospital in June.[30]

Molina's vacancy was not filled except that King was no longer the junior second lieutenant. To replace Gordon as sergeant major, Shaaff selected First Sergeant John F. Knowles of A Company. Knowles was a native of New York City and formerly of the 1st Georgia Volunteers. At age eighteen he had enlisted in Savannah in the Irish Volunteers company in summer 1861 and transferred to the Irish Jasper Greens six months later and then to the sharpshooters. He had been appointed Third Sergeant in August 1862 and had succeeded Charles Pattillo as first sergeant when the latter was commissioned in May 1863.[31]

Colonel J. Cooper Nesbit of the 66th Georgia, whose memory was not the best, recalled that while at Kennesaw the brass band of the sharpshooter battalion, that he referred to as "splendid," would come to the line on quiet evenings and serenade both armies with instrumental and vocal presentations. Sometimes a Yankee band would join in. Nesbit may have been right, but the band could not have been large. Of the twelve men carried on the rolls as musicians beginning in August 1862, only two, Jeremiah Keene and William Mitchell, were still with the battalion by the time they reached Kennesaw. Most of the others had deserted when Walker's brigade left Savannah in May 1863. In deference to Nesbit, it should be noted that three of the original musicians may have been slaves or free blacks and, although present, no longer on the muster rolls because they were not military.[32]

Nesbit also recalled that a raid was conducted into the Union lines one rainy night by a group of 200 volunteers from Walker's division, armed only with revolvers. They went into a camp of US regulars and captured and brought back several officers who had been surprised. According to Nisbet, when the prisoners were brought in, Arthur Shaaff knew some of them from his service in the Old Army. However, while it is true that Stoughton's brigade of regulars in the XIV Corps was directly opposite and close to Gist's brigade during operations at Kennesaw, a table of casualties in the brigade shows one officer killed, sixteen wounded, and none missing in the Atlanta campaign.[33]

The armies began to move again on 1 July. Sherman sent Schofield's corps and McPherson's Army of the Tennessee around Johnston's left. Schofield advanced south to Nickajack Creek and found himself 5 miles in Johnston's rear, 6 miles from the Chattahoochee River and only 4 miles from the vital railroad line. Johnston had no choice but to fall back, but he made it a fighting withdrawal, covering his trains and gaining time to prepare positions on the south bank of the Chattahoochee. On 3 July he abandoned the Kennesaw line and fell back to Smyrna, about 4 miles south of Marietta.

On the same day Sherman got his armies in motion, or soon after, the 1st Sharpshooter Battalion totaled up their combat losses so far in the campaign, possibly a recapitulation from the 30 June muster rolls. The names and numbers, which appeared in the press within a few weeks, were an indication of the severity of the fighting, even for a unit that had been in only two substantial engagements.

> Casualties in the 1st Battalion, Georgia Sharpshooters from May 14 to July 1, 1864, inclusive.
>
> Field and Staff, wounded: Surgeon C. T. Ford, slightly; Sgt. Major A. H. Gordon, dangerously, since died.
>
> Company A, killed: Pvts. W. J. Love and Isaiah Tanner; wounded: Capt. H. D. Twyman, serious; Cpl. E. G. Melton, slight; Pvts. L. B. Burton, severe; N. W. Lee, slight; J. F. Murdock, slight; missing: Pvts. J. B. Lee, H. M. Kittles.
>
> Company B, wounded: 1st Lt. H. Herman, slight; Cpl. Walker Smith, serious; Pvts. J. W. Booth, slight; R. Hurst, severe; M. Roberts, slight; C. Larson, slight; George Kner, severe.
>
> Company C, killed: Pvt. C. Stilwell; wounded: Sgts. R. W. Price and John Thornton, severe; Cpl. W. S. Williams, Pvts. N. M. Williams, severe; L. B. Williams, slight; John Stanfield, slight; W. V. Jones, severe; W. W. Gamble, severe; Edw. Stokes, severe; Henry W. Davis, severe; Lafayette Hayes, slight; missing: Lt. B. Sadler, Sgt. F. Bierhalter, Pvts. J. Stackfleth, E. Mathis, J. A. Lipford.
>
> Company D, killed: Pvt. J. B. Cochran; wounded: Cpl G. W. Layne, slight; Pvts. J. R. Cooper, W. D. Warren, severe; J. W. Peace, slight; W. L. Thomas, severe; S. M. Touchstone, slight; S. D. Chitwood, slight; missing: Cpl J. Reid, Pvt [George] Garner.
>
> Total: killed/mortally wounded: 5; wounded: 31; missing: 9.

An independent report of casualties printed in the *Atlanta Southern Confederacy* newspaper, showed that one other sharpshooter, Private John W.

Armor of C Company, arrived in hospital in Marietta with a wound to the thigh on June 17. The same source showed that Private William L. Thomas, from the preceding list, arrived in Marietta the same day as Armor with a wound in his left foot.

From the foregoing, it may be deduced that since the report of 6 June one man had been killed, Private J. B. Cochran, and eleven wounded, Assistant Surgeon Ford and Privates J. F. Murdock, Luke Williams, Edward Stokes, Henry Davis, Lafayette Hayes, William L. Thomas, S. D. Chitwood, S. M. Touchstone, and J. W. Armor. The names of the missing have been mentioned as the losses occurred. The total loss of 45 men was from a total of 129 effectives at the beginning of the campaign. Private Howell B. Dobson, C Company, a soldier from Berrien County and formerly in the 54th Georgia, who had been reported in the two previous casualty lists as slightly wounded, does not appear on the 1 July list. His service record shows that he was sick in hospital on 31 August 1864.[34]

Many years after the war, Sergeant Robert W. Price's daughter, Miss Beulah Price of Monticello, Jasper County, recalled her father's experience. "He went to Savannah and joined the sharpshooters... He went at 18 years of age. He was twice wounded, the last time at Resaca above Atlanta. Father and Uncle John Price were wounded at about the same time. Neither was in the battle of Atlanta [because] they were both wounded at that time." Miss Price continued that "Uncle John" lost his right arm and right leg at Jonesboro and for the rest of his life had a cork leg and learned to use his left hand. Sergeant Cornelius Hardy wrote after Jonesboro that John Price was "getting along fine" after his wounds, but he (Hardy) complained that "Bob" Price had overstayed his sick furlough at home. In the 1860 census of Jasper County, John W. Price, twenty-two, and Robert W. Price, eighteen, were living with their father, Robert, a farmer. Both sons were listed as farm hands.[35]

Elbert G. Melton, who enlisted in the Georgia State Troops in fall 1861, was one of the three sons of Elbert Melton, Sr., of Cuthbert in Randolph County, aged fifty-nine in 1860 and a native of South Carolina. Young Elbert was eighteen at the time. The other two sons were William P. Melton, twenty-two years old and overseer on his father's farm, and Henry G. Melton, Elbert's twin. In spring 1862 the brothers entered the 47th Georgia Volunteers and then transferred to the sharpshooters. William applied the same qualities that had made him a good overseer and rose to be second sergeant of A Company. Henry was sick much of the time and was in the hospital when Elbert was wounded. Elbert's wound was not serious enough to cause him to leave the ranks and he continued on duty as third corporal of his company. He had also been wounded at Chickamauga.[36]

During the retreat from Kennesaw and the accompanying abandonment of Marietta, several members of the 1st Sharpshooters were captured by the enemy. Some may have been stragglers, others may have been wounded from the hospitals. Among those lost were Privates Stephen D. Chitwood, J. E. Dawson, J. Mills, and John Schmidt, brother of Henry Schmidt, all missing on 3 July. Captured near Marietta or in Cobb County in July, with no specific date given, were Corporal G. W. Layne and Private John Garner. Layne and Chitwood had been included in the report of wounded on 1 July; Garner was erroneously included in the same report as missing. W. H. Mattox of D Company had deserted on the march from Mississippi in August 1863. The advancing Yankee army found him at home in Campbell County that July and took him into custody.

Layne and Mattox took the oath of allegiance almost immediately and were discharged within weeks of their capture. Garner died of pneumonia at Camp Douglas, Illinois, in August. Chitwood, captured for the second time, and Mills and Schmidt remained prisoners until their enlistment in the US volunteers in March 1865. Dawson was a prisoner until his release in May 1865.[37]

One other soldier was captured on 5 July. Private Joseph M. Tuten of B Company had entered service as a substitute for his kinsman, Hardy P. Tuten, in September 1862. He may have been the fortyish Joseph M. Tuten of Ware County in the 1860 census, married, with seven children. By an error in record keeping, Joseph was discharged for disability in May 1863, just as the battalion was departing for Mississippi. When the error was discovered, he rejoined his company at Dalton, only to wind up in the hands of the enemy six months later. Sent to Camp Douglas, Tuten remained there for the rest of the war, but died of chronic diarrhea on 1 May 1865 on the eve of his release. Hardy Tuten did not long survive the exchange. He died at home in Appling County in November 1863, only forty years old.[38]

Johnston held his army on the Smyrna line only two days, easily repelling two small-scale attacks while he did so. On 5 July he learned that Dodge's XVI Corps had maneuvered around his left. The Army of Tennessee pulled back to the west bank of the Chattahoochee River where a chain of defensive positions had been prepared. This time Schofield's corps crossed the river upstream of the Confederate lines and on 9 July Johnston fell back behind the Chattahoochee. Here he took up a line in the outer ring of the defenses of Atlanta along Peachtree Creek. Sherman followed in a wide turning movement to the east and south.

The sharpshooters bid farewell to their friends and former associates in the 47th Georgia on 2 July. General John K. Jackson's brigade was broken up and the 5th and 47th Georgia Volunteers went to the defenses of Charleston. General Jackson went to Florida and the remaining regiments, 5th and 8th Mississippi, 65th Georgia, and 2nd Georgia Sharpshooters were assigned to Gist's brigade. Within a few weeks, the two Mississippi regiments were reassigned to Lowrey's brigade in Cleburne's division.[39]

Some twenty-eight members of the 47th Georgia had come to the 1st Sharpshooters two years before and a few remained, the most prominent of whom was 1st Sergeant William Kersey of A Company. Kersey had succeeded to that position with the selection of former 1st Sergeant John F. Knowles to be Sergeant Major. Kersey was a resident of Randolph County and was enumerated as an eighteen-year-old hand on the farm of his father, Bannister Kersey, near Monticello in 1860. He had begun his military career in the Georgia State Troops in 1861, had been wounded at Chickamauga, and had been a non-commissioned officer since his assignment to the battalion. It will be recalled that a B. Kersey, probably the younger brother of William, had died in Savannah in 1863, shortly after enlisting in the sharpshooters.[40]

Behind Peachtree Creek, Johnston hoped and expected that the nature of the terrain before him would cause a gap to occur between segments of Sherman's advancing front. If the occasion arose, he was prepared to strike against one part of the divided force and drive it back or even destroy it. Johnston's announcement of his intentions to his army on 17 July was greeted with enthusiasm, the men expecting victory. The sharpshooters must have shared in the elation of Gist's brigade in which "the most confident spirit prevailed."[41]

Alas for Johnston, he was removed from command the next day and replaced by General John Bell Hood, a wounded hero of the Army of Northern Virginia, but a deterrent to many of Johnston's proposals since the campaign began at Dalton. When Walker's division marched past Johnston's headquarters that day, the men shouldered arms and the officers saluted; many removed their hats and caps as a sign of respect. General Walker proposed to have the division halt and give a cheer for the retiring general, but Johnston would not allow it. General Stevens wrote a personal note of condolence to Johnston expressing the army's sense of loss. No doubt Arthur Shaaff and his subordinates joined in the sentiment.[42]

On the front, Thomas's Army of the Cumberland forced its way across Peachtree Creek on 19 July and deployed on high ground a few hundred yards south of the creek. Hood signaled the new aggressive tactic of his army by ordering an attack for the next day. Unlike Johnston's plan, Hood directed his attack in hilly, broken terrain, and planned for his divisions to advance en echelon, that is, one after another, rather than all at once. The attack would be made by two corps, Hardee's and Alexander P. Stewart's, with six divisions. Stewart had been selected as the replacement for General Polk, killed in June. Hood's attack was planned for 1:00 P.M., but constant shifting of the line delayed the start time by three hours.

Hardee's corps was on the right of the advance with Walker in the center of three divisions, Bate on the right and General George Maney, commanding Cheatham's division, on the left. Cleburne was in reserve. Bate finally started off at 4:00 P.M. and immediately became entangled in the undergrowth, slowing his advance. He attempted to change his line of advance to get around his enemy's flank but heavy musket and artillery fire deterred him and most of his division never came to grips with the Union forces.

Walker followed Bate's advance by several minutes. There are two versions of Walker's division in this battle. He may have had the brigades of Mercer, Stevens, and Gist aligned right to left, or the division was formed in two lines with Stevens on the left and part of Mercer's brigade on the right in the front line, and Gist on the left and the rest of Mercer on the right in the second line. Gist's brigade was minus the reliable 24th South Carolina that had been sent to reinforce Walthall's division in Stewart's corps but was strengthened by the regiments assigned when John K. Jackson's brigade was broken up.

The Georgia division swept forward "with a rapidity and absence of confusion I have never seen equaled," General Nathan Kimball of Newton's division in the Union IV Corps wrote later. A colonel in Kimball's brigade wrote in his report that the Rebels advanced "firing and yelling, demanding [us] to surrender," so confident were they of success. Newton had had time and forethought enough for his men to erect field fortifications of earth and logs but the work was still in progress and his men had to throw down their tools and take up their muskets when Walker's troops sprang into view. Newton's division was somewhat forward of the units on its left and right, creating a bulge in the line but exposing both his flanks. The Georgians and South Carolinians rushed up to the works and lapped around both ends. Mercer's right drifted off into the growth where Bate was enmeshed. Gist's advance passed Newton and ran into the division on his right. In doing so, it was exposed to Newton's enfilading fire and withdrew. In the alternate version, Gist followed Mercer around Newton's left flank.

In either case, Stevens's brigade, including the sharpshooters, encountered the center of Newton's defenses and took the brunt of their fire. The advance made good progress at first. General Stevens was in the lead, mounted. His horse was killed and as he stepped off the fallen animal he was shot in the head and mortally wounded. Colonel George A. Smith of the 1st Confederate Georgia Regiment succeeded to the command of the brigade. The Confederate troops slowed, began to waver, and then came to a standstill. They continued to fire "heavily but wildly" as their confusion increased. Numerous color-bearers attempted to rally the men but were shot down. Despite the rallying cries of their officers, the Southern infantry withdrew.[43]

The attack was a failure with heavy casualties. General Hardee referred to the Georgia division as "Walker's beaten troops." Hagan told his wife, "The fight on the left of Walker's division was very heavy much worse than wher we was, & our troops suffered badly bucause they [the enemy] was in the works." Private McDermid wrote, "Our division got cut up very bad." A lieutenant in the 66th Georgia in Stevens's brigade wrote his sister that his regiment lost 74 out of 190 men engaged. Hagan's statement lends credence to the placement of Stevens's brigade in the center or on the right of the division formation. Hagan further related his own experience. "We attacked the yankees and drove them back some distance but we finally had to fall back leaving our dead and wounded on the field...I came very near falling into the enimys hands and had to lay down my gun & accutiaments & haversacks & Bedcover. I had to leave all & Swim a creek about 3 hundred yards and made my asscape."[44]

This statement about swimming is perplexing. One possibility was Tanyard Branch, which crossed the defensive line a good half mile west of Newton's right. The more likely is that he penetrated to Peachtree Creek or Clear Creek around Newton's left, which more nearly fits the rightward position of Stevens's brigade.[45]

Private Angus McDermid recorded his experiences at Peachtree Creek in a letter home. "We charged the yankes and we whiped them but I think that we got the most men killed...I run rite among the yankies and [they were] a shooting at me. 2 or 3 of them said surender or I will kill you. I told them no and I went to shooting at...them. I dont see what cept [kept] them from killing me."[46]

Casualties in Shaaff's battalion are difficult to assess. There are no reported combat deaths for 20 July in the compiled service records, but another record shows that Private John F. Hall of D Company was wounded that day. Hall was absent wounded on the muster roll for 31 August 1864, but no specific date of wound is given. Private B. F. Hover, D Company, was reported missing from 20 July but there is no corresponding prisoner of war record.[47]

Two days later Hood tried again. In the Battle of Atlanta or "Hood's

Second Sortie," he sent Hardee's corps in a night march on a wide sweep to the east, hoping to get around Sherman's left flank. As bad luck would have it, Dodge's XVI Corps had been squeezed out of Sherman's tightening encirclement and relocated to the left of the line. Fuller's and Sweeney's divisions were in the process of digging in at their new position when the four Rebel divisions encountered them. Hardee had Bate, Walker, Maney, and Cleburne in line, east to west or right to left.

The fight lasted from noon until after dark on 22 July. On Walker's front, the veteran Union troops and their commanders reacted quickly. In the positions they took, any attack would have to come at them across an open, inclined field. Their concentrated rifle and artillery fire mowed down the attackers. Several lines of blue-coated skirmishers were overrun, but the Rebel masses could not penetrate the main line. Two separate charges were made without effect and with great loss. Only on the left was their success where Cleburne's division overcame two Union defensive lines but could not get through a third.

The Georgia division had formed in line of battle just before noon. General Walker was killed, probably by a sniper's bullet, before the battle commenced. Walker, or General Hugh Mercer, if Walker was already dead, was ordered by Hardee to pivot his front to the right and then advance up the hill in concert with Bate's division. The division had Stevens's brigade, including the sharpshooters, and under its temporary commander, Colonel George A. Smith, on the right, and Gist's on the left. Mercer's brigade, under Colonel Charles Olmstead and a succession of subordinate commanders, was the reserve.

The old Georgia brigade made the pivot smartly but Gist's men, having a greater distance to cover, lagged behind. Smith's men crossed a field covered with underbrush, forded a marshy stream waist deep, and then advanced up the sloping field. Twice they reached the blue line and twice they were driven back. With their left flank uncovered because of Gist's delay, they received enfilading fire on that side and were driven back in confusion, much as had occurred two days before at Peachtree Creek. Colonel Smith was wounded and had his horse killed; Colonel Nisbet of the 66th Georgia succeeded to brigade command.

Then Gist's brigade essayed the advance up the field. They met the same fate as Smith's men. Although they came within 40 yards of the Union line, they could not withstand the fire from three sides. Gist was wounded and his aide, Lieutenant Joseph C. Habersham of Savannah, was mortally wounded. Some accounts have it that at this juncture General Walker rode onto the field, attempted to rally Gist's men, and was killed. The brigade retired, leaving the field strewn with the bodies of the dead and wounded.

Mercer's brigade, under Colonel Olmstead, waited in the tree line for its turn. Olmstead was struck in the head by a shell fragment and command passed to Colonel William Barkuloo of the 57th Georgia. General Mercer ordered Barkuloo to advance. The brigade got as far as the marshy stream, but having already lost men to artillery fire, and having seen the results of the first two attacks, Barkuloo thought it prudent to retire. His brigade was soon ordered off to the left to support Cleburne's more successful effort.

The fragments of Nisbet's brigade gathered themselves for another advance, this time on the left of Bate's division's attack. The outcome was no different. Nisbet was captured and the colors of the 25th Georgia were lost to the 64th Illinois of Fuller's division. As at Peachtree Creek, casualties in the division and the brigade were heavy. Besides the loss of Smith and Nisbet, Colonel William J. Winn of the 25th Georgia and Lieutenant Colonel James S. Boynton of the 30th were wounded and, at the end, command of the brigade fell to Major Arthur Shaaff, the senior officer on the field.[48]

On 22 July the *Republican* had printed a telegram from Captain W. G. Gray informing Mrs. G. H. Johnston, "Major Schaaf [sic], George Johnston, and all the other officers of the battalion are safe," following the battle at Peach Tree Creek. After the battle of Atlanta that same newspaper on 27 July printed a notice from Lieutenant George H. Johnston at East Point, "All of the officers of the First Georgia Battalion Sharpshooters and myself are quite well." On 28 July the *Republican* wrote, "We are without particulars of the late battle. A letter received in this city states that Stevens' brigade suffered considerably. The brigade numbered 1200 men and during two days fight lost 600 killed and wounded. The enemy's press say that their charge was irresistible and that no troops could withstand them." And then, on 29 July, "We learn that after the fall of General Stevens at the late battle, Major Shaaff of the 1st Battalion Sharpshooters was placed in command. Major Shaaff handled the brigade with marked ability and as on previous occasions it distinguished itself for its courage and efficiency." He still may have been commanding the brigade on 31 July because the battalion was headed on that date by Captain Benjamin H. Hardee.[49]

In the sharpshooter battalion, the only known casualties in the battle on 22 July were five men captured. These were Sergeant Major John F. Knowles, First Sergeant Benjamin F. Walker of D Company, Privates Robert A. Beasley and Patrick McDonald of A Company, and Private Lewis Voluntine or Valentine, C Company. The records of two other sharpshooters, Sergeant Christian Meinzer and Private James F. Butler, both of B Company, show they were captured in July but give no specific date. Meinzer, Butler, and Beasley quickly took the oath of allegiance. As prisoners, the other four went to Camp Chase, Ohio, but once there, they suffered varied fates.[50]

Private Lewis Voluntine or Valentine, as he was carried on the muster rolls, was really William Lewis Ballentine. He was born in 1836 in New York, the son of Scottish emigrants William Ballentine, a weaver, and his wife, Jane. The family moved to Canada and then to Georgia, living in Greene and Campbell counties. By 1859 William and his brother John were co-owners of a saloon in Atlanta.

John and another brother, Alexander, enlisted in the Campbell Sharpshooters of Campbell County in 1861. Their company became a part of the 30th Georgia Volunteers and was transferred to Savannah. In August 1862 John was discharged by civil authority, probably for being under age (he was born in 1844). It was in Savannah on 17 August 1862 that William was enlisted in the Georgia sharpshooters by Captain Ross, most likely while on a visit to his brothers. As a soldier, William was frequently sick, being hospitalized and then sent on sick furlough while in Savannah, and hospitalized in Mississippi in 1863. At Jackson, on 16 July 16 1863, brother Alexander was killed in action.

By July 1864 William and his unit were back in Atlanta and there he married Mary Ann Harrison, perhaps his pre-war sweetheart. After being captured on 22 or 23 July, William went to Camp Chase. Sick with dysentery, he was sent to City Point, Virginia, in March 1865 for exchange. He died before the exchange and was buried in an unmarked grave.[51]

Sergeant Major John Knowles lingered at Camp Chase for almost eight months after capture. In March 1865 his release was ordered by President Lincoln and he took the oath of allegiance. One wonders if any political or personal appeal was exerted on his behalf. Sergeant Benjamin Walker contracted smallpox at the prison camp in Ohio in October 1864. He was vaccinated, recovered, and returned to duty. Prison records show that he died of pneumonia in February 1865 but also that he was exchanged in March 1865. However, the prison burial register shows that Sergeant Benjamin Walker of the 1st Georgia Sharpshooter Battalion was interred in the camp cemetery, conclusive enough evidence.

Robert Beasley, a railroad fireman and a blacksmith before the war and seventeen years old in 1860, was wounded at Chickamauga in 1863. It will be remembered that he had erroneously listed as a deserter while in Mississippi. Records indicate he took the oath of allegiance as soon as he was captured in 1864. James F. Butler was one of those convicted deserters who won a presidential pardon in August 1863. He may have been the same as the thirty-five-year-old, Irish-born fireman of the same name enumerated in the Savannah census in 1860. Perhaps he and Beasley had been friends and co-workers before the war. Although in different companies of the battalion, they could have continued their relationship in the army. Butler had also been wounded at Chickamauga. He took the oath of allegiance to the United States on 27 July. Sergeant Meinzer or Meintzer may have been captured at Peachtree Creek. His record indicates that he took the oath of allegiance as a deserter at Chattanooga on 22 July and that he was a resident of Richmond County, Georgia.[52]

Sergeant John W. Hagan, whose letters have been used to trace the experiences of his brigade, was another loss at Atlanta. He, too, was captured on 22 July, along with two captains, a lieutenant, and another sergeant from the 29th Georgia, as he informed his wife in a brief note from Nashville, Tennessee. Like the sharpshooters, he wound up at Camp Chase.[53]

Private Angus McDermid was slightly wounded by a shell fragment during the fight and spent two days in the hospital but survived to tell his family about it. He wrote, "we charged the yankies in their works," and "Our brigade was cut up bad." He remarked there was "more killed and wounded than I ever saw." About the death of his commander, he commented only "old General Walker got killed. I do hate it so bad."[54]

Lieutenant Cuyler King must have had a premonition of a bad outcome from the battle of 22 July, though he would be among the survivors. That morning he penned a brief and almost illegible note to his brother, Mallery, who had been transferred to Savannah: "I owe Capt. Ross of Co. C & [William F.] Cochran of my company $128. Please attend to it for me.... We are about to advance. May God give us the victory to the successful. Gen. Stevens was mortally wounded day before yesterday in a charge against the enemies works on Peachtree St. Road."[55]

As a result of Walker's death and the casualties of 20 and 22 July, Generals Bragg, Hood and Hardee agreed to break up the Georgia division on 24 July. General Mercer returned to Savannah while his brigade, under Colonel Olmstead, passed to Cleburne's division. Gist's brigade of Georgians and Carolinians went to Cheatham's Tennessee division, and the old Walker-Wilson-Stevens brigade was assigned to the division of General William Bate. Brigadier General Henry Rootes Jackson was brought from Savannah as brigade commander. His effective date of command was 28 July; he left Savannah on the twenty-seventh and may have arrived a few days later.[56]

Henry R. Jackson was a man with a long, distinguished career, but not a very impressive military record. He was forty-four years old, a native of Athens, Georgia, a graduate of Yale, and a lawyer by profession. He had been a newspaper editor, a district attorney, a judge, and US minister to Austria.

During the Mexican War he had been colonel of a Georgia regiment of volunteers noted for its unruliness. Made a Confederate brigadier general early in 1861, Jackson served briefly in Virginia and then resigned in the fall of that year to accept a commission from Governor Joseph E. Brown as major general and commander of the Georgia State Troops. W. H. T. Walker had been one of his brigadiers and a number of the sharpshooters had served under him before enlisting in Confederate service.

When the state troops organization was dissolved in April 1862, Jackson was without military position until recommissioned in September 1863 to command troops in another "home guard" organization, the Georgia State Guards under General Howell Cobb. That body of men was dissolved also, in February 1864, but Jackson stayed on in service, filling unimportant posts in the District of Georgia. He was well liked and respected for his civil accomplishments, but his arrival in the Army of Tennessee did not augur inspiring or dramatic leadership for the beat-down Georgia brigade.[57]

The breakup of the division meant also a dissolution of the division staff. Major Joseph B. Cumming, the chief of staff, and Captain William H. Ross both found places on the staff of General Hardee. Cumming eventually went to the staffs of Generals Hood and Johnston, but Ross stayed with Hardee at least until the next January and will be heard from again.[58]

For his brigade staff, General Jackson retained the officers who had served Wilson and Stevens: Lieutenants Josiah Holcombe and Robert Wayne continued as adjutant and inspector. Stevens had twice tried to have them promoted. In March, shortly after taking command of the brigade, and in July, some weeks before his death, Stevens had written to Richmond, asking that the two young officers be advanced to the rank of major in keeping with their staff positions. One of Jackson's first actions after arrival in Atlanta was to renew the application. It received the endorsement of General Bragg in September 1864 but nothing came of it thereafter.[59]

The battle for possession of Atlanta continued unabated through July and August. Sherman already controlled the railroad running north from Atlanta to Chattanooga and had partially destroyed the line running east to Augusta. He next determined to move to East Point, south of the city, and cut the two lines running in that direction, to Macon and Columbus. He sent the Army of the Tennessee from his left, where it had made its stand against Hardee on 22 July, around to his right to make the move on East Point. Hood divined this intention and attempted to intercept the advance at Ezra Church on the Lickskillet Road.

On 28 July the Southern commander, General Stephen D. Lee, newly assigned to lead Hood's old corps, attacked the Union force in its superior defensive position. Two divisions of Stewart's corps, in support, were drawn into the action. So great were the Confederate losses that General Hardee, who had personally experienced the battles of 20 and 22 July, wrote in his report, "No action of the campaign probably did more to demoralize and dishearten the troops engaged in it."[60]

The sharpshooters, with the rest of Bate's division, remained in the defenses of Atlanta and considered themselves well out of it. Meanwhile, the surviving members of C Company mourned the death of Private Henry W. Davis on 26 or 28 July. He had been severely wounded north of Kennesaw in June and brought to hospital in Atlanta. Davis was a resident of Emanuel County, had served in the Georgia State Troops, and came to the sharpshooters from the 32nd Georgia.[61]

Sherman renewed his effort to take East Point on 4 August. Bate's division was sent from Hardee's corps to extend the line of Lee's corps to the left, affording East Point and the railroad greater protection. Bate had been reinforced with the 2nd Brigade of Georgia militia, so he brought five brigades in all to the position. He sited his troops behind earthworks along Utoy Creek with the Georgia militia on the right, connecting to the main Atlanta defenses, then to the left, Finley's Florida brigade, Jackson's Georgia brigade with the sharpshooters, Tyler's Georgia-Tennessee brigade under Thomas B. Smith, and Lewis's Kentucky or Orphan Brigade. The Union attack took place on 6 August. For once the Rebel troops had the advantage of fortifications and could fire on the exposed Yankees as they had done at Kennesaw. The brunt of the fighting fell on the Kentucky and Tennessee defenders who easily repelled their foe.

No losses for the 1st Sharpshooters were recorded at Utoy Creek, but three days before that battle Lieutenant George H. Johnston, the battalion adjutant, was wounded in the right arm while on the lines. The medical report showed that the ball had passed through the deltoid muscle and slightly injured the bone, rendering the arm of little use. He was sent to hospital in Macon and then went home.[62]

The sniping in the lines around Atlanta continued unabated. Private William V. Jones of Blakely in Early County, who had been severely wounded in May, was killed in the trenches on 14 August. Lieutenant Johnston was followed to Savannah in less than two weeks by Lieutenant Stephen P. Norris of B Company, who was wounded for the third time. His arrival at home was reported by the *Daily Morning News* and the *Republican*. The latter paper noted that Norris had been wounded in the thigh at Jackson, Mississippi, in the right thigh at Chickamauga, "from which he had barely recovered when he was wounded the third time in the left thigh, immediately opposite the wound he received at Chickamauga."[63]

That same issue of the *Republican* carried a letter from "V," an officer in the 29th Georgia, written on 14 August and commenting on events of the campaign and conditions in his regiment and the Army of Tennessee. "V" wrote that Norris had received a pretty severe flesh wound that afternoon and that he and Captain John W. Turner, commanding the 29th Georgia, had both been wounded by shell fragments. "V" also reported on a truce between the opposing sides that had occurred on 12 August. The soldiers of the two armies took advantage of the lull to do their usual trading in coffee, tobacco, and newspapers. Major Thomas C. Fitzgibbon of the 14th Michigan approached Major Shaaff, who was commanding the picket line of Jackson's brigade that day, and presented to him the personal effects of Lieutenant William A. "Willie" Ross of the 66th Georgia who had died of wounds inside Union lines on 7 August. Shaaff saw to it that the articles and letters were returned to Ross's family and fiancée in Macon.[64]

The next officer to leave the battalion was Lieutenant Robert P. Wayne of the brigade staff. The record is unclear as to whether or not he was wounded on 15 August, but on the twentieth he was granted sixty days leave and went home. In October he applied for retirement and an extension of his leave for ninety days with permission to travel to Nassau in the Bahamas for his health. His leave was approved in November, but he had not left at the time Savannah fell to the advancing Union army in December.[65]

Other losses occurred in August. Corporal William Haarer of B Company, a German immigrant to Savannah and a former member of the DeKalb Rifles, had been wounded at Chattanooga. He disappeared from his company at Atlanta and was suspected of desertion. In fact, he took the US oath of allegiance at Chattanooga on 22 August. Christopher C. Ketchum of C Company, a native of Whitfield County, had served in the Georgia State Troops and the 54th Georgia before joining the sharpshooters. He was probably the fifteen-year-old laborer, Christian C., on the farm of W. H. Ketchum near Tunnel Hill, Georgia, in 1860. He also left the battalion and took the oath in August.[66]

Sherman made another attempt to cut the railroad south of Atlanta beginning 23 August. This was a larger, bolder effort involving his entire army. Leaving only one army corps to guard his own railroad supply line back to Tennessee, he pulled all of his troops out of the trenches in front of Atlanta on 25 August and sent them in a sweep to the west and south to interdict the rail line at Jonesboro. Hood, who had sent most of his cavalry off on a raid to Tennessee, was in the dark about his adversary's intentions and at first thought they might have given up the siege and retreated. When Hood finally learned that Federal troops were moving on Jonesboro, he sent Hardee's and Lee's corps to intercept them, thinking it was no more than a large raid.

The Union forces, comprising three army corps, crossed the Flint River from the west on 30 August and took up barricaded positions facing east on high ground between the river and the town. Hardee's corps arrived by rail during the night, followed by Lee's. Hardee was in command of both and his corps was led by General Pat Cleburne. They formed battle lines during the day of 31 August and launched an attack on the enemy emplacements beginning about four o'clock in the afternoon. Hardee had orders from Hood to attack as soon as he was in position. Hardee's initial order to his division commanders was to drive forward, wheeling to the right in a clockwise direction. Once Cleburne's movement was well under way, Lee was to advance forward so that the two corps would bring their concentrated effort against the same part of the Union defenses.

Hardee formed a two division front with Cleburne's division under Lowrey on the left and Bate's division under General John C. Brown on the right. Bate had been wounded on 10 August. Cheathams's old division under Maney was the reserve. Lee's corps of two divisions formed Hardee's right, with Stevenson's and Clayton's divisions on the left and right, respectively. Besides the replacement division commanders, many of the officers leading brigades were also temporary or new to their positions.

Brown had Jackson's Georgia brigade and the sharpshooters in the center of his line, with the Florida brigade on its left and the Kentucky brigade on its right. Smith's Georgia-Tennessee brigade was in reserve. During the course of the battle a brigade from Maney's reserve division was brought up behind the Kentucky Orphan Brigade. In the initial attack, Lowrey's division made good progress against light cavalry resistance. But they advanced too rapidly, pulling Brown's division away from its wheeling movement and straight ahead through a swampy ravine with no support on their left flank. This was the situation facing Jackson's Georgia brigade and they were repulsed with heavy losses. A letter report of the battle in a Savannah newspaper said, "The battalion charged up to within thirty yards of the works, but not being properly sustained, fell back. This was repeated three times, when the entire line was ordered to retire." Cuyler King wrote, "We attacked [the enemy] at two o'clock on the 31st he was strongly entrenched. The attack was fruitless & our loss in consequence heavy."[67]

On 1 September the combat was renewed. While Hardee had been fighting, another corps of Sherman's army under General John M. Schofield cut the railroad at Rough and Ready, north of Jonesboro. Hood called Lee's corps back to Atlanta and left Hardee with his single weakened corps to defend Jonesboro. On the second day of the battle, the Federals did the attacking and to good effect. Hardee had Brown in the center with Cheatham's division on the left and Cleburne's on the right, turned back to form a right angle. The brunt of the attack fell on the angle and overran Lewis's Kentucky brigade and Govan's brigade. General Govan was captured, as were 8 pieces of artillery and about 600 men. The line was restored by the transfer of a brigade from Cheatham's reserve. There was no report of the involvement of Jackson's brigade and the sharpshooters. That night Hardee withdrew 6 miles to Lovejoy Station, leaving Jonesboro and the railroad in Federal hands. Atlanta was now cut off from outside support and Hood evacuated the city on 2 September.

In a personal letter to General Cheatham later in the year, Henry R. Jackson gave his version of the first day of battle with a complaint of lack of support.

At Jonesboro, [my] Brigade moved into line of battle on the 31st of August between Tyler's upon the right and Finley's upon the left. Following the movement of Finley's which had been designated as the directing Brigade, it became disconnected from Tyler's. Under orders from Genl. Brown [for] a flank movement to the right, that connection was reestablished. I had advanced but for a few moments again in line of battle, when I was notified by a staff officer that we were "swinging too far to the right," and that the touch must again be to the left... When I reached the point where I expected to touch [Tyler's] left, having marched my command at a double quick, I found numbers of men huddled together in the abandoned skirmish line of the enemy. I cannot speak myself of what occurred upon the left, but have been informed by reliable officers of my command that none of Finley's Brigade could be prevailed upon to advance beyond this line. I commanded Tyler's men to fall in with mine and aid us in the charge. They refused to do so, stating that they were in position by order, and that their Brigade had already been repulsed. As the enemy's fire was still terrific, and our line was concealed from his view by a pine thicket and the crest of a hill, I disbelieved the statement and thinking that command to be still engaged with the enemy and in need of support, I pressed my Brigade forward in beautiful line of battle to a position where it found support neither on the right nor on the left, and where it lost with fearful rapidity more than one third of its numbers.[68]

Indeed, the losses were terrible. Three officers of the 1st Sharpshooter Battalion were killed in action that day, two on duty with the troops and one serving on the staff. They were Lieutenants Josiah Holcombe, General Jackson's adjutant; Henry Herrmann, commanding B Company; and Samuel W. Lawrence, commanding D Company. Cuyler King told his sister, "Poor Lieuts. Lawrence, Hermann & Holcombe of my Battalion were killed. Holcombe was to have been married to Miss Briggs of Columbus this winter and Hermann to a girl in Savannah." Even General Hardee noticed the deaths, telegraphing to his brother, "Dr. Lawrence killed."[69]

Colonel Olmstead, commanding Mercer's old brigade in Cleburne's division, wrote that he saw Brown's division immediately on his right. General Jackson was a familiar figure to Olmstead from Savannah society. "On his staff—his Adjutant General I think—was Joe Holcombe, the son of Mrs. Thomas Holcombe of Savannah—and one of my old school mates [at the Georgia Military Institute] at Marietta. Poor fellow, he was desperately wounded. I saw him as he was being brought from the field and it grieved me beyond measure to be told that his wound was mortal. He died a few hours after."[70]

Holcombe's funeral was conducted in Savannah on 7 September. In the newspaper notice, he was identified as "Major" Holcombe, reflecting the rank for which Generals Stevens and Jackson had recommended him. The funeral was conducted from the residence of Horace Crane. In the following days, notices appeared in the Savannah paper concerning the legacies of some of the battalion's deceased officers. A lawyer applied for letters of administration on the estate of Henry Herrmann; Manuel Molina's widow announced herself as executrix of his estate. Officers and men from other units from the city had been killed at Atlanta and Savannah was in a state of mourning.[71]

The complete list of casualties in the battalion for the first day at Jonesboro was published the day after Holcombe's funeral:

Company A—Killed: Lt. J. L. Holcombe, acting A. A. G.; Wounded: Sgt. W. P. Melton, side, severe; R. T. Love, leg, severe.

Company B—Killed: Lt. H. Herman; Wounded: Sgt. Charles W. Shaw, leg, slight; L. Werm, head, severe; C. Becton, thigh, slight; A. L. Parrott, severe.

Company C—Wounded: Cpl. H. Bennett, leg, amputated; Pvts. W. P. Williams, foot, slight; J. M. Jarrell, leg, slight.

Company D—Killed: Lt. Samuel Lawrence, Sgt. Richard Simpson; Wounded: Sgt. Jonas Johnson, thigh, severe; Pvt. John T. Hall, arm, slight.[72]

No more dramatic story exists to illustrate the fortitude of the men of the sharpshooters than that of Third Corporal Hiram Bennett of C Company. One of fourteen children of Westberry and Elizabeth (Padgett) Bennett of Appling County, Hiram was about seventeen when he enlisted in the Georgia State Troops in October 1861. Upon being mustered out in April 1862, he enlisted in K Company, 54th Georgia, and then transferred to Anderson's sharpshooter battalion in July. He was slightly wounded in the knee at Chickamauga but returned to the ranks and was promoted, probably while the army was at Dalton. Hiram was wounded in the right ankle at Jonesboro, so badly that the foot dangled by a tendon. The plucky soldier cut the remaining tendon, then stuck the stump in the mud to control the bleeding until the litter bearers could get to him. His leg was amputated below the knee soon after.[73]

The deceased Sergeant Simpson was a resident of Mitchell County in south Georgia and had spent a good part of the summer at his home in Camilla on sick furlough, missing the battles of Kennesaw Mountain, Peachtree Creek and Atlanta. He was a former soldier in the 29th Georgia. Curran Becton and A. L. Parrott both came to the sharpshooters in 1862 as conscripts. Becton, sixteen years old in 1860 and a resident of Jefferson County where he farmed near Louisville with his widowed mother, had been wounded at Chickamauga. Parrott might have been Asbury Parrott of Greene County, cousin to W. J. "Billy" Parrott.

Not listed in the report were the captured or missing. They were Privates Nathan W. Lee and Savoy D. Woodward, A Company; Private John Wasden, B Company; Corporal Samuel Boggs and Corporal William and Private Timothy Thornton (cousins), C Company; and Privates Calvin W. Dedge and J. W. Peace, D Company, all captured on 31 August or 1 September.

The Boggs and Thornton families have already been discussed. Calvin Dedge had been a lieutenant in the 11th Georgia Battalion for a month in 1862. He was from Appling County and enlisted in Shaaff's battalion at Savannah in winter 1863. When Walker's brigade moved to Mississippi in May 1863, Dedge was one of the stay behinds in Savannah, but he soon caught up with his unit.

Nathan W. Lee was a farm laborer from the Black Creek area of Screven County and gave his age as thirty in the 1860 census. His military service began in 1862 when he joined a company of the 47th Georgia. John W. Peace had enlisted in the 30th Georgia in 1861 and claimed Clayton County as home. John Wasden was a seventeen-year-old farmer's son in the Pierce County 1860 census. In summer 1861 he made his way to Fort McAllister where he enlisted in the DeKalb Rifles and then transferred to the sharpshooters in 1862. Lee and Peace had both suffered slight wounds earlier in the campaign; Peace and

Wasden had been wounded previously at Chickamauga.

Of the eight prisoners, Nathan Lee and Savoy Woodward were the least fortunate. Lee was shipped off to Camp Douglas, Illinois, where he remained until his discharge in May 1865. Woodward suffered an even worse fate. Possibly a resident of Effingham County, he had enlisted in the 25th Georgia in 1861. He, too, was sent to Camp Douglas, where he died in January 1865 of chronic diarrhea.

Boggs, Dedge, Peace, Wasden, and the two Thorntons benefited from a spur-of-the moment exchange of prisoners at Rough and Ready on 19 and 22 September. Sherman had ordered the expulsion of all citizens of Atlanta who had family members in Confederate military service. They were sent to Rough and Ready to be transported further south. General Hood proposed a prisoner exchange take place at the same location and Sherman agreed to send back not more than 2,000 men, the number who had not yet been transported north, for an equal number of healthy Union soldiers. The actual exchange amounted to 1,200 men. In this way, the six sharpshooters were restored to the thin ranks of their battalion.[74]

Some ten days after the Jonesboro casualty list was published, the Savannah newspapers printed the losses sustained by the sharpshooter battalion while serving around Atlanta. Besides the names of the men killed and wounded on 31 August, the article listed two men killed, three wounded and nine missing. The killed were Privates Joseph T. Lee and William V. Jones; the wounded were Lieutenants Norris and Johnston and First Sergeant Dominique Brown; and the missing were Sergeant Major Knowles, Sergeant Timothy Thornton, Corporal Boggs, and Privates McDonald, John Wasden, Valentine, William Thornton, Dedge and Peace. This list, dated 9 September, was signed by Second Lieutenant T. S. Wayne, acting adjutant.[75]

Missing from this list were the names of Nathan Lee and Savoy Woodward whose status may have been unknown. The list does clarify that William V. Jones was killed in action in August rather than having died of wounds received in June. Lieutenant Robert Wayne's name is not here, suggesting he went home to Savannah because of sickness although he is shown wounded on the 31 August muster roll. Knowles, McDonald, and Valentine are the only three soldiers acknowledged as missing; the fates of Sergeants Walker and Meinzer and Privates Beasley and Butler are not recorded in this list.

Shaaff's few remaining men now prepared to face the most difficult days of their unit's existence.

6

NASHVILLE

Hood held his army at Lovejoy Station until 18 September, expecting another attack by Sherman at any time. While there, the Southern general devised a new plan to harass the Northern supply lines or fall on Sherman's rear if the latter chose to strike out for the coast. Hood then moved his army to Palmetto. President Davis, who visited the army there 25–27 September, concurred in Hood's plan. Although some would argue Hood should have stayed in Sherman's front, there was really little else to do.

Another consequence of Davis's visit was that he finally consented to General Hardee's request to be relieved from the Army of Tennessee. Hardee was sent to Charleston to command the Department of South Carolina, Georgia, and Florida. Cheatham was given command of Hardee's corps, including Bate's division and Jackson's brigade, and General Beauregard was brought from Charleston to coordinate the activities of Hood's army with that of General Richard Taylor, now commanding in the Department of East Louisiana, Mississippi, and Alabama.

Hardee left the army on 29 September. On the night before his departure he was visited and serenaded by the men of his command. They gave him a ringing ovation and as many as could pressed forward to take his hand. Hardee told the men he was sorry to leave them but that they would be in good hands with Generals Cheatham and Cleburne. One soldier, sitting on a tree limb above the crowd, called out, "Yes, General, and Crazy Bill ain't far off," using the nickname by which Bate was known to the Georgia troops. Cuyler King joined a detachment of other men from Bate's division in bidding the general farewell.[1]

Traveling with Hardee as part of his staff, with the official consent of General Hood, was Captain William H. Ross of the 1st Georgia Sharpshooters. As Ross wrote later, "My company [C] was so much reduced by casualties in battle that I had nothing to command. My company numbered only 5 men when I left the army." This statement, although true, was somewhat self-serving. Ross had held staff appointments, as he admitted, for more than a year, and actual command of the company had devolved on its junior officers. Ross stayed with Hardee to the end of the war.[2]

The departure of Ross from the army followed hard on the heels of two other officers' separation from the battalion. On 1 September General Jackson drafted Lieutenant Alfred Bryan to replace the deceased Holcombe as his brigade adjutant and about 19 September General Bate took Major Shaaff to be inspector general on his division staff. Most probably, the general thought the handful of men remaining in the sharpshooters did not need a field officer to command them. Bryan requested a transfer to the 29th Georgia on 6 September, but his application was rejected by General Hood. Previously, he had been detailed in charge of the brigade provost guard.[3]

The muster rolls for 31 August 1864 were not prepared until mid-September because of the exigencies of the service. When they were completed they showed forty-eight officers and men present for duty after excluding casualties at Jonesboro. There were forty-four men absent sick, thirty-seven absent wounded, thirty-four missing or absent in the hands of the enemy, thirteen deserted or absent without leave, two on detail away from the army, and one absent with leave. In addition, one officer and three men were detailed to the brigade provost guard, two men to the division sharpshooters, three men as litter bearers, one man as a pontoon train driver, one as an ambulance driver and one as a hospital orderly. The muster roll for D Company bore a notation that the company's muster roll for June 1864 had been lost on the death of Lieutenant Lawrence.

Company A had present only Lieutenant Schlatter, Corporals Jude B. Waters and Joseph F. Taylor, and eleven privates. In B Company there were Captain Hardee, Lieutenant Thomas Wayne, and eight privates. Lieutenant Cuyler King commanded D Company, with Third Sergeant Henry B. Phillips, Corporal John S. Williamson, eight privates, and the cook Robin, present. It will be recalled that Private John Wasden, B Company; Corporal Samuel Boggs, Corporal William and Private Timothy Thornton, C Company; and Privates Calvin W. Dedge and J. W. Peace, D Company; were returned to the battalion on 22 September, increasing its strength by six.

There were no officers present in C Company; the senior man on duty was Third Sergeant Cornelius M. Hardy, and with him were Corporal William S. Williams, one musician and ten privates. The nominal 1st sergeant of C Company, Peter Derst, was absent in Savannah, apparently still suffering from his wound at Chickamauga. His discharge from service, probably in fall 1864, is in the hands of his descendants, but this author has been unable to obtain or view a copy.

The attentive reader will note that C. M. Hardy is here designated third sergeant whereas he had been second sergeant of his company at the start of the

1864 campaign. For some reason, perhaps clerical error, James A. Thornton was marked as second sergeant on the August 1864 muster roll, even though he had been absent wounded since Chickamauga, and was shown in other records to have retired to the Invalid Corps in April 1864.[4]

Many of the absent wounded were men who had overstayed their sick furloughs; some men who had ordinary furloughs overstayed their time at home also. Hardy wrote bitterly to his sister about the situation. "I would have got a pass if they hadn't to have got to overstaying their time." As for the absent wounded men, Hardy said, "I don't see how M. M. and Bob [Price] stays at home so long. There was men wounded worse than they was, that has been back two months…Bob Price has never had his furlough extended at all." As for the effect on morale, Hardy thought, "What doe such men care for their Country? Nothing. It is enough to discourage a good soldier, to think he has to fight and under go all the hardships of war, for men that is just as able as he is."[5]

Captain Benjamin Hardee's presence with the battalion during and after Jonesboro is unclear. An inspection report dated 17 August 1864 found him absent since 16 August by authority of General Jackson. But the file also notes that that entry was erased. And he signed the muster roll of 31 August. If he was present, he would have succeeded Shaaff as battalion commander. After Hardee, the senior officer remaining on duty was Second Lieutenant Bryan. But with Shaaff and Bryan both on the staff, Cuyler King was the senior officer and became the de facto battalion commander. In fact, King wrote in his journal the following month that he was "still" in command of the battalion.[6]

More officers left the battalion that fall. Captain Willis Gray, the battalion quartermaster, transferred to the Railroad Bureau at the end of September in the face of a program to thin out the number of quartermasters and commissary officers at the unit level. He became assistant chief of the bureau and was still there at the end of January 1865. Major Alfred Hartridge requested the services of his young brother-in-law, Thomas Wayne, at Rose Dew Post on the coast in September, and the order was issued on 23 November. The date Wayne left the battalion is not clear. Cuyler King wrote that he was still with them as late as 20 November and he did not appear on the muster roll of the 27th Georgia Battalion, Hartridge's new unit, at the end of December 1864. He did prepare a list of absentees for Hartridge on 14 February 1865, and he, Hartridge, and Ordnance Sergeant James Leonard, formerly of the sharpshooters, were paroled with the 27th at Greensboro, North Carolina, on 1 May 1865.[7]

Not only officers left the unit. Private James Boggs of C Company, who had been a pontoon driver in August, went back to his old unit, the 32nd Georgia, sometime in the late fall. He fought with that regiment through the

Georgia and Carolinas campaign and surrendered with them at Greensboro in April 1865.

Sergeant Charles W. Shaw, who had been slightly wounded in the leg at Jonesboro, signed a document on 18 October as "Acting Captain, Commanding Company B," indicating there were no commissioned officers in the company. Thomas Wayne should have been with the battalion at that time but if he was acting as adjutant, then Shaw would be senior in the company. Shaw had been hospitalized in Augusta after Jonesboro, but apparently he rejoined the army, and then was sent to hospital again in Montgomery, Alabama, in mid-November. Probably his injured leg made it hard for him to keep up with the fast-moving army. He was captured and paroled in Montgomery when the city fell in May 1865.[8]

When Captain Horace Twyman had been wounded in both legs at Calhoun in May, he had been sent to hospital, first in Marietta, and later in Atlanta. There he was nursed by Charlotte Branch, Hamilton Branch's mother, who was a member of the Savannah Relief Committee. Still later, when he could move, Twyman went home to Virginia to recuperate as best he could. From his home there in Madison County, he wrote a letter to Mrs. Branch on 22 October, telling her of his condition. "I am…still improving, though…helpless as yet. I am wedded to two crutches with but little prospect of escaping them very soon. Pieces of the fractured bones are still coming from my wound and every symptom of continuing for some time. I have high hopes of being able to rejoin my command by the coming Spring campaign but very much fear I will not be fit for Infantry service again." Twyman wrote further that he had heard of the loss of many officers in the battalion and the brigade from Lieutenant Bryan, including the deaths of Herrmann, Holcombe, and Lawrence, who Twyman referred to as "three of the most popular officers in our Batt." It seemed apparent that Twyman would not be coming back to the sharpshooters soon again.[9]

One of Major Shaaff's last acts before leaving the battalion for staff duty was to try to improve the status of officers in the sharpshooters. By letter of 9 September he recommended that Second Lieutenants Thomas S. Wayne, N. Bayard Sadler, and R. Cuyler King be promoted to First Lieutenant to replaced the fallen Henry Herrmann, Josiah Holcombe and Samuel W. Lawrence, respectively, with dates of rank of 31 August 1864. It was Shaaff's intention that the three lieutenants should be company commanders. However, his recommendation ran afoul of adjutant general bureaucracy. His letter was returned from Richmond not once but twice because it was not accompanied by the required company strength reports justifying the presence of first lieutenants. Generals Henry Jackson, John Brown, Frank Cheatham, and Hood all gave positive endorsements to Shaaff's proposal but to no avail. It is likely that Hood approved field promotions for the young men. It will be remembered that Sadler had been a prisoner of war since June and Wayne soon had orders to leave the army. If Hood did approve the promotions, perhaps only King benefited.[10]

General Hood led his army across the Chattahoochee River on 1 October and headed north. Jackson's brigade was composed of the same units as before but losses at Atlanta had caused some consolidations. The 1st Confederate and 66th Georgia regiments were combined under Lieutenant Colonel James C. Gordon of the 1st Confederate, and the 29th and 30th Georgia regiments served together under Lieutenant Colonel William W. Billopp of the 29th. Heading the 25th Georgia was Captain G. W. Holmes, and Major Shaaff was still nominally in command of his battalion. Bate's division had present for duty 231 officers and 2,181 men, of whom 2,064 men were counted as effective. The aggregate present strength amounted to 3,243, including sick and detailed men. Strengths of the individual brigades and units are not available.[11]

As the army moved north toward Dalton, retracing the steps it had taken in the spring, individual corps and divisions captured or attempted to capture Union posts, such as Big Shanty, Allatoona, and Resaca. Hood was in Dalton by 13 October and in Gadsden, Alabama, by the twentieth. He had changed his strategy and decided to move into Tennessee or even Kentucky with a view toward eventually crossing the mountains to join Robert E. Lee in Virginia. The weather turned colder as the troops moved northward and the men began to pull down rail fences for camp fires but General Jackson would not allow his brigade to do so.[12]

Bate's division conducted an operation on 13 October to capture the blockhouse that controlled Mill Creek Gap above Dalton and to destroy the railroad from there as far north as possible. General Bate had returned to the division only three days before after being wounded at Atlanta. His division now consisted of Jackson's Georgia brigade, Finley's Florida brigade under Colonel Robert Bullock, and Tyler's Tennessee-Georgia brigade, still commanded by General Thomas B. Smith.

Bate's artillery bombarded the fort and it surrendered the next day. Meanwhile, most of the infantry worked on tearing up railway. On 15 October they advanced to Tunnel Hill and captured large quantities of supplies, appropriating what they could carry and destroying the rest. The troops had outmarched their rations and went without food from the night of the thirteenth to the evening of the fifteenth. By the time the sharpshooters got to the captured supplies everything was gone but bread, but they procured for themselves enough to last four days. The track was destroyed almost up to the tunnel.

General Jackson wrote later that his brigade had torn up more track around Dalton than the other two brigades combined. At this point Bate received orders to retire and moved off toward LaFayette, his division making up the rear guard of the army.[13]

Nathan Bedford Forrest's cavalry had been ordered to join Hood and the latter moved across north Alabama in anticipation of the linkup. The country was full of bushwhackers. At one point General Cheatham, corps commander, and his staff were riding at the head of the column and were ambushed. Skirmishers were thrown out but the hidden assailants escaped. The weather grew colder with frost forming every night. By 23 October Cuyler King began to suffer from pains in his face and chest as well as hunger and poorly shod feet. He had a tooth pulled on 25 October and had to ride in an ambulance beginning that day. He feared the chest pains might mean pneumonia but it might have been a return of the consumption that had attacked him the year before. Neptune, his servant, was also sick.[14]

Hood reached Decatur on 26 October, made a reconnaissance of the place, then moved to Tuscumbia on the thirtieth where he gathered supplies and waited for Forrest. Now far removed from Chattanooga and thoughts of disrupting Sherman's supply lines, the army's major concerns were food and clothing for the men and the discovery of a place to cross to the north side of the Tennessee River so as to advance on Nashville. Complaints about lack of food and the need for better shoes were staples of Cuyler King's daily journal entries.[15]

The reconnaissance at Decatur was conducted by Cheatham's corps. All three divisions advanced on the defenses of the town, driving the garrison into their forts on 27 October and taking up positions outside. Early the next morning a sortie from the forts got around the left of Cleburne's skirmishers and made a rapid advance along the whole line of that division and Bate's, snapping up prisoners along the way. General Jackson with the 29th Georgia on the extreme right counterattacked and retook the rifle pits. The raiders withdrew with their prisoners. General Robert S. Granger, the Union commander in north Alabama, reported that 120 prisoners were taken during the raid, including five commissioned officers.[16]

Henry Jackson wrote bitterly about the affair at Decatur, laying a large part of the blame for losses in his brigade on his division commander, General Bate. Jackson's account had it that the skirmishers of his brigade had been abandoned when Smith's skirmishers surrendered without a fight. The Georgia men withstood two assaults from the enemy, he wrote, then advanced to reoccupy their former position. At this time an order came from higher headquarters directing them not to advance. They remained in line until withdrawn in the evening. Wrote Jackson, admonishingly, "This affair, in which much gallantry was exhibited, and our loss amounted to fifty men, including some brave officers, has never evoked an official comment." Angus McDermid, taking a more sanguine view of the action, wrote, "My rgt [29th Georgia] was in a little fight only 2 got killed and 9 wounded."[17]

The sharpshooter battalion naturally was involved and may very well have made up a part of the line of skirmishers. The records show that two members of the unit were captured on 28 October, Sergeant Cornelius M. Hardy and Private David B. Forehand, both of C Company. Forehand, whose father had been killed in a fight when David was only five months old, was a married farmer from Burke County and twenty-nine years old in 1861. After six months service in the Georgia State Troops, he enlisted in the "Alexander Greys," a Burke County company of the 32nd Georgia, in May 1862, and then transferred to the sharpshooters. He had been sick for a lengthy period since being in Mississippi in 1863 and had been one of the men detailed to the division sharpshooters in August 1864. Hardy and Forehand both went to the prison compound at Camp Douglas, Illinois, where they remained until discharged in June 1865. Cuyler King confirmed in his journal that the sharpshooters had lost two men at Decatur.[18]

King wrote home from Tuscumbia a few days later, giving a good account of the army's wanderings since it had left Jonesboro. In his words, "We have done some of the tallest marching on the records of this war." King was much disgusted with the reconnaissance at Decatur. "Our corps [Cheatham's] made the demonstration and invested Decatur but the affair was badly managed so that we lost several hundred men when their was no necessity for the loss of a man." As to Hood's intention to enter Tennessee, King was also critical, "I doubt the policy of going into Tennessee at this season of the year, especially as our men are badly clad and at least 1/3 of the army without shoes." And about the food supply, he wrote, "Since we left Palmetto, Neptune [his servant] and myself have been living on 3/4 lb meal and from 8 to 12 oz beef [per day]."[19]

Cuyler had marched on foot all the way from Palmetto and his feet were in bad condition. Although he was only a lieutenant, as battalion commander he was entitled to a horse, but he could not find one. Later, when he was much weakened, Major Shaaff gave him an old horse to ride. King described his own personal appearance, "with my feet on the ground and beard roughly grown out." At another time he gave these details: "My dress consists of a thin, worn out jacket, one thin cotton shirt, drawers of the coarsest cotton and pants with the knee & seat entirely gone—no glove & a pr. of old shoes that let the water and frost to my benumbed feet—I firmly believe if it were not for the overcoat

Geo[rgia, his sister] gave me I should have frozen." He also complained continuously about his lack of adequate footwear. The army received new shoes and clothing on 22 October but Cuyler held back until the men had been supplied; as late as 24 November he was still without shoes. On 2 November he had to have another tooth pulled to relieve the pain in his face.[20]

Angus McDermid attested in his own way to the lack of suitable clothing and equipment. "Father, I am plom bare footed. I haint got a sine of a shoe on my foot nor I dont know when I will hav." As for a blanket, he wrote, "I hav bin without a blanket all the time till in the fight the other day [Decatur]. I got one where their lay a dead yanky so I hav me a good blanket." Happily, Angus was able to report in his next letter that he had acquired a good pair of shoes through normal supply channels.[21]

The sharpshooters arrived at Tuscumbia on 31 October and performed their regular bi-monthly muster that same afternoon. Unfortunately, the results have not survived, but Cuyler King noted that his company, D, had only ten men present. Battalion strength probably did not exceed forty men. Colors were unfurled and the bands played as the army marched through Tuscumbia but the reaction of the populace was cold. On 4 November General Jackson relieved the 25th Georgia from brigade provost duty and assigned that responsibility to King's battalion. He wrote in his journal, "Gen. Jackson…put my Battalion in Charge of the Prisoners. I am now Provost Marshal for the brigade and Batt. The Provost Guard is a very disagreeable position. I wish we could get out of it." Later, the sharpshooters were ordered to round up and arrest all men ages eighteen to forty-five to be sent to corps headquarters. If found fit, these men would be conscripted into Confederate service.[22]

The army remained at Tuscumbia for fourteen days, mainly because of the bad weather and swollen river. The sharpshooters changed camp several times because of sanitary conditions and the need for more firewood, but always remained in the same vicinity. Lieutenant King conferred with Major Shaaff at least once, presumably about battalion administration. King took advantage of the long lull to exercise his new authority as battalion commander. He wrote to Adjutant General Cooper in Richmond recommending that Second Lieutenant Alfred Bryan be promoted to first lieutenant of A Company to replace Horace Crane who had been retired to the Invalid Corps on 10 October.

Perhaps having learned a lesson from Shaaff's letter of recommendations for promotion in September, King had Charles Schlatter, the only officer serving with it, execute a certificate that A Company had thirty-six non-commissioned officers and men present for duty and therefore was authorized a first lieutenant according to army regulations. In their signatures, neither King nor Schlatter indicated whether they were first or second lieutenants but the pencil-written letter is very difficult to read. However, the fact that King recommended Bryan, who had previously been his senior, suggests that the former was now a first lieutenant. As requested, Bryan was promoted on 10 December with his rank backdated to 10 October, the date of Crane's retirement.[23]

Forrest's cavalry joined Hood's army on 14 November. Bate's division now showed a slight increase from sick and wounded men returning to the army. As of 6 November, his strength was 245 officers and 2,220 men present for duty, 2,106 effectives, and 3,249 aggregate present. Not counting the cavalry, Hood's army had 30,000 effectives of all arms, 40,000 present for duty, and 44,000 aggregate present.[24]

About 10 November Lieutenant Schlatter was assigned to duty with the cook wagons. That temporarily left only King and Wayne on duty with the troops in the ranks. King complained to his journal that Wayne spent most of his time at brigade headquarters so that it was very lonely for him in the battalion. If Alfred Bryan was brigade adjutant, it is likely that Wayne preferred the company of his Savannah associate to that of King whom he had known only since joining the army. It was on that day, also, that King finally obtained a horse to ride from Arthur Shaaff.[25]

The sharpshooters crossed to the north bank of the Tennessee River on 13 November. The army was completely across by the eighteenth. Just after Jackson's brigade crossed, the pontoon bridge, which had been a constant source of problems, broke, stranding the division trains and artillery on the south bank. The bridge broke again the next day, this time separating the troops from their rations. Once on the north side, the brigade marched through the town of Florence where they were warmly welcomed by the inhabitants. Cuyler King had the battalion colors unfurled and gave this commentary, "Our old flag when I had [it] unfurled caused great comment & sympathy from the ladies in general—the old thing is so much torn & soiled that it is hard to distinguish its design but still I am proud of it as all my hardships have been endured under its furls."[26] This was most probably the same flag that had been issued under General Beauregard's order in spring 1863. Despite the appeal for a replacement in June 1864, Cuyler's comment indicates that the sharpshooters had been campaigning under its furls for all of their combat operations since their arrival in Mississippi.

On 20 November the army began its northward march into Tennessee in cold, rainy weather. Cheatham's corps took the more northerly route by way of Waynesboro. The other two infantry corps, Lee's and Stewart's, advanced northeast through Lawrenceburg and west of Pulaski where Schofield's Union corps was posted. Bate's division moved with Cheatham's corps, advancing to Columbia, Tennessee, on the Duck River, where it bivouacked on 26 November.[27]

Cuyler King, Tom Wayne, and Dr. C. T. Ford, the battalion surgeon, tried to go to church in Florence on Sunday, the twentieth, but arrived at the service too late. The sharpshooters marched out at 1:00 P.M. on 21 November, having been left behind to escort Bate's division's wagons. The quartermaster in charge soon led them off on the wrong road, following Lee's corps instead of Cheatham's, and they went 5 miles out of their way before discovering the error. The sharpshooters camped in the snow that night and did not catch up to their brigade until the second evening, having had to thread their way through the supply train of the entire army. King recorded that some of his men were so numb with cold that they were unable to remove their outer garments when they reached camp.

Food remained short. On 24 November each man was issued four biscuits and a half pound of beef for his daily ration. The next day they received 8 ounces of uncooked fresh pork and three-quarters of a pound of raw meal per man. King had to hide his new horse's corn to keep the men from stealing it. Sarcastically, he wrote that General Hood had warned the army when they left Florence that bread rations would be short in Tennessee and he had kept his word.[28]

With the Confederate advance, Schofield had pulled back from Pulaski to Columbia. When Bate's and the other divisions arrived there, they engaged in skirmishing for the next two days. Then on 29 November General Hood sent Cheatham's corps, followed by Stewart's, around Schofield's left and northward toward Spring Hill. Forrest's cavalry went ahead to clear the way. Lee's corps was left to occupy the Union troops and make it look as if the Confederates had maintained their position. It is not clear whether Hood planned to cut the road or turnpike at Spring Hill and thereby trap Schofield, or merely move directly to Nashville without engaging the Union force at Columbia.

Cleburne's division was sent first to be placed parallel to the turnpike south of Spring Hill. Bate's division was to form on the left of Cleburne as it came up, and Brown's division would go in on the right. The plan was to have all three in a position to cover the turnpike with fire. Forrest's cavalry had gone ahead to Spring Hill where they became involved in a fight for the town. Through a series of misunderstandings and miscommunications, by now the hallmark of Hood's command, nothing went right. The Confederate line, rather than paralleling the turnpike, at its northern end bent back away from it to the east. And to top matters off, Schofield decided to evacuate Columbia and marched his divisions up the road while the Confederates were getting into place.

As ordered, Bate formed his division in alignment with Cleburne's, with Jackson's brigade, including the 1st Sharpshooters, on the right, Smith's Tennessee brigade on the left, but slightly behind Jackson's, and Bullock's Florida brigade in support. Hood himself ordered Bate to advance to the turnpike and then "sweep" toward Columbia. Cleburne had already started a similar advance before Bate got in line, so the latter had to adjust his movements several times. When he came in sight of the turnpike, he could see it occupied by Federal troops moving north. Major Theodore Caswell's 4th Georgia Sharpshooter Battalion, acting as division skirmishers, began to fire into the enemy, causing them to veer onto a side road on their left. Bate's main line was within 200 yards of the pike.

Cheatham sent an order to Bate to halt and move to connect his right to Cleburne's left. Bate did this with some difficulty, it being already dark. He pulled Smith's brigade in to protect his left, and remained so deployed. Edward Johnson's division of Lee's corps came up on his left later. The Confederate army stayed there all night while Schofield's troops marched passed almost in sight and certainly within earshot. Colonel Ellison Capers of the 24th South Carolina wrote that he could hear the sounds of wheels clearly. Hood and Cheatham were warned several times but neither took any action. Thus passed what might have been a missed opportunity to destroy a large part of the Union army at Spring Hill, and one that might have saved Hood's army much bloodshed the next day. Some modern historians downplay the missed opportunity, but there is no denying the mismanagement, even carelessness, of Hood and his senior commanders.[29]

Cuyler King was as frustrated as anyone else listening to the Union army pass by unmolested. After recounting the trek from before Columbia to the vicinity of Spring Hill, having to march 20 miles to cover 12, he wrote that they formed with Stewart on their left and went in, having "quite a brisk skirmish with the enemy" in which "a few men" were lost. Whether that was in his battalion or in Caswell's sharpshooters he did not specify. Then Bate's division took up a position along the pike and listened while the enemy marched past. Wrote Cuyler, "I was within a few hundred yards of the pike & could—went to sleep about twelve o'clock—hear everything that was going on on the road… It was a criminal mistake on the part of someone in authority for not getting possession of the pike. I doubt if the Battle of Franklin would have been fought if we had acted right."[30]

The 1st Georgia Sharpshooters recorded one casualty at Spring Hill, or perhaps at Columbia. Private John F. Hall of D Company, who may have been wounded at Peachtree Creek and was wounded at Jonesboro, was wounded again, this time in the left foot, on 28 November, and the foot was amputated on the twenty-ninth. Hall was from Clinch County and had served in the 29th Georgia before coming to the sharpshooters. He had been a sergeant early in 1863 but was reduced to private in the spring of that year. After being wounded, he must have been carried with the army because he was captured at Murfeesboro on 5 January 1865. He spent two months in a US Army hospital in Nashville, then was sent to Camp Chase. Hall went to Point Lookout, Maryland, for exchange within a few weeks, but was not finally released until June 1865.[31]

From Spring Hill, Hood's army marched on 30 November to Franklin on the Harpeth River, a distance of 14 miles. After dislodging Wagner's blue division from Winstead Hill, the Confederate soldiers could look 3 miles across a plain to the town. Despite the counseling of Forrest and other commanders to cross the river upstream and get in Schofield's rear, Hood decided on an infantry frontal attack. He had virtually no artillery with him and only two corps up, Lee being still on the road from Columbia with the artillery train.

The drama that followed was the last great charge of the Confederacy and perhaps the most disastrous. Hood deployed his two available corps with Stewart on the right and Cheatham on the left. Stewart had the divisions of Loring, Walthall and French, right to left; Cheatham had Cleburne on the right, Brown in the center, and Bate as his left. Two divisions of Forrest's cavalry corps protected Stewart's right flank, while General James Chalmers's cavalry division was on Cheatham's left. The total infantry in line was about 18,000 men.

Schofield had fortified his position well. He had six infantry divisions in two army corps, perhaps 20,000 men, in a circle of earthworks, bristling with artillery, that completely surrounded the town of Franklin, with the strongest position facing south. Schofield's cavalry was positioned to protect his left flank, where the river was fordable, and his rear. The Union commanders expected Hood would attempt to get around their left and were surprised by the frontal assault when they saw it forming.

The attack stepped off about five o'clock in the darkening winter afternoon. Eighteen brigades were aligned for the advance. The initial assault actually penetrated the center of the first line of Federal defenses but could not break through the main line. For five hours the combatants waged fierce muzzle-to-muzzle and hand-to-hand combat from the opposite sides of the earthworks. The élan of the Southern troops was irrepressible, but as darkness fell and more and more of the men were killed and wounded, the effort sputtered out. By ten o'clock that night the effort had failed. Schofield pulled his men out of Franklin during the night and took the road to Nashville.

On the far left of the Confederate line, Bate was ordered by Cheatham to move through a pass in the ridge, circle to the left, then approach Franklin along the Carter Creek Pike from the southeast, aligning himself with Brown on his right. Bate had to cover a much greater distance than Cleburne or Brown to get in line. When he reached his position, he placed two brigades on line, Jackson on the right and Smith on the left, with Bullock's Florida brigade in the second line. Smith's was the extreme left brigade of the Confederate infantry. The division skirmishers were led by Major Caswell of the 4th Georgia Sharpshooters.

Bate advanced smoothly across the plain with the other divisions, driving in the enemy skirmishers and clearing them from the outer works. Chalmers's cavalry was not in touch with Bate's left as they should have been and Smith's brigade was exposed to an enfilading fire. Bate moved the Florida brigade up on the left to cover that flank. His whole line advanced, Jackson's brigade actually reaching the main enemy works, but the left was driven back. Jackson made repeated efforts during the hours that followed, but could not break the Union line.[32]

Jackson's brigade had been formed, as usual, with the 30th and 29th Georgia regiments on the right and the 1st Sharpshooter Battalion on the left. The 25th Georgia, 1st Confederate, and 66th Georgia regiments made up the center. Cuyler King wrote that "men and officers seemed to move with a confidence that marks the step of victory." The right and center of the brigade rushed past the first Union line and pressed forward to the second. General Jackson's horse would not jump the obstacle, so he rode to the left and discovered there that part of his brigade was in retreat. Wrote Jackson later: "On its extreme [left] had been posted the Battn. of Sharpshooters, distinguished in many previous conflicts for its firmness and gallantry. A number of its men I saw grouped around a brave young officer, facing the enemy's fire but not advancing. I rode back and angrily ordered them forward. The officer hesitated, saying to the effect, '…the entire left of the Division has retreated from the field.'"

Jackson looked to his left and saw that both Smith's and Bullock's brigades were in retreat. The brave young officer was surely Cuyler King. Private James A. McCord of the 30th Georgia added his opinion to General Jackson's. "The larger portion of Genl Bates Div acted very cowardly in the first of the fight. Tyler's [Smith's] & Finley's [Bullock's] and Jackson's left would not charge the works. I was skirmishing in front of Tyler & Finley and they run three times and left me on the hill begging them to come back...".[33]

Hood's losses were terrible. Bate reported 47 men killed, 253 wounded, and 19 missing in his division. Southern losses overall were approximately 1,750 killed, 4,500 wounded, and 700 captured. Six Confederate generals were killed or died of their wounds, five wounded and one captured; forty-five regimental commanders were killed or wounded. In Jackson's brigade, Colonel George A. Smith of the 1st Confederate was killed and Lieutenant Colonel Algernon S. Hamilton of the 66th Georgia was mortally wounded. No losses in the 1st Sharpshooters were recorded. The Army of Tennessee never recovered from the battle at Franklin.[34]

An interesting sidelight on the battle of Franklin was presented by Lieutenant Isaac N. Shannon more than forty years after the war. He wrote that he was a member of a company of special sharpshooters under Lieutenant John M. Ozanne who served in Cheatham's division, led by General John C. Brown at Franklin and Nashville. He said they were armed with Whitworth rifles zeroed for a range of 2,000 yards and were posted in front of the brigade. Shannon noted they had a strength of only five men at Franklin. Recalling that two men of Shaaff's Georgia battalion had been assigned to the "division sharpshooters" in August 1864, one may suspect that they were attached to Ozanne's company or similar unit. In fact, one of the two, David Forehand, had been captured at Decatur, Alabama, while serving as a skirmisher in front of the lines.[35]

Hood's army entered Franklin, following Schofield's evacuation, on the morning of 1 December. Despite his army being much diminished in strength, after a day's rest Hood sent Bate's division east to Murfreesboro to destroy the railroad between there and Nashville. En route, Bate learned that Murfeesboro was occupied by a Union force greater than his division strength of 1,600 effectives. He changed his course and struck the railroad some 5 miles north of the town on 4 December.

Placing the Florida brigade to protect his rear and holding Smith's brigade in reserve, Bate began an artillery bombardment of a blockhouse protecting a bridge, while Jackson's brigade set to work tearing up track. In the evening, a Union force attacked from across the creek. They succeeded in turning Bate's left flank and driving back the Florida brigade, wounding Colonel Bullock. Smith's brigade was brought up to protect the left and Jackson's Georgians were rushed to the support of the Floridians. With a single volley they threw the Yankees back across the creek.[36]

Henry Jackson gave his own account of the events of 4 December. His brigade had torn up about 1,000 yards of rail that day and he feared they were moving too far away from where they had stacked their arms. He informed Bate of the need for his men to fall back on their weapons and the division commander gave his permission. Fortunately, Jackson had almost completed the maneuver when his men were suddenly rushed to the right flank, then returned to camp, then thrust to the front to repel the enemy attack. By now it was dark. Suddenly, and without warning, the Florida regiments came flying into his line, breaking up his left and center, "creating," as Jackson wrote, "a most distressing state of confusion." The general went on, "Some of my command, however, on the right, remained comparatively firm and we poured a partial fire into the enemy. He halted and withdrew beyond a creek."[37]

Bate reported casualties of fifteen killed, fifty-nine wounded, and thirteen missing. There were no recorded losses in the sharpshooter battalion. The next day, 5 December, Bate captured and destroyed three more blockhouses and three bridges and tore up several more miles of track. Later in the day, General Forrest arrived with two divisions of cavalry and two brigades of infantry and assumed command of operations near Murfreesboro. Forrest changed the nature of operations, by Hood's order, from tearing up railroad to capturing the town. On 6 December his combined forces closed up to the Union defenses and dug in.

The whole day of 7 December was taken up with the two sides maneuvering for an advantage. On Forrest's orders, Bate shifted his infantry brigades around several times. Suddenly a Yankee attack materialized in a location where there was a gap between Smith's and the Florida brigades, which were in some hastily thrown up defensive works. Bate sent Major Arthur Shaaff to conduct Jackson's and Sears's brigade to fill the gap. Bate wrote that "Smith's and the right of Jackson's brigade, which was getting in position, drove back in gallant style the right of the enemy line, which was confronting them." General Forrest later wrote that all of the brigades fell back except Smith's. Bate remained with the two brigades of his division until ordered to withdraw by General Forrest, which Bate said he did in a "leisurely" manner. Bate lost 19 killed, 73 wounded ,and 122 missing. The dead included Lieutenant Colonel William W. Billopp of the 29th Georgia. Billopp was not the only loss in the 29th Georgia. Sergeant Angus McDermid, promoted less than a month before, was killed and his body left on the field. When it was recovered the next day for burial, it was stripped of all his personal possessions. Whether the sharpshooters were participants in this action or not, there is scant record of their activities. Cuyler King wrote in his journal on 6 December that his battalion was deployed in the rear of Jackson's brigade to prevent straggling, but they may have been brought up to the line on the seventh.[38]

Typically, Henry Jackson had his own perspective on the proceedings on 7 December. His brigade, he said, moved first to the right, threw up earthworks, was ordered out of them, moved to the left, and dug earthworks again. Then he was ordered further to the left, following General Sears, and "without any explicit instructions," then back to the right to support Smith. When he arrived at the supposed position of Smith's brigade, Jackson found that they "had already retreated in great confusion." He next received an appeal to save the guns and, forming his brigade, advanced against the enemy. The Georgia brigade received fire from the front and from the right flank where the Yankees had occupied the works thrown up by Jackson's men earlier in the day. Jackson was forced to retire, but rallied his men and led them off the field in good order.

Jackson complained that Bate created the crisis by ordering the brigades to the left, giving the enemy an opportunity to occupy the defensive works. When he questioned Bate about the order, that general said the order came from General Forrest, but, said Jackson, Forrest denied any knowledge of the order. The Georgia general said that the division commander had given his brigade no credit at all for being in the fight.[39]

Railroad destruction resumed on 8 December in a heavy snow storm, but little progress was made because the men were not properly dressed for the conditions and the frozen ground made it difficult to take up the rails and ties. Food supplies were in abundance, however, many of the men still were without shoes. Local citizens donated their second-hand shoes to the army but the supply was still insufficient. When Forrest directed Bate on 9 December to return to join Cheatham's corps with the army in front of Nashville, almost one fourth of the men were barefoot. The snow had turned to sleet and the roads were icy; some men marched with bloody feet.[40]

While Hood had been marching across north Alabama and fighting in Tennessee, great events had transpired in Georgia. General Sherman, having decided that Tennessee and his lines of communication were capably defended, had launched his celebrated "March to the Sea." Leaving Atlanta in flames on 15 November, the Union commander struck out for the coast with an army of 60,000 infantry and a few thousand cavalry. His destination was not immediately known on the Southern side and the cities of Augusta and Macon braced themselves for attack. The only force available to oppose Sherman was Wheeler's cavalry, the Georgia militia, and some local troops.

Sherman bypassed the two major cities, instead making his way to Milledgeville, the state capital, and then in a wide swath of destruction toward Savannah. En route, he fought an engagement with the militia at Griswoldville, was temporarily detained by the Georgia Military Institute cadets at the crossing of the Oconee River, and carried on a running engagement with Wheeler. The fight at the Oconee bridge on 24 and 25 November also involved a company of the 27th Georgia Battalion, whose commander was Major Alfred L. Hartridge. The battalion later served in the defenses of Savannah before retreating to South Carolina.

On 13 December Sherman's army captured Fort McAllister, the bastion of the Savannah coast defenses, and on 20 December Savannah itself surrendered. General William J. Hardee, the commander in Georgia, withdrew his forces to South Carolina, hoping to retard Sherman's advance into that state. Still on Hardee's staff was his inspector, Captain William H. Ross. Other members of the sharpshooter battalion were unwilling parties to Sherman's advance.

Private Curran Becton, B Company, had been wounded in the leg at Jonesboro. He was recuperating at home in the Big Creek section of Jefferson County when the Union army arrived there. Becton was captured on 1 December, sent to Point Lookout, Maryland, and released in June 1865. Sergeant Christian Larson, B Company, was a resident of Savannah. He was wounded in the hand at Resaca or Calhoun in May 1864 and went home to recover. His wound must have worsened. When he was captured in Savannah on 21 December, his finger was amputated. He took the oath of allegiance on 19 January 1865 and was sent to the US Army hospital at Hilton Head, South Carolina.

Lieutenant Horace Crane, still on crutches after being wounded in the ankle at Chickamauga, had applied for release from active duty. He was retired to the Invalid Corps on 10 October 1864, then assigned as adjutant of the post at Fort McAllister on 25 November. He was captured there when the fort fell, sent to Fort Delaware as a prisoner, and released in June 1865. Crane's retirement had made possible the promotion of Alfred Bryan, already discussed.

Lieutenant Robert P. Wayne was ordered by General Hardee on 16 December to join the staff of Brigadier General Hugh Mercer in the defenses of Savannah. The latter commanded a motley brigade of 1,200 men in the division of General Ambrose R. Wright on the left of the Confederate line not far from the old sharpshooter Camp Anderson. What capacity Wayne served in, and whether or not he accompanied Hardee's army during the evacuation are unknowns.[41]

On the same day as Bryan's promotion, 10 December, General Jackson penned a ten-page, "private and confidential" letter to General Cheatham stating his unhappiness at serving under General Bate and detailing events as far back as Jonesboro as justification. Many of the paragraphs of the letter have already been quoted or paraphrased here. Jackson was willing, he wrote, to put his concerns in an official document to be forwarded through official channels, and he asked that Cheatham bring the matter to the attention of General Hood. He thought that service under Bate had "already measurably demoralized, and, if continued, will ruin" his brigade. Jackson suggested that the officers and men of his command shared his opinion. He asked that Hood and Cheatham allow him and his troops, now amounting to only 500 or 600 effectives, to be released from Bate's direction to go to "some new field of action."[42]

The letter was probably written the same day Bate's division returned to the army in front of Nashville. With the Army of Tennessee plunging toward its final reckoning, it is unlikely that Cheatham had much time to spend on the complaints of a dissatisfied subordinate, but it is possible that he discussed it with Hood as future events would bear out.

Jackson, in his letter, gave his brigade strength as between 500 and 600 effectives. A return of 13 December for Bate's division showed that the Georgia brigade was the largest in the division. Jackson had 657 effectives and 986 aggregate present, Smith's brigade had 482 effectives and 876 aggregate, and the Florida brigade had 410 effectives and 765 aggregate. Bate could put 1,562 men in line of battle and had 2,658 men in camp. A separate return for 10 December gave Bate 191 officers and 1,659 men present for duty, of whom 1,562 were effectives. Jackson's brigade was composed of the 1st Confederate and 66th Georgia under Lieutenant Colonel Gordon, the 25th Georgia under Captain Joseph E. Fulton, the 29th and 30th Georgia under Colonel William D. Mitchell, and the 1st Sharpshooter Battalion under Lieutenant R. Cuyler King.[43]

In front of Nashville, Hood had aligned his army of approximately 25,000 men, confronting the powerful and well dug in defending force of some 70,000 under General George H. Thomas. Now that Hood had arrived at his goal, he was unsure what to do with it. His enemy had superior numbers, his men were poorly equipped for the winter weather, and his supply line was stretched to the breaking point. He could not bypass Nashville, leaving that powerful bastion in his rear; he was too weak to attack; and retreat would be an admission of failure. His only option, given his pride, his temperament, and the means at his disposal, was to wait for Thomas to attack him and hope to exploit some blunder to his advantage.

Hood deployed his three corps in a 5 mile arc across the south side of the city, interdicting the two railroads to the south, but not having enough men to cut all the major highways. Cheatham's corps with Bate's division and Jackson's brigade was on the right, Lee in the center and Stewart on the left. Thomas waited for the cold weather to moderate slightly, then launched his attack on 15 December. First a feint was made against Cheatham on the right, then the main attack was thrown against Stewart, overwhelming him with numbers and overlapping his flank. Reinforcements sent from the Southern right and center were insufficient to stem the tide.

Hood's whole army fell back to a new, shorter line about 2 miles south of the first. This time Lee was on the right, Stewart in the center, and Cheatham on the left. Thomas applied the same tactic he had used the day before. Attacks went in against Lee while Cheatham's position was pounded with artillery. Late in the day, two infantry corps and the Union cavalry corps were unleashed against Cheatham from three directions. His men could not stand the pressure and his position gave way completely, followed by that of Stewart in the center. As thousands of Southern soldiers fled southeast from the field, only Lee held steady as a rear guard.[44]

General Bate's report of the battle suggests that his division did no fighting on 15 December. In the evening, he was ordered to the left and formed in line of battle on the west side of the Franklin Pike. He observed large numbers of disorganized men streaming to the east. Later, Cheatham moved Bate's division to form on Stewart's left, running west from the Granny White Pike to Shy's Hill, held by Ector's single brigade of French's division. Bate was unable to bring up his artillery because the sudden thaw that day had rendered the ground too soft for even the lightest vehicle. Bate's men dug in in the dark; he complained to Cheatham that his right was in the air because he was unable to find Stewart's left, but his superior told him he had no authority to change the dispositions.

Daylight on the sixteenth confirmed Bate's fears for his line. Stewart's three divisions were several hundred yards in his right rear. Ector's brigade ran from the crown of Shy's Hill north to south, at a right angle to Bate, and that line was continued by Cleburne's division, now under General James A. Smith. Bate's left was on a salient and his right was completely exposed, a most unenviable position. He had his three brigades on line, Jackson on the exposed right, the Florida brigade in the center, and Smith on the left. A hill occupied by Union artillery was directly in front of Shy's Hill and only 400 yards distant. Behind him at a distance of 600 yards ran another range of hills beyond Smith's left, that if occupied by Union artillery would bring fire on his rear. By personal reconnaissance, Bate found a road passable for artillery and brought two guns to the rear of Bullock's brigade where they could cover his exposed right and Stewart's left.

During the morning Union forces began to mass in the woods opposite Bate's line. He threw back one attack, but then Ector's brigade was pulled out of line and put in reserve. Bate was ordered to extend his line to cover the gap. He could do so only by stretching his already thin brigades around the angle of the salient. Soon the heavy artillery bombardment started. As Bate had feared, guns were moved onto the heights on his left and rear and he began to take fire from three directions. Soon, infantry advanced in his front and began to move toward the gap between Jackson's brigade and Stewart's left. Cheatham asked Bate to take over even more of the line on his left so that troops could be pulled out and sent to the extreme left, which was in danger of being turned.

About this time the brigade on the extreme left did give way, and Bate's division began to take musket fire from the rear, wounding and killing his men. Bate went to the angle to encourage his men there, who he knew "to be unsurpassed for gallantry and endurance," to hold on. These were his own Tennessee troops of Smith's brigade whom he had commanded before being promoted to major general. Sensing disaster, Bate ordered his artillery to limber up and take the Franklin Turnpike to the south, his designated escape route, the Granny White Pike, being already cut.

Now came a full infantry assault on the angle on Shy's Hill. Despite heroic efforts, the men could not hold. Colonel William Shy of the 20th Tennessee, for whom the hill was subsequently named, lost his life in the struggle. Only sixty men of Smith's brigade made it to safety. Smith was taken prisoner. Once the breach was made, the Confederate lines on either side fled in confusion. Bate's division melted away except for the 29th and 30th Georgia, under Colonel William D. Mitchell, who fought until surrounded and, presumably, were all captured, including Colonel Mitchell. Frank Roberts of the 2nd Georgia Sharpshooters, in Gist's brigade, Cleburne's division, later wrote, "From our position on the left we could see General Bate's line very distinctly, and when it broke the men seemed to rise like a flock of big birds and fairly fly down the hill."[45]

On the right of Bate's line, Jackson's brigade had been formed in its usual configuration, 29th and 30th Georgia on the right, 25th Georgia, 1st Confederate and 66th Georgia in the center, and 1st Battalion Sharpshooters on the left. During the day on 16 December, the ground in front of the brigade being too rough for the enemy to cross, Jackson's troops had relatively little activity except for their exposure to artillery fire and hot work on the picket line. From their vantage point, the officers and men watched the battle in other locations.

Suddenly, about four o'clock in the afternoon, Lieutenant Bryan and others heard loud cheering in their rear and turned to see Union infantry approaching from where the Florida brigade had given way on their left. Jackson sent Bryan to the right to warn the 29th and 30th Georgia, and another officer, Charles B. Martin, was sent to the left to advise Cuyler King and the sharpshooters. The order was to move out to the right flank. The staff officers returned and found General Jackson and Colonel Gordon trying to get to their horses. Their progress was impeded by the thawed mud which clung to their boots at each step. Gordon left the general on his own and got away. Martin remained with him and they made it to the horses. As they attempted to ride away, however, the general's horse faltered while crossing a fence and he was thrown off.

Jackson pulled off one boot, so as to flee on foot, and was in the process of removing the other, when four blue-coated soldiers apprehended him. Martin turned down the general's collar to hide his stars, but when Jackson pulled the boot back on, the stars were exposed. Three of the soldiers left with the general and one man took charge of Martin. As the two proceeded across a field, the soldier stopped to loot an abandoned knapsack. Martin grabbed his musket, hit him in the head with it, and took off running. Soon he found Gordon with the general's horse. They went as far as Franklin that night, found Jackson's servant, and gave him the horse to return to Savannah if he could make it.[46]

Back on the battlefield, the order to move out by the right flank came too late. The Yankees were among them before they could move. The 29th and 30th Georgia fought until surrounded, as already mentioned, but the 1st Battalion Sharpshooters was caught without a chance. Only scattered men escaped. Lieutenants King and Schlatter and twenty-eight men were captured. Alfred Bryan may have been caught at this time but no record of his capture or imprisonment have been found. The battalion colors may have been captured at this time also. The captive officers were sent to Johnson's Island in Lake Erie, near Sandusky, Ohio. Cuyler King wrote to his sister from there a month later asking for "the substancials [sic] of life" and to let her know he was all right.[47]

The soldier prisoners all went to Camp Chase, Ohio. They were George Abbott, John W. Armor, Anderstokes Best, Zadock Best, Samuel Boggs, William H. Brooks, Louis Brown, William F. Cochran, John W. Edwards, James Green, John J. Griffin, John R. Hurst, James W. Hurt, John B. Leggett, Joshua McHiggs, W. J. "Billy" Parrott, J. W. Peace, H. B. Phillips, Alfred Roath, Thomas C. Robinson, John C. Stephens, Francis L. Taylor, Benjamin Tharpe, W. R. Thomas, Reuben Warren, Jude B. Waters, Luke Williams, and William S. Williams. Martin L. Doyle was picked up near Franklin the next day. He had been assigned as a litter bearer and may have been tending wounded soldiers. William J. Anderson and John F. Hall, both wounded, were captured at Murfreesboro on 5 January. Total loss was thirty-three officers and men. The battalion no longer existed.

Some of these are familiar names. Armor, Hurst, Hurt, Parrott, Peace and Roath had been wounded before. Sam Boggs had been captured at Jonesboro and exchanged at Rough and Ready in September, only to be captured again. The second time there was no exchange. Hall was wounded and lost his foot at Spring Hill. Anderson was treated for a gunshot wound to the right shoulder in Nashville before being sent to Camp Chase; possibly he had been wounded at Spring Hill or Murfreesboro, although his record does not say so, and he and Hall had been left with local residents for convalescence.

The prisoner records of Armor, McHiggs, Phillips, and Waters suggest they enlisted in US service because they were transferred to Chicago in March 1865, the usual course for such "Galvanized Yankees." James Green, Parrott, and W. R. Thomas did enlist in March, and Zadock Best and William Brooks in April 1865. Best and Parrott both deserted in September or October 1865. Hurst and Leggett was paroled in May; Roath, Stephens, and Warren were released in May; and Abbott, Anderson, Doyle, Hall, Hurt, Peace, Robinson, Taylor, Tharpe, and William Williams were released in June 1865. Probably blanketless and probably shoeless, John Griffin, John Edwards, and Luke Williams contracted pneumonia and died at Camp Chase, Griffin on 25 January and Edwards on 31 January. Eighteen-year-old Luke Williams died, probably in the arms of his older brother William, on 5 February. The records of "Stokes" Best, Samuel Boggs, Louis Brown, and William Cochran show no disposition after their arrival at Camp Chase early in January.[48]

Hood's army regained some semblance of order at Columbia and then dragged itself across the Tennessee River and back to Alabama. The return was likened by some to Napoleon's retreat from Moscow. Bate was able to form the remnants of his division into line of battle south of Spring Hill on 18 December and retired across the Tennessee with the rest of Cheatham's corps on Christmas Day. In his after-action report, he made special mention of his three brigade commanders, not omitting Henry Jackson, and also noted the "promptness and gallantry" of his staff, including Major Arthur Shaaff. If there was bad feeling between Bate and Jackson, the former did not allow it to show in official channels.[49]

From Tuscumbia, the army marched to its base at Corinth and Tupelo, Mississippi, the sick and wounded traveling by train. The rear guard closed in to Corinth by New Years Day, 1865, and the army was concentrated around Tupelo in early January. Hamilton Branch wrote to his mother from Corinth on 29 December, "I arrived at this place this morning, dirty, lousey and hungry." His mood and condition were reflective of the whole army's. By a return of 20 January, the Army of Tennessee had roughly 19,000 officers and men present for duty. Cheatham's corps showed an effective infantry strength of 513 officers and 5,197 men. On 6 November he had had an effective strength of 10,500, and on

10 December, 7,200.[50]

From Tupelo on 25 January 1865, in response to an undated query from the adjutant and inspector general's office in Richmond, Lieutenant George H. Johnston sent out a status report on all the officers who were serving or who had served with the battalion. When or how Johnston returned to the army is unknown. He had gone home on wounded sick leave in August 1864. He escaped the capture of Savannah so perhaps he was evacuated with Hardee's army or he could have joined Hood in Alabama or Tennessee. Lieutenant Hamilton Branch had traveled from Savannah to Mobile to Corinth to Tuscumbia in late October and early November. Johnston could have taken the same route, but Cuyler King's journal does not mention his name.

Johnston's report showed that there were only eleven officers carried on the muster rolls but did not tell what duty they were performing. They were Major Shaaff, Assistant Surgeon Ford, and Lieutenant Robert Wayne of the battalion staff; Captain Twyman and Second Lieutenants Bryan and Schlatter, Company A; Captain Ross and Second Lieutenants Sadler and Johnston, Company C; and Captain Dent and Second Lieutenant King, Company D. The ranks of the lieutenants do not reflect the promotions recommended for Schlatter, Sadler, and King by Shaaff in September nor the recorded promotion of Bryan in December. Johnston showed Thomas S. Wayne as transferred with no successor appointed. The name of Stephen Norris of B Company does not appear in the roster at all.

Johnston also reported that Captain Benjamin Hardee was a deserter, that he had been absent sick in Savannah when the city fell and that he remained there. "He is reported to have taken off his uniform and to have taken the oath of allegiance to the U.S. government," he wrote. He noted that there were vacancies in the positions of captain, Company B; 1st lieutenants in all companies; both 2nd lieutenants, Company B; and the junior second lieutenant, Company D, for a total of eight. Then he closed the report with this statement, "It is impossible to give the dates of commission, vacancies &c. as the records of the command were captured in the Atlanta campaign, and I am the only officer now present."[51]

Beyond Johnston's report, the status and remaining strength of the sharpshooter battalion is unknown. Arthur Shaaff for certain, and possibly Alfred Bryan, were the only officers who might have survived Nashville, but they were both filling staff assignments. There was precious little to administer. Indeed, Shaaff was given a thirty-day leave of absence beginning on 10 January, probably to find and care for his wife who had been turned out of Savannah with other officers' families by Sherman, just as had been done at Atlanta. The senior non-commissioned officer present with the battalion would have been First Sergeant William Kersey of A Company, however, he and Privates James Jarrell and Nathan Williams were admitted to hospital in Mississippi with gunshot wounds in early January 1865, suggesting they had been casualties in Tennessee and had been carried back with the army.

Battalion muster rolls for October and December 1864 have not survived, so the present for duty strength of the battalion during the Tennessee campaign cannot be determined. A muster was taken in October; it is unknown if there was anyone to call the roll at the end of December. If one takes the number of men present on 31 August and adds back in all the detailed men and returned prisoners, the possible total for the march to Franklin and Nashville is approximately fifty-five. Taking away losses at Decatur, Alabama, and Murfreesboro of a half dozen, there may have been fifty men to fight at the two major battles. If losses amounted to a dozen at Franklin, there would be fewer than ten men remaining after Nashville.[52]

One former soldier was heard from but not by the battalion. Corporal Washington Wilcox of Henry County, Alabama, had been a member of the "Irwin Invincibles," then the 25th Georgia, and finally, the sharpshooters. Seriously wounded in the thigh at Chickamauga, he had returned to duty at Dalton to reenlist for the war in February 1864 but had been forced to return to hospital. From Eufaula, Alabama, on 16 January 1865, Wilcox wrote to the assistant adjutant general of the Army of Tennessee asking for permission to apply for disability retirement because of his wound. Wilcox had been a twenty-year-old farm laborer living in the household of his father, William "Willcocks," a carpenter, in Henry County in 1860.[53]

The situation in the Carolinas in early 1865 was too desperate to allow an army of almost 20,000 men to remain idle in Mississippi. Sherman had begun his northward march from Savannah and the forces available to deter him were woefully inadequate. Under urging by President Davis, General Beauregard began to send elements of the Army of Tennessee eastward. Hood was removed as army commander, replaced first by General Richard Taylor on 23 January, and then by General Alexander Stewart.

What remained of Hood's forces was barely an army. Many men simply gave up after Nashville and went home. Those that did remain in the ranks took advantage of proximity to their homes to grant themselves leave of absence as they passed. Transport was almost non-existent and the troops had to rely on the railroads for conveyance to the new front. Artillery and small arms had also been lost in the helter-skelter retreat into Mississippi.[54]

The troops traveled by train as much as possible, getting as far as middle Georgia. Sherman had seriously disrupted the rail network in east and central Georgia, so the men had to march overland from Milledgeville to Camak, as in the case of Mercer's old brigade, or from Midway to Mayfield, as did Gist's. From there they could take train to Augusta and then into South Carolina.[55]

The battle for the Carolinas was a race to get a reasonably strong defense force ahead of Sherman's advancing columns. Each time a location was picked for a concentration of Confederate forces, Sherman would pass that place before the Southern commanders could get there. The confusion was compounded by the absence of an overall commander. Beauregard was supervising but not commanding the troops transferred from the west and concentrating at Augusta. Hardee commanded the departmental troops in South Carolina and was, at President Davis's insistence, trying to hold on to Charleston. It was from Charleston that Captain William H. Ross wrote to Congressman Clifford Anderson on 1 February.

The two generals agreed to join forces at Columbia, South Carolina, but Sherman got there first. Hardee finally abandoned Charleston and planned to meet Beauregard at Greensboro, North Carolina, however, Sherman's main army was now interposed between the two Confederate armies. At last, on 21 February, Davis consented to re-appoint General Joseph E. Johnston as commander of the western armies with control over all the troops left to oppose Sherman.

Johnston's first intent was to concentrate at Fayetteville, North Carolina. Beauregard, with the vanguard of Lee's corps under Major General Carter L. Stevenson, was at Charlotte, Stewart's corps was at Newberry, South Carolina, and Cheatham's strung out between Augusta and Newberry. Hardee's command was dispersed along Sherman's right flank from Cheraw to Florence, South Carolina. The 1st Georgia Sharpshooters were with Jackson's brigade, of course, which now, with Stovall's brigade, made up General Henry Clayton's division in Stevenson's corps. Lieutenant Johnston's report from Tupelo on 25 January had shown that Jackson's brigade was in Clayton's division by that date. Perhaps in final response to Henry Jackson's plea of 10 December, or at General Bate's request, one of Hood's final acts as commander of the Army of Tennessee was to remove Jackson's brigade from Bate's division to be replaced by the Louisiana brigade of General Randall Gibson.

By 9 February the brigade and division were at or near Orangeburg Court House, South Carolina. Lieutenant Colonel Gordon was the acting brigade commander, and for a day at least, he was the acting division commander because a more senior Georgia colonel who was acting in General Clayton's place was too intoxicated to give or receive orders. The brigade was a sad shadow of itself. On 23 February it had an effective strength of 81 with 142 total present for duty; on 27 February the effective strength had increased to

101, but there were only 122 present. General Beauregard wrote that the command had been given a brief period to recruit but had to return to duty quickly.[56]

Johnston's attempts to thwart Sherman were hardly more successful than his predecessor's. On 4 March he moved his headquarters to Fayetteville. He planned to strike one of Sherman's two wings, which were operating at some distance from each other, and to do so he decided to concentrate his troops at Smithfield. Sherman reached Fayetteville on 10 March. Johnston moved to Raleigh and ordered Hardee's corps, already at Fayetteville, to fall back but, before doing so, Hardee gave battle at Averasboro on 16 March, losing 700 men and gaining no advantage.

Meanwhile, General Braxton Bragg, commanding a small force of 5,000 men at Goldsboro, concocted a plan to strike at John Schofield's army advancing inland toward Goldboro from Wilmington and Fort Fisher. Bragg's strength was far inferior to Schofield's. He asked for troops from Johnston, who assented to this dilution of his concentration. Johnston sent Bragg the two small divisions of Lee's corps, only 3,000 men, that had just arrived at Smithfield from Charlotte and were normally commanded by Carter Stevenson. For this expedition they were led by General Daniel Harvey Hill who was the senior commander at Smithfield when they arrived.

In the ensuing battle of Kinston, North Carolina, on 8 March, Bragg aligned his 8,000 men against the Union XXIII Corps, 13,000 strong, of General Jacob Cox, the same opponent the Army of Tennessee had faced at Franklin, Tennessee, in November. Bragg placed the division of General Robert Hoke, his original force, on his right, and Hill's "corps" on his left. Hill was to hold in place while Hoke attacked the Union left. When Hoke's attack appeared to be making some headway, Hill was to make a frontal assault on the Union right. The purpose was to drive Cox back, delaying a link up with Sherman.[57]

Hoke's attack met with initial success and he flushed out a small unit of Yankees in advance of their main line. Mistaking this for a general retreat of the Federal force, Hoke called on Bragg to send Hill in pursuit. Hill went off on this pointless mission on Bragg's command and nothing of substance was accomplished beyond Hoke taking 1,000 prisoners. On the ninth, several Confederate actions were initiated but with no positive results.

By the next morning Johnston was calling for his troops to be returned. Bragg complied, but not before Hoke tried another flank movement to his right. Hill was to make a demonstration on the left but not to attack the main line because of "the unwillingness of the men to attack earthworks, their experience in the late campaign not being favorable to such an undertaking." Hill's line advanced as required and took the Yankee skirmish line. As the action continued, Stovall's and Jackson's brigades, which had behaved admirably on the eighth, broke "causelessly." Pettus's brigade and the skirmishers of Hill's division were left exposed in the face of a large Federal force and withdrew.

Hill had 1,300 men under command at Kinston and lost 130. Jackson's Georgia brigade went into action with only 76 effectives; Stovall's had 340. Jackson's brigade suffered ten wounded and one missing, all of them officers. This was both good news and bad for higher level commanders: the junior officers were still willing to lead their men in action but the men refused to fight. It does appear that Hill might have been scape-goating when he blamed his need to retire on the failure of Clayton's brigades. The defection of 400 men from a line of 1,300 would not seem to be disastrous if all the rest held steady, as Hill said they did. In his report, Hill named and thanked all of his staff officers and division and brigade commanders, including General Clayton, but he deliberately omitted mentioning Colonels Henry C. Kellogg and Gordon, leaders of the two offending brigades.[58]

Johnston had his available forces concentrated at Smithfield by mid-March. Bragg provided about 6,500 infantry from the Department of North Carolina, Hardee brought 7,500 infantry from the Department of South Carolina and Georgia, and Alexander Stewart led the 4,000 men of the Army of Tennessee that had reached Johnston's army. Wade Hampton commanded about 5,000 cavalry, including Wheeler's corps. Beauregard had under his charge another 6,000 to 8,000 men protecting the railroad from Danville, Virginia, into the Carolinas. These included two divisions of Cheatham's corps and several brigades of Stewart's. Under Stewart's command with Johnston were Stephen D. Lee's former corps, led by D. H. Hill; Stewart's corps, temporarily entrusted to W. W. Loring; and fragments of Cheatham's corps, commanded by General Bate.

Clayton's division was still part of Hill's corps but there had been some changes in command. Following the battle of Kinston and Hill's displeasure with the behavior of the Georgia troops, Colonel Gordon was relieved from the command of Jackson's brigade and reverted to leading the combined 1st Confederate/66th Georgia Regiment. His replacement was Lieutenant Colonel Osceola Kyle, a lawyer from Coosa County, Alabama, who was nominally an officer of the 46th Alabama in Pettus's brigade of Stevenson's division. Kyle and most of his regiment had been captured at the battle of Baker's Creek in Mississippi in May 1863 and later exchanged.

Major William C. Lester of the 43rd Georgia ascended to the command of Stovall's brigade, although it is not clear whether that happened before or after the battle of Bentonville. In Jackson's Georgia brigade, besides Gordon and his regiment, the units and commanders were 29th and 30th Georgia under Captain Thomas L. Langston of the 66th Georgia, and 25th Georgia and 1st Battalion Sharpshooters led by Captain William J. Whitsitt of the 1st Confederate. On 13 March the brigade had a present for duty strength of 7 officers and 116 men, the effective strength was 103, and the aggregate number of men present was 164.[59]

By 18 March Johnston had finally learned enough of Sherman's intentions to formulate a plan of battle. He would strike at the isolated Union left wing under General Henry Warner Slocum as it marched from Fayetteville to Goldsboro. Johnston planned to hit one corps of Slocum's column at Bentonville, using Hardee's and Stewart's assembled troops for a flank attack while Bragg's division acted as a blocking force on the road. Everything depended on Johnston's ability to bring his forces together at the designated place in a timely manner.

Johnston laid his trap on 19 March, 2 miles south of Bentonville. Stewart's miniscule army was on the Confederate right, facing the road, Hardee's corps was to make up the center when it arrived, and Bragg was already in place across the road, forming the Confederate left. The Union XIV Corps of three divisions, under General Jefferson C. Davis, marched forward until it ran into Bragg's position, but Hardee was not yet in place. Bragg easily repelled the first Federal advance, then asked for reinforcements. Rather than having Hardee take his appointed place, Johnston sent one of his arriving divisions to Bragg. When the other division came up, Hardee launched the main attack with his own and Stewart's troops but it was too late. Two Yankee divisions had had time to deploy, Bragg delayed his participation in the attack, and Hardee frittered away his resources in pursuing elements of Davis's corps that had already been driven from the field.[60]

Hill's (Lee's) corps at Bentonville was near the far right of the Southern line with approximately 2,700 men in his three divisions. Bate, commanding Cheatham's corps, was on his right and Loring, in command of Stewart's corps, on his left. Clayton's division had doubled its effective strength since Kinston with the addition of Alpheus Baker's brigade and brought 867 men to the field. Jackson's brigade could muster only 7 officers and 121 men present for duty, 108 effectives present, and an aggregate strength of 174.[61]

During the early part of the battle Stovall's brigade drove off a weak Union attack on its front. In mid-afternoon a general advance was called for and the corps advanced in two lines with Jackson's and Stovall's brigades in the first line. Resistance was light and the lines advanced through two fortified positions before being ordered to halt and reform. At this time Bate reported the enemy massing in his front and Clayton's division was moved to its right to cover Bate's left. Then, through a miscommunication which seems typical of Southern operations, several units were pulled out of line without the corps commander being notified. The Yankees discovered the error and attacked on the flank through the gap. Only vigorous action diverted a disaster. Clayton's two Georgia brigades, Jackson's and Stovall's, counter-attacked the Yankee unit until it broke and retreated. One more Northern attack at nightfall was also repulsed.[62]

An anecdote from the battlefield of Bentonville underscores the animosity held toward General Bate by many of the Georgia troops after the campaigns for Atlanta and Nashville, and the general's response. The reader will remember the resentment harbored by General Henry R. Jackson, expressed in his letter to General Cheatham on 10 December 1864. Troops of other divisions had come to the habit of derisive cat-calling when around Bate's men. The favorite cry was "Lie down, Bate, we're going to bust a cap," or some such unpleasantry, in recognition of the misfortunes of his division at Franklin, Nashville, and elsewhere.

At the time of the incident described above, when Bate reported the enemy massing in his front at Bentonville, he was riding across a field where the 63rd Georgia of Cleburne's division lay hugging the ground under Yankee fire. General Bate inquired what regiment it was and the answer was given. "Why, boys," said Bate, "you lie mighty close. I came near to riding over you without seeing you. Never tell Bate to lie down any more." In addition to great personal bravery, the general also had a biting sense of humor.[63]

Hill reported losses of 244 in Clayton's division and commended Colonel Kyle in his report; a return for losses from 19–21 March showed 21 killed, 171 wounded and 98 missing in the division, for a total of 290. The only known casualties in Jackson's (Kyle's) brigade were one officer and one private of the 66th Georgia, reported in a local newspaper as wounded in hospital. Johnston remained in position for two days while the rest of Sherman's army converged on him. Finally, in the early morning hours of 22 March, he admitted he could do no more and drew off toward Smithfield. From there he still hoped to retard Sherman's advance or to join forces with Lee if the latter retreated from Virginia.[64]

Following his withdrawal from the battlefield at Bentonville, Johnston concentrated his forces at Smithfield where he was joined by the rest of the troops arriving by rail from Mississippi. He reorganized his army into three corps under Generals Hardee, A. P. Stewart, and S. D. Lee, and named it the Army of Tennessee once more. On 9 April the skeletons of brigades that had survived Franklin and Nashville were reformed as consolidated battalions or regiments. The once proud Walker-Wilson-Stevens-Jackson brigade was reduced to the six-company 1st Confederate Battalion consisting of the remnants of the 1st Confederate Georgia, 25th, 29th, 30th, and 66th Georgia Regiments and the 1st Georgia Sharpshooter Battalion. The combined force amounted to fewer than 500 men and was commanded by Captain William J. Whitsitt. It took its place in the brigade of General Robert J. Henderson, Stevenson's division, Lee's corps.[65]

Sometime early in April, Captain Horace Twyman rejoined the army. As late as 30 March he had been at home in Virginia. He still suffered from his wounds and needed a stick to walk. No doubt he was watching events in the Carolinas and as the army drew nearer to him, he mustered the energy to join its ranks.[66]

On 13 April 1865 General Johnston asked for terms from General Sherman, and on 26 April signed a convention at Greensboro, North Carolina, surrendering his army of some 36,000 men (of whom, Johnston claimed, only 15,000 were effectives). All of them were paroled the next day. The National Archives file slips of the 1st Confederate Battalion show that 344 officers and men, including an unknown number of effectives, were surrendered and paroled in that unit. How many others may have left the army since 9 April cannot be determined. Of those who remained, only a dozen were members of the former 1st Sharpshooter Battalion. Present on the last day of their war were Captain Horace D. Twyman, Assistant Surgeon Cornelius T. Ford, Ordnance Sergeant Nathaniel T. Brewner [Brunner], and Privates William M. Elder, W. H. Gassett, H. Licet, P. Madden, B. B. McDermott, Henry C. Melton, John Morley, M. M. Murrow, and Benjamin F. Peyton. Another soldier, Private M. L. Farris, was probably Quartermaster Sergeant Mortimer L. Faries. Captain Twyman was commander of F Company, while the private soldiers were in companies B and E.[67]

POSTLUDE

THE VETERANS

As the Confederate armies disbanded, the soldiers made their way home. Arthur Shaaff was paroled at Augusta on 1 May 1865. Records indicate he was still on General Bate's staff at the time. A notice in a Savannah newspaper on 8 May reported, "Major Arthur Shaff arrived here this morning by land from Augusta." On 11 August he reported to the provost marshal in Washington, DC, that he was "stopping at Dr. Shaaff, 1st Street, Georgetown, D. C." More officers came home to Savannah during the month, Robert Wayne on 12 May and Alfred Bryan on the sixteenth, possibly after being paroled in North Carolina. Bryan might still have been serving as adjutant of Jackson's brigade because his rank was given as major. Wayne could have accompanied General Hardee's forces when they evacuated Savannah in December 1864. From northern prisoner of war camps others were released, among them Cornelius Hardy on 7 June, Cuyler King on 16 June, Horace Crane and Charles Schlatter on 17 June, and Henry C. Kittles on 20 June. David Forehand also was released on 17 June. He was more fortunate than his two brothers, Berry and William. Berry was killed at Morris Island, South Carolina, in 1863 and William died a prisoner at Point Lookout, Maryland, in April 1865.[1]

The veterans began to pick up the pieces of their lives and to contribute to the building of the New South. By July 1865 Robert Footman had been elected president of the Oglethorpe Lodge of the International Order of Odd Fellows; by November Benjamin Hardee was advertising as agent of the New York-Savannah Steamship Company. Horace Crane went into business with his father and then became a commercial banker. Before his death in 1920 at the age of seventy-nine, he was vice president of the Citizens and Southern Bank, had married twice, and was the father of five children.[2]

General Henry R. Jackson returned to Savannah where he practiced law and was president of the Georgia Historical Society for twenty-five years. In 1866 he took for his second wife Cuyler King's older sister, Florence. During the administration of President Grover Cleveland, he was minister to Mexico. Jackson died in 1898. Robert H. Anderson, founder and first commander of the 1st Georgia Sharpshooters, rose to be brigadier general leading a cavalry brigade under General Joe Wheeler by the end of the war. In 1867 he was appointed police chief of Savannah and held that post until his death in 1888, age fifty-two.[3]

In 1869 John H. Estill, himself a wounded and disabled veteran and owner of the Savannah *Morning News*, published the *Historical Record of the City of Savannah*. Besides a history of the city, it contained a "Roll of Honor" of Savannah men who had fought in the war. Dozens of sharpshooter officers and men, both living and dead, were included; curiously, some well-known names were left out. Neither Arthur Shaaff's nor Alfred Bryan's names were on the roll. Understandably, some members of the battalion who were not Savannah citizens were also omitted.[4]

Many veterans married in the post-war years. In Savannah, former hospital steward Henry Lindner married a widow in 1866, Horace Crane contracted his first marriage, and Robert Wayne married the cousin of Alfred Bryan in 1867. Former Ordnance Sergeant Nicholas T. Brunner married a South Carolina woman in 1868, and former 1st Sergeant Dominique Brown married the widow Barbara Heamerle in 1875.[5]

Elsewhere in Georgia, Cornelius Hardy married a widow in Jasper County in 1870. He farmed until his early death in 1886, brought on by a "disease contracted in the service." George W. Garner married in 1866. He fathered five children and farmed for the next fifty-five years. After the death of his first wife in 1917, Garner remarried in 1919 at the age of seventy-seven. He died in 1921, aged seventy-nine. Hiram Bennett returned to Appling County where he worked as a railroad agent and a woodsman, married twice and fathered several children. After injuring his good leg in a farming accident, he took to his bed and never rose again. The family said he died of "milk leg." Sheppard Foster recovered from his wound and was a businessman and planter in Georgia and Florida after the war. He was a druggist in Savannah and Thomaston for some time and finally settled in Eastman where he spent his last years.[6]

William Lawrence Thomas died in 1912 in Clayton County where he had farmed and operated a country store; he was sixty-nine years old. David Culpepper farmed in Dooly County until his death in 1893, age seventy. James A. Thornton, the disabled veteran, married as soon as the war was over. He became an minister in the Primitive Baptist church and died in 1900, aged about sixty. A strange case was that of Henry Schmidt. After the war he moved from Augusta to Savannah with his family and stayed there for more than twenty years. In 1889 he traveled to Abbeville, South Carolina, to scout out business opportunities. He wrote to his wife several times from Abbeville but after three months the letters stopped and he was never heard from again. He was about fifty-four when he disappeared.[7]

William Henry Ross returned to Macon where he married and resumed business with his father as a cotton merchant. He was a member of the state constitutional convention in 1877, president of the Macon chamber of commerce, and president of a loan and trust association. When he died the day before Washington's Birthday in 1902 after a lengthy illness, the city postponed its annual holiday celebration in order to conduct his funeral with fitting ceremony. His widow died in 1910.[8]

Cuyler King moved to Louisiana after the war and operated a plantation with his brother, John Floyd King. Later, after living in Texas, he returned to Georgia and settled in Macon where he engaged in the cotton business until a few months before his death in 1913. He married in 1888 and fathered a son and a daughter. His widow, Henrietta Nisbet King, lived until 1944. Cuyler's son, Henry Lord Page King, born in 1895, was a US Army general in World War II. His son, H. L. P. King, Jr., now deceased, was an engineer with the Potomac Electric Power Company in Washington, DC. His widow, Eileen, has been the source of much King family information. Another of Cuyler's grandsons, Ranald T. Adams, Jr., is a graduate of the US Military Academy and retired from the Air Force as a lieutenant general.[9]

Others of the veterans also prospered in later life. Alfred Hartridge became a stock broker and an executive of the Savannah streetcar company. He lived in Savannah and New York and accumulated considerable wealth and influence before his death in 1913. The three Kittles brothers of Screven County also did well. Henry read law under former General Ambrose R. Wright in Augusta, became a lawyer, a planter and a county court judge. He died in 1897. William and Peter were partners in a mercantile concern in Sylvania that continued business into the twentieth century.[10]

John Derst, the army baker, founded a bakery in Savannah in 1867 that continues today under his name, Captain John Derst. He became a member of the German Volunteers, a Savannah company, captain of a volunteer fire company, and city alderman. In 1913 Derst revealed that when he came home to Savannah after his army service he saved the flag of his old company, the DeKalb Rifles, from the occupying forces by hiding it in the Planters Hotel. He called it his most prized possession. That flag has been preserved down to modern times and now belongs to the United Daughters of the Confederacy, Chapter 2. Derst died in Savannah 15 July 1928, aged ninety, possibly the last Confederate veteran in Savannah.[11]

George C. Dent and his son James returned to their debt-ridden rice plantation in Glynn County where they struggled for years to pay off their creditors. After George died in March 1884, James carried on alone. When he died in 1913 his widow, Miriam Cohen, and his son, Gratz, turned the place into a dairy farm that prospered sufficiently to satisfy all claims by the time it closed in 1942. James and Miriam's daughter, Ophelia Dent, willed the property to the state of Georgia at her death in 1973, aged eighty-six. Hofwyl-Broadfield is now a state historic park.[12]

Dr. John M. Dent resumed his medical practice after leaving service. The 1870 census found him in Berzelia, Georgia, on the boundary between Richmond and Columbia counties. When he died at age eighty-eight in Waynesboro, Georgia, in 1922, the newspaper obituary detailed his distinguished career but did not mention the sharpshooters.[13]

Arthur Shaaff lived and worked as a bookkeeper in Washington for several years. Then a notice appeared in the *Savannah Daily Morning News*, 28 March 1870: "The friends and acquaintances of Captain H. J. Dickerson and family and of Mr. and Mrs. Arthur Shaaff are invited to attend the funeral of the latter from the home of the former, Tuesday the 29th inst." Lizzie was dead. She left behind one child. The 1870 census for Savannah lists Arthur Shaaff, age three, born in DC, living with Henry M. Branch, clerk in store. "Henry" Branch was Hamilton Branch, married to Elizabeth Shaaff's sister, Marie Eugenia Dickerson.[14]

After Lizzie's death, Arthur spent his last years as trustee of the Southern Life Insurance Company in Savannah. His death followed hers by not many years. He died suddenly and unexpectedly at the Pavilion Hotel in Savannah in July 1874. The register of Laurel Grove Cemetery in Savannah shows Elizabeth L. Shaaff, died 22 March 1870, age twenty-seven, buried 29 March 1870, a native of Savannah, but "died in Georgetown, D. C.," and Arthur Shaaff, died 8 July 1874, age forty-two years and eight months, buried 9 July 1874, a native of Georgetown, DC, residence: Bull and South Broad Streets, Savannah.[15]

A few members of the sharpshooters preceded Shaaff in death, most followed. Many were so young one must conclude they were worn down by their wartime experiences. Alfred Bryan died of consumption in 1875, only thirty-seven years old, and Robert Wayne died on his Liberty County plantation in 1882, forty-one years old. His younger brother Thomas S. Wayne died in 1886, age forty. The Waynes were not long-lived: their sister Julia, the wife of Alfred Hartridge, died at age forty-six in 1884. Lawrence Werm died in 1881, age fifty-six; Benjamin Hardee in an infirmary in 1889, age fifty-four. Dominic Brown killed himself with a pistol in 1882; his age was given as seventy but that would appear to be incorrect. Dr. John T. McFarland died in 1888, age fifty-one, after a distinguished career as director of public health in Savannah.[16]

Almost all the former soldiers were enthusiastic members of the United Confederate Veterans. Many held rank in that organization far superior to any they had as active duty soldiers. Others also embellished their military careers with the passage of years. Private Elbert Mathis was a good and amusing example. As related in these pages, his record shows that he was wounded slightly at Chickamauga and captured in north Georgia in June 1864. Mathis was returned from prison camp to Virginia for exchange in March 1865, probably due to sickness or debility. Despite that, he fathered ten children and lived to be seventy-nine before his death in 1915. An account of his life published later tells that he was captured at Chickamauga, exchanged in April 1864, and thereafter was a member of the Confederate "secret service" until the end of the war.[17]

Some of the old sharpshooters traveled far from Georgia. The widow of J. F. Taylor, formerly of the Irwin Invincibles of Henry County, Alabama, wrote from Chatham, Louisiana, in 1916 that she would like to hear from his comrades to help in documenting her pension claim. Moses Taylor, who was born in 1839 and paroled at Griffin, Georgia, in 1865, died in Carthage, Texas, on 4 January 1926. Other veterans in Texas were Hiram Ricketson, who died in Llano County in 1914, one day before his seventy-eighth birthday, and James Marion Jarrell, who married twice, fathered fourteen children, and died in Childress County in 1908, age sixty-two. A man named N. B. Sadler, who gave his place of birth as New York, was enumerated in Pascagoula, Mississippi, in the 1880 census. He may have been Bayard Sadler, former lieutenant of the sharpshooters. Horace Twyman was also enumerated in 1880 in his ancestral home in Virginia, with his mother, wife, and four children.[18]

John C., twenty-six, and Amos H. Winn, twenty, and their cousin, Allen B. Winn, about twenty, enlisted together in the Campbell Sharpshooters in Campbell County in September, 1861. Their company became part of the 30th Georgia Volunteers. The three young men transferred into Major Anderson's battalion in August 1862. All three fell sick in Mississippi in summer 1863. Allen gave up on army life and deserted when Walker's division made the move to Chickamauga in August 1863. John succumbed to typhoid fever in a hospital in Marietta two months later. Amos remained with his unit and was second corporal of D Company but absent sick in August 1864. After the war he moved to Paulding County, married, and took up farming. On 26 December 1929 Amos Hamilton Winn passed away at the Confederate Soldiers Home in Atlanta, aged about eighty-nine. He was buried in Douglasville.[19]

The last known survivor of the 1st Sharpshooters was William Jasper "Billy" Parrott. Contrary to information contained in his service record, Parrott did not die in Colorado in October 1865. Instead, he deserted from the US Army, probably from Fort Morgan, and turned up at his home in Fayette County, Georgia, two years later. He married and sired a large family. Billy died in Troup County on 29 March 1932, aged about eighty-eight years. His wife had preceded him in death by a month.[20]

In 1914, a brief item appeared in *Confederate Veteran* magazine informing certain Confederate officers of Georgia who had also served in the US Army that they might be entitled to longevity pay due them, their heirs or estates but never disbursed. One of the three named was William D. Smith, husband of Cuyler King's sister, Georgia, another was Arthur Shaaff. Alas, Arthur Shaaff the younger, the son of Arthur and Lizzie, had died in Savannah in 1911 of liver disease, age forty-four, and was buried in the Dickinson family vault with his parents. The only relative listed in his obituary was his aunt, Mrs. H. M. Branch.[21]

Arthur Shaaff, Jr., was not the only member of his family to bear the name. Although it has no direct bearing on this unit history, the author wishes to include here a piece of Shaaff family genealogy that might otherwise go unnoticed.

The Virginia forces in the Civil War included a young soldier named Arthur Shaaff Johns, born in Georgetown, DC, in 1843 to Jane Shaaff and her husband, an Episcopal clergyman named John Johns. "Jane" was Margaretta Jane, sister of Arthur Shaaff, the lawyer. Her husband, John Johns, rose through the ranks of the church to be president of William and Mary College and bishop of Virginia before his death in 1876.

Her son, Arthur S. Johns, first cousin to the Confederate Major Shaaff, was accepted as a cadet at the Virginia Military Institute in 1861, but he was dismissed in October 1862, for violation of regulations. Arthur served subsequently in the 10th Virginia Artillery as lieutenant, acting ordnance officer, and ordnance sergeant. He surrendered at Danville, Virginia, in April 1865, as part of the Appomattox agreement. Young Arthur entered seminary in 1873 and thereafter spent his life as an Episcopal priest. He died in Rockville, Maryland, in 1921, possibly the last to bear the name of the battlefield commander of the 1st Battalion Georgia Sharpshooters.[22]

NOTES

INTRODUCTION

[1]Dana M. Mangham, "Roster of the 2nd Georgia Battalion Sharpshooters, C.S.A.," *Georgia Genealogical Magazine* 35/1–2 (Winter/Spring 1995): 65; William R. Montgomery, *Georgia Sharpshooter: The Civil War Diary and Letters of William Rhadamanthus Montgomery*, ed. George Montgomery, Jr. (Macon GA: Mercer University Press, 1997) 83; "The Battle Near Fredericksburg,"*Savannah Republican,* 27 May 1863, Joseph T. Derry, *Georgia*, extended ed., vol.7 of *Confederate Military History*, ed. Clement A. Evans(1899; reprint, Wilmington NC: Broadfoot Publishing, 1987–1989) 482–83.

[2] Savannah *Daily Morning News*, 30 July 1862.

[3]Dana M. Mangham, *"Oh, For a Touch of the Vanished Hand": Discovering a Southern Family and the Civil War* (Murfreesboro TN: Southern Heritage Press, 2000) 56; Frederick L. Ray, "Shock Troops of the South," *America's Civil War* (July 2002): 36–37; William R. Montgomery to his mother and sister, 7 May, 1863, in Montgomery, *Georgia Sharpshooter*, 84.

[4]Theo. H. Winn to the editor, *Macon Telegraph,* 17 August 1867, reprinted in the *Augusta Chronicle and Sentinel*, 3 May 1868.

[5]Nathaniel Cheairs Hughes, Jr., *General William J. Hardee, Old Reliable* (Baton Rouge LA: Louisiana State University Press, 1965) 281n21.

[6] *Savannah Republican,* 22 February 1864.

[7]Ray, "Shock Troops of the South," 40.

[8]Henry R. Jackson to Benjamin F. Cheatham, 10 December 1864, B. F. Cheatham Papers (microfilm), Tennessee State Library and Archives, Nashville TN; George C. Dent obituary, undated newspaper clipping [March 1884] provided by William D. Temple, Brunswick, Ga.; R. Cuyler King obituary, *Macon Telegraph,* 1 July 1913; Derry, *Georgia*, vol.7 of *Confederate Military History*, 661.

PRELUDE

[1]Alvin L. Duckett, *John Forsyth, Political Tactician* (Athens: University of Georgia Press, 1962) 6; H. B., "Alfred Iverson," in *Dictionary of Georgia Biography*, 2 vols., ed. Kenneth Coleman and Stephen Gurr (Athens: University of Georgia Press, 1983); Etta B. Worsley, *Columbus on the Chattahoochee* (Columbus GA: Columbus Office Supply Co., 1951) 281; Nancy Telfair, *The Columbus, Georgia, Centenary, 1828–1928* (Columbus: Historical Publishing Co., 1929) 97. Strictly speaking, Alfred Iverson, Jr., son of the first wife, was not blood kin to Shaaff but it was "all in the family."

[2]National Law Enforcement Officers Memorial Fund, Inc., "America's Earliest Law Enforcement Casualties" (press release), 5 August 2002.

[3]Shaaff Family File, Walter C. Hartridge, Jr. Collection, collection 1349, Georgia Historical Society, Savannah GA.

[4]George W. Cullum, *Biographical Register of the Officers and Graduates of the United States Military Academy*, 3rd ed., 2 vols. (Boston: Houghton Mifflin, 1891) 1531; US War Department, *The War of the Rebellion, A Compilation of the Official Records of the Union and Confederate Armies*, 128 vols. (Washington, DC: US Government Printing Office, 1880–1901) ser. 1, vol. 30, pt. 4, pp. 491–92, vol. 42, pt. 3, p. 1238, 1364, vol. 46, pt. 2, p. 1179; ser. 4, vol. 1, pp. 575, 1035–36 (Hereafter *OR*. All citations from *OR* are series 1 unless otherwise specified; citations from Cullum refer to graduation numbers, not page numbers.); National Park Service, Civil War Soldiers and Sailors System <http://www.itd.nps.gov/cwss/soldiers.htm.>; Shaaff Family File, Walter C. Hartridge, Jr. Collection, Georgia Historical Society, Savannah GA.

[5]National Archives (NA), Microfilm Publication M233 ("Register of Enlistments in the United States Army, 1798–1914"), roll 28, "Register of Enlistments in the United States Army, 1859–1863," vol. 57, p. 28.

[6]NA, M432 ("1850 Census"), roll 284, "Baltimore, Maryland," 105; NA, M567 ("Letters Received by the Adjutant General's Office, 1822–1860"), roll 527, item S483, Shaaff to the Adjutant General, 5 July 1855; NA, M665 ("Returns from Regular Army Infantry Regiments, June 1821–December 1916"), roll 45, "4th Infantry, January 1860–December 1866"); Francis B. Heitman, *Biographical Register and Dictionary of the United States Army, 1789–1903*, 2 vols. (Washington, DC: US Government Printing Office, 1903) 1:875; William Preston Johnston, *The Life of Gen. Albert Sidney Johnston* (New York: D. Appleton, 1878) 280; Henry C. Wayne to Arthur Shaaff, 16 February 1861; Henry C. Wayne to Alfred Iverson, 16 February 1861; Henry C. Wayne to Charles J. Williams, 28 March 1861, Adjutant General's Letter Books (typescripts), book B44, pt. 1, Georgia Division of Archives and History, Atlanta, Georgia; NA, M266 ("Compiled Service Records of Confederate Soldiers Who Served in Organizations from the State of Georgia" [Hereafter "Confederate Soldiers from Georgia."]), roll 150, "1st Battalion, Sharpshooters," "Arthur Shaaff Service Record"; NA, M347 ("Unfiled Papers and Slips Belonging to Confederate Compiled Service Records" [Hereafter "Unfiled Papers and Slips."]), roll 356, "Arthur Shaaff File"; Shaaff Family File; *OR*, vol. 3, p. 706; vol. 50, pt. 1, p. 566; vol. 52, pt. 2, p. 145.

CHAPTER 1

[1]Public Laws of the Confederate States of America, Passed at the First Congress; 1862. First Session, chap. LXXII. --An Act to organize Battalions of Sharp Shooters, April 21, 1862, Documenting the American South, University of North Carolina Libraries, Chapel Hill, N. C. (electronic edition). <http://docsouth.unc.edu/statutes/statutes.html.>

[2]US War Department, *The War of the Rebellion, A Compilation of the Official Records of the Union and Confederate Armies* 128 vols. (Washington, DC: US Government Printing Office, 1880–1901) ser. 4, vol. 1, pp. 1110–11. Hereafter *OR*.

All citation from *OR* are series 1 unless otherwise specified.

[3]Robert H. Anderson to J. R. Waddy, 1 June 1862, with undated endorsement by J. C. Pemberton, Department of South Carolina and Georgia Collection, Eleanor S. Brockenbrough Library, Museum of the Confederacy, Richmond VA.

[4]Orders, Department of South Carolina and Georgia, November 1861–September 1862, War Department Collection of Confederate Records, RG 109, chap. 2, vol.42, National Archives, Washington, DC; George A. Mercer File, Department of South Carolina and Georgia Collection, Museum of the Confederacy, Richmond VA.

[5]George C. Dent and Alfred L. Hartridge to Waddy, 4 June 1862; Arthur Shaaff and George H. Johnston, Jr., to Waddy, 7 June 1862; S. W. Lawrence to Waddy, 12 June 1862; Anderson to Waddy, 6 June 1862; and Anderson to Waddy, 16 June 1862, Department of South Carolina and Georgia Collection, Museum of the Confederacy, Richmond VA.

[6]R. H. Anderson to J. R. Waddy, 11 June 1862, Department of South Carolina and Georgia Collection, Museum of the Confederacy, Richmond VA.

[7]John Pemberton to Samuel Cooper, 20 June, 11 July 1862, Letters Sent and Received by Gen. J. C. Pemberton, Mar.–Sept. 1862, RG 109, chap. 2, vol.21, Confederate Records, National Archives.

[8]National Archives, mircofilm pubications, M266 ("Compiled Service Records of Confederate Soldiers Who Served in Organizations from the State of Georgia" [Hereafter "Confederate Soldiers from Georgia"]), roll 148, "R. H. Anderson Service Record"; R. H. Anderson to J. R. Waddy, 8 July 1862, Department of South Carolina and Georgia Collection, Museum of the Confederacy, Richmond VA.

[9]*Atlanta Confederacy*, 18 July 1862; Savannah *Daily Morning News*, 30 July 1862; James D. Waddell to wife, 20 June 1862, Waddell-Setze-McClatchey Family Papers, MS 842, Atlanta History Center, Atlanta GA.

[10]Special Order No. 116, 23 July 1862, Orders, Department of South Carolina and Georgia, November 1861—September 1862, RG 109, chap. 2, vol.42; NA, M266 ("Confederate Soldiers from Georgia"), roll 133, "1st [Olmstead's] Georgia, Muster Roll Cards for 1st Company A"; roll 142, Wetter service record; roll 148, "Caption Card for Company B, 1st Sharpshooter Battalion"; Gordon Burns Smith, *The Companies*, vol. 4 of *History of the Georgia Militia, 1783–1861*, 4 vols. (Milledgeville GA: Boyd Publishing, 2000–2001) 269; F. D. Lee and J. L. Agnew, *Historical Record of the City of Savannah* (Savannah GA: Morning News Steam-power Press, 1869) 116; William E. Christman, *Undaunted: The History of Fort McAllister, Georgia* (Atlanta: Georgia Department of Natural Resources, 1996) 5–7, 10, 11–12, 14–17; *OR*, vol. 6, pp. 286, 304; *Savannah Republican,* 30 July 1862. The first two actions at Fort McAllister are not mentioned in *OR*, but they are described in US Navy Department, *Official Records of the Union and Confederate Navies in the War of the Rebellion*, 30 vols. (Washington, DC: US Government Printing Office, 1896–1922) 13:161–62, 221. Hereafter referred to as *ORN*.

[11]Special Order No. 108, 15 July 1862, Orders, Department of South Carolina and Georgia, November 1861–September 1862, RG 109, chap. 2, vol.42, Confederate Records, National Archives.

[12] NA, M266 ("Confederate Soldiers from Georgia"), roll 148, "Caption Cards for 1st Battalion, Sharpshooters, Battalion Return for August 1862"; George C. Dent File, Walter C. Hartridge, Jr. Collection, Georgia Historical Society, Savannah GA. The caption card erroneously shows that B Company was formed from the 32nd and 54th Regiments and the Savannah Guard Battalion. It names no regiments from which C Company was formed.

[13] Lillian Henderson, ed., *Roster of the Confederate Soldiers of Georgia, 1861–1865*, 6 vols. (Hapeville GA: Longino and Porter, 1955–1962) 3:123; http://www.henrylightinfantry.com/history.htm; NA, rolls 148–50, M266 ("Confederate Soldiers from Georgia") C. Bishop, J. McBride, S. Rhymes, J. F. Taylor, B. Tharpe, W. Wilcox service records.

[14] R. H. Anderson to J. R. Waddy, 29 July, 13 August 1862, Department of South Carolina and Georgia Collection, Museum of the Confederacy, Richmond VA.

[15] For a discussion of the formation and service of the Georgia State Troops, see Russell K. Brown, *To the Manner Born: The Life of General William H. T. Walker* (Athens: University of Georgia Press, 1994) 119–28.

[16] George A. Mercer Diary (typescript), 19 August 1862, Mercer Family Papers, Georgia Historical Society, Savannah GA; H. W. Mercer to J. R. Waddy, 16 August 1862, Department of South Carolina and Georgia Collection, Museum of the Confederacy, Richmond VA; General Orders, Department of South Carolina, Georgia and Florida, July 1862–Jan. 1864, RG 109, chap. 2, vol. 43, Confederate Records, National Archives; Henderson, *Confederate Soldiers of Georgia*, 5:638, 719, 720; Savannah *Daily Morning News*, 23 July 1862.

[17] H. W. Mercer to J. R. Waddy, 16 August 1862, Department of South Carolina and Georgia Collection, Museum of the Confederacy, Richmond VA.

[18] William Moody to his wife, 26 August 1862, William Moody Papers, MS 4903z, Southern Historical Collection, University of North Carolina, Chapel Hill; Henderson, *Confederate Soldiers of Georgia*, 5:727.

[19] Mercer Diary, 19 August, 30 October 1862, Mercer Family Papers, Georgia Historical Society, Savannah GA; Descriptive Roll of the 28 Men furnished by 30th Regiment Ga. Vol. For the 1st Battn. Ga. Sharpshooters, George C. Dent file, Walter C. Hartridge Jr. Collection, collection 1349, Georgia Historical Society, Savannah GA; 1859 Savannah Cith Directory (http://www.rootsweb.com/~gachath2/1859SavCity Dir.html); Walter J. Fraser, Jr. *Savannah in the Old South* (Athens: University of Georgia Press, 2003) 326; NA, M266 ("Confederate Soldiers from Georgia"), roll 148, "Battalion Return for August 1862," "Company D Return for September 1862" and "Muster Rolls for August 1862 and October 1862."

[20] NA, M266 ("Confederate Soldiers from Georgia"), roll 148, "Company D Muster Roll for August 1862"; *OR*, vol. 14, p. 625; William Moody to his wife, 26 August 1862, Moody Papers, Chapel Hill NC; William S. Smedlund, *Camp Fires of Georgia's Troops* (Lithonia GA: self-published, 1995) 49. The Grove is the upper extension of the Little Ogeechee.

[21] George W. Cullum, *Biographical Register of the Officers and Graduates of the United States Military Academy*, 3rd ed., 2 vols. (Boston: Houghton Mifflin, 1891)

1794; Stewart Sifakis, *Who Was Who in the Civil War* (New York: Facts on File, 1988) 12; Robert Manson Myers, *The Children of Pride: A True Story of Georgia and the Civil War* (New Haven: Yale University Press, 1972) 1453–54; Joseph H. Crute, Jr., *Confederate Staff Officers, 1861–1865* (Powhatan VA: Derwent Books, 1982) 195.

[22]NA, M653 ("1860 Census"), roll 115, "Chatham County," 219; roll 111, "Bibb County," 522; M266 ("Confederate Soldiers from Georgia"), roll 149–50, Hartridge and Ross service records; Henderson, *Confederate Soldiers of Georgia*, 1:115, 6:795; Spencer Bidwell King, Jr., ed., *Ebb Tide, As Seen Through the Diary of Josephine Clay Habersham, 1863* (Athens GA: University of Georgia Press, 1958) 31n47; *Memoirs of Georgia*, 2 vols. (Atlanta: Southern Historical Association, 1895) 1:371. Gordon Burns Smith, *Counties and Commanders*, Part I, vol. 2 of *History of the Georgia Milita*, 265, quoting the *Charleston Daily Courier*, 28 December 1860.

[23]NA, M653 ("1860 Census"), roll 124, "Glynn County," 228, 229; George C. Dent File and Dent Family File, Walter C. Hartridge Collection, Georgia Historical Society, Savannah GA; Victoria Reeves Gunn, "Hofwyl Plantation" (typescript), (Atlanta GA: Georgia Department of Natural Resources, 1976) 72; Dent Family Genealogy (http: //www. rootsweb. com/~auntjean/ families/dentfam. htm); Brown, *To the Manner Born*, 156; M266 ("Confederate Soldiers from Georgia"), roll 149, Dent service record; Henderson, *Confederate Soldiers of Georgia*, 3:185; Alton J. Murray, *South Georgia Rebels: The True Wartime Experiences of the 26th Regiment Georgia Volunteer Infantry* (St. Mary's GA: self-published, 1976) 17.

[24]NA, M266 ("Confederate Soldiers from Georgia"), roll 150, "R. Wayne Service Record"; M267 ("Compiled Service Records of Confederate Soldiers Who Served in Organizations from the State of South Carolina"), roll 160, "2nd Infantry [2nd Palmetto Regiment]," "R. Wayne Service Record"; M331 ("Compiled Service Records of Confederate General and Staff Officers and Non-Regimental Enlisted Men" [Hereafter "Confederate General and Staff Officers."]), roll 261, "R. Wayne Service Record"; M653 ("1860 Census"), roll 115, "Chatham County, Georgia," 219; Wayne Family File, Walter C. Hartridge Collection, Georgia Historical Society, Savannah GA; *Savannah Republican,* 3 June 1862, 15 January, 3 March, 14 May 1863 (T. S. Wayne); Susan M. Kollock, ed., "Letters of the Kollock and Allied Families, 1826–1884," in *Georgia Historical Quarterly* 34 (1950): 231. See also the service record of Charles S. Pattillo, NA, M266 ("Confederate Soldiers from Georgia"), roll 150, for details on the promotion of Robert Wayne.

[25]NA, M266 ("Confederate Soldiers from Georgia"), roll 149, Footman service record; M331 ("Confederate General and Staff Officers"), roll 96, Footman service record; M653 ("1860 Census"), roll 115, "Chatham County," 230; Myers, *Children of Pride*, 1523; Smith, vol. 2, *History of Georgia Militia*, 276, 277, 331. Footman Family File, Walter C. Hartridge, Jr. Collection, Georgia Historical Society, Savannah GA. NA, M266 ("Confederate Soldiers from Georgia"), roll 149, McFarland service record; M331 ("Confederate General and Staff Officers"), roll 171, McFarland service records; M653 ("1860 Census"), roll 115, "Chatham County," 35; Henderson,

Confederate Soldiers of Georgia, 1:132; Charles H. Olmstead, "Fort Pulaski," *Georgia Historical Quarterly*, 1, 1917): 101; *The Memoirs of Charles H. Olmstead*, ed. Lilla M. Hawes, in *Collections of the Georgia Historical Society*, 14 (Savannah: Georgia Historical Society, 1964) 46, 90; Myers, *Children of Pride*, 936, 1607; *Savannah Republican,* 17 June, 2 and 3 July 1862; Special Order No. 134, 12 August 1862, Department of South Carolina, Georgia and Florida, RG 109, chap. 2, vol.42, Confederate Records, National Archives.

[26]NA, M474 ("Letters Received by the Confederate Adjutant and Inspector General, 1861–1865"), roll 4, "Letters 881– and 891-A-1862," Robert H. Anderson to Thomas Jordan, 9 November 1862.

[27]NA, M266 ("Confederate Soldiers from Georgia"), roll 148, "Caption Cards for 1st Battalion, Sharpshooters," "Field & Staff [F&S] Muster Roll for July and August 1862"; M432 ("1850 Census"), roll 64, "Chatham County," 275; M653 ("1860 Census"), roll 115, "Chatham County," 79, 138, 258; NA, M593 ("1870 Census"), roll 141, "Chatham County," 427; Brunner and Oliveros Family Files, Walter C. Hartridge, Jr. Collection, Georgia Historical Society, Savannah GA; *General Index to Keeper's Record Books, Laurel Grove Cemetery, Savannah, Georgia, 1852–1938*, 4 vols. (Savannah GA: Works Progress Administration, 1939) I: Nathaniel T. Brunner, 20 May 1876; *Savannah Republican,* 15 January, 1 May 1863 (I. Brunner); Oliveros marriage notice, *Savannah Republican,*4 July 1864.

[28]NA, M266 ("Confederate Soldiers from Georgia"), rolls 148–150, D. Brown, P. Derst, Pattillo and Schlatter service records; M432 ("1850 Census"), roll 64, "Chatham County," 238; M653 ("1860 Census"), roll 115, "Chatham County," 152; *Marriages of Chatham County, Georgia*, comp. Genealogical Committee of the Georgia Historical Society, 2 vols. (Savannah: Georgia Historical Society, 1993) 2:17; Derst Family File, Walter C. Hartridge, Jr. Collection, Georgia Historical Society, Savannah GA. Brown was listed as Dominick in the 1860 census and Dominique in his service record.

[29]Monthly returns, Military District of Georgia, August and September 1862, Weekly Field Returns for the Troops in the Military District of Georgia for Monday, 13 October, and Monday, 20 October 1862, Department of South Carolina and Georgia Collection, Museum of the Confederacy, Richmond VA.

[30]*Savannah Republican,* 1 and 2, December 1862.

[31] *Savannah Republican,* 3, 5, 20, and 21 November 1862; *ORN*, 13:454–55; Christman, *History of Fort McAllister*, 18–19; NA, M266 ("Confederate Soldiers from Georgia"), roll 148, "Company D Muster Roll for November and December 1862"; William Moody to wife, 23 November 1862, Moody Papers, Chapel Hill NC. Moody was a day off in his report of the engagement: 19 November 1862, was a Thursday.

[32]NA, M266 ("Confederate Soldiers from Georgia"), rolls 148–50 (service records); *Savannah Republican,* 18 October 1862; NA, M653 ("1860 Census"), roll 112, "Burke County," 888; roll 119, "Dawson County," 51. The family name is spelled variously "Read," "Reed," and "Reid" in the records.

[33]Moody to wife, 7 December 1862, Moody Papers, Chapel Hill NC.

[34]NA, M266 ("Confederate Soldiers from Georgia"), roll 150, service records; M653 ("1860 Census"), roll 111, "Appling County," 36, 50, 84; roll 140, "Wayne County," 315; Henderson, *Confederate Soldiers of Georgia*, 5:646–47, 729–30; Genealogy of Samuel Thornton (http://web3.foxinternet.net/smorgan/assofamily/index_thorn.htm); correspondence with Father James Thornton, Garden Grove, CA. There was a William Thornton, age seventeen, in the Wayne County census, and a William Thornton, age sixteen, in the Appling County census. These individuals may have been the same person enumerated twice.

[35]NA, M266 ("Confederate Soldiers from Georgia"), roll 148, service records; M653 ("1860 Census"), roll 137, "Talbot County," p. 139; Henderson, *Confederate Soldiers of Georgia*, 3:677–78.

[36] *Savannah Republican,* 11 November, 20 December 1862.

[37]NA, M266 ("Confederate Soldiers from Georgia"), rolls 148–50, service records; M432 ("1850 Census"), roll 78, "Monroe County," 62, 73, M653 ("1860 Census"), roll 135, "Randolph County," 618, 672; Henderson, *Confederate Soldiers of Georgia*, 2:290; Frances T. Ingmire, comp., *Randolph County Marriages, 1810–1857* (St. Louis: self-published, 1985).

[38]NA, M266 ("Confederate Soldiers from Georgia"), rolls 148–50, analysis of service reords by the author.

[39]NA, M331 ("Confederate General and Staff Officers"), roll 7, "Robert Anderson Service Record," Anderson to Cooper, 12 October 1862; Anderson to Beauregard, 28 October 1862; Special Orders, Adjutant and Inspector General's Office, October–December 1862, RG 109, chap. 1, vol.11, Confederate Records, National Archives; Thomas Jordan to H. W. Mercer, 22 December 1862, Letters Sent, Department of South Carolina, Georgia and Florida, July 1862–April 1864, RG 109, chap. 2, vol.22, Confederate Records, National Archives.

[40]NA, M331 ("Confederate General and Staff Officers"), roll 7, "Robert Anderson Service Record," Anderson to Beauregard, 28 October 1862.

[41]"Report of Inspection of 1st Battalion Ga. Sharpshooters by Capt. W. S. Basinger, S[avannah] V[olunteer] G[uar]ds, October 31st, 186[2]," Department of South Carolina and Georgia Collection, Museum of the Confederacy, Richmond VA.

[42]General Order No. 10, 19 January 1863, General Orders, Department of South Carolina, Georgia, and Florida, July 1862–Jan. 1864, RG 109, chap. 2, vol.43, Confederate Records, National Archives.

[43]*Arms and Equipment of the Confederacy* (Alexandria VA: Time-Life Books, 1998) 36–37. See also Edward B. Coddington, *The Gettysburg Campaign: A Study in Command* (New York: Charles Scribner's Sons, 1968) 252, for more on firing, loading, and ammunition for the Enfield.

[44]NA, M266 ("Confederate Soldiers from Georgia"), roll 150, Pattillo service record; roll 317, "18th Georgia Battalion (Savannah Volunteer Guard Battalion)," C. S. and R. M. Pattillo service records; M432 ("1850 Census"), roll 66, "Cobb County," 9; M653 ("1860 Census"), roll 117, "Cobb County," 260, 292; Sarah B. Temple, *The First Hundred Years: A Short History of Cobb County in Georgia* (Atlanta: Walter W. Brown Publishing, 1935) 159, 170; Henderson, *Confederate*

Soldiers of Georgia, 1:862; C. S. Pattillo to Governor Joseph E. Brown, 17 February 1862, Incoming Correspondence to Governor Joseph E. Brown, Georgia Division of Archives and History, Atlanta, Georgia, Record Group 1, Subgroup 1, Series 5, Box 42 (Location 3335-08).

[45]NA, M266 ("Confederate Soldiers from Georgia"), roll 150, Oliveros and Schlatter service records; M331 ("Confederate General and Staff Officers"), roll 190, Oliveros service record; *Savannah Republican,* 4 July 1864.

[46]Thomas Jordan to H. W. Mercer, 23 and 31 December 1862; P. T. Beauregard to Samuel Cooper, 30 December 1862, Letters Sent, July 1862–September 1864 RG 109 chap. 2, vol.22; Special Order No. 20, 20 January 1863, Special Orders and Circulars, Department of South Carolina, Georgia, and Florida, September 1862–December 1863, RG 109, chap. 2, vol. 40, Confederate Records, National Archives; Sifakis, *Who Was Who,* 12; NA, M266 ("Confederate Soldiers from Georgia"), roll 150, Shaaff service record.

[47]NA, M266 ("Confederate Soldiers from Georgia"), roll 148, "Caption and Event Cards"; *ORN,* 13:544–45; Christman, *History of Fort McAllister,* 21–28; *Savannah Republican,* 28 and 29 January, 27 February 1863.

[48]*OR,* vol. 14, p. 213; *ORN,* 13:626, 628.

[49]*OR,* vol. 14, pp. 214–17; Leona Frye, "John B. Gallie, 1806–1863," student thesis, (Savannah State-Armstrong State Colleges Joint Graduate Program, Savannah GA, 1977); *Savannah Republican,* 2 February 1863.

[50]*ORN,* 13:628, 630–32; Christman, *History of Fort McAllister,* 28–32.

[51]*OR,* vol. 14, pp. 212, 213, 214–15.

[52] *Savannah Republican,* 13 February 1863; NA, M266 ("Confederate Soldiers from Georgia"), roll 150, "J. Smith and W. D. Warren Service Records;" Service Record"; Descriptive Roll of the 28 Men furnished by 30th Regiment Ga. vol.for the 1st Battn. Ga. Sharpshooters, George C. Dent File, Hartridge Collection, Georgia Historical Society, Savannah GA.

[53]NA, M266 ("Confederate Soldiers from Georgia"), rolls 149–150, service records.

[54]Ibid., roll 150, "Royal (Ryalls) Service Record"; M653 ("1860 Census"), roll 119, "Dooly County," 496; Thomas C. Sutton, "Our Royal Roots," typescript family genealogy, Royal F. Brown, Rochelle GA; *Confederate Reminiscences and Letters, 1861–1865,* 18 vols. to date (Atlanta GA: United Daughters of the Confederacy, 1996–2002) 6:187–88.

[55]NA, M266 ("Confederate Soldiers from Georgia"), rolls 149, "Godwin (Goodman) Service Record"; M432 ("1850 Census"), roll 81, "Randolph County," 368; M653 ("1860 Census"), roll 107, "Jackson County, Fla.," 739; M593 ("1870 Census"), roll 12, "Dale County, Ala.," 268; T9 ("1880 Census"), roll 19, "Lee County, Ala.," 1; Frances T. Ingmire, comp., *Dooly County Marriages, 1839–1884* (St. Louis: self-published, 1985); Thomas C. Sutton, "The Godwin Connection," typescript family genealogy; Henderson, *Confederate Soldiers of Georgia,* 6:541.

[56]NA, M266 ("Confederate Soldiers from Georgia"), rolls 148–50, service records; M653 ("1860 Census"), roll 115, "Chatham County," 79; roll 119, "Dooly

County," 428, 440, 455, 487, 500, 505, 509, 527, 528; Frederick N. Gleaton, "David Culpepper," unpublished family memoir. Henderson, *Confederate Soldiers of Georgia*, 3:698, shows that David Culpepper enlisted in D Company, 32nd Georgia (no date given) and transferred into the sharpshooter battalion in February 1863.

[57]NA, M266 ("Confederate Soldiers from Georgia"), roll 148, "Caption and Event Cards"; Smedlund, *Camp Fires of Georgia's Troops*, 177; Shaaff to Henry C. Wayne, 22 February 1863, Adjutant General's Incoming Correspondence (RG 22, sub-group 1, ser. 17), box 23, Georgia Division of Archives and History, Atlanta, Georgia; William H. Bragg, *Joe Brown's Army: The Georgia State Line, 1862–1865* (Macon GA: Mercer University Press, 1987) 32–35, 45.

[58]*Savannah Republican*, 21 February 1863.

[59]John I. Royal to wife, 22 February 1863, John I. Royal letters, Betty F. Brown and Royal F. Brown papers, Rochelle GA. The author is grateful to William S. Smedlund, Sharpsburg GA for having brought these letters to his attention.

[60]*ORN*, 13:696–98, 716–19; *OR*, vol. 14, pp. 217–20; Christman, *History of Fort McAllister*, 37–41, 46–53; *Savannah Republican*, 2 and 11 March 1863.

[61]NA, M266 ("Confederate Soldiers from Georgia"), roll 148–49, "Companies B, C and D Muster Rolls, March and April 1863," Burns, Mims and Muller service records; *OR*, vol. 14, p. 222; Christman, *History of Fort McAllister*, 55; *Savannah Republican*, 4, 5, 11, 14 March 1863. Henderson, *Confederate Soldiers of Georgia*, 3:464, says Mims's leg was broken at Fort McAllister on 13 December 1864, and he was at home at the end of the war.

[62]John I. Royal to wife, 7 March 1863, Royal letters, Brown papers, Rochelle GA.

[63]*Savannah Republican*, 10 and 20 March 1863; *ORN*, 13:638–39.

[64]Beauregard to Cooper, 30 March 1863, Letters Sent, Department of South Carolina, Georgia, and Florida, 20 March–9 September 1863, RG 109, chap. 2, vol.31, Confederate Records, National Archives.

[65]General Order No. 29, 18 February 1863, Records of General Courts-Martial, Department of South Carolina, Georgia, and Florida, RG 109, chap. 2, vol.182, Confederate Records, National Archives; NA, M266 ("Confederate Soldiers from Georgia"), roll 149, Gleichman and Kiener service records.

[66]NA, M266 ("Confederate Soldiers from Georgia"), roll 149, "Michael Kiener Service Record"; C. M. Hardy to sister, 9 and 10 April 1863, C. M. Hardy Letters (microfilm) Mrs. O. E. Lancaster Collection, Georgia Division of Archives and History, Atlanta GA. The complete Hardy letters have recently been published in *Confederate Reminiscences and Letters*, 18:212–26. William Moody to wife, 12 April 1863, Moody Papers, Chapel Hill NC; John I. Royal to wife, 12 April 1863, Royal letters, Brown papers, Rochelle GA.

[67]*Savannah Republican*, 11 April 1863. The Catholic Cemetery in Savannah contains a grave marked "Micharel Lieve [sic], alias, Kinsey, Co. B, Ga. Sharpshooters," perhaps further adding to the mystery of this man's real name. See *Roster of Confederate Graves*, Centennial Edition, 8 vols., (Atlanta GA: Georgia Division, United Daughters of the Confederacy), vol. I: 111.

[68]General Order No. 21, 1 February 1863 and General Order No. 64, 26 April

1863, Records of General Courts-Martial, Department of South Carolina, Georgia, and Florida, RG 109, chap. 2, vol.182, Confederate Records, National Archives; NA, M266 ("Confederate Soldiers from Georgia"), rolls 148–150, Barrentine, Butler, Englehart, Garrison, Z. Green, and McDaniel service records; Alfred L. Hartridge to George A. Mercer, with endorsements, in Butler's file. Englehart's record indicates he was captured in Mississippi on 15 July 1863, but Hartridge's letter includes his name.

[69]John I. Royal to wife, 12, 18, and 30 April 1863, Royal letters, Brown papers, Rochelle GA; NA, M266 ("Confederate Soldiers from Georgia"), rolls 149–50, Fadden and Pearson service records. Royal referred to Fadden as "John Fans."

[70]Brown, *To the Manner Born*, 140–42; NA, M266 ("Confederate Soldiers from Georgia"), rolls 149–50, Hartridge and Shaaff service records.

[71]NA, M266 ("Confederate Soldiers from Georgia"), roll 150, Twyman service record; M432 ("1850 Census"), roll 958, "Madison County, Virginia," 190.

[72]NA, M266 ("Confederate Soldiers from Georgia"), roll 148, Crane service record; M653 ("1860 Census"), roll 115, "Chatham County," 242; Henderson, *Confederate Soldiers of Georgia*, 1:923; Myers, *Children of Pride*, 1496–97; Olmstead, *Memoirs*, 71–72.

[73]NA, M266 ("Confederate Soldiers from Georgia"), rolls 148, 150, Bryan and Schlatter service records; M653 ("1860 Census"), roll 115, "Chatham County," 43, roll 124, "Glynn County," 215; Myers, *Children of Pride*, 1475; Walter J. Fraser, Jr., *Savannah in the Old South* (Athens: University of Georgia Press, 2003) 306, 310-11 (See also Richard B. Haunton, "Law and Order in Savannah, 1850-1860," *Georgia Historical Quarterly* 56 (March 1972): 1-24; Henderson, *Confederate Soldiers of Georgia*, 3:190, 255; Murray, *South Georgia Rebels*, 221; *OR*, ser. 4, vol.2, p. 274; http: //www. trainweb. org/horseshoecurvenrhs/Altoona_ area.htm.

[74]NA, M266 ("Confederate Soldiers from Georgia"), rolls 149–50, Hardee, Herrmann and T. Wayne service records; M653 ("1860 Census"), roll 115, "Chatham County," 10, 219, 227; Hardee Family File, Walter C. Hartridge, Jr. Collection, Georgia Historical Society, Savannah GA; Henderson, *Confederate Soldiers of Georgia*, 1:149.

[75]NA, M266 ("Confederate Soldiers from Georgia"), roll 150, Pattillo service record.

[76]NA, M266 ("Confederate Soldiers from Georgia"), roll 149, Footman service record; M331 ("Confederate General and Staff Officers"), roll 96, Footman service record.

[77]NA, M266 ("Confederate Soldiers from Georgia"), roll 149, Footman service record, "Abstract of Provisions"; Royal to wife, 22 February 1863, Royal letters, Brown papers, Rochelle GA.

[78]NA, M266 ("Confederate Soldiers from Georgia"), roll 149–50, Gray, McFarland, and Robert Wayne service records; M331 ("Confederate General and Staff Officers"), roll 171 and 261, Robert Wayne and John McFarland service records; M653 ("1860 Census"), roll 115, "Chatham County," 240.

[79]NA, M266 ("Confederate Soldiers from Georgia"), rolls 84, 149, "John M. Dent

service records;" M331 ("Confederate General and Staff Officers"), roll 74, "John M. Dent Service Record;" Joseph Jones, "Roster of the Medical Officers of the Army of Tennessee...," *Southern Historical Society Papers*, vol. 22 (1894): 194. Henderson, *Confederate Soldiers of Georgia*, 6:377; http://www.rootsweb.com/~auntjean/families/dentfam.htm; Albert M. Hillhouse, "Descendants of Dr. John Dent," in *Nuggets and Other Findings in Burke County, Georgia* (Danville KY: Prompt Printing, 1981) 131; Lillian L. Powell, Dorothy C. Odom, and Albert M. Hillhouse, *Grave Markers in Burke County, Georgia* (Waynesboro GA: Chalker Publishing, 1974) 260; Walter A. Clark, *Under the Stars and Bars, or Memories of Four Years Service with the Oglethorpes of Augusta, Georgia* (Augusta: Chronicle Printing Co., 1900) 9–62 passim, 207. Dent's record as a staff officer shows that he was assistant surgeon in the 12th Battalion but the record gives no dates. His grave marker bears the inscription "Co A, 12th Ga Bn."

CHAPTER 2

[1] Russell K. Brown, *To the Manner Born: The Life of General William H. T. Walker* (Athens: University of Georgia Press, 1994) 147–48.

[2] John I. Royal to his wife, 5 May 1863, John I. Royal letters, Betty F. Brown and Royal F. Brown papers, Rochelle GA.

[3] Adamson to father, 7 May 1863, in Richard Bender Abell and Faye Adamson Gecik, eds., *Sojourns of a Patriot: The Field and Prison Papers of an Unreconstructed Confederate* (Murfreesboro TN: Southern Heritage Press, 1998) 154.

[4] National Archives, microfilm publications, M266 ("Compiled Service Records of Confederate Soldiers Who Served in Organizations from the State of Georgia" [Hereafter "Confederate Soldiers from Georgia"]), rolls 149–50, John M. Dent and Shaaff service records; M331 ("Compiled Service Records of Confederate General and Staff Officers and Non-Regimental Enlisted Men" [Hereafter "Confederate General and Staff Officers."]), roll 74, "John M. Dent Service Record."

[5] NA, M266 ("Confederate Soldiers from Georgia"), rolls 148–50, analysis of service records; M653 ("1860 Census"), roll 135, "Randolph County," 642; *Savannah Republican,* 14 and 21 May 1863.

[6] NA, M266 ("Confederate Soldiers from Georgia"), roll 150, Withrow service records; M653 ("1860 Census"), roll 120, "Fannin County," 1056.

[7] NA, M266 ("Confederate Soldiers from Georgia"), roll 148, "Companies A-D Muster Rolls for May and June 1863"; C. C. Wilson to his wife, 15 May 1863, C. C. Wilson Papers, Georgia Historical Society, Savannah GA.

[8] Norman V. Turner, *Brigadier General Claudius C. Wilson: Effingham County, Georgia's, Only Confederate General* (Springfield GA: self-published, 1997) 1–2, 10; Brown, *To the Manner Born*, 141.

[9] R. Cuyler King to his sisters, 12 May 1863, Thomas Butler King Family Papers, Southern Historical Collection, University of North Carolina, Chapel Hill NC; McDermid to parents, 13 May 1863, Angus McDermid letters, Benjamin C. Rountree

papers, Amherst MA. Dr. Rountree published excerpts from this collection as "Letters from a Confederate Soldier" in *Georgia Review* 18 (1964): 267–97.

[10]Brown, *To the Manner Born*, 148–49; US War Department, *The War of the Rebellion, A Compilation of the Official Records of the Union and Confederate Armies* (hereafter *OR*) 128 vols. (Washington, DC: US Government Printing Office, 1880–1901)ser. 1, vol. 14, p. 956 (Herafter *OR*. All citations from *OR* are from series 1 unless otherwise specified.); George A. Mercer Diary (typescript), 31 May 1863 Mercer Family Papers, Georgia Historical Society, Savannah GA.

[11]*OR*, vol. 24, pt. 1, pp. 736–39; C. C. Wilson to his wife, 15 May 1863, C. C. Wilson Papers, Georgia Historical Society, Savannah GA.

[12]Isaac Hermann, *Memoirs of A Confederate Veteran, 1861–1865* (Lakemont GA: CSA Printing and Binding, 1974) 100–101. A Jackson correspondent of the *Savannah Republican* reported that Martin's battery was expected there that day. See "Letter from Jackson," in the paper on 22 May 1863.

[13]*OR*, vol. 24, pt. 1, pp. 785–86; C. C. Wilson to wife, 15 May 1863, C. C. Wilson Papers, Georgia Historical Society, Savannah GA; Ellison Capers to his wife, 17 May 1863, Ellison Capers Papers, South Caroliniana Library, University of South Carolina, Columbia SC; Edwin C. Bearss and Warren Grabau, *The Battle of Jackson, May 14, 1863* in *The Battle of Jackson/The Siege of Jackson/Three Other Post-Vicksburg Actions* (Jackson MS: Jackson Civil War Roundtable, Inc., 1981) 7, 12–13, 19, 35n20. Bearss and Grabau have not included the 25th Georgia in Walker's command in this battle. A new edition of this presentation ("The Battle of Jackson, May 14, 1863") was published as "The Vicksburg Campaign: Grant Moves Inland," in *Blue and Gray Magazine*, 14/1 (October 2000): 6–17, 19, 22, 46–52.

[14]*OR*, vol. 24, pt. 1, pp. 753–54, 759, 785–87, pt. 3, pp. 919–20; Bearss and Grabau, *Battle of Jackson*, 19–20; Hermann, *Memoirs of a Veteran*, 103.

[15]*OR*, vol. 24, pt. 1, pp. 759, 786, pt. 3, pp. 919–20; Bearss and Grabau, *Battle of Jackson*, 20, 23–26; Capers to his wife, 17 May 1863, Capers Papers, South Caroliniana Library, Columbia SC; Eugene W. Jones, Jr., *Enlisted for the War: The Struggles of the Gallant 24th Regiment, South Carolina Volunteers, Infantry, 1861–1865* (Hightstown NJ: Longstreet House, 1997) 85–91.

[16]*OR*, vol. 24, pt. 1, pp. 786–87; Lillian Henderson, ed., *Roster of the Confederate Soldiers of Georgia, 1861–1865*, 6 vols. (Hapeville GA: Longino and Porter, 1955–1962) 3:141; *Savannah Republican*, 28 May (telegram), 6 June (hospital list) 1863; J. A. Thornton to Benjamin Milikin, 11 June 1863, Benjamin Milikin Papers, US Army Military History Institute, Carlisle PA; NA, M266 ("Confederate Soldiers from Georgia"), roll 148–49, "Company A Muster Roll for May and June 1863," service records; C. C. Wilson to wife, 15 May 1863, C. C. Wilson Papers, Georgia Historical Society, Savannah GA; Bearss and Grabau, *Battle of Jackson*, 33.

[17]*Supplement to the Official Records*, ed. Janet Hewett, 81 volumes (Wilmington NC: Broadfoot Publishing, 1997) pt. 1 ("Reports"), 7:261.

[18]*OR*, vol. 24, pt. 3, pp. 883–84, 919–920; Bearss and Grabau, *Battle of Jackson*, 26, 28, 33; NA, M266 ("Confederate Soldiers from Georgia"), roll 150, "Arthur Shaaff

Service Record"; C. C. Wilson to wife, 15 May, 23 June 1863, C. C. Wilson Papers, Georgia Historical Society, Savannah GA; John W. Hagan to wife, 15 May 1863, *Confederate Letters of John W. Hagan*, ed. Bell I. Wiley (Athens: University of Georgia Press, 1957); "Letters from A Confederate Soldier," 275; "From the First Battalion Sharpshooters," *Savannah Republican,* 1 July 1863. Shaaff was reimbursed $200. 00 for the horse the following December while at Dalton GA. See voucher in his file.

[19]Brown, *To the Manner Born*, 153, 156; C. C. Wilson to wife, 3 June, 1 July 1863, C. C. Wilson Papers, Georgia Historical Society, Savannah GA; NA, M266 ("Confederate Soldiers from Georgia"), rolls 149–50, Holcombe, Johnston, R. Wayne service records; M331 ("Confederate General and Staff Officers"), roll 261, "R. Wayne Service Record"; M653 ("1860 Census"), roll 115, "Chatham County," 255, 259; *Savannah Republican,* 15 October 1862; Henderson, *Confederate Soldiers of Georgia* 1:247, 923, 3:427, 4:565; Bowling C. Yates, *History of the Georgia Military Institute, Marietta, Georgia* (Marietta: self-published, 1968) 24. Henderson has confused this George H. Johnston with another of the same name who was from Bibb County and served with the 1st Confederate Georgia Regiment at Pensacola. See Henderson, *Confederate Soldiers of Georgia*, 1:7.

[20]List of Orders, 3 March 1863, container 5, P. G. T. Beauregard Papers, Library of Congress, Washington, DC; NA, M331 ("Confederate General and Staff Officers"), roll 261, "Robert Wayne Service Record"; Howard Michael Madaus and Robert D. Needham, *The Battle Flags of the Confederate Army of Tennessee* (Milwaukee: Milwaukee Public Museum, 1976) 59, 62.

[21]NA, M251 ("Compiled Service Records of Confederate Soldiers Who Served in Organizations from the State of Florida"), roll 41, Sadler service record; M266 ("Confederate Soldiers from Georgia"), roll 150, Sadler service record; *OR*, ser. 4, vol. 1, p. 627.

[22]Robert Manson Myers, *The Children of Pride: A True Story of Georgia and the Civil War* (New Haven: Yale University Press, 1972) 1668–69; "Letters and Papers of Dr. Daniel Turner, A Rhode Islander in South Georgia," Part IV, collected and edited by Richard K. Murdoch, *Georgia Historical Quarterly*, 54, no. 2 (Summer 1970): 245; Marguerite Reddick, comp., *Camden's Challenge: A History of Camden County, Georgia* (St. Mary's GA: Camden County Historical Society, 1976) 583; A. Everett Peterson, "Nicholas Bayard," in *Dictionary of American Biography*, ed. Allen Johnson and Dumas Malone, 10 vols. (New York: Charles Scribner's Sons, 1964) vol. 1, pt 2, p. 68.

[23]NA, M266 ("Confederate Soldiers from Georgia"), roll 149, M331 ("Confederate General and Staff Officers"), roll 63, Cosby service records. See also Joseph Jones, "Roster of the Medical Officers of the Army of Tennessee…," Southern Historical Society Papers, vol. 22 (1894): 185.

[24]NA, M474 ("Letters Received by the Confederate Adjutant and Inspector General, 1861–1865"), roll 58, letter 1348–B-1863, Shaaff to Cooper, 26 May 1863, with endorsements.

[25]NA, M266 ("Confederate Soldiers from Georgia"), roll 148, "Companies B, C

and D Muster Rolls for May and June 1863"; Brown, *To the Manner Born*, 156; C. C. Wilson to wife, 23 June 1863, C. C. Wilson Papers, Georgia Historical Society, Savannah GA; Angus McDermid to parents, 4 July 1863, McDermid letters, Rountree papers, Amherst MA.

[26] "From Johnston's Army," *Savannah Republican,* 2 July 1863; James J. B. White to R. Cuyler King, 24 June 1871, in Bessie Lewis, *King's Retreat Plantation*, vol. 2 of *Plantations of Coastal Georgia*, ed. Mildred Huie and Mildred Wilcox (Brunswick GA: Coastal Printing, 1980) 84–85; NA, M266 ("Confederate Soldiers from Georgia"), roll 150, Twyman service record.

[27] NA, M266 ("Confederate Soldiers from Georgia"), rolls 148–50, analysis of service records.

[28] NA, M266 ("Confederate Soldiers from Georgia"), roll 148, service records; Matt Harris, "Descendants of Thomas Harris" (1999) at http: //www.patch.net/harris/.

[29] NA, M266 ("Confederate Soldiers from Georgia"), roll 149, "J. Mann Service Record"; M653 ("1860 Census"), roll 119, "DeKalb County," 303.

[30] NA, M266 ("Confederate Soldiers from Georgia"), roll 148, M. E. Cobb and W. D. Cobb service records; M653 ("1860 Census"), roll 131, "Randolph County," 638–39.

[31] NA, M266 ("Confederate Soldiers from Georgia"), roll 149, "John Derst Service Record"; M653 ("1860 Census"), roll 115, "Chatham County," 153; Derst Family File, Walter C. Hartridge, Jr. Collection, Georgia Historical Society, Savannah GA.

[32] *Savannah Republican,* 1 June 1863; Savannah *Daily Morning News*, 1 and 20 June 1863; NA, M653 ("1860 Census"), roll 115, "Chatham County," 411; M266 ("Confederate Soldiers from Georgia"), roll 149, service record.

[33] John W. Hagan to wife, 29 May 1863, *Confederate Letters of John W. Hagan*; Joseph B. Cumming, *A Sketch of the Descendants of David Cumming and Memoirs of the War Between the States*, ed. Mary Gairdner Smith Cumming (Augusta: self-published, 1925) 60–61.

[34] *Savannah Republican,* 1 July 1863. The Banners were actually the Tanners.

[35] *Savannah Republican,* 7 July, 19 August 1863; *Savannah City Directory, 1859* <http://www.rootsweb.com/~gachath2/1859SavCitydir.html>.

[36] Edwin C. Bearss, *The Siege of Jackson, July 10–17, 1863*, in in *The Battle of Jackson/The Siege of Jackson/Three Other Post-Vicksburg Actions* (Jackson MS: Jackson Civil War Roundtable, Inc., 1981) 55, 63; Hermann, *Memoirs of a Veteran*, 115; A. P. Adamson, *A Brief History of the Thirtieth Georgia Regiment* (Jonesboro GA: Freedom Hill Press, 1987) 30; C. C. Wilson to wife, 25 July 1863, C. C. Wilson Papers, Georgia Historical Society, Savannah GA.

[37] C. C. Wilson letter to wife, 25 July 1863, C. C. Wilson Papers, Georgia Historical Society, Savannah GA.. Joseph E. Johnston, *Narrative of Operations Directed During the Late War Between the States* (1874; reprint, Bloomington: Indiana University Press, 1959) 205; *OR*, vol. 24, pt. 2, p. 534; Bearss, *Siege of Jackson*, 64.

[38] Russell K. Brown, "Capture of Jackson, Mississippi, (9–16 July 1863)" in David S. and Jeanne T. Heidler, eds., *Encyclopedia of the American Civil War*, 5 vols.

(Santa Barbara CA: ABC-CLIO, 2000) 3:1057–58; Bearss, *Siege of Jackson*, 64, 84; Brown, *To the Manner Born*, 157; Jones, *Enlisted for the War*, 103.

[39]Bearss, *Siege of Jackson*, 81, 84–88; "Gen. Johnston's Movements," *Savannah Republican*, 25 July 1863; C. C. Wilson to wife, 25 July 1863, C. C. Wilson Papers, Georgia Historical Society, Savannah GA.

[40]John W. Hagan to father-in-law, 15 July 1863; John W. Hagan to brothers-in-law, 20 July 1863, *Confederate Letters of John W. Hagan*; Bearss, *Siege of Jackson*, 92–93; *OR*, vol. 24, pt. 2, pp. 641, 649; "Letter from Mississippi," *Savannah Republican*, 30 July 1863; Adamson to sister, 20 July 1863, in Abell and Gecik, eds., *Sojourns of a Patriot*, 165–66.

[41] J. L. Holcombe, "From the Army of the West," *Savannah Republican*, 19 August 1863.

[42]Bearss, *Siege of Jackson*, 89, 90–91.

[43]Ibid., 94, 112n109; *OR*, vol. 24, pt. 3, p. 1008; J. L. Holcombe "From the Army of the West,", *Savannah Republican*, 19 August 1863.

[44]Bearss, *Siege of Jackson*, 96, 97, 100–101, 103; C. C. Wilson to wife, 25 July 1863, C. C. Wilson Papers, Georgia Historical Society, Savannah GA; "Gen. Johnston's Movements," *Savannah Republican*, 25 July 1863; "Letter from Mississippi," *Savannah Republican*, 30 July 1863.

[45]Bearss, *Siege of Jackson*, 94, 105; John W. Hagan to his wife, 23 July 1863, *Confederate Letters of John W. Hagan*; *Savannah Republican*, 13 and 16 July 1863.

[46]J. L. Holcombe "From the Army of the West," *Savannah Republican*, 19 August 1863.

[47]NA, M266 ("Confederate Soldiers from Georgia"), rolls 148–50, service records; "1st Sharpshooter Battalion, D Company Muster Roll, September 1 to October 31, 1863;" George Columbus Dent Papers, collection 213, Georgia Historical Society, Savannah GA; Dent Family File, Hartridge Collection, Georgia Historical Society, Savannah GA; *Memoirs of Georgia*, 2 vols. (Atlanta: Southern Historical Association, 1895) 1:371.

[48]Edwin C. Bearss, *Three Other Post-Vicksburg Actions: Yazoo City, Black River, and Natchez*, in in *The Battle of Jackson/The Siege of Jackson/Three Other Post-Vicksburg Actions* (Jackson MS: Jackson Civil War Roundtable, Inc., 1981) 145–50; *OR*, 24, pt. 2, pp. 667–73; NA, M266 ("Confederate Soldiers from Georgia"), roll 149, Langston service record.

[49]*Marriages of Chatham County, Georgia*, comp. Genealogical Committee of the Georgia Historical Society, 2 vols. (Savannah: Georgia Historical Society, 1993) 2:64; NA, M653 ("1860 Census"), roll 115, "Chatham County, Georgia," 345.

[50] *Savannah Republican*, 20 August 1863.

[51] *Savannah Republican*, 3, 7 August 1863; NA, M266 ("Confederate Soldiers from Georgia"), roll 150, Shaaff service record, vouchers for uniforms dated 23 August and 1 September 1863.

[52]NA, M266 ("Confederate Soldiers from Georgia"), roll 149, Molina service record; M653 ("1860 Census"), roll 115, "Chatham County," 291; *Savannah Republican*, 25 August 1863 (funeral notice), 30 June 1864; Henderson,

Confederate Soldiers of Georgia, 1:135. See *Marriages of Chatham County*, 2:42, for Molina's marriage to Leonora Ross in 1854, and Savannah censuses and city directories for the Rosis/Ross association with the Molinas.

[53]R. Cuyler King to sister, 31 August, 5 September 1863, King Family Papers, Southern Historical Collection, Chapel Hill NC; C. C. Wilson to wife, 3 September 1863, C. C. Wilson Papers, Georgia Historical Society, Savannah GA.

[54]Brown, *To the Manner Born*, 199; R. Cuyler King to sister, 1 September 1863, King Papers, Southern Historical Collection, Chapel Hill NC; C. C. Wilson to wife, 5 September, 3 October, 8 October 1863, C. C. Wilson Papers, Georgia Historical Society, Savannah GA.

[55]NA, M266 ("Confederate Soldiers from Georgia"), roll 148, 150, service records, Savannah *Daily Morning News*, 3 November 1862.

[56]NA, M266 ("Confederate Soldiers from Georgia"), roll 150, Pattillo service record.

CHAPTER 3

[1]Russell K. Brown, *To the Manner Born: The Life of General William H. T. Walker* (Athens: University of Georgia Press, 1994) 161–62; C. C. Wilson to wife, 23 August 1863, C. C. Wilson Papers, Georgia Historical Society, Savannah GA; R. Cuyler King to sister, 29 August, 5 September 1863, Thomas Butler King Family Papers, Southern Historical Collection, University of North Carolina, Chapel Hill NC. The State Road was so called because it had been built by the state of Georgia; most railroad building was privately financed.

[2]C. C. Wilson to his wife, 3 September 1863, C. C. Wilson Papers, Georgia Historical Society, Savannah GA; A. P. Adamson, *A Brief History of the Thirtieth Georgia Regiment* (Jonesboro GA: Freedom Hill Press, 1987) 33.

[3]NA, M266 ("Compiled Service Records of Confederate Soldiers Who Served in Organizations from the State of Georgia" [Hereafter "Confederate Soldiers from Georgia"]), roll 148–50, service records.

[4]Brown, *To the Manner Born*, 162; George W. Brent Journal, 31 August 1863, folder 22, William P. Palmer Collection of Braxton Bragg Papers, Western Reserve Historical Society, Cleveland OH.

[5]C. C. Wilson to wife, 3 September 1863, C. C. Wilson Papers, Georgia Historical Society, Savannah GA; R. Cuyler King to sister, 31 August 1863, King Papers, Southern Historical Collection, Chapel Hill NC; NA, M266 ("Confederate Soldiers from Georgia"), roll 149, "Samuel W. Lawrence Service Record"; M653 ("1860 Census"), roll 124, "Glynn County," 240; Lillian Henderson, ed., *Roster of the Confederate Soldiers of Georgia, 1861–1865*, 6 vols. (Hapeville GA: Longino and Porter, 1955–1962) 3:185; Alton J. Murray, *South Georgia Rebels: The True Wartime Experiences of the 26th Regiment Georgia Volunteer Infantry* (St. Mary's GA: self-published, 1976) 17.

[6]William Moody to wife, 2 September 1863, William Moody Papers, MS 4903z, Southern Historical Collection, University of North Carolina, Chapel Hill; "Letter from the Twenty-fifth Geo.," *Savannah Republican,* 7 September 1863.

[7]C. C. Wilson to wife, 3 September 1863, C. C. Wilson Papers, Georgia Historical Society, Savannah GA; Angus McDermid to parents, 30 August 1863, Angus McDermid letters, Benjamin C. Rountree papers, Amherst MA; R. Cuyler King to sister, 1 and 5 September 1863, King Papers, Southern Historical Collection, Chapel Hill NC.

[8]Brown, *To the Manner Born*, 163, 164.

[9]R. Cuyler King to his sister, 6 September 1863, King Family Papers, Southern Historical Collection, Chapel Hill NC; Brown, *To the Manner Born*, 164; Adamson, *Thirtieth Georgia*, 33.

[10]Ibid.; R Cuyler King to sister, 12 and 15 September 1863, King Family Papers, Southern Historical Collection, Chapel Hill NC.

[11]US War Department, *The War of the Rebellion, A Compilation of the Official Records of the Union and Confederate Armies* (hereafter *OR*) 128 vols. (Washington, DC: US Government Printing Office, 1880–1901)ser. 1,vol. 30, pt. 2, pp. 247–50. Hereafter OR. All citation from OR are series 1 unless otherwise specified. The letter of "J. W. B.," possibly Lieutenant James W. Best, 25th Georgia, giving details of the battle, was published in the *Savannah Republican* on 7 October. It closely follows Wilson's report. The account of "P. W. A.," [Peter Wellington Alexander] a *Republican* correspondent, was published on 26 October.

[12]*OR*, vol. 30, pt. 2, p. 248; Adamson, *Thirtieth Georgia*, 34. In a letter to his wife on 22 September, Wilson wrote that he had only 1,100 men in the battle.

When Lieutenant Colonel James S. Boynton of the 30th Georgia wrote his report he omitted mention of the sharpshooters in the line of battle. The implication is that they had already deployed as skirmishers. By the time they fell in on the brigade left, Boynton was probably too much involved in the action to notice (Report of the 30th Georgia in the Battle of Chickamauga (photocopy), 30th Georgia Regiment File, Chickamauga National Military Park, Chickamauga GA. Boynton'e report is ten manuscript pages and is dated 14 March 1891. In it he wrote that it was substantially the same as the one he had turned in to the brigade commander in 1863 except that locations had been added. This report has not been printed in *OR* or its supplement.).

[13]*OR*, vol. 30, pt. 2, p. 249; Peter Cozzens, *This Terrible Sound: The Battle of Chickamauga* (Urbana: University of Illinois Press, 1992) 137.

[14]*OR*, vol. 30, pt. 2, p. 240.

[15]Ibid., 245, 249.

[16]Ibid., 250; Adamson, *Thirteth Georgia*, 36–37, 53; George A. Mercer Diary (typescript), 3 October 1863, Mercer Family Papers, Georgia Historical Society, Savannah GA; H. J. Lea, "With the Fourth Louisiana Battalion," *Confederate Veteran* vol. 27 (1919): 339; Report of the 30th Georgia, Chickamauga National Military Park, Chickamauga GA; C. C. Wilson to wife, 22 September, 15 October 1863, C. C. Wilson Papers, Georgia Historical Society, Savannah GA.

[17]NA, M266 ("Confederate Soldiers from Georgia"), roll 149–50, Holcombe and Sadler service records; R. Cuyler King to sister, 12 September 1863, King Family Papers, Southern Historical Collection, Chapel Hill NC.

[18]NA, M266 ("Confederate Soldiers from Georgia"), roll 148, Crane service

record; Henderson, *Confederate Soldiers of Georgia*, 1:923; Julia Crane Charlton to Thomas J. Charlton, 28 December 1863, 30 March 1864; H. A. Crane to Thomas J. Charlton, 29 March 1864, Charlton Family Papers, collection 132, Georgia Historical Society, Savannah GA.

[19] *Savannah Republican,* 23 September 1863; Savannah *Daily Morning News,* 25 September, 1 October, 3 October 1863.

[20] *Savannah Republican*, 28 September 1863.

[21] *Savannah Republican*, 26 October 1863.

[22]Henderson, *Confederate Soldiers of Georgia*, 3:557, 572; Descriptive Roll of the 28 Men furnished by 30th Regiment Ga. Vol. for the 1st Battn. Ga. Sharpshooters, George C. Dent File, Walter C. Hartridge, Jr. Collection, Georgia Historical Society, Savannah GA; Joe D. Parrott, Huntsville AL, telephone conversation with author, 19 August 2002; NA, M266 ("Confederate Soldiers from Georgia"), roll 150, "W. J. Parrott Service Record."

[23]NA, M266 ("Confederate Soldiers from Georgia"), roll 150, O'Quinn service record; M653 ("1860 Census"), roll 111, "Appling County," 55; Folks Huxford, comp., *Pioneers of Wiregrass Georgia*, 8 vols. (self-published, 1951–1988) 5:327; Henderson, *Confederate Soldiers of Georgia*, 5:727.

[24]John I. Royal to wife, 24 September 1863, John I. Royal letters, Betty F. Brown and Royal F. Brown papers, Rochelle GA; G. W. Sheppard, Jr., of Warner Robins GA, quoted in Richard A. Baumgartner and Larry M. Strayer, *Echoes of Battle: The Struggle for Chattanooga* (Huntington WV: Blue Acorn Press, 1996) 101; NA, M266 ("Confederate Soldiers from Georgia"), roll 150, Sheppard service record.

[25]NA, M266 ("Confederate Soldiers from Georgia"), roll 149, Gately service record; M653 ("1860 Census"), roll 115, "Chatham County," 67; M593 ("1870 Census"), roll 141, "City of Savannah," 452.

[26]1st Sharpshooter Battalion, D Company Muster Roll, September 1 to October 31, 1863, George C. Dent Papers, Georgia Historical Society, Savannah GA; NA, M266 ("Confederate Soldiers from Georgia"), roll 148, "E. Bryant Service Record"; Henderson, *Confederate Soldiers of Georgia*, 3:477.

[27]NA, M266 ("Confederate Soldiers from Georgia"), roll 150, service record; Barbara Crites, "William Henry Schmidt," http: //genforum.genealogy.com/sc/aiken/messages/236.html.

[28]NA, M266 ("Confederate Soldiers from Georgia"), rolls 148–50, service records.

[29]Joseph T. Derry, *Georgia*, extended ed., vol.7 of *Confederate Military History*, ed. Clement A. Evans(1899; reprint, Wilmington NC: Broadfoot Publishing, 1987–1989) 661; NA, M266 ("Confederate Soldiers from Georgia"), roll 149, Foster service record; Henderson, *Confederate Soldiers of Georgia*, 3:747.

[30]Tabular Statement of the Organization of Walker's Division, Army of Tennessee, undated [October 1863], endorsed on reverse as "Walker's division, Longstreet's Corps," folder 11, Bragg Papers, Cleveland OH; D Company Muster Roll, 31 October 1863, Dent Papers, Georgia Historical Society, Savannah GA; Shaaff to Samuel Cooper, 16 November 1863, in Shaaff Service Record, NA, M266

("Confederate Soldiers from Georgia"), roll 150.

[31]Mallory P. King to R. Cuyler King, 19 October 1863, King Family Papers, Southern Historical Collection, Chapel Hill NC; George C. Dent File, Walter C. Hartridge, Jr. Collection, Georgia Historical Society, Savannah GA.

[32]"Tout le Monde" to the editor, *Savannah Republican,* 12 October 1864.

[33]C. C. Wilson to wife, 8, 11, and 13 October 1863, C. C. Wilson Papers, Georgia Historical Society, Savannah GA. It will be remembered that the men of the brigade had thrown away or lost their personal equipment in Mississippi and it had never been replaced.

[34]Ibid.

[35]C. C. Wilson to wife, 15 and 31 October 1863, C. C. Wilson Papers, Georgia Historical Society, Savannah GA; Ezra J. Warner, *Generals in Gray* (1959; reprint, Baton Rouge: Louisiana State University Press, 1986) 339.

[36]Extracted from Tabular Statement of the Organization of Walker's Division, folder 11, Bragg Papers, Cleveland OH.

[37]Baumgartner and Strayer, *Struggle for Chattanooga*, 177, 178, 181; R. Cuyler King to sister, 29 October 1863, King Family Papers, Southern Historical Collection, Chapel Hill NC; Russell K. Brown, "Battle at Wauhatchie (Brown's Ferry) (28–29 October 1863)" in David S. and Jeanne T. Heidler, eds., *Encyclopedia of the American Civil War*, 5 vols. (Santa Barbara CA: ABC-CLIO, 2000) 4:2076–77.

[38]Edwin R. MacKethan III, ed., *The Story of the Page-King Family of Retreat Plantation, St. Simons Island and of the Golden Isles of Georgia* (Darien GA: published by the editor, 2000) 86–87; correspondence between MacKethan and the author; Bessie Lewis, *King's Retreat Plantation*, vol. 2 of *Plantations of Coastal Georgia*, ed. Mildred Huie and Mildred Wilcox (Brunswick GA: Coastal Printing, 1980) 68; Murray, *South Georgia Rebels*, 17; Warner, *Generals in Gray*, 285–86; NA, M653 ("1860 Census"), roll 124, "Glynn County," 243; M266 ("Confederate Soldiers from Georgia"), roll 149, King service record.

[39]Brown, *To the Manner Born*, 183–84.

[40]C. C. Wilson to wife, 31 October 1863, C. C. Wilson Papers, Georgia Historical Society, Savannah GA; Shaaff to Cooper, 16 November 1863, Shaaff Service Record, NA, M266 ("Confederate Soldiers from Georgia"), roll 150; Brown, *To the Manner Born*, 187–88; J. Cooper Nisbet, *Four Years on the Firing Line*, Bell I. Wiley, ed. (Jackson TN: McCowat-Mercer Press, 1963) xiv, 143–44.

[41]Nisbet, *Four Years on the Firing Line*, 144.

[42]John I. Royal to his wife ("In the Swamp Chickamauga"), 6 November 1863, Royal letters, Brown papers, Rochelle GA.

[43]R. C. King to sister, 22 November 1863, King Family Papers, Southern Historical Collection, Chapel Hill NC; NA, M266 ("Confederate Soldiers from Georgia"), roll 149, Dent service record.

[44]NA, M331 ("Compiled Service Records of Confederate General and Staff Officers and Non-Regimental Enlisted Men" [Hereafter "Confederate General and Staff Officers."]), roll 252, Twyman service record.

[45]NA, M266 ("Confederate Soldiers from Georgia"), roll 150, Patillo service

record.

[46]NA, M266 ("Confederate Soldiers from Georgia"), roll 149; M331 ("Confederate General and Staff Officers"), roll 74, "John Dent Service Records"; NA, M437 ("Letters Received by the Confederate Secretary of War, 1861–1865"), roll 98, letter 192-J-1863, H. H. Jones to Jefferson Davis, 22 June 1863.

[47]R. Cuyler King to sister, 29 October 1863, King Family Papers, Southern Historical Collection, Chapel Hill NC.

[48]Brown, *To the Manner Born*, 188–89.

[49] *Savannah Republican,* 1 December 1863; Horace D. Brown, "William Lawrence Thomas, Army of the Confederacy, 30th Georgia Regiment and First Battalion Georgia Sharpshooters," unpublished family memoir, Miami FL. Mr. Brown is Thomas's grandson; his memoir is based on his grandfather's handwritten reminicsences.

[50]NA, M266 ("Confederate Soldiers from Georgia"), rolls 149–50, service records, M653 ("1860 Census"), roll 124, "Gordon County," 310.

[51]*Savannah Republican,* 18 November, 1 and 15 December 1863.

[52]R. Cuyler King to sister, 2 December 1863, King Family Papers, Southern Historical Collection, Chapel Hill NC; NA, M266 ("Confederate Soldiers from Georgia"), roll 149, King service record.

[53]*OR*, vol. 31, pt. 3, p. 824.

CHAPTER 4

[1]Ezra J. Warner, *Generals in Gray* (1959; reprint, Baton Rouge: Louisiana State University Press, 1986) 291; NA, M331 ("Compiled Service Records of Confederate General and Staff Officers and Non-Regimental Enlisted Men" [Hereafter "Confederate General and Staff Officers."]), roll 236, Stevens service record; C. H. Stevens to "My dear Colonel," 19 April 1864, in Clement H. Stevens Papers, South Caroliniana Library, University of South Carolina, Columbia SC; C. H. Stevens obituary, *Charleston Courier*, 27 July 1864.

[2]J. Cooper Nisbet, *Four Years on the Firing Line*, Bell I. Wiley, ed. (Jackson TN: McCowat-Mercer Press, 1963) 169–70, 175.

[3]Angus McDermid to parents, 26 March, 17 April 1864, Angus McDermid letters, Benjamin C. Rountree papers, Amherst MA.

[4]Adamson to sister, 20 March 1864, in Richard Bender Abell and Faye Adamson Gecik, eds., *Sojourns of a Patriot: The Field and Prison Papers of an Unreconstructed Confederate* (Murfreesboro TN: Southern Heritage Press, 1998) 213–14; *Savannah Republican,* 25 April 1864.

[5]NA, M266 ("Compiled Service Records of Confederate Soldiers Who Served in Organizations from the State of Georgia" [Hereafter "Confederate Soldiers from Georgia"]), roll 150, "Arthur Shaaff Service Record," Shaaff to Cooper, 16 November 1863, 9 January 1864. The command of the 25th Georgia went to its major, William J. Winn.

[6]NA, M266 ("Confederate Soldiers from Georgia"), roll 150, "Arthur Shaaff Service Record," Shaaff to Cooper, 16 November 1863; rolls 231–32, "8th Georgia

Battalion," Leroy Napier and Zach L. Watters service records; M331 ("Confederate General and Staff Officers"), roll 186, "Leroy Napier Service Record"; M653 ("1860 Census"), roll 111, "Bibb County," 569; George W. Cullum, *Biographical Register of the Officers and Graduates of the United States Military Academy*, 3rd ed., 2 vols. (Boston: Houghton Mifflin, 1891) 1807.

[7]Russell K. Brown, *To the Manner Born: The Life of General William H. T. Walker* (Athens: University of Georgia Press, 1994) 205; Richard Irvine Manning to his mother, 28 January 1864, in Williams-Chesnut-Manning Family Papers, South Caroliniana Library, University of South Carolina, Columbia SC; R. Cuyler King to sister, 23 March 1864, Thomas Butler King Family Papers, Southern Historical Collection, University of North Carolina, Chapel Hill NC; Adamson to sister, 6 February 1864, in Abell and Gecik, eds., *Sojourns of A Patriot*, 205.

[8]Frank S. Roberts, "In Winter Quarters at Dalton, Ga., 1863–64," *Confederate Veteran* vol. 26, no. 6, (June 1918): 274.

[9]Joseph E. Johnston, *Narrative of Operations Directed During the Late War Between the States* (1874; reprint, Bloomington: Indiana University Press, 1959) 278; Joseph E. Brown to J. E. Johnston, 10 February 1864, in US War Department, *The War of the Rebellion, A Compilation of the Official Records of the Union and Confederate Armies* (hereafter *OR*) 128 vols. (Washington, DC: US Government Printing Office, 1880–1901) ser. 1, vol. 52, pt. 2, p. 616 (Hereafter *OR*. Citations from *OR* are series 1 unless otherwise specified.); Governor Joseph E. Brown's Letter Book, 1860–65, 597, RG 1, Georgia Division of Archives and History, Atlanta, Georgia; Frank S. Roberts, "Review of the Army of Tennessee at Dalton, Ga.," *Confederate Veteran,* vol. 26(1918): 150.

[10]NA, M266 ("Confederate Soldiers from Georgia"), roll 150, Stephan service record; M347 ("Unfiled Papers and Slips Belonging to Confederate Compiled Service Records" [Hereafter "Unfiled Papers and Slips."]), roll 378, "William Stephan File"; M653 ("1860 Census"), roll 114, "Chatham County," 369; Roberts, "In Winter Quarters," 274. There were three men named William H. Stephens in the Savannah 1860 census. One was an engineeer and another a clothing dealer; the third, a grocer, was most likely the commissary sergeant. In the city directory there were a baker and a clothing dealer.

[11]John I. Royal to his wife, 8 December 1863, John I. Royal letters, Betty F. Brown and Royal F. Brown papers, Rochelle GA; NA, M266 ("Confederate Soldiers from Georgia"), rolls 148, 150, Culpepper and Stokes service records.

[12]*OR*, vol. 31, pt. 3, p. 657; vol. 32, pt. 2, pp. 586, 776; vol. 32, pt. 3, pp. 602, 657, 720, 866.

[13]Walter Brian Cisco, *States Rights Gist: A South Carolina General of the Civil War* (Shippensburg PA: White Mane Publishing, 1991) 116; Nisbet, *Four Years on the Firing Line*, 175.

[14]*OR*, vol. 32, pt. 2, pp. 602, 670.

[15]NA, M266 ("Confederate Soldiers from Georgia"), rolls 148–50, service records; *Savannah Republican,* 22 February 1864.

[16]NA, M266 ("Confederate Soldiers from Georgia"), rolls 148, 150, Coe and Luke

Williams service records; M653 ("1860 Census"), roll 128, "Jasper County," 328; C. M. Hardy to sister, 18 September 1864, C. M. Hardy Letters Mrs. O. E. Lancaster Collection Georgia Division of Archives and History, Atlanta GA.

[17] NA, M266 ("Confederate Soldiers from Georgia"), roll 150, Roath service record.

[18] Army of Tennessee circular, 21 March 1864, cited in Dana M. Mangham, *"Oh, For a Touch of the Vanished Hand": Discovering a Southern Family and the Civil War* (Murfreesboro TN: Southern Heritage Press, 2000) 69–70.

[19] Tabular Statement of the Organization of Walker's Division, folder 11, William P. Palmer Collection of Braxton Bragg Papers, Western Reserve Historical Society, Cleveland OH; *OR*, vol. 31, pt. 3, p. 824; *Savannah Republican,* 14 July 1864.

[20] W. W. Mackall to wife, 5 February 1864, William W. Mackall Papers, Southern Historical Collection, University of North Carolina, Chapel Hill NC; Shaaff Family File, Walter C. Hartridge, Jr. Collection, collection 1349, Georgia Historical Society, Savannah GA; Georgia Smith to R. Cuyler King, 29 August 1863, in Lewis, *King's Retreat Plantation*, 60–61.

[21] See letter of Theo. H. Winn to the editor, *Macon Telegraph,* 17 August 1867, reprinted in *Augusta Chronicle & Sentinel*, 3 May 1868.

[22] NA, M266 ("Confederate Soldiers from Georgia"), rolls 148–50, service records; R. Cuyler King to sister, 23 March 1864, King Family Papers, Southern Historical Collection, Chapel Hill NC.

[23] NA, M266 ("Confederate Soldiers from Georgia"), rolls 148, 150; R. Cuyler King to sister, 23 March 1864, King Family Papers, Southern Historical Collection, Chapel Hill NC.

[24] NA, M266 ("Confederate Soldiers from Georgia"), roll 149, Leonard service record.

[25] Ibid., Kraft service record.

[26] NA, M347 ("Unfiled Papers and Slips"), roll 43, Dominique Brown unfiled slip; War Department endorsement, 8 June 1864, RG 109, chap. 1, vol. 161, p. 223, War Department Collection of Confederate Records, National Archives, Washington, DC.

[27] Christopher Losson, *Tennessee's Forgotten Warriors* (Knoxville: University of Tennessee Press, 1989) 118–19, 133, 135; Thomas L. Connelly, *Autumn of Glory: The Army of Tennessee, 1862–1865* (Baton Rouge: Louisiana State University Press, 1971) 250; Brown, *To the Manner Born*, 205–208; *OR*, vol. 31, pt. 2, pp. 487, 716; vol. 31, pt. 3, pp. 685–86,; vol. 32, pt. 2, pp. 537–38, 560, 670, 813–14. Although most sources are vague on the date of the transfer of brigades among the divisions, Dunbar Rowland, *Military History of Mississippi, 1803–1898* (1908; reprint, Spartanburg SC: The Reprint Company, 1978) 167, 194, states positively that it was 2 February.

[28] Angus McDermid to his parents, 20 February 1864, McDermid letters, Rountree papers, Amherst MA.

[29] *OR*, vol. 32, pt. 1, pp. 8–11; Connelly, *Autumn of Glory*, 294; Nathaniel Cheairs Hughes, Jr., *General William J. Hardee, Old Reliable* (Baton Rouge LA: Louisiana

State University Press, 1965) 194–96; Irving A. Buck, *Cleburne and His Command* (New York: Neale, 1908) 225–27; Losson, *Forgotten Warriors*, 140.

[30]Howard Michael Madaus and Robert D. Needham, *The Battle Flags of the Confederate Army of Tennessee* (Milwaukee: Milwaukee Public Museum, 1976) 102–103, 63; *OR*, vol. 32, pt. 3, p. 647.

[31]George W. Gordon, "The Famous Snowball Battle in the Confederate Army at Dalton, Ga., 1864," in Ben LaBree, ed. *Camp Fires of the Confederacy* (Louisville: Courier-Journal Job Printing Company, 1898) 48–53; Steve Davis, "The Great Snow Battle of 1864," *Civil War Times Illustrated* 15 (June 1976): 32–35; Nisbet, *Four Years on the Firing Line*, 175–76; William G. Bentley, "The Great Snowball Battle," *Civil War Times Illustrated* 5 (January 1967): 22–23; R. Cuyler King to sister, 23 March 1864, King Family Papers, Southern Historical Collection, Chapel Hill NC.

[32]Walker to wife, 2 April 1864, W. H. T. Walker Papers, Duke University, Durham NC; Richard M. McMurry, *John Bell Hood and the War for Southern Independence* (Lexington: University of Kentucky Press, 1982) 100; Roberts, "Review of the Army of Tennessee," 150.

[33]John I. Royal to his wife, 8 December 1863, Royal letters, Brown papers, Rochelle GA; NA, M266 ("Confederate Soldiers from Georgia"), roll 150, Royal service record; Betty Fitzgerald Brown, conversation with author, 9 August 2003.

[34]M266 ("Confederate Soldiers from Georgia"), rolls 148–50, service records; Lillian Henderson, ed., *Roster of the Confederate Soldiers of Georgia, 1861–1865*, 6 vols. (Hapeville GA: Longino and Porter, 1955–1962) 5:89, 644.

[35]Brown, *To the Manner Born*, 219–20, 237, 241.

[36]R. Cuyler King to sister, 6 May 1864, King Family Papers, Southern Historical Collection, Chapel Hill NC; W. W. Mackall to wife, 2 May 1864; Mackall Papers, Southern Historical Collection, Chapel Hill NC; Brown, *To the Manner Born*, 216; Angus McDermid to his mother, 1 May 1864, McDermid letters, Rountree papers, Amherst MA.

CHAPTER 5

[1]E. Merton Coulter, "Thomas Butler King," in *Dictionary of American Biography*, ed. Allen Johnson and Dumas Malone, 10 vols. (New York: Charles Scribner's Sons, 1964) vol. 5, pt. 2, p. 403; Georgia Smith to Cuyler King, 16 May, 6 June 1864, Bessie Lewis, *King's Retreat Plantation*, vol. 2 of *Plantations of Coastal Georgia*, ed. Mildred Huie and Mildred Wilcox (Brunswick GA: Coastal Printing, 1980) 73–75; Cuyler King to sister, 13 September 1864, King Family Papers, Southern Historical Collection, Chapel Hill NC.

[2]NA, M266 ("Compiled Service Records of Confederate Soldiers Who Served in Organizations from the State of Georgia" [Hereafter "Confederate Soldiers from Georgia"]), rolls 149–50, D. Brown, P. Derst, Hardy, Norris and Benjamin Walker service records; Lillian Henderson, ed., *Roster of the Confederate Soldiers of Georgia, 1861–1865*, 6 vols. (Hapeville GA: Longino and Porter, 1955–1962) 3:661; M653 ("1860 Census"), roll 123, "Jasper County," 236–37; C. M. Hardy to sister, 12 June, 7 October 1861, C. M. Hardy Letters, Georgia Division of Archives

and History, Atlanta GA; W. D. Cornell, "Hardy," in *History of Jasper County, Georgia* (Monticello GA: Jasper County Historical Foundation, Inc., 1984) 192. The cousin Cornelius was a soldier in the 32nd Georgia until he died at home in 1864.

[3]1st Battalion Georgia Sharpshooter Muster Rolls, RG 109, War Department Collection of Confederate Records, National Archives, Washington, DC; NA, M266, "Confederate Soldiers from Georgia," roll 116, "Capt. Wheaton's Company (Chatham Artillery)"; roll 136, "1st (Olmstead's) Georgia"; roll 149, "1st Sharpshooter Battalion," "A. H. Gordon Service Record"; M474 ("Letters Received by the Confederate Adjutant and Inspector General, 1861–1865"), roll 66, letter 1320-G-1863, J. A. Maxwell to Samuel Cooper, 11 December 1863, with endorsements; M432 ("1850 Census"), roll 64, "Chatham County," 316; M653 ("1860 Census"), roll 115, "Chatham County," 240.

[4]W. W. Sellers, *A History of Marion County, South Carolina* (1902; reprint, Greenville SC: Southern Historical Press, 1996) 52, 168–69; NA, M266 ("Confederate Soldiers from Georgia"), roll 149, Ford service record; M267 ("Compiled Service Records of Confederate Soldiers Who Served in Organizations from the State of South Carolina"), roll 241, "10th Infantry," "C. T. Ford Service Record"; M331 ("Compiled Service Records of Confederate General and Staff Officers and Non-Regimental Enlisted Men" [Hereafter "Confederate General and Staff Officers."]), roll 96, "C. T. Ford Service Record"; M653 ("1860 Census"), roll 1223, "Marion District, S. C.," 14; Joseph Jones, "Roster of the Medical Officers of the Army of Tennessee..." *Southern Historical Society Papers* 22 (1894): 202.

[5]NA, M331 ("Confederate General and Staff Officers"), roll 63, "T. R. Cosby Service Record."

[6]Hamilton Branch to Charlotte Branch, 18 May 1864, Hamilton Branch Letters, Margaret Branch Sexton Collection, MS 25, Hargrett Rare Book and Manuscript Library, University of Georgia Libraries, Athens GA; John W. Hagan to wife, 16 and 18 May 1864, *Confederate Letters of John W. Hagan*, ed. Bell I. Wiley (Athens: University of Georgia Press, 1957). The Branch letters have been transcribed by Mauriel Phillips Joslyn in *Charlotte's Boys: Civil War Letters of the Branch Family of Savannah* (Berryville VA: Rockbridge Publishing Company, 1996). For the discussion of the Atlanta campaign of 1864 in the following pages, the reader is referred to Albert Castel, *Decision in the West: The Atlanta Campaign of 1864* (Lawrence: University Press of Kansas, 1992).

[7]Castel, *Decision in the West*, 153, 163–64, 168; Russell K. Brown, *To the Manner Born: The Life of General William H. T. Walker* (Athens: University of Georgia Press, 1994) 225–27; A. P. Adamson, *A Brief History of the Thirtieth Georgia Regiment* (Jonesboro GA: Freedom Hill Press, 1987) 39.

[8]Brown, *To the Manner Born*, 227–30; Castel, *Decision in the West*, 178–79.

[9]US War Department, *The War of the Rebellion, A Compilation of the Official Records of the Union and Confederate Armies* (hereafter *OR*) 128 vols. (Washington, DC: US Government Printing Office, 1880–1901)ser. 1, vol. 38, pt. 3, pp. 377, 402, 448, 714 (Hereafter *OR*. All citation from *OR* are series 1 unless otherwise specified.); Eugene W. Jones, Jr., *Enlisted for the War: The Struggles of the Gallant 24th*

Regiment, South Carolina Volunteers, Infantry, 1861–1865 (Hightstown NJ: Longstreet House, 1997) 161–63; Walter Brian Cisco, *States Rights Gist: A South Carolina General of the Civil War* (Shippensburg PA: White Mane Publishing, 1991) 122; Samuel McKittrick to wife, 17 May 1864, Samuel McKittrick Letters, Kennesaw Mountain National Battlefield Park, Kennesaw GA.

[10]*OR*, vol. 38, pt. 3, pp. 378–79, 402, 448.

[11]Hamilton Branch to the editor, *Savannah Republican,* 24 May 1864; Hamilton Branch to his mother, 18 May 1864, Branch Letters, University of Georgia, Athens GA.

[12]Lizzie Shaaff to Hamilton Branch, 25 May 1864, Branch Letters, University of Georgia, Athens GA.

[13]*OR*, vol. 38, pt. 3, p. 714; 13. *Savannah Republican,* 19 and 20 May 1864.

[14]*Savannah Republican,* 28 May, 4 July 1864; NA, M266 ("Confederate Soldiers from Georgia"), roll 150, Twyman service record.

[15]NA, M266 ("Confederate Soldiers from Georgia"), roll 149, Maddox and Mattox service records; Henderson, *Confederate Soldiers of Georgia*, 3:539.

[16]Adamson to father, 31 May 1864, in Richard Bender Abell and Faye Adamson Gecik, eds., *Sojourns of a Patriot: The Field and Prison Papers of an Unreconstructed Confederate* (Murfreesboro TN: Southern Heritage Press, 1998) 229; NA, M266 ("Confederate Soldiers from Georgia"), roll 149, service records.

[17]Brown, *To the Manner Born*, 77–79; M653 ("1860 Census"), roll 136, "Screven County," 149; Dixon Hollingsworth, ed., *The History of Screven County, Georgia* (Dallas TX: Curtis Media Corp., 1989) 203; *Memoirs of Georgia*, 2 vols. (Atlanta GA: Southern Historical Association, 1895) 2:825-26.

[18]NA, M266 ("Confederate Soldiers from Georgia"), roll 149, Lee service record.

[19]Ibid., Doyle and Logan Service Records; M653 ("1860 Census"), roll 115, "Chatham County," 115.

[20]Kevin Thurman (Garner descendant) email to the author, 10 July 2002; Burton J. Bell, *Bi-Centennial History of Gordon County, Georgia* (Calhoun GA: Gordon County Historical Society, 1976) 116; NA, M266 ("Confederate Soldiers from Georgia"), roll 149, Garner service record.

[21]RG 109, chap. 6, vol. 48, p. 183, Confederate Records, National Archives; Angus McDermid to parents, 5 June 1864, Angus McDermid letters, Benjamin C. Rountree papers, Amherst MA.

[22]*Atlanta Confederacy*, 10 June 1864.

[23]John W. Hagan to his wife, 17 June 1864, *Confederate Letters of John W. Hagan*, ed. Bell I. Wiley (Athens: University of Georgia Press, 1957); Angus McDermid to his parents, 24 June 1864, McDermid letters, Rountree papers, Amherst MA; George A. Mercer Diary (typescript), "Journal of Campaign," 15, 16, and 18 June 1864, Mercer Family Papers, Georgia Historical Society, Savannah GA; Walter A. Clark, *Under the Stars and Bars, or Memories of Four Years Service with the Oglethorpes of Augusta, Georgia* (Augusta: Chronicle Printing Co., 1900) 101, 117–24.

[24]NA, M266 ("Confederate Soldiers from Georgia"), rolls 148–50, service

records; M653 ("1860 Census"), roll 115, "Chatham County," 170; *Savannah Republican,* 14 July 1864, repeated in the *Augusta Chronicle & Sentinel,* 3 August 1864; Hamilton Branch to his mother, 19 June 1864, Branch Letters, University of Georgia, Athens GA; Savannah City Directory, 1860.

[25]*Savannah Republican,* 1 and 6 August 1864; NA, M266 ("Confederate Soldiers from Georgia"), roll 148, Bierhalter service record.

[26]*Savannah Republican,* 10 June 1864.

[27]John W. Hagan to his wife, 21 and 22 June 1864, *Confederate Letters of John W. Hagan;* Angus McDermid to parents, 24 June 1864, Angus McDermid letters, Benjamin C. Rountree papers, Amherst MA.

[28]John W. Hagan to wife, 28 June 1864, *Confederate Letters of John W. Hagan;* Henderson, *Confederate Soldiers of Georgia,* 3:465, 492.

[29]Steven H. Newton, "Formidable Only in Flight?," *North and South* No. 4, 3 (April 2000): 45.

[30]NA, M266 ("Confederate Soldiers from Georgia"), rolls 149–50, service records; *Atlanta Intelligencer,* 24 and 26 June 1864; *Savannah Republican,* 25 and 30 June, 1 and 4 July 1864. The registry of Laurel Grove Cemetery, Savannah, shows Gordon's burial date as 21 June.

[31]NA, M266 ("Confederate Soldiers from Georgia"), roll 137, "1st Georgia"; roll 149, Knowles service records; Henderson, *Confederate Soldiers of Georgia,* 1:167. Knowles cannot be found in the 1860 Chatham County census or the 1860 Savannah city directory.

[32]J. Cooper Nisbet, *Four Years on the Firing Line,* Bell I. Wiley, ed. (Jackson TN: McCowat-Mercer Press, 1963) 204; NA, M266 ("Confederate Soldiers from Georgia"), rolls 148–50, service records.

[33]Nisbet, *Four Years on the Firing Line,* 203; *OR,* vol. 38, pt. 1, p. 564.

[34]*Savannah Republican,* 14 July; *Augusta Chronicle and Sentinel,* 3 August 1864; *Atlanta Confederacy,* 17 May 1864, reprinted in Richard A. Baumgartner and Larry M. Strayer, *Kennesaw Mountain, June 1864* (Huntington WV: Blue Acorn Press, 1998) 43; NA, M266 ("Confederate Soldiers from Georgia"), roll 149, Dobson service record.

[35]*Confederate Reminiscences and Letters, 1861–1865,* 18 vols. to date (Atlanta GA: United Daughters of the Confederacy, 1996–2002) 6:119; C. M. Hardy to sister, 18 September 1864, C. M. Hardy Letters, Atlanta GA; NA, M653 ("1860 Census"), roll 128, "Jasper County," 251.

[36]NA, M266 ("Confederate Soldiers from Georgia"), roll 150, service records; M653 ("1860 Census"), roll 135, "Randolph County," 139.

[37]NA, M266 ("Confederate Soldiers from Georgia"), rolls 148–50, service records; correspondence with Barbra Crites in regard to the Schmidt family. The confusion between George and John Garner has already been discussed.

[38]NA, M266 ("Confederate Soldiers from Georgia"), roll 150, Hardy and Joseph Tuten service records; M653 ("1860 Census"), roll 133, "Pierce County," 1025; roll 140, "Ware County," 145; Folks Huxford, comp., *Pioneers of Wiregrass Georgia,* 8 vols. (self-published, 1951–1988) 7:432–33. Joseph Tuten's age is near impossible

to read but his wife was thirty-three and his oldest son was eighteen.

[39]Brown, *To the Manner Born*, 250, 279.

[40]NA, M266 ("Confederate Soldiers from Georgia"), roll 149, "W. Kersey Service Record"; M653 ("1860 Census"), roll 135, "Randolph County," 642; Henderson, *Confederate Soldiers of Georgia*, 5:18.

[41]*OR*, vol. 38, pt. 3, p. 717.

[42]Brown, *To the Manner Born*, 256.

[43]Ibid., 259–60; *OR*, vol. 38, pt. 3, p. 925; Castel, *Decision in the West*, 376.

[44]Brown, *To the Manner Born*, 261; John W. Hagan to wife, 21 July 1864, *Confederate Letters of John W. Hagan*; Angus McDermid to parents, 21 July 1864, McDermid letters, Rountree papers, Amherst MA.

[45]John W. Hagan to wife, 21 July 1864, *Confederate Letters of John W. Hagan*.

[46]Angus McDermid to parents, 21 July 1864, McDermid letters, Rountree papers, Amherst MA.

[47]NA, M266 ("Confederate Soldiers from Georgia"), roll 149, service records; Henderson, *Confederate Soldiers of Georgia*, 3:431.

[48]Brown, *To the Manner Born*, 267–69, 271, 279.

[49]*Savannah Republican,* 22, 27, 28, 29 July 1864; *OR*, vol. 38, pt. 3, p. 664. Johnston's presence at East Point is unexplained.

[50]NA, M266 ("Confederate Soldiers from Georgia"), rolls 148–50, service records.

[51]Thomas A. Valentine, *The Valentine Family of Georgia* (Roswell GA: self-published, 1992) 1b; correspondence with Thomas A. Valentine, May 2003; NA, M266 ("Confederate Soldiers from Georgia"), roll 150, Valentine service record; M432 ("1850 Census"), roll 71, "Greene County," 110; Henderson, *Confederate Soldiers of Georgia*, 3:585.

[52]NA, M266 ("Confederate Soldiers from Georgia"), rolls 148–50, service records; M653 ("1860 Census"), roll 113, "Chatham County," 280, 304; M598 ("Selected Records of the War Department Relating to Confederate Prisoners of War, 1861–1865"), roll 27, "Camp Chase, Ohio, Military Prison, Register of Deaths and Burials, 1863–1865." Marlitta Perkins, "Camp Chase Research Sources," <http://www.geocites.com/campchase/index.html.>

[53]John W. Hagan to his wife, 28 July1864; John W. Hagn to his father, 18 August 1864, *Confederate Letters of John W. Hagan*.

[54]Angus McDermid to parents, 24 July 1864, McDermid letters, Rountree papers, Amherst MA.

[55]Cuyler King to his brother, 22 July 1864, King Family Papers, Southern Historical Collection, Chapel Hill NC.

[56]Brown, *To the Manner Born*, 284; *Savannah Republican,* 28 July 1864.

[57]Theodore H. Jack, "Henry Rootes Jackson," in *Dictionary of American Biography*, ed. Allen Johnson and Dumas Malone, 10 vols. (New York: Charles Scribner's Sons, 1964); John O. Eidson, "Henry Rootes Jackson," in Kenneth Coleman and Charles S. Gurr, eds., *Dictionary of Georgia Biography*, 2 vols. (Athens GA: University of Georgia Press, 1983); Wilbur G. Kurtz, Jr., "The First Regiment of

Georgia Volunteers in the Mexican War," *Georgia Historical Quarterly*, no. 4, 27 (1943): 301–23; Brown, *To the Manner Born*, 91–92, 120–25, 284.

[58]Joseph B. Cumming, *A Sketch of the Descendants of David Cumming and Memoirs of the War Between the States*, ed. Mary Gairdner Smith Cumming (Augusta: self-published, 1925) 72–73; NA, M266 ("Confederate Soldiers from Georgia"), roll 150; M331 ("Confederate General and Staff Officers"), roll 216, Ross service records.

[59]NA, M266 ("Confederate Soldiers from Georgia"), roll 149, Holcombe service record; M331 ("Confederate General and Staff Officers"), roll 261, "Robert Wayne Service Record."

[60]*OR*, vol. 38, pt. 3, p. 699.

[61]NA, M266 ("Confederate Soldiers from Georgia"), roll 149, Davis service record.

[62]Ibid., Johnston service record.

[63]Ibid., rolls 149–50, "Jones and Norris Service Records"; Savannah *Daily Morning News*, 15 August 1864; *Savannah Republican,* 18 August 1864.

[64]*Savannah Republican,* 18 August 1864; Lee Kennett, *Marching Through Georgia* (New York: Harper Collins, 1995) 196–97.

[65]NA, M266 ("Confederate Soldiers from Georgia"), roll 149, service records; M653 ("1860 Census"), roll 141, "Whitfield County," 35; Henderson, *Confederate Soldiers of Georgia*, 5:631.

[66]NA, M331 ("Confederate General and Staff Officers"), roll 261, Wayne service record.

[67]Savannah *Daily Morning News*, 6 September 1864; Cuyler King to sister, 13 September 1864, King Family Papers, Southern Historical Collection, Chapel Hill NC.

[68]H. R. Jackson to B. F. Cheatham, 10 December 1864, B. F. Cheatham Papers (microfilm), manuscript collection 751, Tennessee State Library and Archives, Nashville TN. This letter has been printed in *Supplement to the Official Records*, ed. Janet Hewett (Wilmington NC: Broadfoot Publishing, 1997) pt. 1 ("Reports"), 7:103–106.

[69]NA, M266 ("Confederate Soldiers from Georgia"), roll 149, service records; Savannah *Daily Morning News*, 5 and 6 September 1864; Cuyler King to sister, 13 September 1864, King Family Papers, Southern Historical Collection, Chapel Hill NC; *Savannah Republican,* 2 September 1864. According to the 1860 census, Herrmann had a wife named Anna. See M653 ("1860 Census"), roll 115, "Chatham County," 10.

[70]*The Memoirs of Charles H. Olmstead*, ed. Lilla M. Hawes, in *Collections of the Georgia Historical Society*, 14 (Savannah: Georgia Historical Society, 1964) 154.

[71]Savannah *Daily Morning News*, 7 and 20 September, 15 October 1864.

[72]*Savannah Republican,* 8 September 1864.

[73]NA, M266 ("Confederate Soldiers from Georgia"), roll 148, "H. Bennett Service Record"; M653 ("1860 Census"), roll 111, "Appling County," 54; Huxford, *Pioneers of Wiregrass Georgia*, 5:29; Henderson, *Confederate Soldiers of Georgia*, 5:721;

information from Betty Bennett Joiner, granddaughter, 30 July 2002.

[74]NA, M266 ("Confederate Soldiers from Georgia"), rolls 148–50, service records; M653 ("1860 Census"), roll 125, "Greene County," 537; roll 128, "Jefferson County," 374; roll 133, "Pierce County," 1022; roll 136, "Screven County," 70; M432 ("1850 Census"), roll 75, "Jefferson County," 167b; Henderson, *Confederate Soldiers of Georgia*, 3:567; Kennett, *Marching Through Georgia*, 207–12.

[75]*Savannah Republican,* 19 September 1864.

CHAPTER 6

[1]Nathaniel Cheairs Hughes, Jr., *General William J. Hardee, Old Reliable* (Baton Rouge LA: Louisiana State University Press, 1965) 248–49; Walter A. Clark, *Under the Stars and Bars, or Memories of Four Years Service with the Oglethorpes of Augusta, Georgia* (Augusta: Chronicle Printing Co., 1900) 165–66; 29 September 1864, "Scraps of Journal kept by Capt. R. Cuyler King, 1st Georgia S. S. on the campaign of Hood from Jonesboro, Geo. into Tennessee the autumn of 1864...," Eileen King papers, Rockville MD. Hereafter cited as King Journal.

[2]NA, M331, ("Compiled Service Records of Confederate General and Staff Officers and Non-Regimental Enlisted Men, [Hereafter "Confederate General and Staff Officers"]), roll 216, "William H. Ross Service Record," William Ross to Congressman Clifford Anderson, 1 February 1865.

[3]NA, M266 ("Compiled Service Records of Confederate Soldiers Who Served in Organizations from the State of Georgia" [Hereafter "Confederate Soldiers from Georgia"]), rolls 148, 150, Bryan and Shaaff service records.

[4]Battalion Muster Rolls, RG 109, stack 7W4, B/7/14-15, 2 vols., War Department Collection of Confederate Records, National Archives, Washington, DC; Edward John Derst, III, Savannah, telephone conversation with author, 5 May 2003; M266 ("Confederate Soldiers from Georgia"), roll 150, "James Thornton Service Record."

[5] Mrs. O. E. Lancaster Collection, C. M. Hardy to sister, 18 September 1864, C. M. Hardy Letters (Sophie C. Hardy Family Letters) United Daughters of the Confederacy Collection, Georgia Division of Archives and History, Atlanta GA. "M. M. " is probably "N. M.," referring to Nathan M. Williams who was also absent wounded at this time.

[6]NA, M266 ("Confederate Soldiers from Georgia"), rolls 149, Hardee service record; King Journal, 9 October 1864, Eileen King papers, Rockville MD.

[7]NA, M266 ("Confederate Soldiers from Georgia"), roll 149–50, W. G. Gray and T. S. Wayne service records; rolls 384–85, "27th Georgia Battalion," Hartridge, Leonard and Wayne service records; M347 ("Unfiled Papers and Slips Belonging to Confederate Compiled Service Records" [Hereafter "Unfiled Papers and Slips."]), roll 154, "W. G. Gray Service Record"; Letter from 29th Georgia, 19 August 1864, *Savannah Republican,* 26 August 1864; King Journal, 24 November, 1864, Eileen King papers, Rockville MD.

[8]NA, M266 ("Confederate Soldiers from Georgia"), rolls 148, 150, Boggs and Shaw service records; Lillian Henderson, ed., *Roster of the Confederate Soldiers of Georgia, 1861–1865*, 6 vols. (Hapeville GA: Longino and Porter, 1955–1962)

3:678.

[9]Twyman to Charlotte Branch, 22 October 1864, Hamilton Branch Letters, Margaret Branch Sexton Collection, MS 25, Hargrett Rare Book and Manuscript Library, University of Georgia Libraries, Athens GA.

[10]NA, M474 ("Letters Received by the Confederate Adjutant and Inspector General, 1861–1865"), roll 145, letter 3942-S-1864, Arthur Shaaff to Samuel Cooper, 9 September 1864, with endorsements.

[11]US War Department, *The War of the Rebellion, A Compilation of the Official Records of the Union and Confederate Armies* (hereafter *OR*) 128 vols. (Washington, DC: US Government Printing Office, 1880–1901)ser. 1, vol. 39, pt. 2, pp. 850, 853, Organization and Returns of the Army of Tennessee, 20 September 1864.

[12]Richard M. McMurry, *John Bell Hood and the War for Southern Independence* (Lexington: University of Kentucky Press, 1982) 159–63; King Journal, 10 October 1864, Eileen King papers, Rockville MD.

[13]*OR*, vol. 39, pt. 1, pp. 826–27; King Journal, 15 October 1864, Eileen King papers, Rockville MD; H. R. Jackson to B. F. Cheatham, 10 December 1864, B. F. Cheatham Papers (microfilm), Tennessee State Library and Archives, Nashville TN.

[14]McMurry, *Hood*, 163; King Journal, 16, 17, 23, 25 October 1864, Eileen King papers, Rockville MD.

[15]McMurry, *Hood*, 163–65.

[16]*OR*, vol. 39, pt. 1, pp. 697, 827.

[17]Jackson to B. F. Cheatham, 10 December 1864, Cheatham Papers (microfilm), Tennessee State Library and Archives, Nashville TN; Angus McDermid to parents, 1 November 1864, McDermid letters, Rountree papers, Amherst MA.

[18]NA. M266 ("Confederate Soldiers from Georgia"), roll 149, service records; Henderson, *Confederate Soldiers of Georgia*, 3:758; M432 ("1850 Census"), roll 60, "Burke County," 292; information from Cindy Forehand Watts to the author, 1 July 2002; King Journal, 29 October 1864, Eileen King papers, Rockville MD.

[19]Cuyler King to sister, 1 November 1864, Thomas Butler King Family Papers, Southern Historical Collection, University of North Carolina, Chapel Hill NC.

[20]King Journal, 22 and 28 October; 2, 3, 11, 24 November 1864, Eileen King papers, Rockville MD.

[21]Angus McDermid to parents, 1 and 12 November 1864, McDermid letters, Rountree papers, Amherst MA.

[22]King Journal, 31 October; 4, 7, 27 November 1864, Eileen King papers, Rockville MD.

[23]NA, M474 ("Letters Received by the Confederate Adjutant and Inspector General, 1861–1865"), roll 124, letter 840-K-1864, Cuyler King to Samuel Cooper, Tuscumbia AL, ? November 1864; M266 ("Confederate Soldiers from Georgia"), roll 148, Bryan service record. King's letter may be the source of information on a card showing Alfred Bryan's appointment as adjutant to General Jackson dating from 1 November 1864. The card is misfiled with the service record of Major A[sbury] M. Bryan, Quartermaster, and is the only one pertaining to Lieutenant Bryan's staff duty. See M331 ("Confederate General and Staff Officers"), roll 38.

[24]*OR*, vol. 45, pt. 1, pp. 663, 678.

[25]King Journal, 10 November 1864, Eileen King papers, Rockville MD.

[26]Ibid., 13 and 14 November 1864; McMurry, *Hood*, 166.

[27]Ibid., 169; *OR*, vol. 45, pt. 1, pp. 736, 742.

[28]King Journal, 24, 25, 27 November 1864, Eileen King papers, Rockville MD.

[29]McMurry, *Hood*, 170–73; James Lee McDonough and Thomas L. Connelly, *Five Tragic Hours: The Battle of Franklin* (Knoxville: University of Tennessee Press, 1983) devote a whole chapter to "The Spring Hill Affair," 36–59.

[30]King Journal, 6 December 1864, Eileen King papers, Rockville MD.

[31]NA, M266 ("Confederate Soldiers from Georgia"), roll 149, Hall service record; Henderson, *Confederate Soldiers of Georgia*, 3:431.

[32]*OR*, vol. 45, pt. 1, pp. 742–43; McDonough and Connelly, *Five Tragic Hours*, 140–43.

[33]King Journal, 6 December 1864, Eileen King papers, Rockville MD; Jackson to B. F. Cheatham, 10 December 1864, Cheatham Papers (microfilm), Tennessee State Library and Archives, Nashville TN. The King Journal ends in mid-paragraph with this description of the battle of Franklin. Either he never finished or the rest was lost. James A. McCord to William McCord, 3 December 1864, *Confederate Reminiscences and Letters, 1861–1865*, 18 vols. to date (Atlanta GA: United Daughters of the Confederacy, 1996–2002) 3:221. The original of this letter is at the Woodruff Library, Emory University, Atlanta GA.

[34]*OR*, vol. 45, pt. 1, pp. 686, 743; Connelly and McDonough, *Five Tragic Hours*, 157.

[35]I[saac] N. Shannon, "Sharpshooters with Hood's Army," *Confederate Veteran* 15, no. 3 (March 1907): 123, 125–26; NA, M266 ("Confederate Soldiers from Georgia"), rolls 149–50, Forehand and E. G. Melton service records.

[36]*OR*, vol. 45, pt. 1, pp. 744–45.

[37]Jackson to Cheatham, 10 December 1864, Cheatham Papers (microfilm), Tennessee State Library and Archives, Nashville TN.

[38]*OR*, vol. 45, pt. 1, pp. 745–47, 756; Rountree, "Letters from a Confederate Soldier," *Georgia Review* 18 (1964): 296; King Journal, 6 December 1864, Eileen King papers, Rockville MD.

[39]Jackson to Cheatham, 10 December 1864, Cheatham Papers (microfilm), Tennessee State Library and Archives, Nashville TN.

[40]*OR*, vol. 45, pt. 1, p. 747; *The Memoirs of Charles H. Olmstead*, ed. Lilla M. Hawes, in *Collections of the Georgia Historical Society*, 14 (Savannah: Georgia Historical Society, 1964) 167.

[41]NA, M266 ("Confederate Soldiers from Georgia"), rolls 148–49, service records; M347 ("Unfiled Papers and Slips"), roll 412, "Robert P. Wayne Service Record"; Charles C. Jones, Jr., *The Siege of Savannah in December, 1864…* (Albany NY: Joel Munsell, 1874) 113–14.

[42]Jackson to Cheatham, 10 December 1864, Cheatham Papers (microfilm), Tennessee State Library and Archives, Nashville TN.

[43]*OR*, vol. 45, pt. 1, pp. 668, 679, 680. The slight discrepancy in the addition of

the figures is due to Bate's escort which had thirteen men effective and thirty-one aggregate on 13 December.

[44]Thomas L. Connelly, *Autumn of Glory: The Army of Tennessee, 1862–1865* (Baton Rouge: Louisiana State University Press, 1971) 508–12.

[45]*OR*, 45, pt. 1, pp. 747–50; NA, M266 ("Confederate Soldiers from Georgia"), roll 394, "29th Georgia," "William D. Mitchell Service Record"; Frank S. Roberts, "Spring Hill-Franklin-Nashville, 1864," *Confederate Veteran* 27 (1919): 60.

[46]Charles B. Martin, "Jackson's Brigade in Battle of Nashville," *Confederate Veteran* 17 (1909): 12–13.

[47]Cuyler King to sister, 30 January 1865, King Family Papers, Southern Historical Collection, Chapel Hill NC. Alfred Bryan's name does not appear in a register of prisoners held at Johnson's Island OH the camp to which King and Schlatter were sent and where N. B. Sadler was already held. See NA, M598, roll 82, "Johnson's Island, Ohio, Military Prison, Register of Prisoners, 1862–1865." The absence of his name is not, of course, conclusive evidence.

[48]NA, M266 ("Confederate Soldiers from Georgia"), rolls 148–50, service records. See below for Parrott's status after enlisting in the US volunteers.

[49]*OR*, vol. 45, pt. 1, pp. 750–51.

[50]Hamilton Branch to Charlotte Branch, 29 December 1864, Branch Letters, University of Georgia, Athens GA; *OR*, vol. 45, pt. 1, pp. 664, 678, 679.

[51]Roster of the First Battalion of Georgia Sharp Shooters , 25 January 1865, included with Muster Rolls of 1st Battalion Georgia Sharpshooters (microcopy), RG 109, Confederate Records, National Archives; Hamilton Branch to Charlotte Branch, 30 October; 1, 3, 7 November 1864, Branch Letters, University of Georgia, Athens GA.

[52]NA, M266 ("Confederate Soldiers from Georgia"), rolls 148–50, service records.

[53]Ibid., roll 150, service record; M653 ("1860 Census"), roll 11, "Henry County, Ala.," 116; Letter of Washington Wilcox (typescript), 16 January 1865, Civil War Miscellany-Personal Papers, Georgia Division of Archives and History, Atlanta, Georgia.

[54]Nathaniel Cheairs Hughes, Jr., *Bentonville: The Final Battle of Sherman and Johnston* (Chapel Hill: University of North Carolina Press, 1996) 24–25. This paragraph and those that follow concerning the general activities of the Army of Tennessee are based on Connelly, *Autumn of Glory*, 512–34, passim.

[55]Olmstead, *Memoirs*, 175–76; Eugene W. Jones, Jr., *Enlisted for the War: The Struggles of the Gallant 24th Regiment, South Carolina Volunteers, Infantry, 1861–1865* (Hightstown NJ: Longstreet House, 1997) 247.

[56]*OR*, vol. 47, pt. 2, pp. 1134–35, 1262, 1285, 1286, 1386.

[57]Judith Lee Hallock, *Braxton Bragg and Confederate Defeat*, vol. 2 (Tuscaloosa: University of Alabama Press, 1991) 250–51.

[58]Ibid., 251–52; Connelly, *Autumn of Glory*, 524; *OR*, vol. 47, pt. 1, pp. 1086–89.

[59]*OR*, vol. 47, pt. 2, p. 1386; vol. 47, pt. 3, pp. 698, 734; vol. 24, pt. 2, pp. 102–103.

[60]Connelly, *Autumn of Glory*, 526–27.

[61]*OR*, vol. 47, pt. 1, p. 1089; vol. 47, pt. 2, p. 1437.

[62]*OR*, vol. 47, pt. 1, pp. 1089–91; Hughes, *Bentonville*, 123, 130.

[63]Clark, *Under the Stars and Bars*, 166, 167.

[64]*OR*, vol. 47, pt. 1, pp. 1060, 1091; [Raleigh] *North Carolina Standard*, 24 March 1865; Connelly, *Autumn of Glory*, 527–28.

[65]NA, M266 ("Confederate Soldiers from Georgia"), roll 148, 1st Confederate Georgia Battalion caption cards, Whitsitt card; *OR*, vol. 47, pt. 1, p. 1065.

[66]Joseph F. Waring to Charlotte Branch, 30 March 1865, Branch Letters, University of Georgia, Athens GA.

[67]*OR*, vol. 47, pt. 1, pp. 1088; NA, M266 ("Confederate Soldiers from Georgia"), roll 148, 1st Confederate Georgia Battalion service records.

POSTLUDE

[1]NA, M266 ("Confederate Soldiers from Georgia"), roll 148–50, service records; Joseph H. Crute, Jr., *Confederate Staff Officers, 1861–1865* (Powhatan VA: Derwent Books, 1982) 12; Savannah *Daily Morning News*, 8, 13, 17 May 1865; Henderson, *Confederate Soldiers of Georgia*, 2:939, 5:661.

[2]Savannah *Daily Morning News*, 8 July, 22 November 1865; *Confederate Veteran* 28; no. 11 (November 1920): 428; undated newspaper obituary clipping, clipping album, folder 2, Charlton Family Papers, collection 132, Georgia Historical Society, Savannah GA.

[3]Jack, "Henry Rootes Jackson," in *Dictionary of American Biography*; "Robert Houston Anderson," in Ezra J. Warner, *Generals in Gray* (1959; reprint, Baton Rouge: Louisiana State University Press, 1986).

[4]F. D. Lee and J. L. Agnew, *Historical Record of the City of Savannah* (Savannah GA: Morning News Steam-power Press, 1869) 119–28.

[5]*Marriages of Chatham County, Georgia*, compiled by the Genealogical Committee of the Georgia Historical Society, 2 vols. (Savannah: Georgia Historical Society, 1993) 2:41, 79, 85, 126, 241.

[6]Robert S. Davis, Jr., comp., *Records of Jasper County, Georgia, from the Georgia Division of Archives and History, Atlanta, Georgia* (Greenville SC: Southern Historical Press, 1990) 24; Henderson, *Confederate Soldiers of Georgia*, 3:661; Kevin Thurman, Garner descendant, email with author, 20 July 2002; Betty Bennett Joiner, grandaughter, email with author, 30 July 2002; Joseph T. Derry, *Georgia*, extended ed., vol.7 of *Confederate Military History*, ed. Clement A. Evans(1899; reprint, Wilmington NC: Broadfoot Publishing, 1987–1989) 662.

[7]Horace D. Brown, "William Lawrence Thomas, Army of the Confederacy, 30th Georgia Regiment and First Battalion Georgia Sharpshooters," unpublished family memoir, Horace D. Brown, Miami FL; Frederick N. Gleaton, "David Culpepper," unpublished family memoir, Frederick N. Gleaton, Atlanta GA; Charles Westberry at http://web3.foxinternet.net/smorgan/assofamily/indexthorn.htm; Barbra Crites at http://genforum.genealogy.com/sc/aiken/messages/236.html.

[8]*Macon Telegraph*, 22 February 1902, 22 October 1910.

[9]*Macon Telegraph*, 1 July 1913, 20 May 1944; *Index to Georgia Civil War Confederate Pensions*, trans. Virgil D. White (Waynesboro TN: National Historical Publishing Co., 1996); R. Manning Ancell with Christine M. Miller, *The Biographical Dictionary of World War II Generals and Flag Officers* (Westport CT: Greenwood Press, 1996) 176; *Register of Graduates and Former Cadets of the United States Military Academy, West Point, New York*, 2001 ed., (West Point NY: Association of Graduates, 2001) graduate number 15397 (Class of 1946).

[10]Florence Olmstead, "Old City and Suburban Car Lines," *Georgia Historical Quarterly*, 28 (1944): 140; Hartridge Family File, Walter C. Hartridge, Jr. Collection, Georgia Historical Society, Savannah GA; *General Index to Keeper's Record Books, Bonaventure Cemetery, Savannah, Georgia, 1850–1938*, vol. 1 (Works Progress Administration, 1939); Dixon Hollingsworth, ed., *The History of Screven County, Georgia* (Dallas TX: Curtis Media Corp., 1989) 203; Reminiscences of Mrs. Mamie Lou Kittles Hobby of her father, Henry Kittles, Civl War Micelllany-Personal Papers, Georgia Division of Archives and History, Atlanta, Georgia.

[11]Derst Family File, Walter C. Hartridge, Jr. Collection, Georgia Historical Society, Savannah GA; "Comrades of Savannah, Ga.," *Confederate Veteran* 37, (1929): 224; Gordon Burns Smith, *The Companies*, vol. 4 of *History of the Georgia Militia, 1783–1861*, 4 vols. (Milledgeville GA: Boyd Publishing, 2000–2001) 271; James Mack Adams, "Historic Militia Flag, Lost for Years, Is Returned to Owners," *Savannah Morning News*, 26 June 2002.

[12]George C. Dent obituary, newspaper clipping provided by William D. Temple, Brunswick GA; Victoria Reeves Gunn, "Hofwyl Plantation" (typescript), (Atlanta GA: Georgia Department of Natural Resources, 1976) 72; information from Bill Rivers, Hofwyl-Broomfield State Historic Site Museum, 31 July 2002.

[13]NA, M593, ("1870 Census"), roll 172, "Richmond County," 390; *The* (Waynesboro) *True Citizen*, 25 November 1922; *Augusta Chronicle*, 21 November 1922.

[14]NA, M593, ("1870 Census"), roll 141, "Chatham County," 129; Mauriel Phillips Joslyn, ed., *Charlotte's Boys: Civil War Letters of the Branch Family of Savannah* (Berryville VA: Rockbridge Publishing Company, 1996) 323.

[15]*Augusta Chronicle and Sentinel*, 12 April 1874; Laurel Grove Cemetery register, Savannah GA, Lot 650 (Dickerson family); Shaaff Family File, Walter C. Hartridge, Jr. Collection, collection 1349, Georgia Historical Society, Savannah GA.

[16]*Savannah Morning News*, 2 June 1875; *General Index to Keeper's Record Books, Laurel Grove Cemetery, Savannah, Georgia, 1852–1938*, vol. 1 (Savannah: Works Progress Administration, 1939); *General Index to Keeper's Record Books, Bonaventure Cemetery, Savannah, Georgia, 1850–1938*. vol. 1 (Savannah: Works Progress Administration, 1939); Robert Manson Myers, *The Children of Pride: A True Story of Georgia and the Civil War* (New Haven: Yale University Press, 1972) 1607.

[17]Folks Huxford, comp., *Pioneers of Wiregrass Georgia*, 8 vols. (self-published, 1951–1988) 6:155.

[18]*Confederate Veteran*, vol. 24, no. 3, (March 1916): 143; "Comrades of a Texas

Camp," *Confederate Veteran,* vol. 34, no. 4, (April 1926): 147; JoAnn Hopper at http://www.rootsweb.com/~txburnet/Ricketson.html; Wiley A. Jarrell at http://solaris.cc.vt.edu/pipermail/jarrell-1/1999–June/002979.html; NA, T9 ("1880 Census"), roll 650, "Jackson County, Mississippi," 549C; roll 1377, "Madison County, Virginia," 435D.

[19]NA, M266 ("Confederate Soldiers from Georgia"), roll 150, service records; Henderson, *Confederate Soldiers of Georgia,* 3:542–43; M432 ("1850 Census"), roll 62, "Campbell County," 464–65, M593 ("1870 Census"), roll 168, "Paulding County," 366; T9 ("1880 Census"), roll 160, 472; Georgia Death Index, 1929, certificate 32756K.

[20] Joe D. Parrott, email to author, 7 September 2002; Georgia Death Index, 1932, certificates 7352 and 2911.

[21] "Heirs of Confederate Officers," *Confederate Veteran,* 22 (1914): 215; *Keeper's Record Books, Laurel Grove Cemetery;* Shaaff Family File, Walter C. Hartridge, Jr. Collection, collection 1349, Georgia Historical Society, Savannah GA.

[22]Arthur Shaaff Johns File, Virginia Military Institute Archives, Lexington VA; Shaaff Family File, Walter C. Hartridge, Jr. Collection, Georgia Historical Society, Savannah GA.

BIBLIOGRAPHY

MANUSCRIPTS

Atlanta History Center, Atlanta, Georgia.
    Waddell-Setze-McClatchey Family Papers, Manuscript (Mss.) 842.
Mrs. Betty Fitzgerald Brown and Royal Fitzgerald Brown, Rochelle, Georgia.
    John I. Royal Letters.
Chickamauga-Chattanooga National Military Park, Fort Oglethorpe, Georgia.
    1st Battalion Georgia Sharpshooters File.
    30th Georgia Regiment File.
Eleanor S. Brockenbrough Library, Museum of the Confederacy, Richmond, Virginia.
    Department of South Carolina and Georgia Collection.
Duke University, Durham, North Carolina, Rare Book, Manuscript and Special
    Collections Library.
    Ellison Capers Papers.
    W.H.T. Walker Papers.
Georgia Division of Archives and History, Atlanta, Georgia.
    Adjutant General's Incoming Correspondence (Record Group 22).
    Adjutant General's Letter Books (typescripts).
    C.M. Hardy Letters (Mrs. O.E. Lancaster Collection), (microfilm).
    Civil War Miscellany - Personal Papers (microfilm).
    Georgia Roster Commission Files (Record Group 58-2).
    Governor Joseph E. Brown's Incoming Correspondence (Record Group 1-1).
    Governor Joseph E. Brown's Letter Book, 1860-65.
Georgia Historical Society, Savannah, Georgia.
    Charlton Family Papers.
    George Columbus Dent Papers.
    Walter C. Hartridge, Jr. Collection.
    Mercer Family Papers, George A. Mercer Diary (typescript).
    Savannah Newspaper Digest (Savannah *Daily Morning News*).
    C. C. Wilson Papers.
Hargrett Rare Book and Manuscript Library, University of Georgia Libraries, Athens,
    Georgia.
    Hamilton Branch Letters, Margaret Branch Sexton Collection, Ms. 25.
Kennesaw Mountain National Battlefield Park, Kennesaw, Georgia.
    Samuel McKittrick Letters.
Mrs. Henry Lord Page (Eileen) King, Rockville, Maryland.
    Richard Cuyler King Journal (typescript).
Library of Congress, Manuscripts Division.
    Papers of P.G.T. Beauregard, Manuscript 19007 (microfilm).
National Archives, Washington, D.C.

War Department Collection of Confederate Records, Record Group 109.
>   Letters Sent and Received by General J.C. Pemberton, Mar.-Sep. 1862 (Chapter 2, Vol. 21).
>   Letters Sent, Department of South Carolina, Georgia, and Florida, July 1862-Sep. 1863 (Chapter 2, Vols. 22, 31).
>   Orders, Department of South Carolina and Georgia, Nov. 1861-Sep. 1862 (Chapter 2, Vol. 42).
>   General Orders, Department of South Carolina, Georgia, and Florida, July 1862-Jan. 1864 (Chapter 2, Vols. 41 and 43).
>   Special Orders and Circulars, Department of South Carolina, Georgia, and Florida, Sept. 1862-Dec. 1863 (Chapter 2, Vol. 40).
>   General Court-Martial Orders, Department of South Carolina, Georgia, and Florida, 1863 (Chapter 2, Vol. 182).
>   Orders and Circulars, Department of South Carolina, Georgia, and Florida, 1861-1865 (Entry 73).
>   Orders and Circulars, Department and District of   Georgia, 1861-1865 (Entry 82).
>>   Reports of Casualties in the Army of Tennessee (Chapter 6, Vol. 48).
>>   Muster Rolls of the 1st Battalion Georgia Sharpshooters.
>   Dr. Benjamin C. Rountree, Amherst, Mass.
>>   Angus McDermid Letters.
Southern Historical Collection, University of North Carolina at Chapel Hill.
>   Thomas Butler King Papers, Ms. 1252.
>   William Whann Mackall Papers, Ms. 1299.
>   William Moody Papers, Ms. 4903z.
South Caroliniana Library, University of South Carolina, Columbia.
>   Ellison Capers Papers.
>   Clement H. Stevens Papers.
>   Williams-Chesnut-Manning Family Papers.
Tennessee State Library and Archives, Nashville.
>   Benjamin F. Cheatham Papers, Mss. 750 (microfilm).
U.S. Army Military History Institute, Carlisle, Pa.
>   Benjamin Milikin Papers–James Thornton Letter (photocopy).
Virginia Military Institute Archives, Lexington, Va.
>   Arthur Shaaff Johns File.
Western Reserve Historical Society, Cleveland, Ohio.
>   William P. Palmer Collection of Braxton Bragg Papers, Mss. 2000 (microfilm).
Robert W. Woodruff Library, Emory University, Atlanta, Georgia.
>   Confederate Miscellany–James A. McCord Letter.

NATIONAL ARCHIVES MICROFILM PUBLICATIONS

M233, Register of Enlistments in the United States Army, 1798–1914.

M251, Compiled Service Records of Confederate Soldiers Who Served in Organizations from the State of Florida.

M266, Compiled Service Records of Confederate Soldiers Who Served in Organizations from the State of Georgia.

M267, Compiled Service Records of Confederate Soldiers Who Served in Organizations from the State of South Carolina.

M331, Compiled Service Records of Confederate General and Staff Officers and Non-Regimental Enlisted Men.

M347, Unfiled Papers and Slips Belonging to Confederate Compiled Service Records.

M432, Seventh Census of the United States (1850).

M437, Letters Received by the Confederate Secretary of War, 1861–1865.

M474, Letters Received by the Confederate Adjutant and Inspector General's Office, 1861–1865.

M567, Letters Received by the Adjutant General's Office, 1822–1860.

M593, Ninth Census of the United States (1870).

M598, Selected Records of the War Department Relating to Confederate Prisoners of War, 1861–1865.

M653, Eighth Census of the United States (1860).

M665, Returns from Regular Army Infantry Regiments, June 1821–December 1916. 4th Infantry, January 1860–December 1866.

T9, Tenth Census of the United States (1880).

BOOKS

Abell, Richard Bender, and Faye Adamson Gecik, editors. *Sojourns of a Patriot: The Field and Prison Papers of an Unreconstructed Confederate*. Murfreesboro TN: Southern Heritage Press, 1998.

Adamson, A. P. *A Brief History of the Thirtieth Georgia Regiment*. Jonesboro GA: Freedom Hill Press, 1987.

Ancell, R. Manning, with Christine M. Miller. *The Biographical Dictionary of World War II Generals and Flag Officers*. Westport CT: Greenwood Press, 1996.

Arms and Equipment of the Confederacy. Alexandria VA: Time-Life Books, 1998.

Baumgartner, Richard, and Larry M. Strayer. *Echoes of Battle: The Struggle for Chattanooga*. Huntington WV: Blue Acorn Press, 1996.

_____. *Kennesaw Mountain, June 1864*. Huntington WV: Blue Acorn Press, 1998.

Bearss, Edwin C., and Warren Grabau. *The Battle of Jackson/The Siege of Jackson/Three Other Post-Vicksburg Actions*. Jackson MS: Jackson Civil War Roundtable, Inc., 1981.

Bell, Burton J. *Bi-Centennial History of Gordon County, Georgia*. Calhoun GA: Gordon County Historical Society, 1976.

Bragg, William Harris. *Joe Brown's Army: The Georgia State Line, 1862–1865*. Macon GA: Mercer University Press, 1987.

Brown, Russell K. "Battle at Wauhatchie (Brown's Ferry) (28–29 October 1863)" and "Capture of Jackson, Mississippi, (9–16 July 1863)." In David S. and Jeanne T. Heidler, editors *Encyclopedia of the American Civil War*. 5 volumes. Santa Barbara CA: ABC-CLIO. 2000.

———. *To the Manner Born: The Life of General William H. T. Walker*. Athens: University of Georgia Press, 1994.

Buck, Irving A. *Cleburne and His Command*. New York: Neale, 1908.

Castel, Albert. *Decision in the West: The Atlanta Campaign of 1864*. Lawrence: University Press of Kansas, 1992.

Christman, William E. *Undaunted: The History of Fort McAllister, Georgia*. Atlanta: Georgia Department of Natural Resources, 1996.

Cisco, Walter Brian. *States Rights Gist: A South Carolina General of the Civil War*. Shippensburg PA: White Mane Publishing, 1991.

Clark, Walter A. *Under the Stars and Bars, or Memories of Four Years Service with the Oglethorpes of Augusta, Georgia*. Augusta: Chronicle Printing Co., 1900.

Coddington, Edwin B. *The Gettysburg Campaign: A Study in Command*. New York: Charles Scribner's Sons, 1968.

Confederate Reminiscences and Letters, 1861–1865. 18 vols. to date. Atlanta GA: United Daughters of the Confederacy, 1996–2002.

Connelly, Thomas L. *Autumn of Glory: The Army of Tennessee, 1862–1865*. Baton Rouge: Louisiana State University Press, 1971.

Cozzens, Peter. *This Terrible Sound: The Battle of Chickamauga*. Urbana: University of Illinois Press, 1992.

Crute, Joseph H. *Confederate Staff Officers, 1861–1865*. Powhatan VA: Derwent Press, 1982.

Cullum, George W. *Biographical Register of the Officers and Graduates of the United States Military Academy*. 3rd edition. 2 volumes. Boston MA: Houghton Mifflin Co., 1891.

Cumming, Joseph B. *A Sketch of the Descendants of David Cumming and Memoirs of the War Between the States*. Edited by Mary Gairdner Smith Cumming. Augusta GA: privately printed, 1925.

Davis, Robert S., Jr., compiler. *Records of Jasper County, Georgia, from the Georgia Department of Archives and History*. Greenville SC: Southern Historical Press, 1990.

Derry, Joseph T. *Georgia*. Extended edition. Volume 7 in, *Confederate Military History*. 17 volumes. Edited by Clement Evans. 1899. Reprint, Wilmington NC: Broadfoot Publishing, 1987–1989.

Dictionary of American Biography. 10 volumes. Edited by Allen Johnson and Dumas Malone. New York: Charles Scribner's Sons, 1964.

Dictionary of Georgia Biography. 2 volumes. Edited by Kenneth Coleman and Stephen Gurr. Athens: University of Georgia Press, 1983.

Duckett, Alvin L. *John Forsyth, Political Tactician*. Athens GA: University of Georgia Press, 1962.

[Duncan, Alexander McCrie]. *Roll of Officers and Members of the Georgia Hussars*. Savannah GA: The Morning News Printers. n.d. [ca. 1905].

Durden, Marion Little. *A History of St. George Parish, Colony of Georgia, Jefferson County, State of Georgia*. Swainsboro GA: Magnolia Press, 1983.

Fraser, Walter J. Jr. *Savannah in the Old South*. Athens: University of Georgia Press, 2003.

General Index to Keeper's Record Books, Bonaventure Cemetery, Savannah, Georgia, 1850–1938. 2 volumes. Savannah: Works Progress Administration, 1939.

General Index to Keeper's Record Books, Laurel Grove Cemetery, Savannah, Georgia, 1852–1938. 4 volumes. Savannah: Works Progress Administration, 1939.

Gordon, George W. "The Famous Snowball Battle in the Confederate Army at Dalton, Ga., 1864." In Ben LaBree, editor. *Camp Fires of the Confederacy*. Louisville KY: Courier-Journal Job Printing Company, 1898. 48–53.

Gunn, Victoria Reeves. "Hofwyl Plantation" (typescript). Atlanta GA: Georgia
    Department of Natural Resources, 1976.
Hagan, John W. *Confederate Letters of John W. Hagan*. Edited by Bell I. Wiley. Athens:
    University of Georgia Press, 1957.
Hallock, Judith Lee. *Braxton Bragg and Confederate Defeat*. Volume 2. Tuscaloosa:
    University of Alabama Press, 1991.
Heitman, Francis B. *Biographical Register and Dictionary of the United States Army,
    1789–1903*. 2 volumes. Washington, DC: US Government Printing Office, 1903.
Henderson, Lillian, editor. *Roster of the Confederate Soldiers of Georgia, 1861–1865*. 6
    volumes. Hapeville GA: Longino and Porter, 1955–1962.
Hermann, Isaac. *Memoirs of A Confederate Veteran, 1861–1865*. Lakemont GA: CSA
    Printing and Binding, 1974.
Hillhouse, Albert M. "Descendants of Dr. John Dent." *Nuggets and Other Findings in
    Burke County, Georgia*. Danville KY: Prompt Printing, 1981, 131–32.
History of Jasper County, Georgia. Monticello GA: Jasper County Historical Foundation,
    Inc., 1984.
Hollingsworth, Dixon, editor. *The History of Screven County, Georgia*. Dallas TX: Curtis
    Media Corp., 1989.
Hughes, Nathaniel Cheairs, Jr. *Bentonville: The Final Battle of Sherman and Johnston*.
    Chapel Hill: University of North Carolina Press, 1996.
———. *General William J. Hardee: Old Reliable*. 1965. Reprint, Baton Rouge:
    Louisiana State University Press, 1994.
Huxford, Folks, compiler. *Pioneers of Wiregrass Georgia*. 8 volumes. Self published,
    1951–1988.
Index to Georgia Civil War Confederate Pensions. Virgil D. White, transcriber.
    Waynesboro TN: National Historical Publishing Co., 1996.
Ingmire, Frances T., compiler. *Dooly County, Georgia, Marriages, 1839–1884*. St. Louis:
    self published, 1985.
———. *Jefferson County, Georgia, Marriages, 1806–1857*. St. Louis: self published,
    1985.
_____. *Randolph County, Georgia, Marriages, 1810–1857*. St. Louis: self-published,
    1985.
Johnston, Joseph E. *Narrative of Military Operations Directed During the Late War
    Between the States*. 1874. Reprint, Bloomington: Indiana University Press, 1959.
Johnston, William Preston. *The Life of Gen. Albert Sidney Johnston*. New York: D.
    Appleton, 1878.
Jones, Charles C., Jr. *The Siege of Savannah in December, 1864, and the Confederate
    Operations in Georgia and the Third Military District of South Carolina during
    General Sherman's March from Atlanta to the Sea*. Albany NY: Joel Munsell,
    1874.
Jones, Eugene W., Jr. *Enlisted for the War: The Struggles of the Gallant 24th Regiment,
    South Carolina Volunteers, Infantry, 1861–1865*. Hightstown NJ: Longstreet
    House, 1997.
Joslyn, Mauriel Phillips, editor. *Charlotte's Boys: Civil War Letters of the Branch Family
    of Savannah*. Berryville VA: Rockbridge Publishing Company, 1996.
Kennett, Lee. *Marching Through Georgia*. New York: Harper Collins, 1995.

202   OUR CONNECTION WITH SAVANNAH

King, Spencer Bidwell, Jr. , editor. *Ebb Tide, As Seen Through the Diary of Jospehine Clay Habersham, 1863*. Athens: University of Georgia Press, 1958.

Lee, F. D., and J. L. Agnew. *Historical Record of the City of Savannah*. Savannah GA: Morning News Steam-power Press, 1869.

Lewis, Bessie. *King's Retreat Plantation*. Volume 2 of *Plantations of Coastal Georgia*. Edited by Mildred Huie and Mildred Wilcox. Brunswick GA: Coastal Printing, 1980.

Losson, Christopher. *Tennessee's Forgotten Warriors*. Knoxville: University of Tennessee Press, 1989.

MacKethan, Edwin R., III, editor. *The Story of the Page-King Family of Retreat Plantation, St. Simons Island and of the Golden Isles of Georgia*. As told by Florence Marye. Darien GA: self published, 2000.

McDonough, James Lee. *Chattanooga—A Death Grip on the Confederacy*. Knoxville: University of Tennessee Press, 1984.

McDonough, James Lee, and Thomas L. Connelly. *Five Tragic Hours: The Battle of Franklin*. Knoxville: University of Tennessee Press, 1983.

McMurry, Richard M. *John Bell Hood and the War for Southern Independence*. Lexington: University of Kentucky Press, 1982.

Madaus, Howard Michael, and Robert D. Needham. *The Battle Flags of the Confederate Army of Tennessee*. Milwaukee: Milwaukee Public Museum, 1976.

Mangham, Dana M. *"Oh, For a Touch of the Vanished Hand": Discovering a Southern Family and the Civil War*. Murfreesboro TN: Southern Heritage Press, 2000.

Marriages of Chatham County, Georgia. Compiled by the Genealogical Committee of the Georgia Historical Society. 2 volumes. Savannah: Georgia Historical Society, 1993.

Memoirs of Georgia. 2 volumes. Atlanta GA: Southern Historical Association, 1895.

Montgomery, William R. *Georgia Sharpshooter: The Civil War Diary and Letters of William Rhadamanthus Montgomery*. Edited by George Montgomery, Jr. Macon GA: Mercer University Press, 1997.

Murray, Alton J. *South Georgia Rebels: The True Wartime Experiences of the 26th Regiment Georgia Volunteer Infantry*. St. Mary's GA: self published, 1976.

Myers, Robert Manson. *The Children of Pride: A True Story of Georgia and the Civil War*. New Haven CT: Yale University Press, 1972.

Nisbet, J. Cooper. *Four Years on the Firing Line*. Edited by Bell I. Wiley. Jackson TN: McCowat-Mercer Press, 1963.

Olmstead, Charles H. *The Memoirs of Charles H. Olmstead*. Edited by Lilla M. Hawes. *Collections of the Georgia Historical Society*. 14. Savannah GA, 1964.

Powell, Lillian L., Dorothy C. Odom, and Albert M. Hillhouse. *Grave Markers in Burke County, Georgia*. Waynesboro GA: Chalker Publishing, 1974.

Reddick, Marguerite, compiler. *Camden's Challenge: A History of Camden County, Georgia*. Camden County Historical Society, 1976.

Register of Graduates and Former Cadets of the United States Military Academy, West Point, New York. 2001 edition. West Point, New York: Association of Graduates, 2001.

Roster of Confederate Graves. Centennial Edition. 8 vols. Atlanta GA: Georgia Division, United Daughters of the Confederacy, 1995.

Rowland, Dunbar. *Military History of Mississippi, 1803–1898*. 1908. Reprint, Spartanburg SC: The Reprint Company, 1978.

Scaife, William R. *The Campaign for Atlanta*. Atlanta: self published, 1993.

Sellers, W. W. *A History of Marion County, South Carolina*. 1902. Reprint, Greenville SC: Southern Historical Press, 1996.

Sifakis, Stewart. *Who Was Who in the Civil War*. New York: Facts on File, 1988.

Smedlund, William S. *Camp Fires of Georgia's Troops*. Lithonia GA, privately published, 1995.

Smith, Gordon Burns. *History of the Georgia Militia, 1783–1861*. 4 volumes. Milledgeville GA: Boyd Publishing, 2000–2001.

Supplement to the Official Records. 81 volumes. Edited by Janet Hewett. Volume 7. Wilmington NC: Broadfoot Publishing, 1997.

Telfair, Nancy. *The Columbus, Georgia, Centenary, 1828–1928*. Columbus GA: Historical Publishing Co., 1929.

Temple, Sarah B. *The First Hundred Years: A Short History of Cobb County in Georgia*. Atlanta: Walter W. Brown Publishing, 1935.

US Navy Department. *Official Records of the Union and Confederate Navies in the War of the Rebellion*. 30 volumes. Washington, DC: US Government Printing Office, 1896–1922.

US War Department. *The War of the Rebellion: A Compilation of the Official Records of the Union and Confederate Armies*. 128 volumes. Washington, DC: US Government Printing Office, 1880–1901.

Valentine, Thomas A. *The Valentine Family of Georgia*. Roswell GA: privately printed, 1992.

Warner, Ezra J. *Generals in Gray*. 1959; Reprint, Baton Rouge: Louisiana State University Press, 1986.

Worsley, Etta B. *Columbus on the Chattahoochee*. Columbus GA: Columbus Office Supply Co., 1951.

Yates, Bowling C. *History of the Georgia Military Institute, Marietta, Georgia*. Marietta: privately printed, 1968.

1860 Directory for the City of Savannah. Savannah: John M. Cooper & Co., [1860?]. Microfiche.

PUBLISHED ARTICLES

Adamson, A. P. "Flag of the Thirtieth Georgia Regiment." *Confederate Veteran* 20 (1912): 118.

Bearss, Edwin C. "The Vicksburg Campaign: Grant Moves Inland." *Blue and Gray Magazine* 14/1 (October 2000): 6–17, 19, 22, 46–52.

Britt, Albert S. Jr. and Lilla M. Hawes, editors. "The Mackenzie Papers." Part II. *Georgia Historical Quarterly*, vol. 57 (1973): 85-145.

Davis, Steve. "The Great Snow Battle of 1864." *Civil War Times Illustrated* 15 (June 1976): 32–35.

Jones, Joseph. "Roster of the Medical Officers of the Army of Tennessee…." *Southern Historical Society Papers* 22 (1894): 165–280.

Kollock, Susan M., editor. "Letters of the Kollock and Allied Families, 1826–1884."
    Georgia Historical Quarterly 34 (1950): 227–57.

Kurtz, Wilbur G., Jr. "The First Regiment of Georgia Volunteers in the Mexican War."
    Georgia Historical Quarterly 27 (1943): 301–23.

Lea, H. J. "With the Fourth Louisiana Battalion." *Confederate Veteran* 27 (1919): 339.

Mangham, Dana M. "Roster of the 2nd Georgia Battalion Sharpshooters, C.S.A."
    Georgia Genealogical Magazine 35/1–2 (Winter Spring 1995): 65–82.

Martin, Charles B. "Jackson's Brigade in Battle of Nashville." *Confederate Veteran* 17
    (1909): 11–13.

Murdoch, Richard K. Collector and editor. "Letters and Papers of Dr. Daniel Turner, A
    Rhode Islander in South Georgia." Part IV. *Georgia Historical Quarterly*, vol. 54
    (1970): 244-82.

National Law Enforcement Officers Memorial Fund, Inc., press release, "America's
    Earliest Law Enforcement Casualties," 5 August 2002.

Newton, Steven H. "Formidable Only in Flight?" *North and South* 3 (April 2000): 43–56.

Olmstead, Charles H. "Fort Pulaski." *Georgia Historical Quarterly* 1 (1917): 98–105.

Olmstead, Florence. "Old City and Suburban Car Lines." *Georgia Historical Quarterly*
    28 (1944): 138–42.

Ray, Frederick L. "Shock Troops of the South." *America's Civil War* (July 2002): 34–40.

Roberts, Frank S. "In Winter Quarters at Dalton, Ga., 1863–64." *Confederate Veteran* 26
    (1918): 274–75.

———. "Review of the Army of Tennessee at Dalton, Ga." *Confederate Veteran* 26
    (1918): 150.

———. "Spring Hill-Franklin-Nashville, 1864." *Confederate Veteran* 27 (1919): 58–60.

Rountree, Benjamin, editor. "Letters from A Confederate Soldier." *Georgia Review* 18
    (1964): 267–97.

Shannon, I[saac] N. "Sharpshooters with Hood's Army." *Confederate Veteran* 15 (1907):
    123–27.

UNPUBLISHED ARTICLES

Brown, Horace D. "William Lawrence Thomas, Army of the Confederacy, 30th Georgia
    Regiment and First Battalion Georgia Sharpshooters."

Frye, Leona. "John B. Gallie, 1806–1863." Student thesis. Savannah State-Armstrong
    State Colleges Joint Graduate Program, Savannah GA, 1977.

Gleaton, Frederick N. "David Culpepper."

Sutton, Thomas C. "The Godwin Connection." Typescript genealogy.

———. "Our Royal Roots." Typescript genealogy.

Turner, Norman V. *Brigadier General Claudius C. Wilson: Effingham County,
    Georgia's, Only Confederate General*. Springfield, Georgia: self-published, 1997.

NEWSPAPERS

Atlanta Intelligencer.
Atlanta Southern Confederacy.
Augusta Chronicle & Sentinel.
Charleston Courier.
Macon (Georgia) *Telegraph.*
(Raleigh) *North Carolina Standard.*

(Savannah) *Daily Morning News.*
Savannah Republican.
The (Waynesboro, Georgia) *True Citizen.*

ELECTRONIC SOURCES
Crites, Barbara. "William Henry Schmidt"
    http://genforum.genealogy.com/sc/aiken/messages/236.html.
Harris, Matt. Allen Family Genealogy: "Descendants of Thomas Harris" (1999)
    http://www.patch.net/harris/.
Hopper, JoAnn. Ricketson Genealogy.
    http://www.rootsweb.com/~txburnet/Ricketson.html.
Jarrell, Wiley A. Jarrell Genealogy. http://solaris.cc.vt.edu/pipermail/jarrell-1/1999-
    June/002979.html.
National Park Service. Civil War Soldiers and Sailors System.
    http://www.itd.nps.gov/cwss/soldiers.htm.
Perkins, Marlitta H. "Camp Chase." http://www.geocites.com/campchase/index.
    html
Public Acts of the Confederate States of America, passed at the First Session of the First
    Congress, 1862. Documenting the American South. University of North Carolina
    Libraries, Chapel Hill.
    http://docsouth.unc.edu/statutes/statutes.html.
Railfan's Guide to the Altoona Area http://www.trainweb.org/horseshoecurve-
    nrhs/Altoona_area.htm.
Sons of Confederate Veterans, Camp 1968, Shorterville AL.
    http://www.henrylightinfantry.com/history.htm.
Valentine, Linda. "The Valentine Family and associated lines" (2001).
    http://www.thevalentines.info/ll/Valentin/valentin.htm.
Westberry, Charles. Thornton Genealogy
    http://web3.foxinternet.net/smorgan/assofamily/index_thorn.htm.
1859 Directory for the City of Savannah. Savannah: John M. Cooper & Co., [1859].
    http://www.rootsweb.com/~gachath2/1859SavCityDir.html.

CORRESPONDENCE AND INTERVIEWS
Adams, Ranald T., Jr., Alexandria, Va.
Brown, Betty Fitzgerald, and Royal Fitzgerald Brown, Rochelle, Ga.
Brown, Horace D., Miami, Fla.
Crites, Barbra, Tampa, Fla.
Derst, Edward John, III, Savannah, Ga.
Gleaton, Frederick N., Atlanta, Ga.
Joiner, Betty Bennett, Gainesville, Ga.
King, Eileen (Mrs. H.L.P., Jr.), Rockville, Md.
MacKethan, Edwin R., Grosse Pointe Farms, Mich.
Parrott, Joe D., Huntsville, Ala.
Thornton, Father James, Garden Grove, Cal.
Valentine, Thomas A., Roswell, Ga.
Watts, Cindy Forehand, Conyers, Ga.

Appendix

Roster of Soldiers of the 1st Battalion Georgia Sharpshooters, 1862-1865

Methodology

Taken primarily from National Archives (NARA) Microfilm Publication M266, Compiled Service Records of Soldiers Who Served from the State of Georgia, Rolls 148-150, with supplementary information for selected soldiers from other rolls of the same series, and from Lillian Henderson, compiler, *Roster of the Confederate Soldiers of Georgia, 1861-1865*, six vols. (1955-1964). Also consulted were NARA Microfilms M331, Compiled Service Records of General and Staff Officers and Non-Regimental Enlisted Men, and M347, Unfiled Papers and Slips Belonging to Confederate Compiled Service Records. In a few instances, series for service in other states' units were used.

The basic documents used for compiling the service records were the bi-monthly muster rolls, usually made on the last day of each even-numbered month. Muster rolls available for the sharpshooter battalion are those for August, October and December 1862; February, April, June and December 1863; and February and August 1864. The muster roll for August 1864 was compiled in mid-September 1864, and is the last on file. The muster roll for D Company for October 1863, and a descriptive list of men who transferred from the 30th Georgia Volunteers were found at the Georgia Historical Society in Savannah. Other documents used to compile the service records were monthly returns, hospital returns and muster rolls, prisoner of war reports, inspection reports, general and special orders, and reports of courts-martial.

In 1909, the U.S. War Department began a systematic compilation of individual Confederate service records using the documents noted above. Slips or cards with the name of each man were prepared, one card for each record in which the name was found with the attendant data. Then the cards were collected together by unit to make up the individual service records. Later the cards were microfilmed to be available to the public. The original documents are at the National Archives in Record Group 109, War Department Collection of Confederate Records. To these, the compiler of this roster has added information from selected census schedules, city directories, county histories, genealogies, newspapers, and soldier and family correspondence and reminiscences.

The reader should be aware that the information in these extracts may be a transcription of a transcription. Spelling of names may not be correct, but is what the original War Department transcriber read from the muster rolls; it has usually been copied verbatim into this transcription. In many, but not all, cases of alternate spelling or variations of names, the War Department prepared a separate card for each variant with a cross-reference to the name chosen as correct. Frequently, the name chosen by the transcriber as the lead name was that most used on the muster rolls, but was not always the correct name of the soldier. Names shown in brackets in this roster are from sources other than the muster rolls.

There are 735 name cards for this unit in the M266 files. This compiler believes that approximately 430-450 men actually served in the ranks of the 1st Sharpshooter Battalion. Many of the other cards are for alternate names or spellings, some are for men who served in the DeKalb Rifles but never transferred to the Sharpshooters, some are cards that have been erroneously filed with this unit because of confusion in unit nomenclature or because the unit designation was incorrectly entered on the original document. Some of the alternate names or spellings occur in the original muster rolls, others are misreadings by the War Department transcribers. Most alternative names have not been included in this roster. File entries showing only that the soldier was present at the muster are not included here.

Abbreviations used in the roster

AAG – Assistant Adjutant General
ADC – aide-de-camp
AIG – Assistant Inspector General
GST – Georgia State Troops
MR - Muster Roll
SS - Sharpshooter

The Roster

Abbott, George [A.], Private, D Company: enlisted for 12 mos. 25 Sept. 1861, in Campbell County in G Company (Campbell Grays, Campbell County), 30th Georgia; transferred to 1st SS Battalion; reenlisted for the war 16 Feb. 1864; captured near Nashville 16 Dec. 1864, received at Camp Chase, Ohio 5 Jan. 1865; took the oath of allegiance 12 June 1865; resident of Muscogee County, dark complexion, dark hair, 6 ft. 1/4 in. tall, age 21; descriptive roll: age 18, complexion dark, eyes blue, hair dark, height 5 ft. 9 in., occupation farmer, born Muscogee County.

Alexander, H. [William H.], Private, D Company: enlisted for 12 mos. 8 Oct. 1861, at Camp Black in A Company (Gordon County), 8th Georgia Battalion; transferred to 1st SS Battalion; sick in quarters 31 Dec. 1862; absent without leave, 31 Oct. and 31 Dec. 1863; deserted 27 Aug. 1863, on the move from Mississippi; 14 years old in the Gordon County 1860 census.

Allen, M[orris] H[arris], Private, D Company: enlisted for 12 mos. 25 Sept. 1861, in Clayton County in I Company (Clayton Invincibles, Clayton County), 30th Georgia; transferred to 1st SS Battalion, 1 Aug, 1862; absent sick in Canton, Miss. 19 June 1863; absent sick in Mobile (MRs, 31 October and 31 Dec. 1863); died in General Hospital in Mobile 21 Aug. 1863; age 19, complexion dark, eyes hazel, hair light, height 5 ft. 10 in., occupation farmer, born Randolph County, Ala.; born 1843.

Allen, S[eaborn] M[orris], Private, D Company: enlisted for 12 mos. 25 Sep. 1861 in I Company (Clayton Invincibles, Clayton County), 30th Georgia; transferred to 1st SS Battalion, 1 Aug. 1862; absent sick 31 Dec. 1862; wounded at Chickamauga, Sep. 1863; absent wounded 31 Oct. and 31 Dec. 1863; absent with leave 31 Aug. 1864; age 16, complexion fair, eyes fair, hair light, height 5 ft. 6 in., occupation farmer, born Fayette County; born 11 Sep. 1845, died 22 Nov. 1893. [Erroneously shown on MR as enlisted 8 Oct. 1861 at Camp Black in 8th Georgia Battalion.]

Amey, William, Private, C Company: enlisted for 3 years 26 Mar. 1863, at Savannah; deserted, 30 June 1863.

Anderson, Robert H[ouston], Major, Field & Staff: 2nd Lieutenant, C.S.A., 16 Mar. 1861; ADC to Brig. Gen. Lawton, 24 May 1861; ordered to report to Brig. Gen. W.H.T. Walker at Pensacola as ADC, 31 May 1861; Major A.A.G. 4 Sept. 1861; Major, 1st SS Battalion, 23 July 1862 to rank from 20 June; signs roll as inspector and mustering officer, 31 Aug. 1862; Colonel, 5th Georgia Cavalry, 31 Jan. 1863 to rank from 20 Jan.; Brigadier General of cavalry, 23 July 1864; graduate of West Point, 1857; 2nd Lieutenant, U.S. Army, 1857-1861; born Savannah, 1 Oct. 1835, died there, 8 Feb. 1888.

Anderson, William J., Private, A Company: enlisted for 3 years or the war 4 Mar. 1862 at Reidsville in G Company (Tattnall Invincibles, Tattnall County), 11th Georgia Battalion; converted to 47th Georgia Regiment, 12 May 1862; transferred to 1st SS Battalion 1 Aug. 1862; present in confinement 31 Dec. 1862; appointed 4th Corporal 1 May 1863; appears as 2nd Corporal, absent sick 31 Dec. 1863; appears as 1st Corporal, absent sick in hospital 29 Feb. 1864; sick with chronic diarrhea at Ocmulgee General Hospital, Macon, 15 Aug. 1864; appears as 5th Sergeant, absent sick in General Hospital 31 Aug. 1864; captured as Private, Murfreesboro, Tenn., 4 Jan. 1865; treated at U. S. General Hospital, Nashville, for gunshot wound to the right shoulder, 15 Feb. 1865; confined at Camp Chase, Ohio, and Lookout Point, Md.; name included on a list of sick prisoners released at Pt. Lookout, 5 June 1865; resident of Tattnall County.

Anson, James, Private, C Company: enlisted for 3 years 13 Nov. 1862, at Camp Anderson; deserted 15 Dec. 1862; born Dinwiddie, Va., age 24, light complexion, blue eyes, brown hair, height 5 ft. 9 in.

Anthony, Jesse S., Private, D Company: enlisted as 4th Sergeant for 12 months 25 Sep. 1861 in Clayton County in I Company (Clayton Invincibles, Clayton County), 30th Georgia; transferred to 1st SS Battalion, 1 Aug. 1862; never reported, name appears on a descriptive list of transfers from 30th Georgia; commissioned 2nd Lieutenant, June 1864; captured at Nashville, 16 Dec. 1864; released from Johnson's Island, Ohio, 16 June,

1865; age 22, complexion fair, eyes blue, hair dark, height 5 ft. 8 in., occupation farmer; born Jonesboro 1839.

Armor, John W., Private, C Company: enlisted for 3 years 19 Apr. 1862 at Macon; transferred to 1st SS Battalion from A Company, 54th Georgia Regiment; present in arrest 31 Dec. 1863; pay stopped for rifle, accoutrements and ammunition lost, 29 Feb. 1864; wounded, Lost Mountain, about 17 June 1864; absent without leave 31 Aug. 1864; captured at Nashville 16 Dec. 1864; confined at Camp Chase, Ohio; transferred to Chicago 25 Mar. 1865.

Asbeal [Absell], Anson, Private, C Company: enlisted for 3 years 2 May 1862 at Savannah in I Company (Woodson Guards, Upson County), 32nd Georgia; transferred to 1st SS Battalion, 30 July 1862; detailed as teamster in Quartermaster's Dept., 31 Aug. 1862; died at Camp Anderson of inflammation of the bowels or congestive chill, 22 or 23 or 25 Sept. 1862.

Avera, D. O. P., Private, B Company: conscripted for the war 13 Aug. 1862 at Camp Randolph in Gordon County; transferred to 1st SS Battalion Aug. 1862; absent, wounded at Chickamauga, 31 Dec. 1863; absent wounded in General Hospital 29 Feb. 1864; MR, 31 Aug. 1864 shows him killed at Chickamauga but supposed to have been wounded; casualty report shows him mortally wounded.

Ballard, James, Private, C Company: enlisted for 3 years 6 May 1862 in Savannah in I Company (Woodson Guards, Upson County), 32nd Georgia; transferred to 1st SS Battalion, 330 July 1862; detailed as teamster in Quartermaster's Dept., 31 Oct. 1862; absent sick in hospital, Jackson, Miss., 30 June 1863; present sick, 31 Dec. 1863; absent sick in Atlanta, 29 February 1864; absent sick in General Hospital, 31 Aug. 1864; signed receipts for clothing 1 May and 30 Sept. 1864.

Ballard, Joseph, Private, C Company: enlisted as Private in I Company, 6th Regiment, GST, 18 Oct. 1861; mustered out Apr. 1862; enlisted for 3 years 18 Apr. 1862 in Savannah in I Company (Woodson Guards, Upson County), 32nd Georgia; transferred to 1st SS Battalion, 30 July 1862; detailed for extra duty in Quartermaster's Dept., 28 Feb. 1863; present sick, 31 Dec. 1863; absent sick in General Hospital, 31 Aug. 1864; signed receipt for clothing, 29 Sept. 1864.

Barrentine, D[octor], Private, A Company: enlisted for 3 years or the war 4 Mar. 1862 at Homersville in F Company (Appling Rangers, Appling County), 11th Georgia Battalion; converted to 47th Georgia Regiment, 12 May 1862; transferred to 1st SS Battalion 30 Aug. 1862; absent without leave, 30 Sept. 1862; in confinement, 31 Oct. 1862; deserted from camp, 7 Dec. 1862; rejoined from desertion, 14 Jan. 1863; under court-martial, 31 Mar. 1863; court-martial results published in Gen. Order #64/24, Headquarters, Dept. of South Carolina, Georgia and Florida, 26 Apr. 1863; absent in arrest in Savannah, 30 June 1863; absent sick in hospital in Atlanta, 29 Feb. 1864; absent sick in hospital in Forsyth, 31 Aug. 1864; admitted to Ocmulgee Hospital, Macon with pneumonia and ascites, 1 Nov. 1864, discharged from hospital, 15 Nov. 1864; place of residence, Appling County; 47 years old, dark complexion, gray eyes, light hair, height 6 ft..

Baugh, E[phraim] J., Private, D Company: enlisted for 12 months 25 Sept. 1861 in Fayette County in H Company (Fayette Volunteers, Fayette County), 30th Georgia; transferred to 1st SS Battalion, 1 Aug. 1862; discharged by civil authority on 18 Nov. 1862, being under age; age 18, complexion dark, eyes black, hair black, height 5 ft. 6 in., occupation farmer, born Chambers [or Montgomery] County, Ala., 29 Nov. 1844.

Baxter, W.E., Private, B Company: conscripted for the war 27 July 1862 at Camp Randolph in Gordon County; transferred to 1st SS Battalion Aug. 1862; received 10 day furlough, 10 Sept. 1862; dropped, 30 Sept. 1862; deserted since last muster, 31 Oct. 1862; born Mobile, Ala., age 16, light complexion, light hair, blue eyes, height 5 ft. 2 in.

Beacher, L., Private, A Company: enlisted for 3 years or the war at Homersville Mar. 4, 1862; transferred to 1st SS Battalion from F Company (Appling Rangers, Appling County), 47th Georgia; absent sick in Savannah, Aug. 31, 1862; absent sick in Springfield, Sept. 30, 1862; deserted, Oct. 31, 1862; age 17, complexion dark, eyes blue, hair dark, born in Appling County.
[Possible full name: William Lumpkin Beacher or Betcher; enlisted 10 Sep. 1863 in I Company, 27th Georgia; surrendered 26 Apr. 1865 at Greensboro, N.C.; born Georgia 1845.]

Beasley, Robert A., Private, A Company: enlisted for 1 year 6 Aug, 1861 at Savannah in D Company (City Light Guards), 1st (Olmstead's) Georgia; transferred to 1st SS Battalion, 13 Aug. 1862; present in arrest, 31 Aug. 1862; present in confinement, reenlisted for the war, 31 Oct. 1862; absent in Savannah, 31 Dec. 1862; wounded at Chickamauga, Sep. 1863; admitted wounded to Ocmulgee Hospital, Macon, 25 Sept. 1863, discharged 26 Sept. 26; reenlisted for the war, 16 Feb. 1864; captured at Chatham County [sic], 22 July 1864; took oath of allegiance to U.S. at Louisville, Ky., 27 July 1864; absent in hands of the enemy, 31 Aug. 1864; place of residence, Chatham County, age 19, complexion dark, hair dark, eyes grey, height 5 ft. 9 in., occupation blacksmith, born Georgia, 17-year-old railroad fireman in Chatham County 1860 census.
[included with this record]
Burdeshaw, Robert A., received as deserter from rebel army, 25 July 1864; took oath of allegiance and discharged as prisoner, 27 July 1864.

Beckworth [Beckwith], Simon, Private, C Company: enlisted as Private in E Company, 5th Regiment, GST, 12 Oct. 1861; mustered out Apr. 1862; enlisted for 3 years 10 May 1862 at Savannah in G Company (Emanuel County), 32nd Georgia; transferred to 1st SS Battalion, 30 July 1862; absent on special service with Lt. Holcombe, 30 Apr. 1863; wounded at Chickamauga, Sep. 1863; absent sick in General Hospital, 31 August 1864; born Georgia ca. 1844.

Becton, Curran, Private, B Company: conscripted for the war 13 Aug. 1862 at Camp Randolph in Gordon County; transferred to 1st SS Battalion Aug. 1862; wounded at Chickamauga, Sep. 1863; absent, wounded at Chickamauga, 31 Dec.1863; absent wounded in General Hospital, 29 Feb. 1864; absent, wounded at Jonesboro, 31 Aug. 1864; captured at Big Creek, Ga., 1 Dec. 1864; prisoner at Point Lookout, Md.; released

24 June 1865; place of residence, Jefferson County; complexion fair, hair brown, eyes blue, height 5 ft. 7 1/4 in.; 16 years old in the Jefferson County 1860 census.

Bennett, Hiram, Private, Corporal, C Company: enlisted 3 Oct. 1861 as Private in A Company, 1st Regiment, GST; mustered out Apr. 1862; enlisted for 3 years 18 Apr. 1862 at Savannah in K Company (Appling County), 54th Georgia; transferred to 1st SS Battalion, 30 July 1862; wounded at Chickamauga, Sep. 1863; absent sick in Atlanta 31 Dec. 1863; absent sick in Atlanta, 24 Feb. 1864; wounded at Jonesboro, leg amputated, 31 Aug. 1864; appears as 3rd Corporal, absent wounded in St. Mary's, 31 Aug. 1864; patient in Floyd House Hospital, Macon, with gunshot wound requiring amputation of the right leg, 3 Oct. 1864; paroled as Private, Thomasville, 22 May 1865; post office, Scriven, Ga.; 15 yuears old in the Appling County 1860 census.

Best, Anderstoke[s], Private, C Company: enlisted for 3 years 6 May 1862 at Savannah in E Company (Berrien County), 54th Georgia; transferred to 1st SS Battalion, 1 Aug. 1862; resigned as Corporal and returned to ranks, 15 Apr. 1863; captured 16 Dec. 1864 at Nashville; prisoner at Camp Chase, Ohio, 2 Jan. 1865; released, 16 May 1865; place of residence Scriven County [sic]; complexion dark, hair dark, eyes blue, height 5 ft. 6 in., age 21; 18-year-old farm laborer in the Berrien County 1860 census.

Best, Zadock, Private, C Company: enlisted 6 Oct. 1861 as Private in K Company, 5th Regiment, GST; mustered out, Apr. 1862; enlisted for 3 years 6 May 1862 at Savannah in E Company (Berrien County), 54th Georgia; transferred to 1st SS Battalion, 1 Aug. 1862; absent on sick furlough, 31 Oct. 1862; present on extra duty with provost guard, 31 Dec. 1863; detailed as litter bearer, 31 Aug. 1864; captured at Nashville, 16 Dec. 1864; received Camp Chase, Ohio, 4 Jan. 1865; enlisted in E Company, 5th U.S. Volunteer Infantry, 22 Apr. 1865; deserted 17 Aug. 1865.

Bierhalter, Frank [Francis C.], Private, B Company, Sergeant, C Company: enlisted for 14 months 7 June 1861 at Savannah in DeKalb Rifles (A Company, 1st (Olmstead's) Georgia); 4th Corporal, Sep. 1861; 3rd Corporal, Apr. 1862; Private, June 1862; transferred to 1st SS Battalion, 23 July 1862; 4th Sergeant, C Company, 30 Sept. 1862; captured Marietta, 16 June 1864; received at Rock Island, Ill., 27 June 1864; in the hands of the enemy, 31 Aug. 1864; enlisted in U.S. Army for frontier service, 6 Oct. 1864.

Bishop, Cleveland, Private, A Company: enlisted for 12 months 8 Aug. 1861 in Henry County, Ala., in Irwin Invincibles; became E Company (Henry Light Infantry), 25th Georgia, Dec. 1861; transferred to 1st SS Battalion, 1 Aug. 1862; reenlisted for the war, 31 Oct. 1862; appears as 3rd Corporal, 31 Dec. 1863; appears as Private, absent in hospital, 29 Feb. 1864; absent in the hands of the enemy, 31 Aug. 1864.
[included with this record]
Bishop, C., Corporal, 1st Georgia Battalion: captured 15 or 30 July 1863 at Snyder's Bluff, Miss., near Jackson, Tenn. [sic]; enlisted in 7th [Indiana?] Cavalry at Camp Morton, Ind., Aug. 1863.

Blakely, R.A.F., Private, B Company: conscripted for the war 12 Aug. 1862 at Camp Randolph in Gordon County; transferred to 1st SS Battalion Aug. 1862; wounded,

Jackson, Miss., July 1863; admitted as patient to French's division hospital, Lauderdale, Miss., 12 July 1863; absent sick in General Hospital, 31 Dec. 1863 and 29 Feb. 1864; absent sick, 31 Aug. 1864.

Blatz, John, Private, B Company: enlisted for the war 7 June 1861 at Savannah in DeKalb Rifles (A Company, 1st (Olmstead's) Georgia); transferred to 1st SS Battalion, 23 July 1862; sent to General Hospital, 23 Sept. 1862; deserted at Savannah, 5 May 1863; age 28, complexion light, eyes gray, hair light, height 5 ft. 5 in., occupation gardener, born in Germany.

Bodie, Alsa, Private, C Company: enlisted for 3 years 7 May 1862 at Savannah in F Company (Jeff Davis Guards, Clay County), 32nd Georgia; transferred to 1st SS Battalion, 30 July 1862; died of typhoid fever at Camp Anderson, 27 Sept. 1862.

Boggs, Barney, Private, C Company: enlisted as Private in D Company, 6th Regiment, GST, 18 Oct. 1861; mustered out, Apr. 1862; enlisted for 3 years 18 Apr. 1862 at Savannah in B Company (Talbot County), 32nd Georgia; transferred to 1st SS Battalion, 30 July 1862; assigned as company cook, 31 Oct. 1862; wounded, Jackson, Miss., July 1863; admitted as patient to French's Division Hospital, Lauderdale, Miss., 28 July 1863; absent sick in Talbot County, 31 Dec. 1863; absent sick in Columbus, Ga., 29 Feb. 1864; absent sick in General Hospital, 31 Aug. 1864; unfit for field service and detailed by Spec. Field Order No. 115/5, Headquarters, Army of Tennessee in the field, 29 Sept. 1864; 18-year-old student in the Talbot County 1860 census.

Boggs, James, Private, C Company: enlisted as Private in D Company, 6th Regiment, GST, 18 Oct. 1861; discharged for disability, 18 Jan. 1862; enlisted for 3 years 6 May 1862 in Savannah in B Company (Talbot County), 32nd Georgia; transferred to 1st SS Battalion; wounded at Chickamauga, Sep. 1863; absent sick in Talbot County, 31 Dec. 1863; absent sick in Macon, 29 Feb. 1864; detailed as driver for pontoon train, 31 Aug. 1864; returned to 32nd Georgia, Dec. 1864; surrendered at Greensboro, N.C., 26 Apr. 1865; 20-year-old student in the Talbot County 1860 census.

Boggs, Samuel, Private, Corporal, C Company: enlisted as Private in D Company, 6th Regiment, GST, 18 Oct. 1861; mustered out, Apr. 1862; enlisted for 3 years 18 Apr. 1862 in Savannah in B Company (Talbot County), 32nd Georgia; transferred to 1st SS Battalion, 30 July 1862; absent sick in convalescent camp, 21 Aug. 1862; absent sick in convalescent camp at Whitesville, 30 Sept. 1862; present 31 Oct. 1862; wounded, Jackson, Miss., July 1863; admitted as patient to French's Division Hospital, Lauderdale, Miss., 19 July 1863; absent sick in Talbot County, 31 Dec. 1863; absent sick in Columbus, 29 Feb. 1864; patient at Walker Hospital, Columbus, 30 Mar. 1864, "to be returned to his command;" appears as 4th Corporal, absent in the hands of the enemy, 31 Aug. 1864; captured Jonesboro, 31 Aug. 1864; exchanged at Rough and Ready, 19 or 22 Sept. 1864; captured at Nashville, 16 Dec. 1864; prisoner received at Camp Chase, Ohio, 2 Jan. 1865; 17 years old in the Talbot County 1860 census.

Bone, Manning, Private, D Company: enlisted for 12 months 25 Sep. 1861 in Campbell County in F Company (Campbell Sharpshooters, Campbell County), 30th Georgia; transferred to 1st SS Battalion, 1 Aug. 1862; never reported, replaced by Jacob McGuire; name appears on a descriptive list of transfers from 30th Georgia; deserted, took oath of allegiance and released at Louisville, Ky., 3 Aug. 1864; age 18, complexion fair, eyes blue, hair light, height 5 ft. 7 in., born Campbell County, occupation farmer.

Booth, John W., Private, B Company: enlisted for the war 14 Aug. 1861 at Fort McAllister in DeKalb Rifles (A Company, 1st (Olmstead's) Georgia); transferred to 1st SS Battalion, 23 July 1862; wounded at Chickamauga, Sep. 1863; wounded, Resaca or Calhoun, Ga., 14 or 16 May, 1864; absent wounded, 31 Aug. 1864.

Bowden, John C., Private, C Company: enlisted for 3 years 6 May 1862 at Savannah in B Company (Talbot County), 32nd Georgia; transferred to 1st SS Battalion, 30 July 1862; absent sick in hospital in Savannah, 31 Aug. 1862; present sick in quarters in camp, 31 Oct. 1862; absent sick in hospital in Benton, Miss., 30 June 1863; admitted as patient to Loring's Division Hospital, Macon, Miss., 16 July 1863; absent sick in Miss., 31 Dec. 1863; absent sick in General Hospital, 31 Aug. 1864.

Bowers, James A., Private, C Company: enlisted 17 Oct. 1861 as Private, C Company, 1st Battalion, GST; mustered out Apr. 1862; enlisted for 3 years 5 May 1862 at Macon in A Company (Lamar Infantry, Bibb County), 54th Georgia; transferred to 1st SS Battalion; discharged by civil authority on 13 Feb. 1863, being under age.

Boyle, Dennis, Private, Corporal: B Company: enlisted for 4 months 18 July 1861 at Tybee Island in Capt. Way's company; enlisted for the war 26 Sep. [or 26 Dec.] 1861 at Fort McAllister in DeKalb Rifles (A Company, 1st (Olmstead's) Georgia); 4th Corporal, June 1862; transferred to 1st SS Battalion, 23 July 1862 as 4th Corporal; absent sick furlough, 27 Oct. to 2 Nov. 1862; appears as 3rd Corporal, 31 Dec. 1862; appears as 2nd Corporal, 30 June 1863; died of cramps in hospital at Kingston, Ga., 28 Aug. 1863.
[another Dennis Boyle, possibly the same man: enlisted 25 Nov. 1861 in the Chatham Artillery; absent without leave, 31 Dec. 1861 and 28 Feb. 1862; dropped, 7 May 1862.]

Bradley [Bradler], J[oseph], Private, D Company: enlisted for 12 months 25 Dec. 1861 at Savannah in E Company (Alapaha Guards, Clinch County), 29th Georgia; transferred to 1st SS Battalion; present sick, 30 June 1863; absent sick in Atlanta, 31 Oct. 1863; absent sick, 29 Feb. 1864; signed receipt for clothing, 18 July 1864; absent sick, 31 Aug. 1864.

Brannon, Daniel, Private, A Company: enlisted for 12 months 24 Aug. 1861 at Savannah in F Company (Altamaha Scouts, Liberty County), 25th Georgia; transferred to 1st SS Battalion, 30 July 1862; absent sick at Whitesville, 30 Sept. 1862; absent sick in Savannah, reenlisted for the war, 31 Oct. 1862; absent, wounded at Jackson, Miss., 14 May 1863; patient at General Hospital, Point Clear, Baldwin County, Ala., 31 Aug. 1863; absent sick at Savannah, 31 Dec. 1863; absent sick in hospital in Savannah, 29 Feb. 1864; retired, 13 Apr. 1864; attached to Marshall Hospital, Columbus, 16 June 1864; disability retired from service, 20 Oct. 1864; reexamined, 24 Oct. 1864; born Carlisle, England, 1833.

Brewer, James R., Private, B Company: enlisted for the war 1 Sep. 1861 at Fort McAllister in DeKalb Rifles (A Company, 1st (Olmstead's) Georgia); detached on special duty at the shipyard in Savannah, June 1862; transferred to 1st SS Battalion, 23 July 1862; absent detailed as ship's carpenter, 13 May 1862; discharged as over age, 20 Nov. 1862.

Brickman, Caspar, Private, B Company: enlisted for the war 6 Mar. 1862 at Fort McAllister in DeKalb Rifles (A Company, 1st (Olmstead's) Georgia); transferred to 1st SS Battalion, 23 July 1862; killed Chickamauga, 20 Sept. 1863.

Brodbacker, Frank, Private, B Company: enlisted for 12 months 14 Aug. 1861 at Fort McAllister in DeKalb Rifles (A Company, 1st (Olmstead's) Georgia); transferred to 1st SS Battalion, 23 July 1862; deserted, 21 Aug. 1862; dropped, 30 Sept. 1862.

Bromm, Lewis [Louis], Private, B Company: enlisted for 14 months 7 June 1861 at Savannah in DeKalb Rifles (A Company, 1st (Olmstead's) Georgia); transferred to 1st SS Battalion, 23 July 1862; detailed as company cook, 28 Feb. 1863; deserted at Savannah, 5 May 1863; age 20, complexion light, eyes blue, hair red, height 5 ft. 6 in., occupation baker, born in Germany.

Brooks, William H., Private, B Company: enlisted for the war 1 Mar. 1862 at Fort McAllister in DeKalb Rifles (A Company, 1st (Olmstead's) Georgia); absent in General Hospital in Augusta, 1 May, 1862; absent on sick leave, 30 June 1862; transferred to 1st SS Battalion, 23 July 1862; detailed as company cook, 28 Feb. 1863; absent sick in Yazoo City, 13 June 1863; attached to French's Division Hospital, Lockhart, Miss., as cook on extra duty, 9 Aug. 1863; company cook, 31 Aug. 1864; captured from D Company, Nashville, 16 Dec. 1864; received at Camp Douglas, Ohio, 24 Dec. 1864; applied for oath of allegiance, Feb. 1865; mustered into U.S. volunteer service, 3 Apr. 1865.

Brown, Dominique [Dominick], 2nd Sergeant, 1st Sergeant, B Company: enlisted for the war 7 June 1861 at Savannah in DeKalb Rifles (A Company, 1st (Olmstead's) Georgia); 2nd Sergeant, 1 Sep. 1861; 1st Sergeant, 30 June 1862; transferred to 1st SS Battalion as 1st Sergeant, 23 July 1862; recommended for promotion to Ensign by Major Shaaff, 1 Apr. 1864; promotion denied by War Dept., 8 June 1864; wounded at Atlanta, Aug. 1864; admitted to Ocmulgee Hospital, Macon, 9 Aug. 1864; absent wounded, 31 Aug. 1864; born in Baden, Germany, 36-year-old shoemaker in the Chatham County 1860 census; died by his own hand in Savannah, 10 Oct. 1882, age 70 [sic].

Brown, E.J., Private, A Company: enlisted for 3 years 4 Mar. 1862 in Effingham County in I Company (Empire State Guards, Effingham County), 11th Georgia Battalion; converted to 47th Georgia Regiment, 12 May 1862; transferred to 1st SS Battalion 30 July 1862; absent sick in General Hospital in Savannah, 30 Sept. 1862; absent sick at Whiteville, 31 Oct. 1862; absent sick at Whiteville, 30 June 1863; signed receipt for clothing in hospital at Guyton, Ga., 22 July 1863; absent sick in Savannah, 31 Dec. 1863;

absent sick in hospital in Augusta, 29 Feb. 1864; 22-year-old painter in Effingham County 1860 census.

Brown, John, colored, Chief Cook, A Company: joined 4 Aug. 1862, colored man belonging to Durham; identified as slave belonging to Durham, 31 Oct. 1862; dropped by order of Major Shaaff because of illegal enlistment, 29 Feb. 1864.

Brown, Louis, Private, Corporal, B Company: conscripted for the war 13 Aug. 1862 at Camp Randolph in Gordon County; transferred to 1st SS Battalion Aug. 1862; wounded, Jackson, Miss., July 1863; patient at Loring's Division Hospital, Lauderdale, Miss., 18 Aug. 1863; captured as Corporal at Nashville, 16 Dec. 1864; received at Camp Chase, Ohio, 6 Jan. 1865; place of residence, Upson County, Ga.; complexion florid, hair black, eyes blue, height 5 ft. 8 3/4 in., age 24.

Brunner [Bruner, Brewner], N[athaniel] T., Ordnance Sergeant, Field & Staff: enlisted as Private for 60 days 31 May 1861 at Savannah in A Company, Savannah Volunteer Guards; reenlisted for 6 months 27 August 1861; reenlisted for the war 10 May 1862; transferred to 1st SS Battalion by Spec. Order No. 338, District of Georgia, 15 Aug. 1862; assigned duty as Ordnance Sergeant by Gen. Order No. 13, 1st SS Battalion, 17 Aug. 1862; detailed on ordnance duty at Division Headquarters, 29 Feb. 1864; admitted sick to St. Mary's Hospital, Montgomery, Ala., 13 Nov. 1864; admitted with ulcers to Ocmulgee Hospital, Macon, 19 Jan. 1865; returned to duty, 3 Feb. 1865; 39-year-old railroad engineer in the Chatham County 1870 census; residence Savannah, born in Beaufort, S. C., died in Savannah, 20 May, 1876, age 46.

Bryan, Alfred, Brevet [Jr.] 2nd Lieutenant, 2nd Lieutenant, A Company: joined 3 Sept. 1862, appointed 4 Oct. 1862, date of rank, 6 July 1862; promoted 2nd Lieutenant, 30 June 1863; wounded at Chickamauga, Sep. 1863; admitted with dysentery to Ocmulgee Hospital, Macon, and transferred to Savannah, 4 Nov. 1863; absent sick in Savannah, 31 Dec. 1863; leave approved by Spec. Order No. 81/1, Headquarters Army of Tennessee, 23 Mar. 1864; detailed in charge of brigade provost guards, 31 Aug. 1864; requested transfer to B Company, 29th Georgia, 6 Sept. 1864, transfer disapproved by order of Gen. Hood; acting assistant adjutant general, Jackson's Brigade, 7 Nov. 1864; promoted 1st Lieutenant, Jackson's Brigade, 10 Dec. 1864, date of assignment, 1 Sept. 1864, date of commission, 10 Oct. 1864; present at Tupelo, Miss., 25 Jan. 1865; died in Savannah 1 June 1875, age 37; 22-year-old clerk in the Chatham County 1860 census.

Bryant, E[lijah W.], Private, D Company: enlisted for 3 years 29 Sept. 1861 at Thomasville in H Company (Thomas County Volunteers), 29th Georgia; transferred to 1st SS Battalion, 1 Aug. 1862; wounded at Chickamauga, Sep. 1863; absent sick in hospital, 31 Dec. 1863; died in hospital at Marietta, 25 Nov. 1863; MR for Foard Hospital, Newnan, 31 Dec. 1863, shows died there, 10 Dec. 1863.

Burden, J.C., Private, C Company: absent sick in hospital since 1 Aug. 1862. No other record.

Burke, John, Private, A Company: enlisted for 4 months 18 July 1861 in Capt. Way's company (Forest City Rangers); mustered out, 18 Nov. 1861, MR shows him a boilermaker in Augusta; enlisted for the war 5 Jan. 1862 at St. Simon's Island in E Company (Irish Volunteers), 1st (Olmstead's) Georgia; transferred to 1st SS Battalion, 10 Aug. 1862; deserted from Camp Anderson, 16 Oct. 1862; absent without leave, 31 Dec. 1862; age 22, complexion ruddy, eyes blue, hair auburn, height 5 ft. 7 in., born in Ireland.

Burks, D[avid A.], Private, D Company: enlisted for 12 months 25 Sept. 1861 at Henry County in E Company (Bartow Invincibles, Henry County), 30th Georgia, transferred to 1st SS Battalion, Aug. 1862; absent on furlough from 25 Aug. to 4 Sept. 1862; absent sick in Savannah, 31 Oct. 1862; absent sick in Jonesboro, 31 Dec. 1862 and 28 Feb. 1863; absent sick in Canton, Miss., since 19 June 1863; absent sick, 31 Oct. and 31 Dec. 1863; admitted with chronic diarrhea to Ocmulgee Hospital, Macon, 29 July 1864; transferred 5 Aug. 1864; absent sick, 31 Aug. 1864; residence Clayton County; age 23, complexion dark, eyes black, hair black, height 5 ft. 11 in., occupation farmer, born Henry County.

Burks, J[ohn H.], Private, D Company: enlisted for 12 months 25 Sept. 1861 at Henry County in E Company (Bartow Invincibles, Henry County), 30th Georgia; 4th Sergeant, 16 May 1862; transferred to 1st SS Battalion, 1 Aug. 1862; sent to hospital in Macon, 1 Aug. 1862; absent sick, 31 Aug. 1862; absent sick in Macon, 31 Oct. 1862, 31 Dec. 1862 and 28 Feb. 1863; absent sick in Savannah since 5 May 1863; absent sick in Atlanta, 31 Oct., 1863; present sick, 31 Dec. 1863; absent sick, 29 Feb. 1864; age 24, complexion dark, eyes black, hair black, height 5 ft. 11 in., occupation farmer, born Henry County, 1 Sep. 1838.

Burns, J., Private, C Company: employed as painter in the Quartermaster's Department, 30 Sept. 1862. No other record.

Burns [Beirne, Berne], Lackey, Private, Corporal, A Company: enlisted for the war 16 Nov. 1861 in Savannah in E Company (Irish Volunteers), 1st (Olmstead's) Georgia; transferred to 1st SS Battalion, 10 Aug. 1862; present sick in quarters, 31 Oct. 1862; 3rd Corporal, 1 May 1863; captured near Jackson, Miss., July 1863; sent to Snyder's Bluff, Miss., 30 July 1863; appears as 1st Corporal, absent without leave, 31 Dec. 1863; appears as Private, deserted, 29 Feb. 1864.

Burns, William H., Private, C Company: enlisted for 3 years 1 Mar. 1862 at Green Island in C Company, Savannah Volunteer Guard Battalion; transferred to 1st SS Battalion, 15 Aug. 1862; deserted, 30 June 1863; captured Chickamauga, 20 Sept. 1863; forwarded to Louisville, Ky., for exchange, 1 Oct. 1863; received at Camp Douglas, Ill., October 1863; absent without leave, 31 Dec. 1863; deserted to the enemy 19 Sept. 1863, during the battle of Chickamauga, (MR, 29 Feb. 1864).

Burton, L[ewis] B[rown], Private, A Company: enlisted for 3 years or the war 2 Sept. 1861 in Bibb County in L Company (Calhoun Repeaters, Calhoun County), 25th Georgia; transferred to 1st SS Battalion, 1 Aug. 1862; sick in hospital in Jackson, Miss., 30 June 1863; admitted to Loring's Division Hospital, Lauderdale, Miss., 22 Aug. 1863;

extra duty as nurse at Loring's Division Hospital from 1 Sept. 1863; returned to duty, 27 Oct. 1863; absent on furlough from hospital, 29 Feb. 1864; wounded, Resaca or Calhoun, Ga., 14 or 16 May, 1864; absent wounded in hospital in Columbus, 31 Aug. 1864; captured at Macon as Sergeant, Apr. 1865.

Butler, James F., Private, B Company: enlisted for the war 7 June 1861 at Savannah in DeKalb Rifles (A Company, 1st (Olmstead's) Georgia); transferred to 1st SS Battalion, 23 July 1862; deserted, 23 Dec. 1862; court-martial results in Gen. Order No. 21/2/6, Dept. of South Carolina, Georgia and Florida, 1 Feb. 1863; sentenced to 1 year in ball and chain for desertion, 28 Feb. 1863; absent in arrest at Oglethorpe Barracks, Savannah, 30 June 1863; incarcerated in Chatham County jail, 1 Aug. 1863; recommended for presidential amnesty and pardon by Major A.L. Hartridge by letter of 7 Aug. 1863; absent, gunshot wound to the right leg, 20 Sept. 1863; wounded at Chickamauga, 31 Dec. 1863; absent wounded in Savannah, 29 Feb. 1864; captured, July 1864; took oath of allegiance to U.S., 27 July 1864; absent in the hands of the enemy, 31 Aug. 1864; place of residence Chatham County; complexion dark, hair dark, eyes blue, height 5 ft. 9 in.; born Cork, Ireland, 35-year-old fireman in the Chatham County 1860 census.

Callahan, E.W., Private, B Company: enlisted for the war 7 Aug. 1862 at Garden City; died of dropsy at camp near Dalton, 6 Dec. 1863.

Campbell, [Thomas], see Finn, John H.

Cannington, J.H., Private, A Company: enlisted for 3 years or the war 9 Mar. 1863 at Camp Jordan; reenlisted for the war, 29 Feb. 1864.

Carolina, Negro Cook, D Company: joined for the war 23 Aug. 1862; enlisted by master as company cook, 30 Sept. 1862; absent with leave, 31 Dec. 1863; deserted while on leave, 1 Jan. 1864.

Carter, W.J., Private, B Company: enlisted for the war 1 May 1863 at Savannah; absent sick at Benton, Miss., 30 June 1863; joined as William Carter by transfer from Navy, 31 Dec. 1863; absent sick, left at Benton, Miss., 29 Feb. 1864; absent sick, 31 Aug. 1864.

Cason, Lewis F., Private, B Company: enlisted for the war 10 Sep. 1861 at Fort McAllister in DeKalb Rifles (A Company, 1st (Olmstead's) Georgia); transferred to 1st SS Battalion, 23 July 1862; absent sick in General Hospital, 31 Dec. 1863; died at Blackshear, Pierce County, 30 Aug. 1864.

Chapman [Chatman], J[ames] D[avid], Private, D Company: enlisted for 12 months 25 Sept. 1861 in Campbell County in F Company (Campbell Sharpshooters, Campbell County), 30th Georgia; transferred to 1st SS Battalion, 2 Aug. 1862; absent sick in Savannah, 31 Dec. 1862; present sick in hospital, 28 Feb. 1863; transferred from General Hospital No. 1, Savannah, to General Hospital, Whitesville, with gonorrhea, 5 May 1863; present sick, 30 June 1863; absent in hospital in Atlanta, 31 Oct. 1863; deserted from hospital, 26 Nov. 1863; absent, 31 Dec. 1863; age 20, complexion dark, eyes black, hair brown, height 5 ft. 11 in., occupation farmer, born Monroe County.

Chitwood, S[tephen] D., Private, D Company: enlisted for 12 months 31 Dec. 1861 at Franklin County in G Company (Stephens Volunteers, Berrien County), 29th Georgia; transferred to 1st SS Battalion, 1 Aug. 1862; leave of absence, sick in Macon, 10-19 Aug. 1862; absent, 31 Aug. 1862; sent to General Hospital, Savannah, 30 Sept. 1862; absent without leave, 30 Apr. 1863; absent without leave since 14 May (MR, 30 June 1863); captured, 14 May 1863; paroled prisoner in camp at Demopolis, 5 June 1863; reenlisted for the war, 29 Feb. 1864; wounded, north Georgia, 7-30 June 1864; absent in the hands of the enemy since 3 July (MR, 31 Aug. 1864); captured near Marietta, prisoner at Camp Douglas, Ill., 18 July 1864; enlisted I Company, 5th U.S. Volunteers, 1 Apr. 1865.

Clancey, Edward, Private, B Company: enlisted for the war 26 Aug. 1862 at Fort McAllister in DeKalb Rifles (A Company, 1st (Olmstead's) Georgia); transferred to 1st SS Battalion; given up to the Navy as a deserter, 8 Sept. 1862; claimed by the Navy (MR, 31 Oct. 1862).

Clark, Charles, Private, C Company: enlisted Apr. 1863 as substitute for Alexander Faucett, deserted.
[No service record for Charles Clark with 1st Sharpshooter Battalion MRs.]

Cobb, M[arcus] E., Private, A Company: enlisted for 3 years or the war 23 Jan. 1863 in Randolph County; died at Yazoo City of brain fever, 7 June 1863; 15 years old in the Randolph County 1860 census;.

Cobb, W[illiam] D., Private, A Company: enlisted for 3 years or the war 23 Jan. 1863 in Randolph County; died at Canton of brain fever, 2 June 1863; 23 years old in the Randolph County 1860 census.

Cochran, B[urris] J., Private, D Company: enlisted for 3 years or the war 1 Mar. 1863 in Bryan County; absent sick, 31 Oct. 1863 to 29 Feb. 1864; killed, Lost Mountain, Ga., 18 June 1864; named in bounty voucher in file of C.W. Dedge.

Cochran, William F. [W. Frank], Private, D Company: enlisted for 12 months 27 July 1861 at Savannah in A Company (Thomasville Guards, Thomas County), 29th Georgia; transferred to 1st SS Battalion, 1 Aug. 1862; wounded, Jackson, Miss., July 1863; admitted with icterus [jaundice] to Floyd House and Ocmulgee Hospitals, Macon, 28 Nov. 1863; reenlisted for the war, 29 Feb. 1864; captured at Nashville, 16 Dec. 1864; received as prisoner at Camp Chase, Ohio, 4 Jan. 1865.

Coe, F.M., Private, C Company: enlisted for 3 years or the war 1 Dec. 1863 at Dalton; absent sick at Atlanta, 29 Feb. 1864; absent without leave, 31 Aug. 1864.

Coile James, Private, A Company: enlisted for 1 year 6 Aug. 1861 at Savannah in D Company (City Light Guards), 1st (Olmstead's) Georgia; transferred to 1st SS Battalion; absent without leave, 31 Aug. 1862; reenlisted for the war, deserted from Camp Anderson, 26 Aug. 1862 (MR, 31 Oct. 1862); born Cavan, Ireland, 19-year-old laborer in Chatham County 1860 census. Pension application of James Coyle referred to in this file.

Coleman, Thomas, Private, A Company: enlisted 25 July 1861 in Capt. J.B. Read's company; mustered out, 25 Jan. 1862; enlisted for 3 years or the war 14 Feb. 1862 at Savannah in A Company (Irish Jasper Greens), 1st (Olmstead's) Georgia; transferred to 1st SS Battalion; absent without leave, 31 Oct. 1862; deserted from Camp Anderson 16 October 1862; age 23, complexion ruddy, hair dark, height 6 ft. 1 in., occupation laborer, born in Ireland; born in Kerry, Ireland, 24-year-old laborer in Chatham County 1860 census.

Comaskey, James, Private, A Company: joined 6 Oct. 1862 as substitute for O.B. Waters; reenlisted for the war, 31 Oct. 1862; captured at Jackson, Miss., 14 May 1863; absent without leave, 30 June 1863; paroled at Demopolis, Ala., 5 June 1863; absent sick at Montgomery, Ala., 31 Dec. 1863; reenlisted for the war, present sick in General Hospital, 29 Feb. 1864.

Conway, W.H.T., Private, B Company: enlisted for the war 26 Feb. 1863 at Savannah; absent, sent to General Hospital, 12 Apr. 1863; died at General Hospital, 10 May 1863.

Cook, William J., Private, A Company: enlisted for 3 years or the war 30 Mar. 1863, at Decatur; transferred from C.S. Navy, sick at Yazoo City, 30 June 1863; absent sick at Montgomery, 31 Dec. 1863; absent sick in hospital at Savannah, 29 Feb. 1864; patient in Empire Hospital, Atlanta, 30 Apr. 1864; absent sick in General Hospital, 31 Aug. 1864.

Cooper, Dennis A.R.J., Private, C Company: enlisted for 3 years 8 Nov. 1862 at Camp Anderson; present sick in hospital, 31 Dec. 1862; absent sick in hospital at Canton, 30 June 1863; present sick in hospital at Atlanta, 31 Dec. 1863; absent sick in hospital, Atlanta, 29 Feb. 1864; absent sick, 31 Aug. 1864.

Cooper, J[ohn] R[andolph], Private, D Company: enlisted for 3 years 7 May 1862 at Camp Smith in B Company (Littlefield Volunteers, Gordon County), 8th Georgia Battalion; transferred to 1st SS Battalion; wounded, Jackson, Miss., July 1863; absent sick, 31 Oct. and 31 Dec. 1863; reenlisted for the war, absent sick, 29 Feb. 1864; wounded, Resaca or Calhoun, Ga., 14 or 16 May, 1864; absent wounded, 31 Aug. 1864; 19 years old in the Gordon County 1860 census.

Cooper, R[obert] C., Private, D Company: enlisted for 3 years 5 Oct. 1861 at Savannah [sic] in B Company (Littlefield Volunteers, Gordon County), 8th Georgia Battalion; transferred to 1st SS Battalion; present sick, 30 June 1863; absent without leave, 31 Oct. and 31 Dec. 1863; deserted 26 July 1863 on the retreat from Jackson, Miss. (MR, 29 Feb. 1864); 16-year-old farm laborer in the Gordon County 1860 census.
[Included in this record]
Cooper, K.C., Private, B Company, 1st SS Battalion: captured near Jackson, Miss., July 1863; received as prisoner at Camp Morton, Ind., 7 Aug. 1863; died of dysentery, 1 or 7 Nov. 1863.
[Included in this record]

Cooper, R., Private, D Company, 1st SS Battalion: enlisted for 3 years 1 Mar. 1862 at Savannah; attached Walker's Division Hospital, Lauderdale, Miss., 2 Aug. 1863; present, 31 Aug. 1863.

Cosby, T[homas] R., Assistant Surgeon, Field & Staff: commissioned 16 Nov. 1861, entered service from Virginia; assigned to Orleans Battery, Louisiana Artillery, Fort Livingston, La.; on duty in Jackson, Miss., Nov. 1862; signed for forage in Walker's division as Asst. Surg., 1st SS Battalion, 30 June 1863; requested medical supplies at Vernon, Miss., July 1863; present, 29 Feb. 1864; assigned to 45th Miss., Mar, 1864; promoted Surgeon, 1 June 1864 to rank from 30 Mar.; assigned to 1st and 4th Florida, Sep. 1864.

Cox, James A., Private, B Company: conscripted for the war 7 Aug. 1862 at Camp Randolph in Gordon County; transferred to 1st SS Battalion Aug. 1862; admitted to Floyd House and Ocmulgee Hospitals with intermittent fever, 7 Nov. 1863, returned to duty, 11 Nov. 1863; died at General Hospital, Kingston, Ga., 8 Feb. 1864; post office Euharlee.

Cox, M.J., Private, B Company: conscripted for the war 12 Aug. 1862 at Camp Randolph in Gordon County; transferred to 1st SS Battalion Aug. 1862; absent sick in Upson County from 17 Dec. 1862 (MR, 31 Dec. 1862 and 28 Feb. 1863); absent sick in Upson County from 28 Nov. 1862, (MR, 30 Apr. and 30 June 1863); absent sick at Thomaston, Upson County, 31 Dec. 1863; paid commutation, Mar. 1864.

Crane, Horace A., Jr., Senior 2nd Lieutenant, 1st Lieutenant, A Company: enlisted as 3rd Sergeant, B Company, 8th Georgia, 21 May 1861; commissioned 2nd Lieutenant 1st SS Battalion, 1 Aug. 1862, joined 7 Aug., date of rank 2 July 1862; absent on special service, 30 Sept. 1862; promoted 1st Lieutenant, vice Twyman, 30 June 1863, date of rank, 20 Jan. 1863; wounded at Chickamauga, 19 Sept. 1863; absent sick furlough, 31 Dec. 1863; gunshot wound above the ankle, compound fracture, unhealed and unfit for service, Savannah, 12 July 1864; absent by medical authority, inspection report, 17 Aug. 1864; absent on surgeon's certificate to 20 Oct. (MR, 31 Aug. 1864); absent wounded, inspection report, 17 Sept. 1864; retired to Invalid Corps 10 Oct. 1864; assigned as post adjutant, Fort McAllister, totally disabled, 25 Nov. 1864; captured, Fort McAllister, 13 Dec. 1864; retired, no successor, inspection report, Tupelo, Miss., 25 Jan. 1865; sent to Fort Delaware, 7 Feb. 1865; took oath of allegiance and released, 17 June 1865; born St. Mary's, Ga.,1841, died Savannah, 8 Sep. 1920, age 79; 18-year-old clerk in the Chatham County 1860 census.

Crawford, James A., Private, C Company: enlisted for 3 years 18 Apr. 1862 at Macon in A Company (Lamar Infantry, Bibb County), 54th Georgia; transferred to 1st SS Battalion 30 July 1862; absent sick in convalescent camp, 31 Aug. 1862; absent on sick leave furlough, 31 Oct. 1862; deserted from Camp Anderson, 13 Jan. 1863.

Crow[e], J.H. [J.S.], Private, D Company: enlisted for the war 1 May 1863 at Savannah in place of William Lightbourne, who transferred to C.S. Navy; mortally[?] wounded at

Chickamauga, Sep. 1863; absent wounded, 31 Oct. and 31 Dec. 1863; absent sick, 29 Feb. 1864; absent wounded, 31 Aug. 1864.

Crumbley, J.C., Private, A Company: enlisted for 3 years or the war 3 May 1862 at Doctor Town in F Company (Altamaha Scouts, Liberty County), 25th Georgia; transferred to 1st SS Battalion, 30 July 1862; absent sick in Savannah, 31 Aug. 1862; sick at Whitesville, 30 Sept. 1862; transferred back to 25th Georgia, 21 Oct. 1862; took the oath of allegiance at Thomasville, 11 May 1865, as J. Crumley, 1st Georgia SS Battalion [see below]; complexion dark, hair dark, eyes grey, height 5 ft. 1 in.

Crumley, (Connally) [sic], Jesse, Corporal, Private, C Company: enlisted 3 Oct. 1861 as Private in A Company, 1st Regiment, GST; mustered out Apr. 1862; enlisted for 3 years 18 Apr. 1862 at Savannah in K Company (Appling County), 54th Georgia; transferred to 1st SS Battalion; promoted Corporal, 17 Aug. 1862; appears as Private, 31 Dec. 1862; wounded at Chickamauga, Sep. 1863.

Culpepper, David, Private, C Company: enlisted for 3 years 6 Feb. 1863 in Dooly County; present sick, 31 Dec. 1863; absent sick in Dooly County, 29 Feb. 1864; absent sick on 60 days furlough from 29 Aug. 1864; 38-year-old farmer in the Dooly County 1860 census; born Crisp County, 15 Nov. 1823, died there, 13 Aug. 1893.

Dannenfelser, Martin M., Musician, Private, B Company: enlisted for the war 7 June 1861 at Savannah in DeKalb Rifles (A Company, 1st (Olmstead's) Georgia); transferred to 1st SS Battalion, 23 July 1862; discharged by civil authority, Oct. 19, 1862.

Darvie [Davie, Davis], Richard, Private, A Company: enlisted for 3 years or the war 8 Aug. 1861 at Savannah in G Company (Brown Light Infantry, Screven County), 25th Georgia; transferred to 1st SS Battalion, 1 Aug. 1862; present sick in quarters, 31 Aug. 1862; present sick in hospital, 31 Oct. 1862; transferred to C.S. Navy, by special order, 30 June 1863; captured, Richmond, Va., 3 Apr., paroled, 27 Apr. 1865.

Davis, Henry W., Private, C Company: enlisted for 3 years 7 May 1862, at Savannah in G Company (Emanuel County), 32nd Georgia; transferred to 1st SS Battalion, 30 July 1862; present sick in camp, 31 Oct. 1862; absent sick on furlough, 31 Dec. 1862; absent sick on furlough since 1 Nov. 1862 (MR, 28 Feb. 1863); present sick in Atlanta [sic], 31 Dec. 1863; wounded, north Georgia, 7-30 June 1864; died of wounds at General Hospital, 26 or 28 July 1864.

Davis, McDonald [or Davis McDonald], Private, D Company: enlisted for 12 months 25 Sept. 1861 at Campbell County in G Company (Campbell Grays, Campbell County), 30th Georgia; transferred to 1st SS Battalion, 1 Aug. 1862; absent sick at Savannah Medical Hospital, 28 Feb. and 30 Apr. 1863; absent sick in Savannah since Feb. 1863 (MRs, 30 June and 31 Oct. 1863); absent sick, 31 Dec. 1863 and 29 Feb. 1864; absent wounded, 31 Aug. 1864; age 18, complexion dark, eyes gray, hair black, height 5 ft. 5 in., occupation farmer, born DeKalb County; 16 years old in the Campbell County 1860 census.

Dawson, J[ohn] E. [or C.], Private, D Company: enlisted for 3 years 5 Oct. 5, 1861 at Camp Black in B Company (Littlefield Volunteers, Gordon County), 8th Georgia Battalion; absent on sick furlough, 28 May to 13 June 1863; transferred to 1st SS Battalion, Aug. 1862; appears as Corporal, 30 Apr. 1863; appears as 3rd Corporal, 31 Oct. and 31 Dec. 1863; reenlisted for the war, 16 Feb. 1864; captured in Marietta, 3 July 1864; received at Camp Douglas, Ill., 18 July 1864; appears as Private, absent in the hands of the enemy since 3 July (MR, 31 Aug. 1864); applied for oath of allegiance at Camp Douglas, Mar. 1865; discharged 16 May 1865; home, Calhoun, Ga; 20 years old in the Gordon County 1860 census.

Deckert [Deckker], John [E.], Private, B Company: enlisted for 14 months 7 June 1861 at Savannah in DeKalb Rifles (A Company, 1st (Olmstead's) Georgia); transferred to 1st SS Battalion, 23 July 1862; deserted at Savannah, May 5, 1863; age 28, complexion light, eyes blue, hair red, height 5 ft. 4 in., occupation tailor, born in Germany.

Dedge, C[alvin] W., Private, D Company: enrolled 4 Mar. 1862 as Junior 2nd Lieutenant, F Company, 11th Georgia Battalion; resigned, 12 Apr. 1862; enlisted for the war 15 Mar. 1863 at Savannah; absent without leave from 5 May 1863; G.W. Dodge [sic] employed as nurse at General Hospital, Canton, Miss., from 7 June 1863; deserted, 4 May 1863, was taken sick en route to company and reported to hospital, Canton, Miss., 28 May, 1863; returned to duty, 18 Aug. 1863; deserted, 28 Aug. 1863; returned to duty, 15 Oct. 1863; reenlisted for the war, 16 Feb. 1864; signed commutation 4 Mar. 1864; captured Jonesboro, Ga., 31 Aug. 1864; absent in the hands of the enemy since 1 Sept. 1864; exchanged at Rough and Ready, Ga., 19 or 22 Sept. 1864; 22-year-old farmer in the Ware County 1860 census.

Dedwilder [Dedwylie], W[illiam] C.L., Private, B Company: conscripted for the war 25 July 1862 at Camp Randolph in Gordon County; transferred to 1st SS Battalion Aug. 1862; died at Lauderdale Springs, Miss., 16 Aug. 1863; claim filed on behalf of Sarah Dedwiler, widow, Glascock County, Georgia, by William Walton, attorney, agent in Richmond of the Georgia Relief and Hospital Association.

DeGeorge, Phillip [George, P.D.], Private, C Company: enlisted for 3 years 6 May 1862 at Savannah in I Company (Effingham County), 54th Georgia; transferred to 1st SS Battalion, 1 Aug. 1862; absent sick in hospital in Savannah, 31 Aug. 1862; present sick in quarters in camp, 31 Oct. 1862; discharged 2 Nov. 1862, by order of Brig. Gen. Mercer.

Dent, George C[olumbus], Captain, D Company: enrolled in Brunswick as Captain, Glynn Guards (13th Georgia), 14 Aug. 1861; assigned as artillery on St. Simon's Island, 19 Aug. 1861; designation changed to A Company, 13th Georgia, 15 Oct. 1861; company transferred to Savannah, early 1862; designation changed to 26th Georgia, ca. 1 Mar. 1862; company converted to cavalry and assigned 3rd Georgia Cavalry Battalion, 1 Apr. 1862; "retired," 12 May 1862; appointed Captain, 1st SS Battalion, 23 June 1862; absent on 24 hour leave, 30 Sep. 1862; absent on furlough, 9 Dec. 1862; wounded at Jackson, Miss., 15 July 1863; absent sick, wounded at Jackson (MR, 31 Oct. 1863); requested by Gen. Gilmer for duty in Dept. of S.C., Ga. and Fla., 25 Jan. 1864; requests light duty, 29 Jan. 1864; ordered to report to Gen. Gilmer by Spec. Order No. 38/24, Adjutant and

Inspector General's Office, 15 Feb. 1864; absent sick, 29 Feb. 1864; assigned to duty as assistant inspector of artillery, Military District of Georgia, Gen. Order No. 10, 24 Mar. 1864; assigned as assistant inspector to 3rd Military District of South Carolina (Col. Olmstead), 12 May 1864; relieved from duty as inspector and assigned to command at Red Bluff, by Gen. Order No. 149, 7 July 1864; signed voucher for quarters in Savannah, 27 Aug. 1864; absent, detached by order Secretary of War, 31 Aug. 1864; surrendered, 10 May 1865; paroled Thomasville, Ga., 23 May 1865; 38-year-old farmer in Glynn County 1860 census; born South Carolina, 1 May 1822, died Glynn County 4 Mar. 1884.

Dent, John M[arshall], Assistant Surgeon, Field & Staff: enlisted 10 Apr. 1862 in Augusta in A Company (Oglethorpe Light Infantry, Richmond County), 12th Georgia Artillery Battalion; commissioned as Assistant Surgeon 4 Sept. 1862; Assistant Surgeon, 12th Georgia Artillery Battalion, no date; assigned to 1st SS Battalion by Spec. Order No. 47, District of Georgia, 16 Feb. 1863; absent on 30 day sick furlough from 4 Apr. 1863; reported, 3 May 1863; signed voucher for forage, 20 July to 30 Sep. 1863; resigned, 19 Oct. 1863; replaced by C.T. Ford; born Augusta, 22 July 1836, died Burke County, 20 Nov. 1922.

Derst, John, Private, B Company: enlisted for the war 6 Mar. 1862 at Fort McAllister in DeKalb Rifles (A Company, 1st (Olmstead's) Georgia); transferred to 1st SS Battalion, 23 July 1862; absent sick in Canton, Miss. from 25 June 1863; baker at Walker's Division Hospital from 5 July 1863; detailed by order of Gen. Hardee, 31 Oct. 1863; on roll of extra duty men at Newton, Miss., 31 Dec. 1863; cook at Newton, Miss., 30 Nov. 1863; absent sick at Newton, Miss., 31 Dec. 1863; cook by order Gen. Hardee, 31 Jan. 1864; absent sick at Newton, Miss., 29 Feb. 1864; absent sick, 31 Aug. 1864; born Hesse-Darmstadt, Germany, 22-year-old baker in the Chatham County 1860 census; died Savannah, 15 July 1928.

Derst, Peter, 1st Sergeant, B/C Company: enlisted for the war 7 June 1861 at Savannah in DeKalb Rifles (A Company, 1st (Olmstead's) Georgia); transferred to 1st SS Battalion 23 July 1862; Private, B Company, transferred to C Company by Spec. Order No. 12, Sharpshooter Battalion, 14 Aug. 1862, and appointed 1st Sergeant, 18 Aug.; absent on special service with Lt. Holcombe, 30 Apr. 1863; wounded at Chickamauga, Sep. 1863; absent sick in Savannah, 31 Dec. 1863 and 29 Feb. 1864; present at Savannah General Hospital, 29 Feb. 1864; absent wounded in Savannah, 31 Aug. 1864; operator of a shaving saloon, 1860 Savannah city directory.

Dickinson, Jacob K., Private, C Company: enlisted as Private in I Company, 6th Regiment, GST, 18 Oct. 1861; mustered out Apr. 1862; enlisted for 3 years 18 Apr. 1862 at Savannah in I Company (Woodson Guards, Upson County), 32nd Georgia; transferred to 1st SS Battalion, 21 Aug. 1862; absent with leave from 20 Aug. 1862; absent without leave from 27 Aug. 1862; transferred back to I Company, 32nd Georgia. 31 Oct. 1862; present in Macon hospital with dropsy, 23 Sep. 1863; surrendered at Greensboro, N.C., 26 Apr. 1865.

Dobson, Howell B., Private, C Company: enlisted for 3 years 6 May 1862 at Savannah in E Company (Berrien County), 54th Georgia; transferred to 1st SS Battalion, 1 Aug. 1862;

absent sick at convalescent camp from 21 Aug. 1862, detailed as cook in hospital, 30 Aug. 1862; absent sick in General Hospital, 31 Dec. 1862; absent sick in General Hospital at Whitesville since 18 Dec. (MR, 28 Feb. 1863); absent sick in General Hospital at Guyton, 30 Apr. 1863; absent in General Hospital at Whitesville as nurse since 20 Apr. (MR, 30 June 1863); present on special service at Whitesville Hospital, 31 Dec. 1863; nurse at Guyton General Hospital since 25 Apr. 1863 (MR, Jan. 31, 1864); discharged from Guyton, 1 Feb. 1864; wounded, Resaca or Calhoun, Ga., 14 or 16 May, 1864[?]; absent sick in General Hospital, 31 Aug. 1864.

Dodson, J[ohn] E., Private, D Company: enlisted for 12 months 25 Sept. 1861 at Clayton County in I Company (Clayton Invincibles, Clayton County), 30th Georgia; transferred to 1st SS Battalion, 1 Aug. 1862; absent, detailed for extra duty in the Quartermaster Dept., 31 Oct. and 31 Dec. 1862, 28 Feb. through 30 June 1863, and 31 Oct. 1863; detailed as teamster, 31 Dec. 1863; reenlisted for the war, 29 Feb. 1864; absent in the Quartermaster Dept., 31 Aug. 1864; detailed to the Quartermaster Dept., 16 Sep. 1864; age 28, complexion dark, eyes black, hair black, height 5 ft. 6 in., occupation farmer, born Henry County.

Donnelly, T[homas] J., Private, A Company: enlisted 30 May 1861; reenlisted for 3 years or the war 14 Feb. 14, 1862 at Savannah in A Company (Irish Jasper Greens), 1st (Olmstead's) Georgia; transferred to 1st SS Battalion, 30 July 1862; absent sick in Whitesville, 31 Aug. 1862; deserted at Savannah 9 May 1863; age 25, complexion fair, eyes blue, hair dark, height 5 ft. 8 in.

Doughtry, M[itchell], Private, A Company: enlisted 8 Aug. 1861 in D Company (Ogeechee Rifles, Screven County), 25th Georgia; transferred to 1st SS Battalion, 1 Aug. 1862; provided Edward Eagan as substitute; discharged 11 Aug. 1862.

Douglass, M[ichael] W., Private, A Company: enlisted for 3 years or the war 4 Mar. 1862 at Homersville in F Company (Appling Rangers, Appling County), 11th Georgia Battalion; converted to 47th Georgia Regiment, 12 May 1862; transferred to 1st SS Battalion, 30 July 1862; absent sick at Whitesville, 31 Aug. 1862; absent on sick furlough for 30 days, 31 Oct. 1862; present sick, 30 June 1863; reenlisted for the war, 29 Feb. 1864.

Doyle, Martin L., Private, A Company: enlisted for 3 years or the war 16 Mar. 1863 at Savannah as substitute for P.R. Kittles; attached as cook at Bragg Hospital, Newnan, Ga., 1 Nov. 1863; absent sick at Newnan, Ala. [sic], 31 Dec. 1863; absent sick in hospital at Newnan, Ga., 29 Feb. 1864; detailed to litter corps, 31 Aug. 1864; captured near Franklin, Tenn., 17 Dec. 1864; received as prisoner at Camp Chase, Ohio, 4 Jan. 1865; took oath of allegiance, 12 June 1865; residence Chatham County; complexion florid, hair dark, eyes gray, age 45; 33-year-old railroad clerk in the Chatham County 1860 census, born Roscommon, Ireland.

Draeger, Charles, Private, B Company: enlisted for 12 months 7 Aug. 1861 at Fort McAllister in DeKalb Rifles (A Company, 1st (Olmstead's) Georgia); transferred to 1st SS Battalion, 23 July 1862; deserted 9 Dec. 1862; arrested, 1 Mar. 1863; deserted at

Savannah, 5 May 1863; born Germany, 32 years old, dark complexion, brown hair, gray eyes, height 5 ft. 5 in.
[included in this file]
Dräger, Karl, or Draggers, Charles, Private, Atlanta Home Guard, took oath of allegiance at Chattanooga, 22 Aug. 1864; received as prisoner at Louisville, Ky., 26 Sept. 1864; residence Demplin, Prussia; complexion light, hair brown, eyes blue, height 5 ft. 5 in.
Dragers, Charles, received as prisoner at Louisville, 1 Sep. 1864; discharged, 4 Sept. 1864; residence Fulton County.

Driggers, John, Private, B Company: enlisted for the war 9 May 1862 at Fort McAllister in DeKalb Rifles (A Company, 1st (Olmstead's) Georgia); transferred to 1st SS Battalion, 23 July 1862; absent on furlough, 25 to 31 Oct. 1862; captured at Clinton, Miss., 8 July 1863, or Jackson, Miss., 10 July 1863, or Warren County, Miss., 11 July 1863; received at Gratiot Prison, St. Louis, Mo., 16 July 1863; received at Camp Morton, Ind., 2 Aug. 1863; deserted, missing on retreat from Missionary Ridge (MR, 31 Dec. 1863); transferred for exchange, 26 Feb. 1865.

Duignan [Degnan], Mathew, Private, A Company: enlisted 10 Aug. 1861 at Savannah in A Company (Irish Jasper Greens), 1st (Olmstead's) Georgia; reenlisted for 3 years or the war 14 Feb. 1862 at Savannah; transferred to 1st SS Battalion, Aug. 1862; sick at Whitesville, 30 Sept. 1862; captured at Clinton, Miss., as Private, 1st Georgia Battery, 8 July 1863; received at Gratiot Prison, St. Louis, Mo., 26 July 1863; sent to Camp Morton, Ind., 1 Aug. 1863; enlisted in U.S. service, Aug. 1863; absent without leave (MR, 31 Dec. 1863); deserter, 29 Feb. 1864.

Dunn, John, Private, B Company: enlisted for the war 1 May 1863 at Savannah, joined by transfer from C.S. Navy; admitted to U.S. General Hospital, Chattanooga, with gun shot wound to right knee joint, 20 Sept. 1863; absent, wounded, in the hands of the enemy, 31 Dec. 1863; absent, wounded at Chickamauga, in the hands of the enemy, 29 Feb. 1864; absent in the hands of the enemy, captured at Chickamauga, 31 Aug. 1864.

Easen, William F., Private, B Company: conscripted for the war 27 July 1862 at Camp Randolph in Gordon County; transferred to 1st SS Battalion Aug. 1862; absent, sent to General Hospital in Savannah, 3 Sept. 1862; absent, sent to General Hospital, 15 Oct. 1862; absent, sent to General Hospital in Atlanta, 25 Oct. 25 (MR, 31 Dec. 1862 and 28 Feb. 1863); died in Cass County, Ga., 18 Mar. 1863.

Edwards, John W., Private C Company: enlisted for 3 years 6 Feb. 1863 in Dooly County; absent sick in hospital in Canton, Miss., 30 June 1863; patient in General Hospital, Marion, Miss., 30 June 1863; present sick, 29 Feb. 1864; admitted with chronic diarrhea to Ocmulgee Hospital, Macon, 16 June, discharged 30 June 1864; captured at Nashville, 16 Dec. 1864; received as a prisoner at Camp Chase, Ohio, 4 Jan. 1865; died of pneumonia, 31 Jan. 1865; 31-year-old farmer in the Dooly County 1860 census.

Egan [Eagan], Edward, Private, A Company: enlisted for 3 years or the war 11 Aug. 1862 at Savannah as substitute for M. Doughtry; absent sick in hospital, 31 Dec. 1862; transferred from General Hospital No. 1 at Savannah to hospital at Macon with syphilis and gonorrhea, 10 Feb. 1863; absent sick at Savannah, 28 Feb. 1863; absent sick in hospital, 30 Apr. 1863; absent sick at Atlanta, 30 June 1863; absent without leave, 31 Dec. 1863; deserted, 31 Aug. 1864.

Ehrlish [Ehrlich], Abraham, Private, B Company: enlisted for the war 7 June 1861 at Savannah in DeKalb Rifles (A Company, 1st (Olmstead's) Georgia); transferred to 1st SS Battalion, 23 July 1862; present, detailed as mail carrier, 28 Feb. 1863; captured at Jackson 14 May and sent to Demopolis, 5 June 1863; absent at parole camp, Meridian, Miss., 30 June 1863; arrested as a deserter, 26 Aug. 1863; wounded at Chickamauga, Sep. 1863; patient in General Hospital No. 1, Savannah, 1 Dec. 1863; absent, wounded at Chickamauga, 31 Dec. 1863 and 29 Feb, 1864; absent wounded, 31 Aug, 1864.

Elder, William [M.], Private, D Company: enlisted for 12 months 25 Sep. 1861 in Fayette County [or 23 Apr. 1862 in Chatham County] in H Company (Fayette Volunteers, Fayette County), 30th Georgia; transferred to 1st SS Battalion, 1 Aug. 1862; discharged by civil authority for under age, 18 Nov. 1862; reenlisted 1863; surrendered at Greensboro, N.C., 26 Apr. 1865; age 18, complexion fair, eyes blue, hair light, height 5 ft. 7 in., occupation farmer, born Randolph County, Ala.

Elkins, J[ohn] H., Private, D Company: enlisted for 12 months 4 Oct. 1861 at Thomasville in I Company (Seventeenth Patriots, Thomas County), 29th Georgia; transferred to 1st SS Battalion, 1 Aug. 1862; wounded, Chickamauga, 19 Sep. 1863, leg amputated [sic]; absent wounded, 31 Oct. and 31 Dec. 1863; absent sick, 29 Feb. 1864; wounded, New Hope Church, 25 May 1864 [sic]; detached as prison guard at Americus [Andersonville], 1864; absent wounded, 31 Aug. 1864; present with E Company, Troops and Defenses of Macon, 30 Nov. and 31 Dec., 1864; admitted to Hood Hospital, Cuthbert, Ga., Mar. 12, 1865, with gun shot wound to right thigh from Chickamauga; ulcer improving, 31 Mar. 1865.

Englehart, Frank, Musician, Private, B Company: enlisted for the war 26 Aug. 1861 at Fort McAllister in DeKalb Rifles (A Company, 1st (Olmstead's) Georgia); transferred to 1st SS Battalion, 23 July 1862; deserted 23 Dec. 1862; sentenced to 1 year in ball and chain for desertion, 28 Feb. 1863; captured, Jackson, Miss., 15 July 1863; received at Camp Morton, Ind., 7 Aug. 1863; recommended for presidential amnesty and pardon by Major A.L. Hartridge by letter of 7 Aug. 1863 (see service record of James F. Butler); enlisted in 7th [Ind.?] Cavalry, Aug. 1863; deserted, missing on retreat from Missionary Ridge, 31 Dec. 1863.

Erkel [Eckel], George, Musician, B Company: enlisted for the war 10 Mar. 1862 at Fort McAllister in DeKalb Rifles (A Company, 1st (Olmstead's) Georgia); transferred to 1st SS Battalion, 23 July 1862; deserted at Savannah, 5 May 1863; age 27, complexion light, eyes blue, hair light, height 5 ft. 6 in., occupation butcher, born in Germany.

Faries, M[ortimer] L., Quartermaster Sergeant, Field & Staff: Private in 1st Georgia Cavalry Battalion, 1861-62; enlisted for the war 12 Apr. 1862 in Savannah in B Company, Savannah Volunteer Guard Battalion; transferred to 1st SS by department special order, Aug. 1862; assigned as Quartermaster Sergeant by Battalion Gen. Order

No. 4, 8 Aug. 1862 to be effective from 1 Aug.; present on all MR through 29 Aug. 1864; 26-year-old grist mill superintendent in the Chatham County 1860 census.

Faucett, Alexander, Private, C Company: enlisted for 3 years 25 Mar. 1863 at Savannah; provided Charles Clark as substitute, Apr. 1863; discharged; born Ireland, 20-year-old clerk in the Chatham County 1860 census.

Faulk, Henry, Private, C Company: enlisted 17 Oct. 1861 as Private, C Company, 1st Battalion, GST; mustered out Apr. 1862; enlisted for 3 years 24 Apr. 1862 at Macon in A Company (Lamar Infantry, Bibb County), 54th Georgia; transferred to 1st SS Battalion; deserted, May 1863.

Faulkner, John, Private, B Company: enlisted for the war 25 Apr. 1862 at Fort McAllister in DeKalb Rifles (A Company, 1st (Olmstead's) Georgia); transferred to 1st SS Battalion, 23 July 1862; deserted, 20 Aug. 1862; absent without leave, 30 Aug. 1862; claimed by the C.S. Navy, 8 Sept. 1862; given up to the navy as a deserter, 30 Sept. 1862.

Finn, John H., Private, C Company: enlisted for 3 years 6 Feb. 1863 in Dooly County; Thomas Campbell was substitute for John H. Finn in Apr. 1863 but deserted; 32-year-old laborer in the Dooly County 1860 census. [No service record for Thomas Campbell with 1st Sharpshooter Battalion records.]

Fischer, Frederick, Private, B Company: enlisted for the war 12 Aug. 1861 at Fort McAllister in DeKalb Rifles (A Company, 1st (Olmstead's) Georgia); transferred to 1st SS Battalion, 23 July 1862; absent, sent to Savannah sick on 7 Oct. 1862; died of dysentery at Savannah, 28 Nov. 1862.

Fitzgerald, George, Musician, C Company: enlisted for 3 years 8 Apr. 1863 at Savannah; deserted, 30 June 1863.

Flowers, E.J., Private, A Company: enlisted for 3 years or the war 15 May 1862 at Doctor Town in F Company (Altamaha Scouts, Liberty County), 25th Georgia; transferred to 1st SS Battalion, 30 July 1862; absent sick at Whitesville, 31 Aug. 1862; absent without leave, 31 Oct. 1862; absent sick, 31 Dec. 1862 and 28 Feb. 1863; absent sick in Atlanta, 30 June 1863 and 31 Dec. 1863; absent sick in Augusta, 29 Feb. 1864; absent sick in General Hospital, 31 Aug. 1864.

Footman, Robert H[abersham], Captain and Assistant Quartermaster, Field & Staff: commissioned 11 Aug. 1862 to rank from 16 July; absent in Savannah on quartermaster business, 30 Sept. 1862; transferred to 5th Gerogia Cavalry by Spec. Order No. 84, District of Georgia, 25 March 1863; replaced by W.G. Gray; assigned to 18th Georgia Battalion, July 1863; assigned to Gen. J.A. Walker's brigade, Sep. 1864; assigned to Gen. R.H. Anderson's cavalry brigade, Feb. 1865; paroled at Hillsboro, N.C., 1 May 1865; born 1833 near Tallahassee, Fla.; died 7 Sep. 1896, age 63, Guyton, Ga.; 27-year-old insurance broker in the Chatham County 1860 census.

Ford, C[ornelius] T., Assistant Surgeon, Field & Staff: enrolled 4 Sep. 1861 as 1st Lieutenant at Georgetown in G Company, 10th South Carolina; assigned to duty as Captain, 6 June 1862; on recruiting duty in S.C., 20 Feb. 1863; resigned 14 May 1863; commissioned Assistant Surgeon 11 July 1863 to rank from 8 Aug.; left with sick in Jackson, Miss., 14 July 1863; ordered to Army of Tennessee, 31 Oct. 1863; joined 1st SS Battalion, Apr. 1864; reports received by Inspector of Hospitals, 21 Apr. and 22 Aug. 1864; wounded, north Georgia, 7-30 June 1864; remaining by inspection report at Tupelo, Miss., 25 Jan. 1865; surrendered at Greensboro, N.C. with 1st Confederate Georgia Battalion, 26 Apr. 1865; 25-year-old medical student in Marion District, S.C. 1860 census.

Forehand, David B., Private, C Company: enlisted as Private in B Company, 5th Regiment, GST, 22 Oct. 1861; 1st Corporal, 28 Jan. 1862; mustered out Apr. 1862; enlisted for 3 years 21 Apr. 1862 at Savannah in K Company (Alexander Greys, Burke County), 32nd Georgia; transferred to 1st SS Battalion, 30 July 1862; absent sick at convalescent camp from 10 Aug. 1863; patient at St. Mary's Hospital, LaGrange, 1 Jan. 1864; detailed as division sharpshooter, 31 Aug. 1864; captured at Decatur, Ala., 28 Oct. 1864; received as prisoner at Camp Douglas, Ill., 4 Nov. 1864; discharged on oath of allegiance, 17 June 1865; place of residence, Burke County, complexion fair, hair light, eyes blue, height 5 ft. 9 in.; 26-year-old planter in the Burke County 1860 census.

Fortner, Obediah S., Private, C Company: enlisted for 3 years 14 Apr. 1863 at Savannah; discharged, 30 June 1863.

Foster, Sheppard A., Private, C Company: enlisted as Private in I Company, 6th Regiment, GST, 4 Nov. 1861; 4th Corporal, 11 Dec. 1861; mustered out Apr. 1862; enlisted for 3 years 18 Apr. 1862 at Savannah in I Company (Woodson Guards, Upson County), 32nd Georgia; transferred to 1st SS Battalion, 21 Aug. 1862; absent sick in hospital at Yazoo City, 30 June 1863; captured at Chickamauga, 19 September 1863; patient in prison hospital, Nashville, 29 Sept. 1863; received as prisoner at Camp Morton, Ind., 5 Nov. 1864; absent without leave (MR, 31 Dec. 1863); deserted to the enemy during the battle of Chickamauga on 19 Sept. 1863 (MR, Feb. 29, 1864); transferred to City Point, Va. for exchange, 4 Mar. 1865; admitted to Recovery and Wayside Hospital or General Hospital No. 9, Richmond, 11 Mar. 1865.

Friend, Elmer, Private, D Company: enlisted for the war 7 Feb. 1862 at Savannah in A Company (Chatham County), 13th Georgia Battalion; transferred to 1st SS Battalion, Aug. 1862; transferred to C.S. Navy by spec. order of Gen. H.W. Mercer, 1 May 1863.

Gallagher [Galagher], Frank, Private, C Company: enlisted for 3 years 26 July 1861 at Thomasville in A Company (Thomasville Guards, Thomas County), 29th Georgia; transferred to 1st SS Battalion, 26 July 1862; deserted from Camp Jordan, 27 Mar. 1863.

Gamble, William W., Private, C Company: enlisted for 3 years 6 Feb. 1863 in Dooly County; present sick, 31 Dec. 1863; wounded, Resaca or Calhoun, Ga., 14 or 16 May, 1864; absent sick, 31 Aug. 1864; patient with gun shot wound to the upper left thigh in

Floyd House and Ocmulgee Hospitals, Macon, 2 Sep. 1864; post office, Vienna, Ga.; 25-year-old farmer in the Dooly County 1860 census.

Gardner, William, Private, B Company: enlisted for 12 months 19 Aug. 1861 at Fort McAllister in DeKalb Rifles (A Company, 1st (Olmstead's) Georgia); detached on special duty as carpenter in the Savannah shipyard, 30 June 1862; transferred to 1st SS Battalion, 23 July 1862; absent detailed as ship's carpenter from 13 May 1862 on all MR through 29 Feb. 1864; died at Augusta, 31 Aug. 1864.

Garner, George W., Private, D Company: enlisted for 12 months 5 Oct. 1861 in Calhoun County in B Company (Littlefield Volunteers, Gordon County), 8th Georgia Battalion; transferred to 1st SS Battalion, Aug. 1862; present in arrest, 30 June 1863; reenlisted for the war, 16 Feb. 1864; absent in the hands of the enemy from 17 May 1864; 18-year-old farm laborer in the Gordon County 1860 census.

Garner, John, Private, D Company: enlisted for the war 20 Jan. 1863 at Camp Anderson; present in arrest, 30 June 1863; reenlisted for the war, 16 Feb. 1864; captured near Marietta, July 1864; received as a prisoner at Camp Douglas, Ill., 18 July 1864; died of pneumonia, at Camp Douglas, 4 Aug. 1864; absent in the hands of the enemy since 3 July (MR, 31 Aug. 1864).

Garner, William M., Private, B Company: conscripted for the war 25 July 1862 at Camp Randolph in Gordon County; transferred to 1st SS Battalion Aug. 1862; died of diarrhea in General Hospital at Savannah, 19 Jan. 1863.

Garrison, Robert D., Private, B Company: enlisted for the war 24 Aug. 1861 at Fort McAllister in DeKalb Rifles (A Company, 1st (Olmstead's) Georgia); transferred to 1st SS Battalion, 23 July 1862; deserted, 23 Dec. 1862; in Chatham County jail under sentence of death by court-martial, Spec. Order No. 21/2/6, dated 1 Feb. 1863; sentence "respited" for 21 days by Spec. Order No. 51/1, 26 Feb. 1863; sentence suspended by Spec. Order No. 75/8, 30 Mar. 1863; in Chatham County jail under sentence of death by court-martial, 30 Apr. 1863; in arrest in Chatham County jail, 30 June 1863; recommended for presidential amnesty and pardon by Major A.L. Hartridge by letter of 7 Aug. 1863 (see service record of James F. Butler); transferred to the Maryland Line, 17 Mar. 1864; served in C Company, 2nd Maryland Battalion.

Gaskin, John, Private, B Company: conscripted for the war 11 Aug. 1862 at Camp Randolph in Gordon County; transferred to 1st SS Battalion Aug. 1862; admitted with intermittent fever to Floyd House and Ocmulgee Hospitals, Macon, 7 Nov. 1863, released 23 Nov.; present sick, 29 Feb. 1864; absent sick, 31 Aug. 1864; post office Douglass.

Gassett, William [H.], Private, C Company: enlisted as Private in D Company, 6th Regiment, GST, 18 Oct. 1861; mustered out, Apr. 1862; enlisted for 3 years 18 Apr. 1862 at Savannah in B Company (Talbot County), 32nd Georgia; transferred to 1st SS Battalion, 30 July 1862; absent on furlough, 30 Sept. 1862; absent sick at home in Taylor County, 31 Oct. 1862; present, detailed as litter bearer, 31 Aug. 1864; born Talbot County, 14 June 1841.

[Lillian Henderson, *Roster of the Confederate Soldiers of Georgia*, Vol. 3: 681, shows another soldier, William B. Garrett, transferred to the SS Battalion at the same time as Gassett. There is no record of Garrett in the SS records. Either they were the same man or their records were merged by the NARA transcribers.]

Gately, Patrick, Private, C Company: enlisted for 3 years 30 Apr. 1862 at Savannah in D Company (Screven County), 54th Georgia; transferred to 1st SS Battalion, 1 Aug. 1862; absent sick in Savannah, 31 Dec. 1862; absent, taken prisoner at Jackson and paroled, 30 June 1863; deserted, 28 Aug. 1863; killed at Chickamauga, 19 Sept. 1863; born Roscommon, Ireland, 35-year-old laborer in the Chatham County 1860 census.

Gill, William B., Private, B Company: enlisted for the war 9 Apr. 1862 at Fort McAllister in DeKalb Rifles (A Company, 1st (Olmstead's) Georgia); transferred to 1st SS Battalion, 23 July 1862; absent, sent to General Hospital, 27 Sep. 1862; absent, detailed to General Hospital in Savannah, 11 Oct. (MR, 31 Dec. 1862); absent detailed on special service in General Hospital in Savannah, 28 Feb. and 30 Apr 1863; detailed as nurse in General Hospital in Savannah, 30 June 1863; detailed as hospital nurse, 31 Dec. 1863 and 29 Feb. 1864; absent sick, 31 Aug. 1864; patient with remittent fever at Ocmulgee Hospital, 28 Aug. to 19 Nov. 1864; patient with hypertension of the heart at Floyd House Hospital, 12 Dec. 1864; appointed watchman for 60 days at the armory in Macon, 29 Dec. 1864; reappointed, 7 Apr. 1865; captured at Macon, 30 Apr. 1865.

Gleichman, Charles, Private, B Company: enlisted for the war 6 Mar. 1862 at Fort McAllister in DeKalb Rifles (A Company, 1st (Olmstead's) Georgia); transferred to 1st SS Battalion, 23 July 1862; died by his own hand at Camp Anderson, 22 Jan. 1863.

Goff, J.D. [Isaiah], Private, D Company: enlisted for 12 months 29 Sept. 1861 in Thomasville in H Company (Thomas County Volunteers), 29th Georgia; transferred to 1st SS Battalion, 1 Aug. 1862; absent at the convalescent camp, Springfield, 31 Aug. and 30 Sept. 1862; absent sick at Yazoo City from 13 June 1863; absent sick, 31 Oct. and 31 Dec. 1863; present; reenlisted for the war, 29 Feb. 1864; absent sick, 31 Aug. 1864; signed receipt at Blackie Hospital, Augusta, Ga., 12 Oct. 1864.

Goodman [Godwin, Goodwin], Sparknin [Sparkman] N., Private, C Company: enlisted for the war 6 Feb. 1863 in Dooly County; absent sick in hospital at Yazoo City, 30 June 1863; no later record; born in Ga., ca. 1827; 33-year-old farmer in the Jackson County, Fla. 1860 census.

Gordon, A[lfred] H., Sergeant Major, Field & Staff: enlisted for 30 days 31 May 1861 at Savannah in the Georgia Hussars; age 24, furnished his own horse and equipment; mustered out, 30 June; enlisted for the war 26 Feb. 1862 at Savannah in the Chatham Artillery; appears as Corporal, 28 Feb. 1863; present, 30 Apr. 1863; admitted with dysenteria, Floyd House and Ocmulgee Hospitals, Macon, 2 Dec. 1863; patient at General Hospital No. 2, Savannah, 31 Dec. 1863; absent in hospital in Savannah, 29 Feb. 1864 [only SS MR on which name appears]; sent from General Hospital No. 1 to General Hospital No. 2 in Savannah, 17 Mar. 1864; mortally wounded at Calhoun, Ga., 16 May,

1864; died in Atlanta about 21 June 1864; 25-year-old commission merchant in Chatham County 1860 census.

Grauss, William, Private, B Company: enlisted for the war 10 Apr. 1862 at Fort McAllister in DeKalb Rifles (A Company, 1st (Olmstead's) Georgia); transferred to 1st SS Battalion, 23 July 1862; present, 31 Aug. 1862 to 30 Apr. 1863; deserted 5 May 1863 at Savannah; age 26, complexion dark, eyes gray, hair dark, height 5 ft. 11 in., occupation baker, born in Germany.

Gray [Grey], H[ines] H[olt], Private, D Company: enlisted for 12 months 4 Oct. 4, 1861 at Thomasville in K Company (Seventeenth Patriots, Thomas County), 29th Georgia; transferred to 1st SS Battalion, 1 Aug. 1862; present sick in hospital, 31 Dec. 1862; wounded and missing, Chickamauga, Sep. 1863; absent wounded, 31 Oct. and 31 Dec. 1863; absent sick, 29 Feb. 1864; wounded, Kennesaw Mountain, 27 June 1864 [sic]; absent wounded, Aug. 31, 1864.

Gray, W.G. [Willis, Willie], Assistant Quartermaster, Field & Staff: enlisted for the war 20 Feb. 1862 at Savannah in the Chatham Artillery; requested discharge on expiration of term of service, 31 July 1862; discharged by Gen. Mercer as a non-resident on the certificate of the British vice counsel in Savannah, 2 Aug. 1862; requested appointment, 14 Mar. 1863; recommended for appointment by Brig. Gen. Mercer, identifying him as native of Scotland and merchant in Savannah, 30 Mar. 1863; appointed Assistant Quartermaster 30 Apr. 1863 to rank from 1 Mar. 1863; on leave, 4 Mar. 1864; absent on duty with a commission, 25 Aug. 1864; requests transfer in letter to Quartermaster Gen. A.R. Lawton, 29 Aug. 1864; transferred to Railroad Bureau by Spec. Order No. 224, Adjutant and Inspector General's Office, 21 Sep. 1864; paid as assistant chief, Railroad Bureau, 15 Nov. 1864 and 31 Jan. 1865; transferred, no replacement, on inspection report, Tupelo, Miss., 25 Jan. 1865.

Green, James, Private, C Company: enlisted as Private in C Company, 6th Regiment, GST, 22 Oct. 1861; mustered out, Apr. 1862; enlisted for 3 years 6 May 1862 at Savannah in B Company (Talbot County), 32nd Georgia; transferred to 1st SS Battalion, 30 July 1862; absent sick at home in Taylor County, 31 Oct. 1862; absent sick in hospital in Selma, Ala., 30 June 1863; patient with turned ankle at Floyd House and Ocmulgee Hospitals, Macon, 23 Nov. 1863; absent without leave, 31 Dec. 1863; absent sick in Macon, 29 Feb. 1864; present, detailed to brigade provost guard, 31 Aug. 1864; captured at Nashville, 16 Dec. 1864; received at Camp Chase, Ohio, 4 Jan. 1865; enlisted in U.S. service, 20 Mar. 1865.

Green, Zachariah [Zach, Jack], Private, B Company: enlisted for 12 months 14 Oct. 1861 at Fort McAllister in DeKalb Rifles (A Company, 1st (Olmstead's) Georgia); transferred to 1st SS Battalion, 23 July 1862; deserted, 23 Dec. 1862; court-martial results in Gen. Order No. 21/2/4, Dept. of South Carolina, Georgia and Florida, 1 Feb. 1863; sentence "respited" for 21 days by Spec. Order No. 51/1, 26 Feb. 1863; sentence suspended by Spec. Order No. 75/8, 30 Mar. 1863; absent in Chatham County jail under sentence of death by court-martial, 28 Feb. and 30 Apr. 1863; absent in arrest in Chatham County jail, Savannah, 30 June 1863; recommended for presidential amnesty and pardon by

Major A.L. Hartridge by letter of 7 Aug. 1863; wounded and captured at Chickamauga, 19 Sept. 1863; received at Camp Douglas, Ill., 4 Oct. 1863; deserted at Chickamauga (MR, 31 Dec. 1863); transferred and enlisted in U.S. volunteers, 3 Apr. 1865.

Griffin, John J., Private, D Company: enlisted for 12 months 4 Oct. 1861 at Thomasville in I Company (Seventeenth Patriots, Thomas County), 29th Georgia; transferred to 1st SS Battalion, 1 Aug. 1862; admitted with intermittent fever to Floyd House and Ocmulgee Hospitals, Macon, 28 Nov. 1863; absent on leave, 29 Feb. 1864; captured at Nashville, 16 Dec. 1864; received at Camp Chase, Ohio, 4 Jan. 1865; died of pneumonia, 25 Jan. 1865; buried at Camp chase Cemetery, grave #883.

Haarer [Harrer], William, Private, Corporal, B Company: enlisted for the war 7 Aug. 1861 at Fort McAllister in DeKalb Rifles (A Company, 1st (Olmstead's) Georgia); transferred to 1st SS Battalion, 23 July 1862; absent on special service in Savannah arresting deserters, 31 Aug. 1862; appointed Corporal, 4 May 1863; wounded at Chickamauga, Sep. 1863; appears as 2nd Corporal, absent, wounded at Chickamauga, 31 Dec. 1863; patient at General Hospital No. 1, Savannah, 31 Dec. 1863; absent wounded at Savannah, 29 Feb. 1864; took oath of allegiance to U.S. at Chattanooga, 22 Aug. 1864; deserted to the enemy, 31 Aug. 1864; residence, Wurttemberg, Germany, complexion light, hair black, eyes dark, height 5 ft. 10 in.

Hall, John F., Private, Corporal, Sergeant, D Company: enlisted for 12 months 27 July 1861 at Savannah in A Company (Thomasville Guards, Thomas County), 29th Georgia; transferred to 1st SS Battalion as 3rd Corporal, 1 Aug. 1862; appears as Sergeant, 30 Apr. 1863; appears as Private, 30 June 1863; absent in hospital in Atlanta, 31 Oct. 1863; reenlisted for the war, 29 Feb. 1864; wounded, 20 July 1864; wounded at Jonesboro, 31 Aug. 1864; absent wounded, 31 Aug. 1864; wounded at Spring Hill, Tenn., 28 Nov. 1864; left foot amputated, 29 Nov. 1864; captured Murfreesboro, Tenn., 4 Jan. 1865; patient at U.S. Army General Hospital No. 1, Nashville, 10 Feb. 1865; received as prisoner at Camp Chase, Ohio, 12 Mar. 1865; transferred to Pt. Lookout, Md. for exchange, 31 Mar. 1865; released, 5 June 1865.

Ham, Benjamin, Private, B Company: enlisted for the war 3 Mar. 1862 at Fort McAllister in DeKalb Rifles (A Company, 1st (Olmstead's) Georgia); transferred to 1st SS Battalion, 23 July 1862; absent on detached service in pursuit of deserters, 31 Dec. 1862; present, detailed on extra duty as brigade butcher, 30 June 1863, last muster roll on which name entered; 23 years old in the 1860 Bryan County census.

Hamrick, Noah R., Private, D Company: enlisted for 12 months 25 Sep. 1861 in Clayton County in I Company (Clayton Invincibles, Clayton County), 30th Georgia; transferred to 1st SS Battalion, 1 Aug. 1862; never reported, name appears on a descriptive list of transfers from 30th Georgia; absent sick at home, 31 Dec. 1862; pension record shows sick in hospital at end of war; age 19, complexion fair, eyes blue, hair light, height 6 ft. 1 in., occupation farmer, born Lincoln County.

Hancock, William, Private, A Company: enlisted for 1 year 8 Aug. 1861 at Savannah in D Company (Ogeechee Rifles, Screven County), 25th Georgia; transferred to 1st SS

Battalion, 30 July 1862; absent on sick furlough for 30 days, 31 Oct. 1862; died of fever at Canton, Miss., 4 June 1863.

Hardee, Benjamin H[opkins], 1st Lieutenant, Captain, B Company: enrolled for the war as 2nd Lieutenant, 7 June 1861 at Savannah in DeKalb Rifles (A Company, 1st (Olmstead's) Georgia); 1st Lieutenant, Dec. 1861; transferred to 1st SS Battalion with his company, 23 July 1862; 1st lieutenant 4 Oct. 1862 to rank from 11 July 1862; signed roll as 1st Lieutenant, commanding company, 31 Aug. 1862; absent on 24 hour leave, 30 Sept. 1862; absent on detached service in pursuit of deserters, 31 Dec. 1862; signed roll as company commander, 30 Apr. 1863; appointed captain 30 Apr. 1863 to rank from 20 Jan. or 28 Apr. 1863; on detail by Spec. Order No. 100/7, Army of Tennessee, 11 Apr. 1864; absent sick at Savannah when city fell, reported to have taken off his uniform and taken the oath of allegiance, inspection report at Tupelo, Miss., 25 Jan. 1865; nephew of Gen. William J. Hardee; born 1835, died Savannah, 6 Mar. 1889, age 54; 26-year-old commission merchant in the Chatham County 1860 census.

Hardy, Cornelius [Marion], Sergeant, C Company: served in Arkansas state troops, 1861; enlisted as Private in B Company, 6th Regiment, GST, 8 Feb. 1862; mustered out, Apr. 1862; enlisted as 5th Sergeant for 3 years 18 Apr. 1862 in A Company (Jasper and Jones Counties), 32nd Georgia; transferred to 1st SS Battalion, 30 July 1862; appears as 2nd Sergeant, 31 Aug. 1862; present, sick in quarters, 31 Dec. 1862; captured Decatur, Ala., 28 Oct. 1864; received at Camp Douglas, Ill., 4 Nov. 1864; released 7 June 1865; place of residence, Jasper County, complexion fair, hair light, eyes gray, height 5 ft. 11 in.; 26 years old in the Jasper County 1860 census; died 1886.

Hartridge, Alfred L[amar], Captain, B Company: enrolled for the war 7 June 1861 at Savannah as 2nd Lieutenant in DeKalb Rifles (A Company), 1st (Olmstead's) Georgia; 1st Lieutenant, 7 Aug. 1861; Captain, 11 Nov. 1861; transferred to 1st SS Battalion with his company, 23 July 1862 Aug. with new date of rank, 21 June 1862; absent on 10 days leave, 31 Aug. 1862; absent on detached service for general court martial in Savannah, 31 Dec. 1862; absent by authority of Brig. Gen. Mercer, 9 Apr. 1863; promoted Major of Artillery, 30 June [Apr.?] 1863, to rank from 15 Nov. 1862; commander of Rose Dew Post, 1863-64; assigned as commander, 27th Georgia Battalion, 29 Nov. 1864; paroled at Greensboro, N.C., 1 May 1865; xx-year-old clerk in Chatham County 1860 census; born South Carolina, 17 Feb. 1837, died Savannah, 13 Apr. 1913, age 76.

Harwood, J.F., Private, B Company: conscripted for the war 23 July1862 at Camp Randolph in Gordon County; transferred to 1st SS Battalion Aug. 1862; absent sick in General Hospital, 31 Dec. 1863 and 29 Feb.; died at Montgomery, Ala., 8 July 1864.

Haschkell, William [Wilhelm] B., Private, B Company: enlisted for the war 9 Aug. 1861 at Fort McAllister in DeKalb Rifles (A Company, 1st (Olmstead's) Georgia); transferred to 1st SS Battalion, 23 July 1862; captured 10 or 14 July 1863 near Jackson, Miss.; received at Camp Morton, Ind., 7 Aug. 1863; enlisted in 32nd Indiana, Aug. 1863; missing on the retreat from Big Black River, Miss. (MR, 31 Dec. 1863).

Hays, John, Musician, D Company: enlisted for the war 13 Apr. 1863 at Savannah; deserted at Canton, Miss., 24 May 1863, and dropped from the rolls, 30 June 1863.

Hays, J.T., Private, A Company: enlisted for 3 years or the war 26 Jan. 1863 in Randolph County; died of congestive fever at Yazoo City, 9 June 1863.

Hays, La Fayette, Private, C Company: enlisted for 3 years 30 Apr. 1862 at Savannah in B Company, 54th Georgia; transferred to 1st SS Battalion, Aug. 1862; present, sick in quarters, 31 Dec. 1862; absent sick in General Hospital, Savannah, 30 Apr. 1863; absent sick in hospital, Yazoo City, 30 June 1863; admitted to Loring's Division Hospital, Macon, Miss., 16 July 1863; present [sic] sick in Macon, Ga., 31 Dec. 1863; absent sick in Macon, 29 Feb. 1864; wounded, north Georgia, 7-30 June 1864; deserted to the enemy, 16 Aug. 1864.

Heffernan, Hugh, Corporal, Private, A Company: enlisted for 60 days 30 May 1861, reenlisted for 6 months 10 Aug. 1861, reenlisted for 3 years or the war 14 Feb. 1862 in Savannah in B Company (Irish Jasper Greens), 1st (Olmstead's) Georgia; 4th Corporal, Feb. 1862; 1st Corporal, Apr. 1862; reduced to ranks for absence without leave, 12 June 1862; transferred to 1st SS Battalion, Aug. 1862; appears as 1st Corporal, absent sick in Savannah, 31 Aug. 1862; present in arrest, 30 June 1863; captured near Jackson, Miss., 15 or 17 July 1863; received at Camp Morton, Ind., 7 Aug. 1863; enlisted in 7th Ind. Cav. [sic], Aug. 1863; appears as Private, absent without leave, 31 Dec. 1863; deserter, 29 Feb. 1864; age 22, complexion fair, eyes gray, hair light, height 5 ft. 9 in.

Heine, Henry, Private, B Company: enlisted for the war 30 Aug. 1862 in Savannah as substitute for A.P. Wetter; absent without leave, 31 Aug. 1862; absent sick in Savannah from 1 Oct. 1862; absent sick in Savannah from 8 Oct. (MR, 31 Dec. 1862); captured near Jackson, Miss., 17 July 1863; received at Camp Morton, Ind., 7 Aug. 1863; deserted, missing on the retreat from Jackson (MR, 31 Dec. 1863); released on oath of allegiance, 22 May 1865; residence Savannah, complexion florid, hair sandy, eyes blue, height 5 ft. 4 in.

Heisler, David, Private, B Company: conscripted for the war 13 Aug. 1862 at Camp Randolph in Gordon County; transferred to 1st SS Battalion Aug. 1862; absent, sent to General Hospital, Savannah, 25 Nov. 1862; present sick, 29 Feb. 1864; patient at Ocmulgee Hospital, Macon, 8 Apr. to 3 May 1864; absent sick, 31 Aug. 1864.

Herrmann, Henry, 2nd Lieutenant, 1st Lieutenant, B Company: enrolled for the war 7 June 1861 in Savannah in DeKalb Rifles (A Company, 1st (Olmstead's) Georgia); by voucher, 2nd lieutenant, DeKalb Rifles, Oct. 1861; transferred to 1st SS Battalion 23 July 1862; 2nd lieutenant from 4 Oct. 1862 with date of rank 1 July 1862; absent on 10 days furlough from 23 Sep. 1862; signed roll as lieutenant commanding company, 31 Dec. 1862; appointed 1st lieutenant 30 Apr. 1862 with date of rank from 28 Apr. 1862; present on special service in charge of brigade provost guard, 31 Dec. 1863; absent on furlough for 14 days, 29 Feb. 1864; signed as 1st Lieutenant, commanding company, 17 Mar. 1864; wounded, Calhoun, Ga., 16 May, 1864; killed at Jonesboro, Ga., 31 Aug. 1864; born Prussia, 32-year-old grocer in Chatham County 1860 census.

Herrnstadt, Solomon, Private, B Company: enlisted for 14 months 7 June 1861 at Savannah in DeKalb Rifles (A Company, 1st (Olmstead's) Georgia); transferred to 1st SS Battalion, 23 July 1862; absent, sent to General Hospital in Savannah, 27 Dec. 1862; died in General Hospital in Savannah, 2 Jan. 1863.

Heuer, Charles, Private, B Company: enlisted for the war 14 Aug. 1861 at Fort McAllister in DeKalb Rifles (A Company, 1st (Olmstead's) Georgia); transferred to 1st SS Battalion, 23 July 1862; absent, sent to General Hospital in Savannah, 15 Feb. 1863; absent, sent to hospital in Yazoo City, 13 June 1863; absent, sick in General Hospital, 31 Dec. 1863; patient at French's Division Hospital, Shelby Springs, Ala. from 27 Aug. (MR, 31 Dec. 1863); absent sick, 31 Aug. 1864; patient with hypertrophy of the heart at unnamed hospital, 22 Dec. 1864.
[Another record, possibly the same man: Brewer, Charles, Private, B Company: admitted with pteplismus to 1st Mississippi CSA Hospital, Jackson, Miss., 27 Aug. 1863; returned to duty, 11 Feb. 1864; no other record.]

Heyer, Frederick, Private, B Company: enlisted for the war 6 May 1862 at Fort McAllister in DeKalb Rifles (A Company, 1st (Olmstead's) Georgia); transferred to 1st SS Battalion, 23 July 1862; absent on special service arresting deserters in Savannah, 31 Aug. 1862; deserted at Camp Anderson, 13 Jan. 1863; present in arrest since 1 Mar. (MR, 30 Apr. 1863); transferred to the C.S. Navy by order of Gen. Mercer, 1 May 1863.

Hillebrandt, Peter P., Private, B Company: enlisted for 14 months 7 June 1861 at Savannah in DeKalb Rifles (A Company, 1st (Olmstead's) Georgia); transferred to 1st SS Battalion, 23 July 1862; patient at Jackson's Cavalry Division Hospital, Old Marion, Miss., 31 Aug. 1863; absent sick in General Hospital, 31 Dec. 1863; absent sick, 31 Aug. 1864; admitted to General Hospital No. 11, Charlotte, N.C., with rheumatism on 4 Mar., and typhoid on 18 Apr. 1865; paroled there, May 1865.

Holcombe, Josiah L[aw], 1st Lieutenant, C Company: enlisted as 1st Sergeant, 21 May 1861 in B Company, 8th Georgia; commissioned 2nd Lieutenant, 14 Aug. 1861; resigned, 1 Dec. 1861; appointed 1st Lieutenant, 1st SS Battalion, 4 Oct. 1862 with date of rank of 13 July 1862; absent on 24 hours leave from 28 Sep. 1862; absent on special service arresting deserters, 30 Apr. 1863; absent on detached service by order of Col. Wilson, 30 June 1863; ordnance officer on the staff of Wilson's brigade since 17 June (report of 18 Nov. 1863); admitted to Floyd House and Ocmulgee Hospitals, Macon, with chronic diarrhea, 2 Dec. 1863; absent on detached service, 31 Dec. 1863; patient at General Hospital No. 2, Savannah, 31 Dec. 1863; on extra duty as acting assistant adjutant general to Gen. Stevens, 29 Feb. 1864; absent on 14 days leave by Spec. Order No. 103, Army of Tennessee, 14 Apr. 1864; assigned as acting assistant adjutant general by Col. Nisbet, 25 Aug. 1864; detailed on Gen. Jackson's staff, 31 Aug. 1864; recommended for assignment as assistant adjutant general with promotion to captain or major, 20 Mar., 14 July, 16 Aug. 1864; killed Jonesboro, 31 Aug. 1864; age at death, 26; 22-year-old clerk in the Chatham County 1860 census.

Hover, B[enjamin] F., Sergeant, Private, D Company: enlisted for the war 6 Feb. 1862 in Savannah in A Company (Chatham County), 13th Georgia Battalion; transferred to 1st SS Battalion as 5th sergeant, Aug. 1862; absent, sent to General Hospital, Savannah, 30 Sep. 1862; absent sick in Savannah as private, 31 Oct. 1862; absent sick in hospital in Atlanta, 31 Oct. 1863; reenlisted for the war, 16 Feb. 1864; missing since 20 July (MR, 31 Aug. 1864).

Hubbard, W.H., Private, D Company: enlisted for the war 18 Apr. 1863 at Savannah; deserted at Demopolis, Ala., 12 May 1863; dropped from the rolls, 30 June 1863; captured in Montgomery, in jail in Macon, Sep. 1863; no later entries.

Hughes, D.N., Private, A Company: enlisted [in C.S. Navy?] for 3 years or the war in Decatur [County?] February 1863; transferred to 1st SS Battalion, 30 June 1863; absent without leave, 31 Dec. 1863; deserter, 29 Feb. 1864.

Hurst, John R., Private, B Company: conscripted for the war 13 Aug. 1862 at Camp Randolph in Gordon County; transferred to 1st SS Battalion Aug. 1862; wounded, Jackson, Miss., July 1863; wounded, Resaca or Calhoun, Ga., 14 or 16 May, 1864; patient at St. Mary's hospital, La Grange, 1864; transferred to Thomaston, 19 June 1864; absent wounded, 31 Aug. 1864; captured at Nashville, 16 Dec. 1864; received at Camp Chase, Ohio, 6 Jan. 1865; paroled at Camp Chase for exchange via New Orleans, 2 May 1865.

Hurt [Hart], J[ames] W., Private, Sergeant, D Company: enlisted for 12 months 25 Sep. 1861 in Campbell County in F Company (Campbell Sharpshooters, Campbell County), 30th Georgia; transferred to 1st SS Battalion, 2 Aug. 1862; appears as 4th Corporal, 31 Oct. 1863; reenlisted for the war, 18 Feb. 1864; absent with leave, 31 Aug. 1864; captured at Nashville, 16 Dec. 1864; received at Camp Chase, Ohio, 4 Jan, 1865; took oath of allegiance, 12 June 1865; residence Campbell County, complexion dark, hair dark, eyes gray, height 6 ft. 1 in., age 21; from descriptive list: age 19, complexion dark, eyes blue, hair dark, height 6 ft. 1 in., occupation farmer, born Spartanburg, S.C.

Isaacson, Joseph, Private, C Company: enlisted for 3 years 16 Apr. 1862 at Savannah in I Company (Woodson Guards, Upson County), 32nd Georgia; transferred to 1st SS Battalion, 20 Aug. 1862; deserted from camp on 2 or 4 Sep. 1862; born in Germany, residence in Randolph County, age 37, occupation printer, light complexion, dark eyes, brown hair, height 5 ft. 7 in.

Ivey, Wesley, Private, C Company: enlisted for 3 years 6 Feb. 1863 in Dooly County; absent sick in hospital in Jackson, Miss., 30 June 1863; discharged 23 Jan. 1864; age 34; 23-year-old [sic] farm laborer in the Dooly County 1860 census.

Jackson, B.C., Private, B Company: conscripted for the war 13 Aug. 1862 at Camp Randolph in Gordon County; transferred to 1st SS Battalion Aug. 1862; absent sick in General Hospital in Savannah, 31 Aug. 1862; discharged by certificate of disability, 18 Oct. 1862.

Jackson, John J., Private, A Company: enlisted 4 Mar. 1862, in I Company (Empire State Guards, Effingham County), 11th Georgia Battalion; became 47th Georgia Regiment, 12 May 1862; transferred to 1st SS Battalion, 1 Aug. 1862; died in Marietta Hospital, 10 Jan. 1864.

Jarrell, James M[arion], Private, C Company: enlisted for 3 years 6 May 1862 at Savannah in F Company (Jeff Davis Guards, Clay County), 32nd Georgia; transferred to 1st SS Battalion, 30 July 1862; absent sick at home in Taylor County, 31 Oct. 1862; absent on sick furlough, 31 Dec. 1864; absent, wounded at Jonesboro, Aug. 1864; admitted with wound to Way Hospital, Meridian, Miss., 14 Jan., 15 and 22 Mar. 1865; born in Bibb County, 31 May 1845, died in Childress County, Tex., 15 Apr. 1908.

Jim, Musician, C Company: enlisted on 1 Aug. 1862; pay due through 31 Aug. 1862; no other record.

Johnson, James, Private, D Company: enlisted for 12 months 1 Dec. 1861 at Stockton in E Company (Alapaha Guards, Clinch County), 29th Georgia; transferred to 1st SS Battalion, 1 Aug. 1862; absent sick in Savannah, 31 Aug. 1862; absent sick in hospital, 28 Feb. 1863; absent sick, 31 Dec. 1863; reenlisted for the war, 16 Feb. 1864; absent sick, 31 Aug. 1864; patient at Floyd House and Ocmulgee Hospitals, Macon, suffering from chorea, rendering locomotion extremely difficult, with great debility, 19 Oct. 1864; born Houston County, 1832; pension record shows him at home on sick furlough at end of war.

Johnson, Jonas, Private, Sergeant, D Company: enlisted for 12 months 4 Oct. 1861 at Thomasville in I Company (Seventeenth Patriots, Thomas County), 29th Georgia; transferred to 1st SS Battalion, 1 Aug. 1862; present sick, 30 June 1863; absent without leave, 26 Aug. to 5 Oct. 1863; reenlisted for the war, 16 Feb. 1864; absent, wounded at Jonesboro, appears on roll as 5th sergeant, 31 Aug. 1864; patient with gunshot wound and compound fracture of the femur at Floyd House and Ocmulgee Hospitals, Macon, 2 Nov. 1864.

Johnston [Johnson], George H[ouston], Jr., Jr. 2nd Lieutenant, C Company: enlisted for 30 days 31 May 1861 at Savannah in the Georgia Hussars; age 23; furnished his own horse and equipment; mustered out, 30 June; enlisted as Private 7 Dec. 1861 in the Chatham Artillery; applied for commission, 19 Feb. 1862; discharged 17 July 1862 to accept commission in !st SS Battalion; appointed 4 Oct. 1862 to rank from 7 July 1862; recommended for appointment as battalion adjutant, 1 Apr. 1863; on special service as acting adjutant, 30 Apr. 1863; detailed as adjutant for battalion, 30 June 1863; admitted with bronchitis to Floyd House and Ocmulgee Hospitals, Macon, 2 Dec. 1863; absent sick, 31 Dec. 1863; patient at General Hospital No. 2, Savannah, 31 Dec. 1863; on extra duty as acting adjutant for the battalion, 29 Feb. 1864; absent by medical authority by inspection report of 17 Aug. 1864; patient at Floyd House and Ocmulgee Hospitals with gunshot wound to the right arm, 7 Sep. 1864, ball passing through the deltoid and slightly injuring the humerus, giving little use of the arm; absent wounded from 3 Aug. by inspection report of 17 Sep. 1864; only officer present with the battalion at Tupelo, Miss.,

25 Jan. 1865; born 2 Mar. 1839, died 17 May, 1904; 22-year-old bookkeeper in the Chatham County 1860 census.

Jones, William V. [Wiley], Private, C Company: enlisted as Private in C Company, 5th Regiment, GST, 16 Oct. 1861; mustered out Apr. 1862; enlisted for 3 years 16 Apr. 1862 at Savannah in F Company (Jeff Davis Guards, Clay County), 32nd Georgia; transferred to 1st SS Battalion, 30 July 1862; absent sick in General Hospital in Savannah, 30 Apr. and 30 June 1863; patient with hernia at Floyd House and Ocmulgee Hospitals, Macon, 25 Sep. 1863; readmitted 14 Oct., released 15 Oct. 1863; present sick in Macon [sic], 31 Dec. 1863; absent sick in Newnan, 29 Feb. 1864; wounded, Resaca or Calhoun, Ga., 14 or 16 May, 1864; killed at Atlanta, 14 Aug. 1864; post office, Blakely.

Jordan [Gordon], Henry W., Private, A Company: enlisted for 3 years 29 Apr. 1862 at Causton's Bluff in F Company (Appling Rangers, Appling County), 11th Georgia Battalion; converted to 47th Georgia Regiment, 12 May 1862;; transferred to 1st SS Battalion 1 Aug. 1862; absent without leave, 31 Aug. and 30 Sep. 1862; present sick, 31 Oct. 1862; absent in search of deserters by authority of district headquarters, 30 Apr. 1863; sent on special service and deserted, 9 May 1863; deserted, 14 June 1864; complexion dark, eyes dark, height 5 ft. 10 in.

Keene, Jeremiah, Musician, A Company, enlisted for 3 years or the war Apr. 7, 1863 at Savannah; absent without leave, June 30 and Dec. 31, 1863; reenlisted for the war, Feb. 16, 1864; present, to have $20 deducted from his pay for expenses in bringing him back from absence without leave, Feb. 29, 1864; patient at Blunt School Hospital, Macon, Ga., June 23, 1864.

Keith, E[li], Private, Sergeant, D Company: enlisted for 12 months 13 Sep. 1861 in Bibb County in K Company (Chattahoochee Volunteers, Campbell County), 30th Georgia; transferred to 1st SS Battalion, 1 Aug. 1862; 4th Sergeant; killed at Chickamauga as Color Sergeant, 19 Sep. 1863; age 19, complexion fair, eyes blue, hair red, height 5 ft. 10 in., occupation clerk, born Marion District, S.C.

Kent, W[illiam] A., Private, A Company: enlisted for 3 years or the war 3 Jan. 1862 at Camp Wilson in G Company (Brown Light Infantry, Screven County), 25th Georgia; transferred to 1st SS Battalion, 1 Aug. 1862; absent without leave, 31 Oct. 1862; captured near Jackson, Miss., 20 July 1863; received at Camp Morton, Ind., 7 Aug. 1863; enlisted in 7th [Ind.?] Cavalry, Aug. 1863; absent without leave, 31 Dec. 1863; deserter, 29 Feb. 1864; age 19, complexion fair, eyes blue, hair light, height 5 ft. 3 in., born Effingham County.

Kersey, B[annister], Private, A Company: enlisted for 3 years or the war 9 Mar. 1863 at Camp Jordan; admitted with typhoid fever to General Hospital No. 1, Savannah, 30 Apr. 1863; died, 6 May 1863; 15-year-old farm hand in the Randolph County 1860 census.

Kersey, William, Private, 1st Sergeant, A Company: enlisted 21 Oct. 1861 as 3rd Corporal, K Company, 7th Regiment, GST; mustered out 20 Apr. 1862; enlisted for 3 years or the war 25 Apr. 1862 in Randolph County in B Company (Randolph Light

Guards, Randolph County), 11th Georgia Battalion; converted to 47th Georgia Regiment, 12 May 1862; transferred to 1st SS Battalion 1 Aug. 1862; 2nd Corporal from 1 Sep. 1862; absent sick in hospital, 31 Oct. 1862; appointed 2nd Sergeant, 1 May 1863; absent sick in Dover, Ga., 31 Dec. 1863; absent detailed on conscript duty, 1 Mar. 1864; reenlisted for the war,2 Mar. 1864; absent sick in General Hospital, appears on roll as 1st Sergeant, 31 Aug. 1864; wounded patient in Way Hospital, Meredian, Miss., 10 Jan. 1865; patient in St. Mary's Hospital, West Point, Miss., 13 Jan. 1865; furloughed for 60 days by medical evaluation board, 23 Jan. 1865; 18-year-old farm hand in the Randolph County 1860 census.

Kessel, John [Johann], Private, B Company: enlisted for the war 6 Mar. 1862 at Fort McAllister in DeKalb Rifles (A Company, 1st (Olmstead's) Georgia); transferred to 1st SS Battalion, 23 July 1862; deserted at Savannah, 5 May 1863; age 27, complexion dark, eyes gray, hair dark, height 5 ft. 5 in., occupation gardener, born in Prussia.

Ketchum, Christopher C., Private, C Company: enlisted 26 Dec. 1861 as Private, D Company, 1st Battalion, GST; mustered out Apr. 1862; enlisted for 3 years 23 Apr. 1862 at Macon in A Company (Lamar Infantry, Bibb County), 54th Georgia; transferred to 1st SS Battalion July 1862; absent sick at the convalescent camp at Savannah since 25 Aug. (MR, 31 Aug. 1862); present sick in quarters in camp, 31 Oct. 1862; present sick in hospital, 31 Dec. 1862; absent sick in hospital in Jackson, Miss., 30 June 1863; present at hospital convalescent camp, Rome, Ga., 31 Oct. 1863; present sick in Macon, Ga., 31 Dec. 1863; present sick, 29 Feb. 1864; deserted, 16 Aug. 1864; took oath of allegiance to U.S., 25 Aug. 1864; absent, deserted to the enemy, 31 Aug. 1864; residence Whitfield County, complexion dark, hair sandy, eyes blue, height 5 ft. 9 in.; 15-year-old laborer in the Whitfield County 1860 census.

Kiener [Keiner], Michael, Private, B Company: enlisted for the war 11 Jan. 1862 at Fort McAllister in DeKalb Rifles (A Company, 1st (Olmstead's) Georgia); transferred to 1st SS Battalion, 23 July 1862; confined in Chatham County jail under charges of desertion of 1 day, 28 Feb. 1863; court-martialed by Gen. Order No. 29/4/1, Department of South Carolina, Georgia and Florida, dated 18 Feb. 1863; respite of 21 days from sentence by Spec. Order No. 66-9, 17 Mar. 1863; executed by sentence of court martial, 10 Apr. 1863.

King, R[ichard] Cuyler, 2nd Lieutenant, D Company: enlisted 14 Aug. 1861 in Glynn Guards (13th Georgia), 14 Aug. 1861; assigned as artillery on St. Simon's Island, 19 Aug. 1861; appears as 2nd Corporal, 31 Aug. 1861; company transferred to Savannah, early 1862; designation changed to A Company, 26th Georgia, ca. 1 Mar. 1862; Sergeant, Ordnance Sergeant, up to Mar. 1862; company converted to cavalry and assigned 3rd Georgia Cavalry Battalion, 1 Apr. 1862; mustered out, 12 May 1862; appointed 2nd Lieutenant 1st SS Battalion 4 Oct. 1862 to rank from 8 July; absent on surgeon's certificate, 21 Jan. 1863; absent sick, 28 Feb. 1863; present on detached service with C Company, 30 Apr. 1863; admitted to Floyd House and Ocmulgee Hospitals, Macon, with phthisis pulmonitis, 6 Dec. 1863; absent sick in hospital, 31 Dec. 1863; recommended for promotion to 1st Lieutenant, 9 Sep. 1864; signed as Lieutenant commanding 1st SS Battalion, 30 Nov. 1864; captured at Nashville as 1st Lieutenant, 16 Dec. 1864; prisoner at Johnson's Island, Ohio, 22 Jan. 1864; released on oath of allegiance, 16 June 1865; residence St. Simon's Island, complexion dark, hair dark, eyes dark, height 5 ft. 6 in., age 23; 18 years old in the Glynn County 1860 census; died in Macon, 30 June 1913.

King, William, Corporal, Private, A Company: enlisted for 3 years or the war 14 May 1862 at Camp Deptford in A Company (Irish Jasper Greens), 1st (Olmstead's) Georgia; transferred as Corporal to 1st SS Battalion, Aug. 1862; reduced to the ranks, 31 Aug. 1862; transferred to the C.S. Navy, 30 June 1863.

Kittles [Kettles, Kelley], Henry C., Private, A Company: enlisted for 1 year 8 Aug. 1861 at Savannah in D Company (Ogeechee Rifles, Screven County), 25th Georgia; transferred to 1st SS Battalion, 30 July 1862; absent sick in Screven County, 31 Aug. 1862; absent, 31 Oct. 1862; absent sick in Atlanta, 31 Dec. 1863; reenlisted for the war, 29 Feb. 1864; captured at Adairsville, Ga., 17 May 1864; received at Rock Island, Ill., 27 May 1864; absent in the hands of the enemy, 31 Aug. 1864; released on oath of allegiance, 20 June 1865; residence Screven County, complexion dark, hair black, eyes gray, height 5 ft. 9 in.; 16 years old in the Screven County 1860 census; born 1842, died 1897, postwar lawyer and judge.

Kittles [Kettles], P[eter] R., Private, A Company: enlisted for 1 year 17 Aug. 1861 at Savannah in K Company (Ogeechee Rifles, Screven County), 25th Georgia; transferred to 1st SS Battalion, 30 July 1862; present sick in quarters, 28 Feb. 1863; furnished [Martin L.] Doyle as substitute and discharged, 11 Mar. 1863; 23-year-old farmer in the Screven County 1860 census; postwar merchant.

Klein, Jacob [Jakob], Private, B Company: enlisted for the war 7 June 1861 at Savannah in DeKalb Rifles (A Company, 1st (Olmstead's) Georgia); transferred to 1st SS Battalion, 23 July 1862; transferred to C.S. Navy, 1 May 1863.

Kner, George, Private, B Company: enlisted for the war 7 June 1861 at Savannah in DeKalb Rifles (A Company, 1st (Olmstead's) Georgia); transferred to 1st SS Battalion, 23 July 1862; absent on special service in Savannah arresting deserters, 31 Aug. 1862; detailed at teamster in quartermaster's department, 28 Feb. 1863 - 29 Feb. 1864; wounded, north Georgia, 16 May–6 June 1864; absent wounded, 31 Aug. 1864.

Knight, Wiley, Private, B Company: enlisted for the war 14 Aug. 1861 at Fort McAllister in DeKalb Rifles (A Company, 1st (Olmstead's) Georgia); transferred to 1st SS Battalion, 23 July 1862; present as a carpenter, 31 Aug. 1862; present, employed as a carpenter in the quartermaster's department, 30 Sep. 1862; absent on detached service in pursuit of deserters, 31 Dec. 1862; absent sent to hospital in Yazoo City, 13 1863; wounded at Chickamauga, Sep. 1863; absent, wounded at Chickamauga, 31 Dec. 1863 and 29 Feb. 1864; patient at Empire Hotel Hospital, Atlanta, 30 Apr. 1864.

Knowles, John F., Sergeant, Sergeant Major, A Company, F&S: enlisted for 12 months 25 July 1861 at Oglethorpe Barracks in E Company (Irish Volunteers), 1st (Olmstead's) Georgia; 4th Corporal, Dec. 1861; 3rd Corporal, Jan. 1862; mustered out, 25 Jan. 1862; enlisted for 3 years or the war 14 Feb. 1862 at Savannah in A Company (Irish Jasper

Greens), 1st Georgia; transferred to 1st SS Battalion, Aug. 1862; appears as 3rd Sergeant on roll for 31 Aug. 1862; appointed 1st Sergeant, 1 May 1863; reenlisted for the war, 29 Feb. 1864; captured near Atlanta as Sergeant Major, 22 July 1864; received at Camp Chase, Ohio, 2 Aug. 1864; absent in the hands of the enemy, 31 Aug. 1864; released by presidential order, 17 Mar. 1865; residence New York, N.Y., complexion light, hair dark, eyes blue, height 5 ft. 7 1/2 in., age 21.

Kraft, Justus, Private, Hospital Steward, B Company, F&S: enlisted for the war 7 Aug. 1861 at Fort McAllister as hospital steward in DeKalb Rifles (A Company, 1st (Olmstead's) Georgia); transferred to 1st SS Battalion, 23 July 1862; absent sick in Savannah, 31 Aug. 1862; on extra duty as hospital steward, 31 Oct. 1862; detailed as hospital steward, 28 Feb.; appointed hospital steward by warrant dated 19 Nov. 1863.

Krail, William, Private, B Company: enlisted for the war 7 June 1861 at Savannah in DeKalb Rifles (A Company, 1st (Olmstead's) Georgia); transferred to 1st SS Battalion, 23 July 1862; captured near Jackson, Miss., 17 July 1863; received at Camp Morton, Ind., 7 Aug. 1863; enlisted in 33rd Indiana, Aug. 1863; deserted, missing on the march from Jackson (MR, 31 Dec. 1863).

Landgraf, [Charles] Andrew, Private, D Company: enlisted for the war 26 Feb. 1863 at Camp Jordan; present sick, 30 June 1863; patient at General Hospital, Pt. Clear, Baldwin County, Ala., 31 Aug. 1863; absent sick at Macon, Miss., 31 Oct. 1863; absent sick in General Hospital, 31 Dec. 1863 through 31 Aug. 1864; born Germany, 30-year-old "flowerist" in the Chatham County 1860 census.

Lane, Abraham, Private, B Company: conscripted for the war 11 Aug. 1862 at Camp Randolph in Gordon County; transferred to 1st SS Battalion Aug. 1862; detailed to work at Fort Boggs, 28 Feb. 1863; absent sick in Yazoo city from 1 June 1863; absent sick in General Hospital, 31 Dec. 1863 and 29 Feb. 1864; absent wounded, 31 Aug. 1864; surrendered at Tallahassee, Fla., 10 May and paroled at Thomasville, Ga., 22 May 1865.

Lane, Alfred, Private, C Company: enlisted 10 Oct. 1861 as Private, K Company, 2nd Regiment, GST; mustered out Apr. 1862; enlisted for 3 years 21 Apr. 1862 in Savannah in B Company (Appling County), 54th Georgia; transferred to 1st SS Battalion, Aug. 1862; present sick in hospital in camp, 31 Oct. 1862; deserted from Camp Jordan, 29 Mar. 1863; not on muster roll for 30 June 1863; present sick in Atlanta, 31 Dec. 1863; absent sick in Atlanta, 29 Feb. 1864; absent sick, 31 Aug. 1864.

Langford, [T.] Jefferson, Private, C Company: enlisted for 3 years 6 May 1862 at Savannah in I Company (Woodson Guards, Upson County), 32nd Georgia; transferred to 1st SS Battalion; absent with leave, returned to I Company, 32nd Georgia, 31 Aug. 1862; sick in General Hospital, Savannah, Sep. 1862.

Langston, W[illiam] F., Private, D Company: enlisted for 12 months 25 Sep. 1861 in Campbell County in I Company (Clayton Invincibles, Clayton County), 30th Georgia; transferred to 1st SS Battalion, 1 Aug. 1862; absent on 36 hours leave to go to Savannah, 30 Sep. 1862; absent sick in Yazoo City from 13 June 1863; captured at Yazoo City and paroled, 13 July, died of typhoid fever 15 July 1863; Edward B. Langston of Jonesboro, Clayton County, Ga., claimed accrued pay and allowances, 24 Dec. 1863; reported died 26 July 1863 in General Hospital, Yazoo City (MR, 29 Feb. 1864); hair dark, eyes dark, height 6 ft. 6 in.

Larson, Christian, Sergeant, Private, B Company: enlisted for the war 7 June 1861 at Savannah in DeKalb Rifles (A Company, 1st (Olmstead's) Georgia); transferred to 1st SS Battalion as 5th Sergeant, 23 July 1862; reduced to Private, 18 Oct. 1862; absent sick in Savannah from 5 May 5 1863; present as company cook, 29 Feb. 1864; wounded, Resaca or Calhoun, Ga., 14 or 16 May, 1864; absent wounded, 31 Aug, 1864; captured in Savannah, 21 Dec. 1864; gunshot wound to the right hand, 4th finger amputated, 22 Dec. 1864; sent from Fort Pulaski to take oath of allegiance, 19 Jan. 1865; in hospital at Hilton Head, S.C., 6 Mar. 1865.

Lawrence, S[amuel] W., 1st Lieutenant, D Company: enrolled in Brunswick as 1st Lieutenant, Glynn Guards (13th Georgia), 14 Aug. 1861; assigned as artillery on St. Simon's Island, 19 Aug. 1861; designation changed to A Company, 13th Georgia, 15 Oct. 1861; company transferred to Savannah, early 1862; designation changed to 26th Georgia, ca. 1 Mar. 1862; company converted to cavalry and assigned 3rd Georgia Cavalry Battalion, 1 Apr. 1862; "retired," 12 May 1862; appointed 1st Lieutenant, 1st SS Battalion, 4 Oct. 1862 to rank from 14 July 1862; absent on leave, 31 Oct. 1863; absent sick in hospital, 31 Dec. 1863; absent sick, 29 Feb. 1864; granted leave by Spec. Order No. 63/1, Army of Tennessee, 5 Mar. 1864; signed voucher as 1st Lieutenant, commanding company, 31 Mar. 1864; killed Jonesboro, Ga., 31 Aug. 1864; born S.C., 28-year-old physician in the 1860 Glynn County census.

Lawrence, W.B. [W.S.], Private, D Company: enlisted for the war 1 May 1862 in Screven County in D Company (Screven County), 54th Georgia; transferred to 1st SS Battalion, 19 Aug. 1862; discharged by civil authority for being under age, 21 Sep. 1862.

Layne [Lane], G[eorge] W., Private, Corporal, D Company: enlisted for 12 months 25 Sep. 1861 in Campbell County in F Company (Campbell Sharpshooters, Campbell County), 30th Georgia; transferred to 1st SS Battalion, 2 Aug. 1862; appears as 2nd Corporal, 31 Oct. 1863; absent sick in Calhoun, 31 Dec. 1863; absent sick, 29 Feb. 1864; wounded, Resaca or Calhoun, Ga., 14 or 16 May, 1864; captured in Cobb County; took oath of allegiance at Chattanooga, 11 July 1864; discharged at Louisville, Ky., 16 July 1864; absent wounded, 31 Aug. 1864; complexion ruddy, hair auburn, eyes hazel, height 5 ft. 9 in.; from descriptive list: age 18, complexion fair, eyes hazel, hair brown, height 5 ft. 10 in., occupation farmer, born Lincoln County.

Lee, Joseph B., Private, A Company: enlisted for 3 years or the war 4 Mar. 1862 at Savannah in D Company (Screven Guards, Screven County), 11th Georgia Battalion; converted to 47th Georgia Regiment, 12 May 1862; transferred to 1st SS Battalion 1 Aug. 1862; absent sick at Whitesville, 31 Aug 1862; present sick, on extra duty with quartermaster's department, 31 Oct. 1862; present on duty with quartermaster's department, 31 Dec. 1862; present, detailed as teamster in quartermaster's department, 28 Feb. 1863; detached to ordnance department, 16 Apr. 1863; absent on special service by district special order, 30 Apr. 1863; absent on detached duty in the ordnance department, 30 June 1863; present, reenlisted for the war, 29 Feb. 1864; captured Adairsville, Ga., 18 May 1864; received at Rock Island, Ill., 27 May 1864; absent in the hands of the enemy, 31 Aug. 1864; took oath of allegiance, 17 June 1865; residence Ogeechee, Screven County, complexion dark, hair dark, eyes blue, height 5 ft. 11 in., age 36.

Lee, N[athan] W., Private, A Company: enlisted for 3 years or the war 12 May 1862 at Causton's Bluff in D Company (Screven Guards, Screven County), 47th Georgia; transferred to 1st SS Battalion 30 July 1862; absent sick in Savannah, 31 Aug. 1862; detached to ordnance department, 16 Apr. 1863; absent on special service by district special order, 30 Apr. 1863; absent on detached duty in the ordnance department, 30 June 1863; present, reenlisted for the war, 29 Feb. 1864; wounded, north Georgia, 16 May–6 June 1864; captured Jonesboro, Ga., 31 Aug. 1864; received at Camp Douglas, Ill., 1 Nov. 1864; discharged 12 May 1865; residence Screven County, complexion fair, hair light, eyes blue, height 5 ft. 10 in.; 30-year-old farm laborer in the Screven County 1860 census.

Lee, Thomas J., Private, A Company: enlisted as Private 9 Oct. 1861 in F Company, 1st Regiment, GST; mustered out Apr. 1862; enlisted for 3 years 25 Apr. 1862 in Randolph County in B Company (Randolph Light Guards, Randolph County), 11th Georgia Battalion; converted to 47th Georgia Regiment, 12 May 1862; transferred to 1st SS Battalion 1 Aug. 1862; absent sick at Benton, Miss., 30 June 1863; died at Medical College Hospital in Atlanta, 20 Oct. 1863 or died in Atlanta, 15 Dec. 1863, of wound to the head received at Chickamauga, 29 [sic] Sep. 1863; killed at Atlanta, July-Aug. 1864; 20-year-old farmer in the Randolph County 1860 census.

Leggett, John B., Private, B Company: enlisted for the war 27 Feb. 1862 at Fort McAllister in DeKalb Rifles (A Company, 1st (Olmstead's) Georgia); transferred to 1st SS Battalion, 23 July 1862; absent on sick furlough, 25 Oct. to 9 Nov. 1862; captured at Nashville, 16 Dec. 1864; sent to Camp Chase, Ohio, 4 Jan. 1865; paroled for exchange, 2 May 1865.

Leonard, James M., Sergeant, B Company: enlisted for the war 7 June 1861 at Savannah in DeKalb Rifles (A Company, 1st (Olmstead's) Georgia); transferred to 1st SS Battalion, 23 July 1862; present, promoted Sergeant, 31 Oct. 1862; absent, detailed on special service in pursuit of deserters, 31 Dec. 1862; wounded at Chickamauga, Sep. 1863; pay voucher shows rank of 2nd Sergeant, Feb. 1864; requested by Major A.L. Hartridge to be Ordnance Sergeant at Rose Dew Post, 8 Feb. 1864; approved, 24 Feb. 1864; appointed Ordnance Sergeant, 2 Mar. 1864; paroled as Ordnance Sergeant, 27th Georgia Battalion, 1 May 1865 at Greensboro, N.C.; born North Sea, Mass., complexion dark, hair dark, eyes blue, height 5 ft. 4 1/4 in., age 25, occupation carriage painter.

Licet [Liecet, Lycett], H., Private, D Company: enlisted for 3 years 12 May 1862 at Thomasville in I Company (Berry Infantry, Floyd County), 29th Georgia; transferred to 1st SS Battalion, 1 Aug. 1862; absent sick on surgeon's furlough, 31 Aug. 1862; absent, sent to Thomasville, 30 Sep. 1862; absent sick in Thomasville, 31 Oct. 1862; present, company cook, 30 June 1863; present, medical wagon driver near Dalton, 31 Dec. 1863;

present, on extra duty with the medical department, 29 Feb. 1864; surrendered 26 Apr. 1865, Greensboro, N.C.

[Another record, probably the same man: Licet, Samuel, Private, D Company: unfit for field service, detailed as teamster by Special Field Order No. 154, Army of Tennessee, 20 May 1864; name does not appear on any muster roll.]

Lightbourne, William, Sergeant, Private, D Company: enlisted for 3 years 6 Feb. 1862 at Savannah in A Company (Chatham County), 13th Georgia Battalion; transferred to 1st SS Battalion as 2nd Sergeant, Aug. 1862; present, reduced to Private, 28 Feb. 1863; transferred to C.S. Navy by special order of Gen. Mercer, 1 May 1863.

Lightfoot, W[illiam] T., Private, A Company: enlisted for 3 years or the war 4 Mar. 1862 at Reidsville in G Company (Tattnall Invincibles, Tattnall County), 11th Georgia Battalion; converted to 47th Georgia Regiment, 12 May 1862; transferred to 1st SS Battalion Aug. 1862; absent, deserted from Camp Anderson, 7 Dec. 1862; name appears on no muster rolls between Dec. 1862 and Aug. 1864; absent, deserted 30 June 1864; age 31, dark complexion, gray eyes, dark hair, height 6 ft.

Lindner, Henry W., Corporal, Sergeant, B Company: enlisted for the war 3 Sep. 1861 at Fort McAllister in DeKalb Rifles (A Company, 1st (Olmstead's) Georgia); transferred to 1st SS Battalion as 4th Sergeant, 23 July 1862; absent on special service arresting deserters in Savannah, 31 Aug. 1862; sent to General Hospital in Savannah, 27 Sep. 1862; wounded at Chickamauga, Sep. 1863; appears as 3rd Sergeant, hospital steward, 31 Aug. 1864; 33-year-old gardener in the Chatham County 1860 census, born Prussia.

Lipford, James A., Private, C Company: enlisted 22 Oct. 1861 in C Company, 6th Regiment, GST; mustered out, Apr. 1862; enlisted for 3 years 8 Apr. 1862 at Savannah in A Company (Jasper and Jones Counties), 32nd Georgia; transferred to 1st SS Battalion, 30 July 1862; absent sick at General Hospital in Savannah, 30 Sep. 1862; present sick in hospital in camp, 31 Oct. 1862; deserted, 30 June 1863; present, joined from desertion, 31 Dec. 1863; captured Lost Mountain, near Marietta, 18 June 1864; received at Camp Morton, Ind., 28 June 1864; absent in the hands of the enemy, 31 Aug. 1864; released on oath of allegiance, 22 May 1865; complexion light, hair light, eyes dark, height 5 ft. 9 3/4 in.

Little, Andrew J., Private, C Company: enlisted 22 Oct. 1861 in B Company, 6th Regiment, GST; mustered out, Apr. 1862; enlisted for 3 years 18 Apr. 1862 at Savannah in A Company (Jasper and Jones Counties), 32nd Georgia; transferred to 1st SS Battalion, 30 July 1862; present sick in hospital, 31 Dec. 1862; wounded, Jackson, Miss., July 1863; admitted to French's Division Hospital, Lauderdale, Miss., 13 July 1863; present sick in Jones County, 31 Dec. 1863; absent sick in Atlanta, 29 Feb. 1864; retired to Invalid Corps. 18 Apr. 1864; absent wounded, application made for retirement, 31 Aug. 1864.

Logan, Luke, Private, C Company: enlisted for 3 years 15 Aug. 1862 at Savannah in F Company (Jeff Davis Guards, Clay County), 32nd Georgia; transferred to 1st SS Battalion, Aug. 1862; present on extra duty in the medical department, 31 Oct. and 31

Dec. 1862; present, detailed in the hospital, 30 June 1863; admitted to Walker's Division, Lauderdale, Miss., 9 Aug. 1863; patient at French's division hospital, Lauderdale, 18 Sep. 1863; pay for Sep. 1863 shows occupation as hospital nurse; admitted to Breckinridge's Division Hospital No. 2, Lauderdale Springs, 15 Dec. 1863; present sick at Atlanta, 31 Dec. 1863; present on extra duty in the medical department of the battalion, 29 Feb. 1864; captured at Dalton, Ga., 13 May 1864; received at Rock Island, Ill., 16 June 1864; detailed, sent home and supposed to be captured, 31 Aug. 1864; request for status by Mrs. Margaret Logan, wife, forwarded by General Lafayette McLaws, Savannah, to General Samuel Cooper, Richmond, 30 Sep. 1864; transferred for exchange, 2 Mar. 1865; school teacher in the 1859 Savannah city directory; 45-year-old railroad clerk in the Chatham County 1860 census, born Galway, Ireland.

Long [Lang], Richard G., Private, A Company: enlisted for 3 years or the war 4 Mar. 1862 at Homersville in F Company (Appling Rangers, Appling County), 11th Georgia Battalion; converted to 47th Georgia Regiment, 12 May 1862; transferred to 1st SS Battalion 30 July 1862; present sick in hospital, 31 Oct. 1862; absent sick in Yazoo City, 30 June 1863; mortally wounded at Chickamauga, 19 Sep. 1863.

Love, Joseph, Private, C Company: enlisted as Private in E Company, 5th Regiment, GST, 12 Oct. 1861; mustered out, Apr. 1862; enlisted for 3 years 7 May 1862 at Savannah in G Company (Emanuel County), 32nd Georgia; transferred to 1st SS Battalion, 30 July 1862; absent on 24 hour leave, 1 Oct. 1862; deserted from Camp Jordan, 30 Mar. 1863; absent sick in hospital in Canton, Miss., 30 June 1863; present sick in Atlanta, 31 Dec. 1863; patient on register of Ocmulgee Hospital, Macon, 15, 18, 22, 25 July 1864; patient with pleuritis at Floyd House Hospital, Macon, 31 Aug. 1864; absent sick, 31 Aug. 1864; surrendered at Augusta, Ga., 27 May 1865.

Love, R.T., Private, A Company: enlisted for 1 year 1 Sep. 1861 in Calhoun County in L Company (Calhoun Repeaters, Calhoun County), 25th Georgia; transferred to 1st SS Battalion, 1 Aug. 1862; absent sick at Whitesville, 31 Aug. 1862; absent sick in the convalescent camp at Springfield, 30 Sep. 1862; absent sick in hospital, 31 Dec. 1862; present sick in quarters, 28 Feb. 1863; admitted with intermittent fever to Floyd house and Ocmulgee Hospitals, Macon, 7 Nov. 1863; absent sick in Atlanta, 31 Dec. 1863; admitted with diarrhea to Ocmulgee Hospital, 21 Jan. 1864, returned to duty, 4 Feb.; admitted with diarrhea to Ocmulgee Hospital, 24 June 1864, returned to duty, 8 July; wounded at Jonesboro, 31 Aug. 1864.

Love, W.J., Private, A Company: enlisted for 3 years 1 May 1862 in Calhoun County in L Company (Calhoun Repeaters, Calhoun County), 25th Georgia; transferred to 1st SS Battalion, 30 July 1862; transferred with syphilis from General Hospital No. 1, Savannah, to General Hospital, Augusta, 25 Apr. 1863; absent sick in hospital, 30 Apr. 1863; absent sick at Whitesville, 30 June 1863; absent sick in Atlanta, 31 Dec. 1863; absent on furlough from Macon Hospital, reenlisted for the war, 29 Feb. 1864; killed, Resaca or Calhoun, Ga., 14 or 16 May, 1864.

Lovin, E[lijah] W., Private, D Company: enlisted for 12 months 25 Sep. 1861 in Campbell County in F Company (Campbell Sharpshooters, Campbell County), 30th

Georgia; transferred to 1st SS Battalion, 2 Aug. 1862; absent on furlough from 26 Aug. to 4 Sep. 1862; deserted at Savannah, 10 Apr. and absent without leave, 30 Apr. 1863; dropped from the rolls, 10 June 1863; age 19, complexion fair, eyes dark, hair brown, height 5 ft. 8 in., occupation farmer, born Campbell County.

Loyd, Jasper, Private, D/B Company: enlisted for 12 months 25 Sep. 1861 in Fayette County in H Company (Fayette Volunteers, Fayette County), 30th Georgia; transferred to 1st SS Battalion, 1 Aug. 1862; present sick in quarters, 31 Dec. 1862; captured Ringgold, Ga., 27 Nov. 1863; sent to Rock Island, Ill, 12 Dec. 1863; reported absent without leave, 31 Dec. 1863; reported absent sick, 29 Feb. 1864; released on oath of allegiance, 22 June 1865; residence Fayetteville, Fayette County, complexion dark, hair black, eyes gray, height 5 ft. 6 1/2 in., age 30; from descriptive list: age 28, complexion dark, eyes gray, hair dark, height 5 ft. 7 in., occupation farmer, born Fayette County.

Lundy [Lunday], Edwin R., Private, C Company: enlisted for 3 years 10 May 1862 at Savannah in K Company (Alexander Greys, Burke County), 32nd Georgia; transferred to 1st SS Battalion, 30 July 1862; attached as carpenter, 13 Oct. 1862; present sick in hospital, 31 Dec. 1862; admitted to Breckinridge's Division Hospital, Lauderdale Springs. Miss., 21 June 1863; absent sick in hospital in Canton, Miss., 30 June 1863; wounded at Chickamauga, Sep. 1863; absent sick in Atlanta, 31 Dec. 1863; present sick, 29 Feb. 1864; surrendered at Thomasville, Ga., 23 May 1865, paroled, 24 May.

Madden, P[eter], Private, D Company: enlisted for the war 1 Aug. 1862 in Chatham County; failed to return from 5 hours leave, 10 Aug. 1862; deserted from Camp Pemberton on 5 Aug. (MR, 31 Oct. 1862); appears on no other muster roll, but a P. Madden is on the roll of the 1st Confederate Georgia Battalion, surrendered at Greensboro, N.C., 26 Apr. 1865, with former service in 1st SS Battalion; born Wicklow, Ireland, 26-year-old laborer in the Chatham County 1860 census.
[Included with this record: deserted from B Company, 1st Georgia Regiment, 21 Sep. 1863.]

Maddox, G[eorge] C., Private, D Company: enlisted for 12 months 4 Oct. 1861 at Thomasville in I Company (Seventeenth Patriots, Thomas County), 29th Georgia; transferred to 1st SS Battalion, 1 Aug. 1862; wounded and captured, 19 Sep. 1863; received Camp Morton, Ind, 22 Oct. 1863; absent, wounded at Chickamauga, 31 Oct. 1863; absent wounded in the hands of the enemy, 31 Dec. 1863; absent sick, 29 Feb. 1864; absent in the hands of the enemy since the battle of Chickamauga (MR, 31 Aug. 1864); released on oath of allegiance, 12 June 1865; residence Thomas County, complexion dark, hair brown, eyes gray, height 5 ft. 9 in.

Malcolmson, Thomas, Private, B Company: enlisted for the war 7 June 1861 at Savannah in DeKalb Rifles (A Company, 1st (Olmstead's) Georgia); transferred to 1st SS Battalion, 23 July 1862; present, on extra duty as teamster in quartermaster's department, 30 Sep. and 31 Oct. 1862; absent in pursuit of deserters, 31 Dec. 1862; on extra duty as teamster in quartermaster's department, 28 Feb. 1863 to 31 Aug. 1864.

Mann, John A[sa] O[liver], Private, C Company: enlisted for 3 years 24 Oct. 1862 at Atlanta; absent sick in hospital in Canton, Miss., 30 June 1863; admitted to Breckinridge's Division Hospital No. 1, Lauderdale Springs, Miss., 17 July 1863, furloughed 2 Sep.; discharged for disability, no date; died in Decatur or DeKalb County, Ga., 1 Nov. 1863; last pay to mother, Mrs. Malinda Mann, 24 Nov. 1863; born Elbert County, age 28, occupation lawyer, complexion dark, hair light, eyes blue, height 5 ft. 11 in.; 27-year-old attorney in the DeKalb County 1860 census.

Mann, Robert, Private, C Company: enlisted for 3 years 5 Nov. 1862 at Camp Anderson; wounded at Chickamauga, Sep. 1863; admitted wounded to Floyd House and Ocmulgee Hospitals, Macon, 24 Sep. 1863, released on 30 day furlough, 28 Sep.; present sick at Atlanta, 31 Dec. 1863; appears on no muster roll after 28 Feb. 1864; post office Dawson [Terrell County].

Martin, William, Private, C Company: enlisted for 3 years 6 May 1862 in Savannah in I Company (Woodson Guards, Upson County), 32nd Georgia; transferred to 1st SS Battalion, 30 July 1862; detailed as company cook, 31 Oct. and 31 Dec. 1862; absent sick in hospital in Canton, Miss., 30 June 1863; absent without leave, 31 Aug. 1864.

Mathias [Mathis], John J., Private, C Company: enlisted for 3 years 6 May 1862 in Savannah in E Company (Berrien County), 54th Georgia; transferred to 1st SS Battalion, 1 Aug. 1862; received clothing at St. Mary's Hospital, LaGrange, Ga., 6 Aug. 1964; absent sick, 31 Aug. 1864; returned to duty from St. Mary's Hospital, 19 Sep. 1864.

Mathis, Elbert, Private, C Company: enlisted for 3 years 2 May 1862 in Savannah in E Company (Berrien County), 54th Georgia; transferred to 1st SS Battalion, Aug. 1862; absent on sick furlough, 31 Dec. 1862; wounded at Chickamauga, Sep. 1863; present sick in Appling County, Ga., 31 Dec. 1863; absent sick in Appling County, Ga., 29 Feb. 1864; captured Marietta, 15 June 1864; received Rock Island, Ill., 24 June 1864; absent in the hands of the enemy, 31 Aug. 1864; transferred for exchange, 25 Feb. 1865; received at Richmond, Va., 5 Mar. 1865; paid at Camp Winder, Va., General Hospital, 7 Mar. 1865; born in Lowndes County, 1836, died 1915, age 79.

Mattox [Maddox], W[illiam] H., Private, D Company: enlisted for 12 months 25 Sep. 1861 in Campbell County in F Company (Campbell Sharpshooters, Campbell County), 30th Georgia; transferred to 1st SS Battalion, 2 Aug. 1862; sent to General Hospital in Savannah, 30 Sep. 1862; absent without leave, 31 Oct. and 31 Dec. 1863; deserted on the march from Mississippi, 26 Aug. 1863 (MR, 29 Feb. 1864); captured Campbell County, 17 July or 3 Aug. 1864, discharged on oath of allegiance, 4 Aug.; complexion light, hair dark, eyes gray, height 5 ft. 7 in.; from descriptive list: age 20, complexion fair, eyes blue, hair light, height 5 ft. 8 in., occupation farmer, born Carroll County.

McBride, James, Private, A Company: enlisted for 12 months 8 Aug. 1861 in Henry County, Ala., in Irwin Invincibles; became E Company (Henry Light Infantry), 25th Georgia, Dec. 1861; transferred to 1st SS Battalion, 30 July 1862; died of dysentery in hospital in Atlanta, 13 Dec. 1863; 16 years old in the Henry County, Ala., 1860 census.

McCann, Green, Private, B Company: conscripted for the war 12 Aug. 1862 at Camp Randolph in Gordon County; transferred to 1st SS Battalion Aug. 1862; absent, sent to convalescent camp at Springfield, 31 Aug. 1862; furloughed for 9 days to go to Green County, 22 Sep. 1862; on extra duty with the quartermaster department, 31 Oct. 1862; discharged on certificate of disability for bad leg, 5 Dec. 1862; age 26, occupation farmer, residence Upson County, complexion light, hair light, eyes gray, height 5 ft. 9 in.

McConnell, John E., Private, C Company: enlisted for 3 years 6 May 1862 in Savannah E Company (Berrien County), 54th Georgia; transferred to 1st SS Battalion, 1 Aug. 1862; present sick in hospital in camp, 31 Dec. 1862; on duty as company cook, 28 Feb. to 30 June 1863; died of chronic diarrhea at Fair Grounds Hospital No. 1, Atlanta, Sep. 20, 1863.
[another record, probably the same man: McConnell, John M., Private, C Company: died of chronic dysentery in hospital in Atlanta, date not given, report received, 8 Feb. 1863 [sic].]

McCook, Alexander R., Private, C Company: enlisted as 1st Corporal in C Company, 5th Regiment, GST, 25 Oct. 1861; discharged 7 Mar. 1862; enlisted for 3 years 7 May 1862 in Savannah in E Company (Washington County), 32nd Georgia; transferred to 1st SS Battalion, 30 July 1862; deserted 27 or 29 Sep. 1862; born in Randolph County, age 24, light complexion, grey eyes, dark hair, height 6 ft.

McDaniel, Miles, Private, B Company: conscripted for the war 23 July 1862 at Camp Randolph in Gordon County; transferred to 1st SS Battalion Aug. 1862; deserted 23 Dec. 1862; court-martialed by Gen. Order No. 21/2/5, Dept. of South Carolina, Georgia & Florida, 1 Feb. 1863; 21 day respite in execution of sentence granted by Spec. Order No. 51-2, 26 Feb. 1863; absent in Chatham County jail under sentence of death by court-martial, 28 Feb. 1863; sentence suspended by Spec. Order No. 73-8, 30 Mar. 1863; absent in arrest in Chatham County jail, 30 June 1863; refer to service record of James F. Butler for information on amnesty and pardon; absent, wounded at Chickamauga, 31 Dec. 1863; absent wounded, reported deserted from hospital, 29 Feb. 1864; absent sick, 31 Aug. 1864; surrendered at Augusta, 2 May 1865; took oath of allegiance, 14 May 1865; residence Jefferson County, Ky., complexion fair, hair brown, eyes gray, height 5 ft. 11 in.

McDermott [McDermart, McDermit, McDurman], B.B., Private, D Company: enlisted for 12 months 5 Oct. 1861 at Camp Black in A Company (Gordon County), 8th Georgia Battalion; transferred to 1st SS Battalion, Aug. 1862; detached in the Quartermaster Dept., 31 Oct. 1863; present, detailed as blacksmith, 31 Dec. 1863; on extra duty in the quartermaster department, 29 Feb. 1864; absent, on duty as brigade blacksmith, 31 Aug. 1864.

McDermott, James, Musician, B Company: enlisted for the war 8 Apr. 1863 in Savannah; deserted, 16 Apr. 1863.

McDonald, Patrick, Private, A Company: enlisted for the war 20 Sep. 20, 1861 in Savannah in E Company (Irish Volunteers), 1st (Olmstead's) Georgia; transferred to 1st

SS Battalion, 15 Aug. 1862; absent sick in hospital, 31 Dec. 1862; present sick in quarters, 28 Feb. 1863; patient with syphilis at General Hospital No. 1, Savannah, 3 May 1863; absent sick at Whitesville, Ga., 30 June 1863; present, reenlisted for the war, 29 Feb. 1864; captured near Atlanta, 22 July 1864; received Camp Chase, Ohio, 2 Aug. 1864; absent in the hands of the enemy, 31 Aug. 1864; released, 8 or 13 May 1865; residence Chatham County, complexion florid, hair light, eyes blue, height 5 ft. 7 1/2 in.

McFarland, J[ohn] T[heodore], Assistant Surgeon, F&S: enrolled 31 May 1861 in Savannah as 1st Lieutenant in C Company (Republican Blues), 1st (Olmstead's) Georgia; appointed Assistant Surgeon, 8th Georgia, 5 June 1861; resigned 28 Oct. 1861; re-commissioned, 17 Feb. 1862 and assigned to 1st Georgia; surrendered at Ft. Pulaski, Ga., 11 Apr. 1862; prisoner at Ft. Columbus, N.Y., 2 June 1862; released July 1862; assigned to 1st SS Battalion, 13 Aug. 1862; transferred to 5th Georgia Cavalry, 28 Feb. 1863; Senior Surgeon, Gen. B.H. Robertson's cavalry brigade, Dec. 1863; promoted Surgeon 1 June 1864 to rank from 20 Jan. 1863; commander Walker Hospital, Columbus, Ga., Feb. 1865; Surgeon, Gen. R.H. Anderson's cavalry brigade, Apr. 1865; born Savannah, 23 Feb. 1836, died Savannah 10 Feb. 1888, age 51; 23-year-old physician in the Chatham County 1860 census.

McGuire, D[aniel] J., Private, D Company: enlisted for 12 months 22 Aug. 1861 in A Company (Thomasville Guards, Thomas County), 29th Georgia; transferred to 1st SS Battalion, 1 Aug. 1862; on extra duty with quartermaster's department, 31 Oct. 1862 to 30 June 1863; detached in the Quartermaster Dept., 31 Oct. 1863; present sick, 31 Dec. 1863; granted 40 days furlough for chronic diarrhea and debility for past 4 months by Medical Examining Board, Dalton, 9 Feb. 1864; absent sick, 29 Feb. and 31 Aug. 1864; patient at Ladies' Hospital, Montgomery, Ala., 15 Nov. 1864; admitted with catarrhus, Ocmulgee Hospital, Macon, 9 Apr. 1865; readmitted with chronic diarrhea, 18 Apr., returned to duty, 28 Apr.; captured and paroled, Apr. 1865; residence Thomasville.

McGuire, J[acob] B., Private, D Company: enlisted for 12 months 25 Sep. 1861 in D Company (Huguenin Rifles, Bibb County), 30th Georgia; transferred to 1st SS Battalion, 1 Aug. 1862 in exchange for Private Manning Bone; teamster in the quartermaster department, 31 Aug. 1862; present sick in quarters, 31 Dec. 1862; absent in hospital in Atlanta, 31 Oct. 1863; patient at Foard Hospital, Newnan, Ga., 31 Dec. 1863; absent sick, 31 Dec. 1863 and 29 Feb. 1864.

McHiggs, Joshua [Isaac], [Higgs, Mack C.], Private, A Company: enlisted for 1 year 14 Aug. 1861 in Savannah in F Company (Altamaha Scouts, Liberty County), 25th Georgia; transferred to 1st SS Battalion, 1 Nov. 1862; reenlisted for the war, 29 Feb. 1864; captured at Nashville, 16 Dec. 1864; received at Camp Chase, Ohio, 4 Jan. 1865; enlisted in U.S. Army, transferred to Chicago, Ill., 20 Mar. 1865.

McSwain, Roderick, Private, B Company: enlisted for the war 1 Sep. 1861 at Fort McAllister in DeKalb Rifles (A Company, 1st (Olmstead's) Georgia); transferred to 1st SS Battalion, 23 July 1862; deserted since muster of 31 Aug., dropped from the roll, 23 Oct. 1862.

Meinzer, Christian, Private, Sergeant, B Company: enlisted for the war 7 June 1861 at Savannah in DeKalb Rifles (A Company, 1st (Olmstead's) Georgia); transferred to 1st SS Battalion, 23 July 1862; appears as 2nd Corporal, 31 Aug. 1862; appears as 1st Corporal, 31 Dec. 1862; took oath of allegiance as deserter at Chattanooga, 22 July 1864; took oath at Louisville, 27 July 1864; appears as 3rd Sergeant, absent in the hands of the enemy, 31 Aug. 1864; residence Richmond County, complexion light, hair light, eyes hazel, height 5 ft. 5 in.

Melton, E[lbert] G., Private, Corporal, A Company: enlisted as Private, 21 Oct. 1861 in K Company, 7th Regiment, GST; mustered out 20 Apr. 1862; enlisted for 3 years 16 May 1862 at Causten's Bluff in B Company (Randolph Light Guards, Randolph County), 47th Georgia; transferred to 1st SS Battalion 1 Aug. 1862; absent on 30 days sick furlough, 31 Oct. 1862; absent on sick furlough, 31 Dec. 1862; wounded at Chickamauga, Sep. 1863; present, reenlisted for the war, 29 Feb. 1864; wounded, Resaca or Calhoun, Ga., 14 or 16 May, 1864; appears as 3rd Corporal, detailed to division sharpshooters by order of Gen. Brown, 31 Aug. 1864; admitted wounded to Floyd House & Ocmulgee Hospitals, Macon, 25 Sep. 1864, granted 30 days furlough, 26 Sep.; post office, Ward's Station; 17 years old in the Randolph County 1860 census.

Melton, H[enry] C., Private, A Company: enlisted as Private, 21 Oct. 1861 in K Company, 7th Regiment, GST; mustered out 20 Apr. 1862; enlisted for 3 years 16 May 1862 at Causten's Bluff in B Company (Randolph Light Guards, Randolph County), 47th Georgia; transferred to 1st SS Battalion 1 Aug. 1862; absent sick in Dover, Ga., 31 Dec. 1863; present, reenlisted for the war, 29 Feb. 1864; granted 60 days furlough by Medical Examining Board, Dalton, for chronic diarrhea and debility for past 3 months in Cannon Hospital, 15 June 1864; absent sick in hospital, 31 Aug. 1864; town: Notchaway; 17 years old in the Randolph County 1860 census.

Melton, William P., Private, Sergeant, A Company: enlisted as Private 21 Oct. 1861 in K Company, 7th Regiment, GST; mustered out, 20 Apr. 1862; enlisted for 3 years 25 Apr. 1862 in Randolph County in B Company (Randolph Light Guards, Randolph County), 11th Georgia Battalion; converted to 47th Georgia Regiment, 12 May 1862; transferred to 1st SS Battalion 1 Aug. 1862; appears as 5th Sergeant from 29 Aug. (MR, 31 Oct. 1862); absent on special service, 28 Feb. 1863; appears as 3rd Sergeant, 30 June 1863; reenlisted for the war, 16 Feb. 1864; appears as 2nd Sergeant, absent, wounded at Jonesboro, 31 Aug. 1864; 22-year-old overseer in the Randolph County 1860 census.

Metzger, Aaron, Private, B Company: enlisted for the war 7 June 1861 at Savannah in DeKalb Rifles (A Company, 1st (Olmstead's) Georgia); transferred to 1st SS Battalion, 23 July 1862; captured near Jackson, Miss., July 1863; received at Camp Morton, Ind., 7 Aug. 1863; released on oath of allegiance, 15 Aug. 1863; deserted, missing on the retreat from Jackson (MR, 31 Dec. 1863).

Middleton, George W., Private, C Company: enlisted 10 Oct. 1861 as Private, K Company, 2nd Regiment, GST; mustered out Apr. 1862; enlisted for 3 years 21 Apr. 1862 in Savannah in B Company (Appling County), 54th Georgia; transferred to 1st SS

Battalion, 30 July 1862; present sick in Atlanta, 31 Dec. 1863; died of pneumonia in Institute Hospital, Atlanta, 6 Jan. 1864.

Mills, J[ohn F. C.], Private, D Company: enlisted for 12 months 1 Oct. 1861 in Franklin County in G Company (Stephens Volunteers, Berrien County), 29th Georgia; transferred to 1st SS Battalion, 1 Aug. 1862; admitted 1st Mississippi C.S.A. Hospital, Jackson, 13 July 1863, sent to General Hospital, 14 July; absent sick, 31 Dec. 1863; reenlisted for the war, 16 Feb. 1864; captured near Marietta, 3 July 1864; received at Camp Douglas, Ill., 18 July 1864; applied for oath of allegiance, 17 Aug. 1864; enlisted E Company, 6th U.S. Volunteers, 25 Mar. 1865.

Mills, T[homas], Private, D Company: enlisted for 12 months 1 Oct. 1861 in Franklin County in G Company (Stephens Volunteers, Berrien County), 29th Georgia; transferred to 1st SS Battalion, 1 Aug. 1862; absent on sick furlough in Franklin County, 31 Dec. 1862; absent without leave, 30 Apr. 1863; reenlisted for the war, 16 Feb. 1864.

Mimmes, J.R., Private, D Company: enlisted for 12 months 1 Sep. 1861 in Savannah in 30th Georgia; transferred to 1st SS Battalion, Aug. 1862; absent on furlough, 31 Aug. 1862; dropped from the roll 10 Sep. 1862, never having reported.
[This man's name does not appear on the descriptive roll of 28 men transferred from the 30th Georgia, nor is he in Henderson, *Roster of the Confederate Soldiers of Georgia*. There is no one named Mimmes, Mimms, or Mims in the 30th Georgia in the NARA master index of Civil War Confederate soldiers. This may be an erroneous entry for J.J. Mims (see below).]

Mims, _____, Musician, C Company: due pay from 1 Aug. (MR, 31 Aug. 1862); no further record.

Mims, J[ames] J. [or I.], Private, D Company: enlisted for 12 months 25 Sep. 1861 in Stockton in E Company (Alapaha Guards, Clinch County), 29th Georgia; transferred to 1st SS Battalion, 1 Aug. 1862; absent sick at the convalescent camp in Springfield, 31 Aug. 1862; absent, sent to General Hospital in Savannah, 30 Sep. 1862; absent sick in Canton, Miss., 30 June 1863; absent in hospital in Atlanta, 31 Oct. 1863; present sick, 31 Dec. 1863; absent sick, 29 Feb. 1864; absent without leave, 31 Aug. 1864; wounded, leg broken at Fort McAllister, 13 Dec. 1864 [sic]; born in Georgia; home on leave at end of war.

Mitchell, William, Musician, C Company: enlisted for 3 years Apr. 29, 1863 at Savannah; present, on extra duty as orderly at battalion headquarters, 31 Dec. 1863 and 29 Feb. 1864; captured at Macon, 21 Apr. 1865.

Molina, Manuel, 2nd Lieutenant, D Company: enlisted 31 May 1861 for 60 days at Savannah in 2nd Republican Blues company; appointed 7th Sergeant in Chatham Artillery to rank from 16 May 1861; appointed 2nd Lieutenant, 1st SS Battalion, 4 Oct. to rank from 4 July 1862; absent sick in Savannah, 31 Aug. and 30 Sep. 1862; absent on general court-martial duty, Savannah, 30 Apr. 1863; absent on sick leave, 14 Apr. to 3 May 1863; 26 days leave granted by Spec. Order No. 7/1, Army of Tennessee, 31 July

1863; died, 28 June 1864; born Spain, 35-year-old cigar dealer in Chatham County 1860 census; age at death, 41.

Moody, William, Corporal, C Company: enlisted 3 Oct. 1861 as 3rd Sergeant in A Company, 1st Regiment, GST; mustered out Apr. 1862; enlisted for 3 years 18 Apr. 1862 at Savannah in K Company (Appling County), 54th Georgia; transferred to 1st SS Battalion July 1862, with date of rank as 3rd Corporal from 20 July; killed at Chickamauga, 19 Sep. 1863; born in 1841; 21-year-old hired laborer in the Appling County 1860 census.

Morel[l], J. I[rwin], Private, Sergeant, A Company: enlisted for 3 years 4 Mar. 1862 in Effingham County in I Company (Empire State Guards, Effingham County), 11th Georgia Battalion; converted to 47th Georgia Regiment, 12 May 1862; transferred to 1st SS Battalion 1 Aug. 1862; appears as 4th Corporal, 30 Apr. 1863; appears as 5th Sergeant since 28 Apr. (MR, 30 June 1863); reenlisted for the war, 16 Feb. 1864; died of chronic diarrhea in Effingham County, 6 or 20 Mar. 1864; 16 years old in Effingham County 1860 census.

Morgan, A.L., Private, B Company: conscripted for the war 9 Aug. 1862 at Camp Randolph in Gordon County; transferred to 1st SS Battalion Aug. 1862; absent on 10 day furlough, 30 Sep. 1862; present, company cook, 28 Feb. and 30 Apr. 1863; absent, left sick in Montgomery, Ala., 5 May 1863; absent sick in General Hospital, 31 Dec. 1863; absent, left sick in Montgomery, Ala., 29 Feb. 1864.

Morgan, G.W., Private, B Company: conscripted for the war 9 Aug. 1862 at Camp Randolph in Gordon County; transferred to 1st SS Battalion Aug. 1862; absent, sent to the convalescent camp at Springfield, 31 Aug. 1862; discharged on certificate of disability, 16 Oct. 1862.

Morley, John, Private, D Company: enlisted for the war 17 Apr. 1863 at Savannah; absent, wounded at Chickamauga (MR, 31 Oct. 1863); absent with leave, 31 Dec. 1863; Spec. Order No. 8/1, District of Georgia, 8 Jan. 1864, shows him a prisoner; reenlisted for the war, 16 Feb. 1864; surrendered, Tallahassee, Fla., 10 May 1865; paroled, Albany, Ga., 15 May 1865.
[Another John Morley, or the same man: enlisted at Savannah 17 Apr. 1862 by Capt. Dent; surrendered at Greensboro, N.C., 26 Apr. 1865, with 1st Confederate Georgia Battalion; former service in 1st SS Battalion.]

Morton, D[avid] M., Private, A Company: enlisted for 3 years 4 Mar. 1862 in Effingham County in I Company (Empire State Guards, Effingham County), 11th Georgia Battalion; converted to 47th Georgia Regiment, 12 May 1862; transferred to 1st SS Battalion 30 July 1862; discharged by civil authority for being under age, 15 Oct. 1862; 15 years old in Effingham County 1860 census.

Müller, Frederick, Private, B Company: enlisted for the war 7 Aug. 1861 at Fort McAllister in DeKalb Rifles (A Company, 1st (Olmstead's) Georgia); transferred to 1st SS Battalion, 23 July 1862; deserted, 21 Aug. 1862; dropped from the roll, 30 Sep. 1862.

Muller, William, Private, C Company, enlisted Mar. 1, 1862 at Green Island; transferred to 1st SS Battalion from B Company, Savannah Volunteer Guard Battalion, Aug. 1862; absent sick at the convalescent camp, Springfield, since Aug. 21, Aug. 31, 1862; absent sick in Savannah, Oct. 31, 1862; absent sick in General Hospital in Savannah, Apr. 30, 1863; absent in the quartermaster department, Savannah, by order of Gen. Mercer, June 30, 1863; admitted with dysentery to Floyd House and Ocmulgee Hospitals, Macon, Dec. 6, 1863; present sick in Atlanta, Dec. 31, 1863; present, on extra duty in the assistant adjutant general's office, brigade headquarters, Feb. 29, 1864.

Mullins, J[onathan] A., Private, A Company: enlisted for 3 years 4 Mar. 1862 in Randolph County in B Company (Randolph Light Guards, Randolph County), 11th Georgia Battalion; converted to 47th Georgia Regiment, 12 May 1862; transferred to 1st SS Battalion 1 Aug. 1862; absent without leave, 30 Sep. 1862; in confinement for loss of equipment, 31 Oct. 1862; deserted from Camp Anderson, 13 Dec. 1862; transferred to E Company, 13th Georgia, by Spec. Order No. 295/9, Adjutant and Inspector General's Office, Richmond, 12 Dec. 1863; born in Monroe County, age 26, dark complexion, black eyes, dark hair, height 5 ft. 8 in.; 24-year-old farmer in the Randolph County 1860 census.

Mumm, John, Sergeant, Private, B Company: enlisted for 14 months 7 June 1861 at Savannah in DeKalb Rifles (A Company, 1st (Olmstead's) Georgia); transferred to 1st SS Battalion, 23 July 1862; deserted, 21 Aug. 1862; dropped from the roll, 30 Sep. 1862; received at Fort Mifflin, Pa., as a rebel deserter, 2 July 1863, released 3 Oct. 1863.

Mundorf, Frederick, Private, B Company: enlisted for the war 15 Aug. 1861 at Fort McAllister in DeKalb Rifles (A Company, 1st (Olmstead's) Georgia); transferred to 1st SS Battalion, 23 July 1862; discharged by the justice of the inferior court, 3 Sep. 1862.

Murdock, John F., Private, A Company: enlisted for 3 years 25 Apr. 1862 in Randolph County in B Company (Randolph Light Guards, Randolph County), 11th Georgia Battalion; converted to 47th Georgia Regiment, 12 May 1862; transferred to 1st SS Battalion 1 Aug. 1862; absent sick in Griffin County, 31 Dec. 1863; present, reenlisted for the war, 29 Feb. 1864; present, company cook, 31 Aug. 1864; wounded, north Georgia, 7-30 June 1864; 25-year-old overseer in the Randolph County 1860 census.

Murdock, T[homas] J., Private, A Company: enlisted for 3 years 4 Mar. 1862 in Randolph County in B Company (Randolph Light Guards, Randolph County), 11th Georgia Battalion; converted to 47th Georgia Regiment, 12 May 1862; transferred to 1st SS Battalion 1 Aug. 1862;; absent sick in Savannah, 31 Dec. 1862; died of typhoid pneumonia at General Hospital No. 1, Savannah, 3 or 8 Jan. 1863; 22-year-old farm hand in the Randolph County 1860 census.

Murphy, Nicholas, Private, B Company: enlisted for the war 19 Aug. 1861 at Fort McAllister in DeKalb Rifles (A Company, 1st (Olmstead's) Georgia); transferred to 1st SS Battalion, 23 July 1862; employed in the quartermaster department as a teamster, 30 Sep. 1862; present, on extra duty as a teamster, 31 Oct. 1862; present, on special duty as teamster in quartermaster's department, 28 Feb. 28 to 30 June 1863; absent sick in General Hospital, 31 Dec. 1863 and 29 Feb. 1864; absent, detailed as a teamster by order of Gen. Johnston, 31 Aug. 1864; reported in Savannah, 3 May 1865; born Ireland, residence Savannah, age 50, complexion florid, hair brown, eyes blue, height 5 ft. 10 in.

Murrow, M[artin] M., Private, D Company: enlisted for the war 4th Corporal 25 Sep. 1861 in Campbell County in G Company (Campbell Grays, Campbell County), 30th Georgia; 5th Sergeant, May 1862; transferred to 1st SS Battalion, 1 Aug. 1862; absent sick in Yazoo City from 13 June 1863; reenlisted for the war, 16 Feb. 1864; surrendered at Greensboro, N.C., 26 Apr. 1865, with 1st Confederate Georgia Battalion; age 19, complexion light, eyes blue, hair light, height 5 ft. 11 in., occupation farmer, born Cobb County.

Nally, F[ountain] A. [or G.], Private, D Company: enlisted for 12 months 1 Oct. 1861 in Banks County in G Company (Stephens Guards, Berrien County), 29th Georgia; transferred to 1st SS Battalion, 1 Aug. 1862; discharged on surgeon's certificate for disability (going blind), 6 Dec. 1862, born Franklin County, age 23, complexion dark, hair black, eyes black, height 5 ft. 5 in.
[A pension record for Nally, F.A., shows enlisted 16 Sep. 1861 in B Company (Ochlockonee Light Infantry, Thomas County), 29th Georgia; discharged for blindness at Camp Anderson, 3 Nov. 1862; born Banks County, 1832.]

Newman[s], A[ndrew] J., Private, A Company: enlisted for 3 years or the war 4 Mar. 1862 at Reidsville in G Company (Tattnall Invincibles, Tattnall County), 11th Georgia Battalion; converted to 47th Georgia Regiment, 12 May 1862; transferred to 1st SS Battalion Aug. 1862; sick in hospital, 31 Oct. 1862; died at Camp Anderson of typhoid pneumonia, 12 Dec. 1862.

Nobles, James, Private, B Company: conscripted for the war 9 Aug. 1862 at Camp Randolph in Gordon County; transferred to 1st SS Battalion Aug. 1862; discharged on certificate of disability, Dec. 1862, a weak, nervous man who should never have been conscripted, unable to perform duty for the past 60 days; surrendered, Albany, Ga., 29 May 1865; born Lumpkin County, age 31, complexion dark, hair dark, eyes black, height 5 ft. 8 in.

Nobles, R., Private, B Company: conscripted for the war 9 Aug. 1862 at Camp Randolph in Gordon County; transferred to 1st SS Battalion Aug. 1862; discharged on certificate of disability, 28 Oct. 1862.

Norris, Stephen P., Sergeant, 2nd Lieutenant, D/B Company: enlisted for the war 1 Mar. 1862 at Green Island, Ga. in C Company, Savannah Volunteer Guard Battalion; transferred to 1st SS Battalion as 3rd Sergeant, Aug. 1862; sent to General Hospital in Savannah, 30 Sep. 1862; appears as 2nd Sergeant, 31 Dec. 1862; appears as 1st Sergeant, 28 Feb. 1863; wounded at Jackson, miss., July 1863; absent, wounded at Chickamauga (MR, 31 Oct. 1863); absent wounded in Savannah, 31 Dec. 1863; patient at General Hospital No. 2, Savannah, 31 Dec. 1863 and 29 Feb. 1864; absent sick, 29 Feb. 1864; examined for promotion to 2nd Lieutenant, 30 Mar. 1864; recommended by Major Shaaff for promotion to 2nd Lieutenant, B Company for conspicuous gallantry and wound at Chickamauga, 1 Apr. 1864; recommended for promotion for valor as 2nd Lieutenant, B Company, 11 Apr. 1864; appointed 28 Apr. to rank from 21 Apr. 1864; wounded at Atlanta, Aug. 1864; absent on medical authority from 15 Aug. on inspection report of 17 Aug. 1864; absent wounded, 31 Aug. 1864; absent wounded from 14 Aug. on inspection report of 17 Sep. 1864; born in Savannah and resident of that city; 18-year-old mechanic's apprentice in the Chatham County 1860 census.

Odum, H.J., Private, A Company: enlisted for 3 years or the war 4 Mar. 1862 in Cuthbert in 13th Georgia; transferred to 1st SS Battalion, Dec. 1863; died in hospital in Virginia, 23 Dec. 1863, before reporting; 22-year-old farmer in the Randolph County 1860 census.

Ogletree, H.F., Private, B Company: conscripted for the war 12 Aug. 1862 at Camp Randolph in Gordon County; transferred to 1st SS Battalion Aug. 1862; absent sick in General Hospital, 29 Feb. 1864; absent sick, 31 Aug. 1864.

Oliveros, E[sidro] J., Sergeant Major, Field & Staff: assigned as Assistant Surgeon, 57th Georgia, dropped, 6 May 1862; enlisted 16 May 1862 at Savannah in B Company, Savannah Volunteer Guard Battalion; transferred to 1st SS Battalion, 15 July 1862; assigned duty by Spec. Order No. 8, SS Battalion, 8 Aug. 1862, to be effective from 1 Aug.; absent on special service as acting assistant surgeon by Spec. Order No. 666, District of Georgia, 10 Dec. 1862; transferred and assigned duty as assistant surgeon by Spec. Order No. 681, District of Georgia, 25 Dec. 1862; appointed Assistant Surgeon 4 Apr. 1863 to rank from 16 Dec. 1862; assigned as chief of board of surgeons at Orangeburg to examine conscripts in the 3rd Military District of South Carolina, Feb. 1863; transferred to Charleston, Dec. 1863; relieved, 16 Dec. 1864; born St. Augustine, Fla., 1836; 14 years old in the 1850 Chatham County census.

Olsen, James, Private, B Company: enlisted for the war 11 Mar. 1862 at Fort McAllister in DeKalb Rifles (A Company, 1st (Olmstead's) Georgia); transferred to 1st SS Battalion, 23 July 1862; captured near Jackson, Miss., July 1863; received at Camp Morton, Ind., 7 Aug. 1863; deserted, missing on the retreat from Jackson (MR, 31 Dec. 1863).

O'Quinn, George W., Private, C Company: enlisted 3 Oct. 1861 as Private in A Company, 1st Regiment, GST; mustered out Apr. 1862; enlisted for three years 18 Apr. 1862 in Savannah in K Company (Appling County), 54th Georgia; transferred to 1st SS Battalion, 30 July 1862; present sick in quarters, 31 Dec. 1862; color bearer, killed at Chickamauga, 20 Sep. 1863; born Appling County, 1 July 1844; 15 years old in the Appling County 1860 census.

Owens, William Oscar, Private, Corporal, A Company: enlisted for the war as Musician, 12 May 1862 at Fort Brown in B Company (Irish Jasper Greens), 1st (Olmstead's) Georgia; transferred to 1st SS Battalion, 11 Aug. 1862; absent sick in Montgomery, Ala., 31 Dec. 1863; reenlisted for the war, 16 Feb. 1864; appears as 2nd Corporal, 29 Feb. 1864; died of chronic dysentery in Atlanta, 7 Apr. 1864.

Parrott, A.L., Private, B Company: conscripted for the war 13 Aug. 1862 at Camp Randolph in Gordon County; transferred to 1st SS Battalion Aug. 1862; transferred with acute rheumatism from General Hospital No. 1, Savannah, to Whitesville, 7 Apr. 1863; absent sick, sent to General Hospital in Guyton, 30 Apr. 1863; absent sick in General Hospital, 31 Dec. 1863 and 29 Feb. 1864; absent, wounded at Jonesboro, 31 Aug. 1864; patient at Ocmulgee Hospital, Macon, with flesh wound to the right hypochondria region, wounding the right lobe of the head, 28 Sep. 1864; admitted to Receiving and Wayside Hospital or General Hospital No. 9, Richmond, Va., 2 Mar. 1865; surrendered, Augusta, 18 May 1865; died Colquitt County, 7 Jan. 1922.

Parrott, W[illiam] L. [Jasper], Private, D Company: enlisted for 12 months 25 Sep. 1861 in Fayette County in H Company (Fayette Volunteers, Fayette County), 30th Georgia; 1st Corporal, 1 May 1862; transferred to 1st SS Battalion, 1 Aug. 1862; absent, wounded at Chickamauga (MR, 31 Oct. 1863); absent sick, 29 Feb. 1864; captured 16 Dec. 16, received at Camp Chase, Ohio, 6 Jan. 1865; enlisted in B Company, 6th U.S. Volunteers, 16 Mar. 1865; transferred to Chicago, Ill., 20 Mar. 1865; deserted in Colorado, 1 Oct. 1865; age 18, complexion dark, eyes dark, hair dark, height 5 ft. 8 in.; occupation farmer, born Fayette County; died Troup County, 29 Mar. 1932.

Patrick, Cornelius, Private, C Company: enlisted for 3 years Feb. 12, 1863 in Dooly County; E. Stiles accepted as his substitute, Apr. 1863.

Pattillo, Charles S., 1st Sergeant, 2nd Lieutenant, A/B Company: enlisted for 3 years or the war 10 May 1862 at Fort Boggs in B Company, Savannah Volunteer Guard Battalion; transferred to 1st SS Battalion, 19 Jul. 1862; appears as 1st Sergeant, A Company with date of rank of 1 Aug. (MR, 31 Aug. 1862); absent on 30 days sick furlough, 31 Oct. 1862; recommended for promotion to 2nd Lieutenant, B Company, vice R. Wayne by Major Anderson, 13 Dec. 1862; transferred to B Company as acting 2nd Lieutenant by battalion Spec. Order No. 25, 5 Apr. 1863; appointed 8 June with rank from 2 May 1863; signed pay voucher, 30 Oct. 1863; signed forage voucher, 10 Nov. 1863; died at Marietta, Ga., Oct. 20 or Nov. 18, 1863: see record of Stephen P. Norris for Arthur Shaaff's statement of death date; 18-year-old clerk in the Cobb County 1860 census.

Peace, J[ohn] W., Private, D Company: enlisted for 12 months 25 Sep. 1861 in I Company (Clayton Invincibles, Clayton County), 30th Georgia; transferred to 1st SS Battalion, 1 Aug. 1862; wounded at Chickamauga, Sep. 1863; absent wounded, 31 Oct. and 31 Dec. 1863; reenlisted for the war, 16 Feb. 1864; wounded, north Georgia, 7-30 June 1864; captured at Jonesboro, Ga., 1 Sep. 1864; exchanged at Rough and Ready, Ga., 19 or 22 Sep. 1864; captured at Nashville, 16 Dec. 1864; sent to Camp Douglas, Ill., 21 Dec. 1864; discharged, 15 June 1865; residence Clayton County.

Peacock, James M., Private, B Company: enlisted for the war 27 Sep. 1861 at Fort McAllister in DeKalb Rifles (A Company, 1st (Olmstead's) Georgia); transferred to 1st SS Battalion, 23 July 1862; sent to General Hospital, Savannah, 20 Aug. 1862; deserted from hospital, dropped from the roll, 7 Oct. 1862; born in Liberty County, age 36, dark complexion, black eyes, height 5 ft. 9 in.

Pearman, William, Private, B Company: conscripted for the war 13 Aug. 1862 at Camp Randolph in Gordon County; transferred to 1st SS Battalion Aug. 1862; absent sick in General Hospital, 31 Dec. 1863 and 29 Feb. 1864; admitted to St. Mary's hospital, 30 June 1864, granted 30 days leave for rheumatism with edema of the lower extremities on 7 July with orders to return on 9 Aug.; absent sick, 31 Aug. 1864; post office, Greensboro, Greene County.

Pearson, Donald B., Private, C Company: enlisted for 3 years Jan. 1, 1863 at Macon; James Fadden accepted as substitute, Apr. 1863; Fadden deserted from camp, Apr. 30, 1863.

Peyton [Paton], Benjamin, Private, C Company: enlisted for 3 years 6 Feb. 1863 in Dooly County; absent sick in hospital in Canton, Miss., 30 June 1863; present sick in Atlanta, 31 Dec. 1863; present sick, 29 Feb. 1864; admitted with ascites to Ocmulgee Hospital, Macon, 8 Apr. 1864, granted 60 days furlough, 16 Apr. absent sick, 31 Aug. 1864; post office, Drayton, Ga.; surrendered at Greensboro, N.C., 26 Apr. 1865; 20-year-old farm laborer in the Dooly County 1860 census.

Phillips, H.B., Private, Sergeant, D Company: enlisted for 12 months 5 Oct. 1861 at Camp Black in A Company, 8th Georgia Battalion; transferred to 1st SS Battalion, Aug. 1862; wounded, Jackson, Miss., July 1863; patient at French's Division Hospital, Lauderdale, Miss., 31 Aug. 1863; absent, wounded at Jackson, appears as 4th Sergeant (MR, 31 Oct. 1863); absent sick in hospital, 31 Dec. 1863; reenlisted for the war, 16 Feb. 1864; captured at Nashville, 16 Dec. 1864; received at Camp Chase, Ohio, 6 Jan. 1865; transferred to Chicago, 20 Mar. 1865; 19-year-old farm laborer in the Gordon County 1860 census.

Phillips, Samuel P., Private, B Company: enlisted for the war 3 Mar. 1862 at Fort McAllister in DeKalb Rifles (A Company, 1st (Olmstead's) Georgia); transferred to 1st SS Battalion, 23 July 1862; present as carpenter, 31 Aug. 1862; deserted at Savannah, 5 May 1863; age 31, complexion sallow, eyes gray, hair light, height 5 ft. 5 in., occupation farmer, born in Bryan County.

Pickard, R.M., Private, Company B: conscripted for the war 13 Aug. 1862 at Camp Randolph in Gordon County; transferred to 1st SS Battalion Aug. 1862; transferred to 32nd Georgia, 8 Sep. 1862.

Price, Robert W., Sergeant, C Company: enlisted as 4th Sergeant, 22 Oct. 1861 in C Company, 6th Regiment, GST; mustered out, Apr. 1862; enlisted for 3 years 18 Apr. 1862 at Savannah in A Company (Jasper and Jones Counties), 32nd Georgia; transferred to 1st SS Battalion; appointed 3rd Sergeant, 17 Aug. 17, 1862; wounded, Resaca or Calhoun, Ga., 14 or 16 May, 1864; absent wounded, 31 Aug. 1864.

Pundt, Peter, Private, B Company: enlisted for 12 months 15 Aug. 1861 at Fort McAllister in DeKalb Rifles (A Company, 1st (Olmstead's) Georgia); transferred to 1st SS Battalion, 23 July 1862; deserted 20 Aug. 1862; dropped from the roll, 30 Sep. 1862.

Ragan, Thomas A., Private, A Company: enlisted as Private, 21 Oct. 1861 in K Company, 7th Regiment, GST; mustered out 20 Apr. 1862; enlisted for 3 years or the war 25 Apr. 1862 in Randolph County in B Company (Randolph Light Guards, Randolph County), 11th Georgia Battalion; converted to 47th Georgia Regiment 12 May 1862; transferred to 1st SS Battalion 1 Aug. 1862; appears as 4th Corporal ranking from 1 Sep. (MR, 31 Oct. 1862); appears as Private, 30 Apr. 1863; employed as nurse since 7 Aug. at Nott General Hospital, Mobile, Ala., 31 Oct. 1863; absent sick in Mobile, 31 Dec. 1863 and 29 Feb. 1864; absent without leave, 31 Aug. 1864; 19-year-old farmer in the Randolph County 1860 census.

Ramsey, Owen, Private, C Company: enlisted for 3 years Mar. 26, 1863 in Savannah; provided William Amey as substitute.

Reddick, John, Private, C Company: enlisted as Private in B Company, 5th Regiment, GST, 22 Oct. 1861; mustered out Apr. 1862; enlisted for 3 years 21 Apr. 1862 at Savannah in K Company (Alexander Greys, Burke County), 32nd Georgia; transferred to 1st SS Battalion, 30 July 1862; died at Guyton Hospital, Whitesville, of chronic diarrhea. 18 Oct. 1862; father Nicholas Reddick claimed pay due, 22 Nov. 1862; born Burke County; residence Sardis, age 23, complexion dark, hair dark, eyes blue, height 6 ft. 1/2 in., occupation farmer; 21 years old in the Burke County 1860 census.

Reed [Read, Reid], J[ames] A., Private, Corporal, D Company: enlisted for 12 months 5 Oct. 1861 at Camp Black in A Company (Gordon County), 8th Georgia Battalion; Corporal; transferred to 1st SS Battalion, Aug. 1862; died of typhoid fever at General Hospital in Savannah, 11 Oct. 1862; appears as 5th Corporal, 30 Apr. 1863; mother Elizabeth Read of Dawson County filed claim for pay, 25 May 1863; appears as 1st Corporal, 31 Oct. 1863; reenlisted for the war, 16 Feb. 1864; absent in the hands of the enemy from 17 May 1864; 15-year-old farm laborer in 1860 Dawson county census [part of this record belongs with J.D. Reed, below].

Reed [Read, Reid], J[ohn] D., Private, Corporal, D Company: enlisted for 12 months 5 Oct. 1861 at Camp Black in A Company (Gordon County), 8th Georgia Battalion; transferred to 1st SS Battalion, Aug. 1862; died of typhoid fever, 17 Jan. 1863; appears as Corporal, 28 Feb. 1863; 17-year-old farm laborer in 1860 Dawson county census [part of this record belongs with J.A. Reed, above].

Rhymes [Rimes], Stephen [B.], Corporal, Private, A Company: enlisted for 3 years or the war 16 Apr. 1862 in Henry County, Ala. [sic] in L Company (Calhoun Repeaters, Calhoun County), 25th Georgia; transferred to 1st SS Battalion, 1 Aug. 1862; appears as 2nd Corporal, 31 Aug. 1862; appears as 4th Sergeant since 1Sep. (MR, 31 Oct. 1862); absent sick and deserted in Apr. (MR, 30 June 1863); sent on special service 9 May and deserted (MR, 31 Dec. 1863); returned on 1 Dec. and reduced to Private, reenlisted for the war, 29 Feb. 1864; deserted on 14 June 1864(MR, 31 Aug. 1864); age 36, complexion fair, eyes blue, hair light, height 5 ft. 9 in.; 40-year-old farm laborer in the Henry County, Ala., 1860 census.

Richard, Musician, A Company: present, due pay, Aug. 31, 1862; no further record.

Rickertson, Hiram, Private, B Company: conscripted for the war 11 Aug. 1862 at Camp Randolph in Gordon County; transferred to 1st SS Battalion Aug. 1862; absent sick in Benton, Miss. from 4 June 4 1863; patient from 20 Oct. 1863 at Guyton General Hospital; absent sick in General Hospital, 31 Dec. 1863 and 29 Feb. 1864; absent sick, 31 Aug. 1864; paroled at Thomasville, 25 May 1865; born in Ware County, 21 Apr. 1836, died in Burnet County, Tex., 22 Feb. 1918.

Roath [Routh], Alfred, Private, A Company: enlisted for 1 year 17 Aug. 1861 at Savannah in D Company (Ogeechee Rifles, Screven County), 25th Georgia; transferred to 1st SS Battalion, 1 Aug. 1862; wounded at Chickamauga, Sep. 1863; absent sick in Savannah, 31 Dec. 1863; detached in Screven County by civil authority as witness in a murder case, 29 Feb. 1864; detailed to brigade provost guard, 31 Aug. 1864; captured at Nashville, 16 Dec. 1864; received at Camp Chase, Ohio, 6 Jan. 1865; took oath of allegiance, 15 May 1865; residence Screven County, age 33, complexion dark, hair dark, eyes hazel, height 5 ft. 5 in.; 50 years old in the Wayne County 1880 census.

Roberts, E.W., Private, B Company: conscripted for the war 11 Aug. 1862 at Camp Randolph in Gordon County; transferred to 1st SS Battalion Aug. 1862; absent sick in Coffee County from 6 Nov. (MRs, 31 Dec. 1862 and 28 Feb. 1863); died in Coffee County, 18 Mar. 1863.

Roberts, Mark, Private, B Company: enlisted 13 Oct. 1862 at Decatur; joined from camp of instruction at Decatur, 31 Dec. 1862; absent sick in Coffee County since 3 Jan. 1863; wounded at Chickamauga, Sep. 1863; absent, wounded at Chickamauga, 31 Dec. 1863; present sick, $12 stoppage of pay for expenses in being arrested while absent without leave, 29 Feb. 1864; wounded, Resaca or Calhoun, Ga., 14 or 16 May, 1864; absent wounded, 31 Aug. 1864.

Roberts, Robert, Private, B Company: conscripted for the war 11 Aug. 1862 at Camp Randolph in Gordon County; transferred to 1st SS Battalion Aug. 1862; died of heart disease at Camp Anderson, 2 Jan. 1863.

Robin, Cook, D Company: enlisted by master for the war 23 Aug. 1862 at Camp Anderson; appears as company cook (colored), 30 June 1863; present, 31 Aug. 1864.

Robinson [Roberson], B.A., Private, D Company: enlisted for 12 months 5 Oct. 1861 at Camp Black in A Company (Gordon County), 8th Georgia Battalion; transferred to 1st SS Battalion, Aug. 1862; absent on sick furlough in Calhoun, Ga., 31 Dec. 1862; discharged by civil authority, 4 Apr. 1863.

Robinson, Thomas C., Private, Corporal, B Company: conscripted for the war 9 Aug. 1862 at Camp Randolph in Gordon County; transferred to 1st SS Battalion Aug. 1862; 4th Corporal from 1 June 1 1863; nurse from 16 Sep. 1863 at Buckner Hospital, Newnan, Ga.; absent sick in General Hospital, appears as 3rd Corporal, 31 Dec. 1863; absent sick, appears as 1st Corporal, 31 Aug. 1864; captured at Nashville, 16 Dec. 1864; received at Camp Chase, Ohio, 6 Jan. 1865; released on oath of allegiance, 12 June 1865.

Ross, William H[enry], Captain, C Company: commissioned as 1st Lieutenant, C Company (Floyd Rifles, Bibb County), 2nd Georgia Battalion, 20 Apr. 1861; commissioned as Lieutenant Colonel, commanding 1st Battalion, GST, 1 Nov. 1861; mustered out, Apr. 1862; appointed Captain, 1st SS Battalion, 23 July 1862 to rank from 22 June; detailed as enrolling officer, Spec. Order No. 251/4, Dept. of South Carolina, Georgia and Florida, 13 Dec. 1862; absent on special duty, 31 Dec. 1862; absent inspecting command at Oglethorpe Barracks, 28 Feb. 1863; absent mustering by inspection report No. 57, Dept. of South Carolina, Georgia and Florida, 28 Feb. 1863; out patient at Floyd House & Ocmulgee Hospitals, Macon, 3 Dec. 1863; absent sick, 31 Dec. 1863; on extra duty as acting assistant inspector general, Walker's Division since 15 Nov. 1863 (MR, 29 Feb. 1864); absent, assigned duty as acting assistant inspector general on Gen. Hardee's staff, 23 Aug. 1864 and 31 Jan. 1865; received clothing at Charleston, S.C., 10 Oct. 1864; paroled 1 May 1865 at Greensboro, N.C.; 23-year-old commission merchant in the Bibb County 1860 census; died in Macon, Feb. 21, 1902.

Rutledge, Andrew J., Private, C Company: enlisted for 3 years 21 Apr. 1862 at Savannah in A Company, 54th Georgia; transferred to 1st SS Battalion, Aug. 1862; absent without leave, never reported, 31 Aug. 1862; deserted, 10 Sep. 1862.

Ryalls [Royal], John J. [Isom, Isham], Private, C Company: enlisted for 3 years 6 Feb. 1863 in Dooly County; absent sick at Atlanta, 29 Feb. 1864; died of chronic diarrhea in Dawson Hospital, Greensboro, Ga., 9 Mar. 1864; 32-year-old farmer in Dooly County 1860 census; born North Carolina, 7 Nov. 1826.

Rye, William [G.], Private, C Company: enlisted for 3 years 19 Apr. 1862 at Macon in A Company (Lamar Infantry, Bibb County), 54th Georgia; transferred to 1st SS Battalion, Aug. 1862; absent without leave, never reported, 31 Aug. 1862; present, 31 Oct. 1862; deserted, June 30, 1863; shown present with A Company, 54th Georgia, 29 Feb. 1864.

Sadler, N[icholas] Bayard, 2nd Lieutenant, C Company: enlisted 12 July 1861 for 12 months at Jacksonville in H Company, 2nd Florida, age 23; detached by order of the Secretary of War, Dec. 1861; drill master in Fla., 10 Jan. and 28 Feb. 1862; absent in Fla.; on detached duty, 30 Apr. 1862; detached by order of the Secretary of War, 30 June 1862; transferred, 31 Oct. 1862; appointed 2nd Lieutenant, 1st SS Battalion, 4 Oct. 1862 to rank from 3 July; wounded at Chickamauga, Sep. 1863; absent sick, 31 Dec. 1863; absent sick in hospital in Marietta, 29 Feb. 1864; captured at Big Shanty near Marietta, 15 June 1864; received at Johnson's Island, Ohio, 22 June 1864; absent in the hands of the enemy, 31 Aug. 1864; recommended for promotion to 1st Lieutenant, 9 Sep. 1864; released on oath of allegiance, 15 June 1865; residence Savannah, age 25, complexion fair, hair light, eyes gray, height 6 ft.

Sailer, Charles, Private, B Company: joined/conscripted for the war by Lt. Hardee 24 Mar. 1863 at Savannah; discharged by civil authority, 1 Apr. 1863.

Schaffer, Peter, Private, Corporal, B Company: enlisted for the war 7 June 1861 at Savannah in DeKalb Rifles (A Company, 1st (Olmstead's) Georgia); transferred to 1st SS

Battalion, 23 July 1862; appears as Corporal ranking from 20 Oct. 1862; deserted at Savannah, 5 May 1863; age 19, complexion light, eyes gray, hair light, height 5 ft. 6 in., occupation baker, born in Germany.

Schlatter, Charles L., [Jr.], 1st Sergeant, Sergeant Major, 2nd Lieutenant, D/A Company/F&S: enlisted as 3rd Corporal for 60 days 29 May 1861 in Brunswick Rifles; became L Company, 13th Georgia, 13 Aug. 1861; reenlisted for 12 months 7 Sep. 1861 at St. Simon's Island, Ga.; designation changed to K Company, 15 Oct. 1861; designation changed to 26th Georgia, ca. 1 Mar. 1862; company converted to cavalry and assigned 3rd Georgia Cavalry Battalion, 1 Apr. 1862; in A Company, 26th Georgia; mustered out, 12 May 1862; enlisted 1 Aug. 1862 in C Company, Savannah Volunteer Guard Battalion; transferred to 1st SS Battalion as 1st Sergeant, 2 Aug. 1862; promoted Sergeant Major, 1 Jan. 1863; transferred to A Company as 2nd Lieutenant, 4 May 1863; appointed 2nd Lieutenant 30 May with rank from 2 May 1863; wounded at Chickamauga, Sep. 1863; signed roll as company commander, 31 Dec. 1863, 29 Feb. and 31 Aug. 1864; appears on vouchers as company commander, 31 Jan. and 31 Mar. 1864; granted leave by Spec. Order No. 58/5, Army of Tennessee, 29 Feb. 1864; captured at Nashville, 16 Dec. 1864; received at Johnson's Island, Ohio, 22 Dec. 1864; released on oath of allegiance, 17 June 1865; residence, Waresboro, Ga., complexion florid, hair dark, eyes hazel, height 5 ft. 6 in., age 23; born Pa., 18-year-old civil engineer in the 1860 Glynn County census.

Schmauch, Charles, Private, B Company: enlisted for the war 22 Aug. 1861 at Fort McAllister in DeKalb Rifles (A Company, 1st (Olmstead's) Georgia); transferred to 1st SS Battalion, 23 July 1862; deserted at Savannah, 11 Apr. [sic] 1863; detailed as orderly for commanding officer, 30 Apr. 1863; absent without leave, 30 June.

Schmidt [Smith], Henry, Private, Corporal, B Company: enlisted for the war 17 Aug. 1861 at Fort McAllister in DeKalb Rifles (A Company, 1st (Olmstead's) Georgia); transferred to 1st SS Battalion, 23 July 1862; absent, sent to General Hospital in Savannah, 31 Aug. 1862; wounded at Chickamauga, Sep. 1863; granted 40 days furlough by a medical examining board at Cannon Hospital, Dalton, 6 Dec. 1863, for gun shot wound to the right hip on 19 Sep. 1863; absent on special service in the quartermaster's department in Augusta by order of the secretary of war, 31 Dec. 1863, 29 Feb. 1864 and 31 Aug. 1864; appears as 4th Corporal, 31 Dec. 1863; appears as 2nd Corporal, 31 Aug. 1864; residence Augusta; born Hanover, Germany, ca. 1835, disappeared in Abbeville, S.C., 1889.

Schmidt, John, Private, B Company: enlisted for the war 19 Aug. 1861 at Fort McAllister in DeKalb Rifles (A Company, 1st (Olmstead's) Georgia); transferred to 1st SS Battalion, 23 July 1862; absent sick, sent to Canton, Miss., 25 June 1863; captured at Kennesaw near Marietta, 3 July 1864; received at Camp Douglas, Ill., 18 July 1864; absent in the hands of the enemy, 31 Aug. 1864; enlisted in I Company, 5th U.S. Volunteers, 29 Mar. 1865.

Schnee, Lewis [Louis], Private, B Company: enlisted for the war 17 Aug. 1861 at Fort McAllister in DeKalb Rifles (A Company, 1st (Olmstead's) Georgia); transferred to 1st SS Battalion, 23 July 1862; on extra duty as cook in hospital, 31 Aug. to 31 Oct. 1862;

detailed as cook in hospital, 28 Feb. 1863; deserted at Savannah, 5 May 1863; age 35, complexion dark, eyes black, hair black, height 5 ft. 9 in., occupation gardener, born in France.

Schreiber, Frederick, Private, B Company: enlisted for 12 months 22 Aug. 1861 at Fort McAllister in DeKalb Rifles (A Company, 1st (Olmstead's) Georgia); transferred to 1st SS Battalion, 23 July 1862; deserted, 21 Aug. 1862; dropped from the rolls, 30 Sep. 1862; born Wurttemburg, Germany, 29-year-old shoemaker in Chatham County 1860 census.

Shaaff, Arthur, Captain, Major, A Company/F&S: appointed 2nd Lieutenant, C.S. Army, 16 Mar. 1861; appointed Captain, C.S. Army, 30 Sep. 1861; assigned as ordnance officer, Sibley's Texas Brigade, 3 Oct. 1861; relieved from duty and ordered to report to Richmond, 27 Oct. 1861; arrived in Savannah as 1st Lieutenant, 24 Dec. 1861; on detached service with examining board, Savannah, June 1862; transferred to Major Anderson's command, 18 July 1862; appointed Captain, 23 July 1862 with rank from 20 June; assumed command, A Company, 1st SS Battalion, 1 Aug. 1862; absent on special service in Savannah, 30 Sep. 1862; absent on sick furlough, 12 Dec. 1862; signed muster roll as captain commanding battalion, 28 Feb. 1863; granted 30 days leave from 28 Mar. 1863; appointed Major 30 Apr. 1863 to rank from 20 Jan.; wounded at Chickamauga, Sep. 1863; absent from command with leave, in Savannah, 31 May 1864; assistant inspector general on Major General Bate's staff, 19 Sep. 1864; granted leave of absence for 30 days, Spec. Order No. 5/8, Army of Tennessee, 10 Jan. 1865; paroled in Augusta, 1 May 1865; 2nd Lieutenant, U.S. Army, 1855-1861; born Georgetown, D. C. ca. 1830, died in Savannah 8 July 1874, age 42.

Shaw, Charles W., Private, Sergeant, B Company: enlisted for the war 7 June 1861 at Savannah in DeKalb Rifles (A Company, 1st (Olmstead's) Georgia); transferred to 1st SS Battalion, 23 July 1862; appears as Corporal, Aug. 31, 1862; appointed 5th Sergeant, 20 Oct. 1862; absent, sent to hospital in Canton, Miss., 25 June 1863; absent sick in General Hospital, 31 Dec. 1863 and 29 Feb. 1864; wounded at Jonesboro, 31 Aug. 1864; received clothing at Augusta, 1 Oct. 1864; signed as acting captain, company commander, 18 Oct. 1864; admitted to Stonewall Hospital, Montgomery, Ala., 15 Nov. 1864; paroled at Montgomery, 25 May 1865; complexion fair, hair light, eyes blue, height 5 ft. 8 in.

Sheer [Scheer], Henry, Private, B Company: enlisted for the war 7 June 1861 at Savannah in DeKalb Rifles (A Company, 1st (Olmstead's) Georgia); 5th Sergeant, 1 Nov. 1861; detached on special service in the Ordnance Dept., Apr. 1862; transferred to 1st SS Battalion, 23 July 1862; absent on special service in the ordnance dept. since 18 Mar (MRs, 31 Aug. 1862 to 31 Dec. 1863); absent in the ordnance department in Macon, 29 Feb. 1864; received as a prisoner at Louisville, Ky., 1 Apr. 1864; present at Macon Arsenal, June 1864; took oath of allegiance at Chattanooga, 22 Aug. 1864; deserted to the enemy, (MR, 31 Aug. 1864); captured at Philadelphia, Pa. [sic], took oath of allegiance, 26 Sep. 1864; complexion light, hair dark, eyes blue, height 5 ft. 11 in. [Record refers to the personal papers of R.M. Cuyler].

Sheppard, Green, Private, C Company: enlisted for 3 years 6 Feb. 1863 in Dooly County; died in field hospital at Chickamauga, 19 or 23 Sep. 1863; 36-year-old farmer in the Dooly County 1860 census.

Sikes, William A[shley], Private, A Company: enlisted for 1 year 14 Aug. 1861 at Savannah in F Company (Altamaha Scouts, Liberty County), 25th Georgia; transferred to 1st SS Battalion, 30 July 1862; appears as 4th Corporal ranking from 29 Aug. 1862; appears as 4th Sergeant ranking from 1 May 1863; reenlisted for the war, 16 Feb. 1864; appears as Private, 31 Aug. 1864; reported at Savannah as a rebel deserter, 25 Apr. 1865; residence Savannah, age 23, complexion dark, hair dark, eyes gray, height 5 ft. 6 in.

Simmons, R[ichard] E., Private, A Company: enlisted for 1 year 14 Aug. 1861 at Savannah in F Company (Altamaha Scouts, Liberty County), 25th Georgia; transferred to 1st SS Battalion, 30 July 1862; absent sick in Savannah, 31 Aug. 1862; absent sick at Springfield, 30 Sep. 1862; transferred back to 25th Georgia, 21 Oct. 1862.

Simmons, William, Private, C Company: enlisted 17 Oct. 1861 as Private in C Company, 1st Battalion, GST; mustered out, Apr. 1862; enlisted for 3 years 25 Apr. 1862 at Macon in D Company (Screven County), 54th Georgia; transferred to 1st SS Battalion, 30 July 1862; under age, discharged by civil authority, Feb. 20, 1863; born Screven County, 10 Feb. 1827 [sic], died there 1904.

Simpson, R[ichard] M. [R.N.], Corporal, Sergeant, D Company: enlisted for 3 years 29 Sep. 1861 at Thomasville in H Company (Thomas County Volunteers), 29th Georgia; transferred to 1st SS Battalion as 2nd Corporal, 1 Aug. 1862; appears as 3rd Sergeant, 28 Feb. 1863; absent sick at Canton, Miss. from 19 June 1863; absent sick in hospital in Atlanta, 31 Oct. 1863; reenlisted for the war, 16 Feb. 1864; granted 60 days furlough from Floyd House & Ocmulgee Hospitals for chronic diarrhea, 23 May 1864; killed at Jonesboro, 31 Aug. 1864; post office Camilla.

Smith, A[llen] D., Private, D Company: enlisted for the war 9 May 9, 1862 in Screven County in H Company (Thomas County Volunteers), 29th Georgia; transferred to 1st SS Battalion, 1 Aug. 1862; assigned as quartermaster department teamster, 30 Sep. 1862; absent on special service in Yazoo City from 13 June 13 1863; absent sick, 31 Dec. 1863 and 29 Feb. 1864; absent without leave, 31 Aug. 1864; home on sick furlough at end of war.

Smith, A.N., Private, B Company: conscripted for the war 8 Aug. 1862 at Camp Randolph in Gordon County; transferred to 1st SS Battalion Aug. 1862; wounded, Jackson, Miss., July 1863; patient from 13 July 1863 at French's Division Hospital, Lauderdale, Miss.; absent, wounded at Jackson, Miss., 31 Dec. 1863; determined unfit for past 60 days due to fracture of the right ulna with great loss of tissue rendering the limb entirely useless, Institute Hospital, Atlanta, 12 Feb. 1864; received payment as discharged soldier, 22 Feb. 1864; absent sick in General Hospital, 29 Feb. 1864; absent wounded, 31 Aug. 1864; born Fayette County, age 27, complexion dark, hair black, eyes gray, height 5 ft. 9 in., occupation farmer.

Smith, J[oseph B.], Corporal, Sergeant, D Company: enlisted for the war 1 May 1862 in Chatham County in I Company (Clayton Invincibles, Clayton County), 30th Georgia; transferred to 1st SS Battalion as 1st Corporal, 1 Aug. 1862; appears as Sergeant, 31 Oct. 1862; killed by the explosion of a shell at Genesis Point, 12 Feb. 1863; age 22, complexion fair, eyes blue, hair light, height 5 ft. 7 in., occupation mason.

Smith, J.H.G., Private, D Company: enlisted for the war 9 May 1863 in Savannah in place of Elmer Friend; present sick, 30 June 1863; admitted as patient to 1st C.S.A. Hospital, Jackson, Miss., 13 July 1863, transferred to General Hospital, 14 July; absent sick, 31 Oct., 31 Dec. 1863 and 29 Feb. 1864.

Smith, John M., Corporal, C Company: enlisted in C Company, 6th Regiment, GST; mustered out, Apr. 1862; enlisted for 3 years 18 Apr. 1862 at Savannah in A Company (Jasper and Jones Counties), 32nd Georgia; transferred to 1st SS Battalion as 1st Corporal, 30 July 1862; absent on sick furlough, 30 Sep. 1862; drew clothing at Nott General Hospital, Mobile, Ala., 29 July 1863; absent sick in Jasper County, 31 Dec. 1863 and 29 Feb. 1864; present at Gilmer Hospital, Atlanta, 30 June 1864; absent sick in Forsyth, 31 Aug. 1864.

Smith, Nathan, Private, B Company: conscripted for the war 13 Aug. 1862 at Camp Randolph in Gordon County; transferred to 1st SS Battalion Aug. 1862; died of congestion at Camp Anderson, 14 Oct. 1862.

Smith, R.A., Private, B Company: conscripted for the war 13 Aug. 1862 at Camp Randolph in Gordon County; transferred to 1st SS Battalion Aug. 1862; furloughed for 29 days from 22 Sep. 1862 to go to Greene County; supplied Patrick Tarney as substitute.

Smith, Walker, Private, B Company: enlisted for the war 1 May 1863 at Savannah; joined by transfer from C.S. Navy; wounded, north Georgia, 16 May–6 June 1864; absent wounded, 31 Aug. 1864; discharged as Corporal with amputated left thigh resulting from gun shot wound, 7 Dec. 1864; born Jasper County, age 22, complexion fair, hair light, eyes gray, height 5 ft. 6 in., occupation farmer, post office Forsyth.
[another Walker Smith or the same man: enlisted 5 May 1862 in A Company (Jasper and Jones Counties), 32nd Georgia; wounded, leg amputated, 1863.]

Spears [Spear], William J., Private, C Company: enlisted as Private in C Company, 5th Regiment, GST, 16 Oct. 1861; mustered out Apr. 1862; enlisted for 3 years 16 Apr. 1862 at Savannah in F Company (Jeff Davis Guards, Clay County), 32nd Georgia; transferred to 1st SS Battalion, 30 July 1862; deserted 27 Sep. 1862; born in Henry County, Ala., age 31, light complexion, dark hair, dark eyes, height 5 ft. 10 in., residence in Randolph County, Ga.

Spell, James M., Private, B Company: conscripted for the war 11 Aug. 1862 at Camp Randolph in Gordon County; transferred to 1st SS Battalion Aug. 1862; absent sick in Ware County from 9 Oct. 1862 to 29 Feb. 1864; absent sick, 31 Aug. 1864.

Stackfleth, Julius, Corporal, Private, B/C Company: enlisted for the war 7 June 1861 at Fort Savannah in DeKalb Rifles (A Company, 1st (Olmstead's) Georgia); transferred to 1st SS Battalion, 23 July 1862; transferred from B Company to C Company as Private, 17 Aug. 1862; absent at General Hospital in Savannah, 30 Sep. 1862; on extra duty as company cook, 31 Dec. 1863; absent sick in Dalton, 29 Feb. 1864; captured at Marietta, 16 June 1864; received at Camp Morton, Ind., 26 June 1864; absent in the hands of the enemy, 31 Aug. 1864; released on oath of allegiance, 10 June 1865; residence Chatham County, complexion light, hair sandy, eyes blue, height 5 ft. 10 3/4 in.; born Hanover, Germany, 30-year-old hotel clerk in the Chatham County 1860 census.

Stancel, Henry J. [M.J.], Private, C Company: enlisted for 3 years 6 Feb. 1863 in Dooly County; wounded, Jackson, Miss., July 1863; absent sick in Atlanta, 31 Dec. 1863; absent sick in Dalton, 29 Feb. 1864; patient at Blackie Hospital, Madison, Ga., 29 Feb. 1864; absent, 31 Aug. 1864; 37-year-old farmer in the Dooly County 1860 census.

Stanfield, J[ohn], Private, C Company: enlisted 6 Feb. 1863 at Doctor Town; wounded, north Georgia, 16 May–6 June 1864; absent wounded, 31 Aug. 1864; name appears on no other muster rolls.

Stephan, William, Private, Sergeant, B Company: enlisted for the war 7 June 1861 at Savannah in DeKalb Rifles (A Company, 1st (Olmstead's) Georgia); receipts for pay as Commissary Sergeant at Genesis Point, Feb. and Mar. 1862; transferred to 1st SS Battalion, 23 July 1862; appears as 3rd Sergeant, 31 Aug. 1862; absent sick in General Hospital, 31 Dec. 1863; appears as Commissary Sergeant, 29 Feb. 1864; appears as 2nd Sergeant and Commissary Sergeant, 31 Aug. 1864.
[Included with this file]
Stevens, William P., Private, A Company, 1st Georgia Battalion, captured, Macon, 20/21 Apr. 1865.

Stephens, John C., Private, B Company: conscripted for the war 13 Aug. 1862 at Camp Randolph in Gordon County; transferred to 1st SS Battalion Aug. 1862; received blanket at Empire Hospital, Atlanta, 26 Sep. 1863; absent sick in General Hospital, 31 Dec. 1863; patient at General Hospital No. 1, Savannah, 31 Dec. 1863; captured at Nashville, 16 Dec. 1864; received at Camp Chase, Ill., 4 Jan. 1865; released on oath of allegiance, 15 May 1865; residence Chatham County, complexion dark, hair black, eyes dark, height 5 ft. 9 1/2 in., age 28.

Stephens, Jonas, Private, B Company: conscripted for the war 13 Aug. 1862 at Camp Randolph in Gordon County; transferred to 1st SS Battalion Aug. 1862; absent on furlough, 28 Oct. to 3 Nov. 1862; detailed as company cook, 31 Dec. 1862 to 30 June 1863; present sick in camp, 31 Dec. 1863; absent sick in General Hospital, 29 Feb. 1864; absent sick, 31 Aug. 1864.

Stewart, Franklin M., Private, B Company: enlisted for 12 months 19 Aug. 1861 at Fort McAllister in DeKalb Rifles (A Company, 1st (Olmstead's) Georgia); transferred to 1st SS Battalion, 23 July 1862; discharged for under age, 27 Nov. 1862; age 17, complexion light, hair yellow, eyes blue, height 5 ft. 6 1/2 in. [place of birth too faint to read, possibly Clarke County].

Stewart, J[ames] R., Private, D Company: enlisted for 12 months 25 Sep. 1861 in Campbell County in F Company (Campbell Sharpshooters, Campbell County), 30th Georgia; transferred to 1st SS Battalion, Aug. 1862; absent sick in General Hospital, 28 Feb. 1863; killed at Chickamauga, 20 Sep. 1863; age 18, complexion fair, eyes blue, hair light, height 5 ft. 8 in., occupation farmer, born Campbell County.

Stiles, Edward, Private, C Company: enlisted for 3 years 12 Feb. 1863 in Dooly County; deserted, 30 June 1863.

Stilwell, Columbus [Fin], Private, C Company: enlisted for 3 years 6 May 1862 in Savannah in I Company (Woodson Guards, Upson County), 32nd Georgia; transferred to 1st SS Battalion, 20 July 1862; name appears on voucher, 4 Mar. 1864; killed in action at Resaca or Calhoun, Ga., 14 or 16 May 1864.

Stokes, Edward, Private, C Company: enlisted for 3 years 20 Feb. 1863 in Dooly County; wounded, north Georgia, 7-30 June 1864; absent wounded, 31 Aug. 1864; 35-year-old farmer in the Dooly County 1860 census.

Stone, J.R., Private, B Company: conscripted for the war 25 July 1862 at Camp Randolph in Gordon County; transferred to 1st SS Battalion Aug. 1862; died of pneumonia at Yazoo City, Miss., 18 or 23 June 1863.

Sutton, Jasper N., Private, C Company: enlisted for 3 years 6 Feb. 1863 in Dooly County; absent sick in hospital in Canton, Miss., 30 June 1863; wounded at Chickamauga, Sep. 1863; absent sick in Atlanta, 31 Dec. 1863; died in Dooly County, 30 Jan. 1864; 30-year-old farmer in the Dooly County 1860 census.

Swindle, G[eorge] W., Private, A Company: enlisted for 1 year 14 Aug. 1861 in Savannah in F Company (Altamaha Scouts, Liberty County), 25th Georgia; transferred to 1st SS Battalion, 1 Nov. [sic] 1862; absent sick at Springfield, 30 Sep. 1862; absent sick at Yazoo City, 30 June 1863; absent without leave, 17 Feb. 1864; died in Liberty County, Feb. 1864; not on MR for Aug. and Oct. 1862].

Swindle, John J., Private, A Company: enlisted for 1 year 26 Oct. 1861 at Tybee Island in I Company F Company (Altamaha Scouts, Liberty County), 25th Georgia; transferred to 1st SS Battalion, 30 July 1862; absent sick in Savannah, 31 Aug. 1862; absent sick in Springfield, 30 Sep. 1862; absent sick in hospital, 31 Oct. and 31 Dec. 1862; present sick, 30 June 1863; died of fever in hospital in Miss., Sep. 1863.

Swords, Henry, Private, A Company: enlisted for 3 years or the war 22 Sep. 1862 at Waynesville; transferred from the Mercer Partizans, Capt. Hopkins, by Spec. Order No. 47, District of Georgia, Jan. 1863; deserted from Capt. Hopkins, 9 Oct. 1862, arrested 24 Jan. 1863; wounded at Chickamauga, Sep. 1863; absent sick in Dover, Ga., 31 Dec. 1863; reenlisted for the war, 29 Feb. 1864.

Tanner, A[sberry] C., Private, A Company: enlisted for 3 years or the war 29 Apr. 1862 at Causton's Bluff in F Company (Appling Rangers, Appling County), 11th Georgia Battalion; converted to 47th Georgia Regiment, 12 May 1862; transferred to 1st SS Battalion 30 July 1862; absent without leave, 31 Aug. 1862; present sick in quarters, 31 Dec. 1862; absent without leave, 30 Apr. 1863; deserted at Savannah on 8 Apr. (MR, 30 June 1863); returned from absence, 1 Jan. 1864; reenlisted for the war, 29 Feb. 1864; absent sick in General Hospital, 31 Aug. 1864; age 28, complexion dark, eyes dark, hair dark, height 5 ft. 10 in.
[another record, possibly the same man: Tanner, O.B., Private, A Company: absent without leave on regimental return for 30 Sep. 1862; name appears on no muster roll.]

Tanner, Green, Private, A Company: enlisted for 3 years or the war 4 Mar. 1862 at Homersville or in Coffee County in F Company (Appling Rangers, Appling County), 11th Georgia Battalion; converted to 47th Georgia Regiment, 12 May 1862; transferred to 1st SS Battalion 30 July 1862; absent sick in Savannah, 31 Aug. 1862; absent sick at Springfield, 31 Oct. 1862 to 28 Feb. 1863; deserted at Savannah, 4 May 1863; patient at Jackson's Cavalry Division Hospital, Old Marion, Miss., 31 Aug. 1863; absent sick in Savannah, 31 Dec. 1863; absent, furloughed by Medical Board from 1 Feb. to 1 Sep. 1864; complexion light, eyes gray, hair light, born Appling County.

Tanner, Isaiah, Private, A Company: enlisted for 3 years or the war 4 Mar. 1862 at Homersville in F Company (Appling Rangers, Appling County), 11th Georgia Battalion; converted to 47th Georgia Regiment, 12 May 1862; transferred to 1st SS Battalion 30 July 1862; absent without leave, 31 Aug. and 31 Oct. 1862; present sick in quarters, 28 Feb. 1863; absent without leave, 30 Apr. 1863; deserted at Savannah, 8 Apr. or 4 May 1863; killed, north Georgia, 16 May–6 June 1864; age 25, complexion light, eyes gray, hair light, height 5 ft. 11 in., born Appling County.
[another record, possibly the same man: Tanner, W., Private, A Company: absent without leave on regimental return for 30 Sep. 1862; name appears on no muster roll.]

Tarney, Patrick, Private, B Company: enlisted for the war 13 Aug. 1862 in Gordon County as substitute for R.A. Smith; deserted, dropped from the rolls, and claimed as deserter from Montgomery Guards, 16 Oct. 1862.

Taylor, Francis L., Private, A Company: enlisted for 3 years or the war 2 Sep. 1861 in Calhoun County in L Company (Calhoun Repeaters, Calhoun County), 25th Georgia; transferred to 1st SS Battalion, 1 Aug. 1862; reenlisted for the war, 16 Feb. 1864; captured at Nashville, 16 Dec. 1864; received at Camp Chase, Ohio, 6 Jan. 1865; released on oath of allegiance, 12 June 1865; residence Newton County, complexion dark, hair dark, eyes blue, height 5 ft. 9 1/2 in., age 21.

Taylor, J[oseph] F., Private, Corporal, A Company: enlisted for 12 months 8 Aug. 1861 in Henry County, Ala., in Irwin Invincibles; became E Company (Henry Light Infantry), 25th Georgia, Dec. 1861; transferred to 1st SS Battalion, 30 July 1862; absent sick in Savannah, 31 Aug. 1862; absent sick in hospital, 31 Dec. 1862; absent sick in Savannah, 28 Feb. 1863; absent on 30 day sick leave from 16 Apr. 1863; absent sick in Atlanta, 30

June 1863; absent sick in Henry County, 31 Dec. 1863; reenlisted for the war, 16 Feb. 1864; appears as 4th Corporal, present, 31 Aug. 1864; sent from command, 18 Jan. 1865; admitted wounded to Way Hospital, Meridian, Miss., 20 Jan. 1865; admitted for debility to Hood Hospital, Cuthbert, Ga., 26 Jan. 1865; treated and discharged, 12 Feb. 1865; occupation farmer.

Taylor, Moses C., Private, C Company: enlisted for 3 years 6 May 1862 at Savannah in I Company (Woodson Guards, Upson County), 32nd Georgia; transferred to 1st SS Battalion, 30 July 1862; absent without leave, 31 Dec. 1863; deserted at West Point, Ga., 27 Aug. 1863, while en route from Morton, Miss., to Tenn. (MR, 29 Feb. 29, 1864); paroled at Griffin, Ga., 1865; born 14 Nov. 1839, died Carthage, Tex., 4 Jan. 1926.

Tharpe [Thorp], Benjamin A., Private, A Company: enlisted for 12 months 8 Aug. 1861 in Henry County, Ala., in Irwin Invincibles; became E Company (Henry Light Infantry), 25th Georgia, Dec. 1861; transferred to 1st SS Battalion, 30 July 1862; wounded at Chickamauga, Sep. 1863; admitted wounded to Floyd House & Ocmulgee Hospitals, Macon, 27 Sep. 1863, released on 30 days furlough, 28 Sep.; absent sick in Henry County, Ala., 31 Dec. 1863; absent on sick furlough from hospital in Columbus to 29 Feb. 1864, and for 30 days from 11 Mar. 1864; absent sick in General Hospital in Columbus, 31 Aug. 1864; captured at Nashville, 16 Dec. 1864; received at Camp Chase, Ill., 6 Jan. 1865; released on oath of allegiance, 12 June 1865; residence Muscogee County, complexion dark, hair dark, eyes hazel, height 5 ft. 10 in., age 28; 20-year-old farmer in the Henry County, Ala., 1860 census.

Thomas, James A., Private, B Company: enlisted for the war 30 Apr. 1862 at Fort McAllister in DeKalb Rifles (A Company, 1st (Olmstead's) Georgia); transferred to 1st SS Battalion, 23 July 1862; discharged by civil court, 3 Dec. 1862.

Thomas, James M., Private, B Company: conscripted for the war 13 Aug. 1862 at Camp Randolph in Gordon County; transferred to 1st SS Battalion Aug. 1862; deserted at Savannah, 5 May 1863; paroled at Thomasville, Ga., 23 May 1865; age 33, complexion light, eyes blue, hair light, height 5 ft. 5 1/2 in., born in Ware County.

Thomas, W[illiam] L[awrence], Private, D Company: enlisted for 12 months 25 Sep. 1861 in Clayton County in I Company (Clayton Invincibles, Clayton County), 30th Georgia; transferred to 1st SS Battalion, 1 Aug. 1862; patient with intermittent fever in General Hospital No. 1, Savannah, 5 May 1863, transferred to General Hospital, Whitesville; absent sick in Selma, Ala., from 3 May 1863; reenlisted for the war 16 Feb. 1864; wounded, Lost Mountain, about 17 June 1864; paid at Macon, Ga., 18 July 1864; age 20, complexion dark, eyes black, hair black, height 5 ft. 9 in., occupation farmer; born 10 June 1842, Spalding County; occupation, mill hand; postwar grocer; died 1912, Experiment, Ga.

Thomas, W[illiam] R., Private, D Company: enlisted for 12 months 25 Sep. 1861 in Clayton County in I Company (Clayton Invincibles, Clayton County), 30th Georgia; transferred to 1st SS Battalion, 1 Aug. 1862; absent sick in Savannah Medical Hospital, 28 Feb. 1863; reenlisted for the war, 16 Feb. 1864; captured at Nashville, 16 Dec. 1864;

received at Camp Douglas, Ill., 24 Dec. 1864; mustered into 6th U.S. Volunteers, 25 Mar. 1865; age 18, complexion fair, eyes blue, hair light, height 5 ft. 9 in., occupation mechanic, born Meriwether County.

Thompson, W. H., Private, D Company: enlisted for 3 years 10 Dec. 1861 at Cass Station in A Company (Gordon County), 8th Georgia Battalion; transferred to 1st SS Battalion; died of typhoid fever at Camp Anderson, 5 Oct. 1862.

Thornton, James A., Sergeant, C Company: enlisted 3 Oct. 1861 as 2nd Corporal in A Company, 1st Regiment, GST; mustered out Apr. 1862; enlisted for 3 years 18 Apr. 1862 at Savannah in K Company (Appling County), 54th Georgia; transferred to 1st SS Battalion; appointed 4th Sergeant from 17 Aug. 1862; absent sick in General Hospital in Savannah, appears as 3rd Sergeant, 31 Oct. 1862; wounded and disabled at Chickamauga, 19 Sep. 1863; absent sick in Appling County, 31 Dec. 1863 and 29 Feb. 1864; retired to Invalid Corps as Private, 13 Apr. 1864; absent wounded in Appling County, 31 Aug. 1864; surrendered at Tallahassee, 10 May 1865; paroled, 15 May; 23 years old in the Appling County 1860 census; postwar Baptist preacher; born Appling County, 9 June 1840, died Ware County, Ga., 28 June 1900.

Thornton, Jonathan [John C.], Private, Corporal, C Company: enlisted 3 Oct. 1861 as 1st Corporal in A Company, 1st Regiment, GST; mustered out Apr. 1862; enlisted for 3 years 18 Apr. 1862 at Savannah in K Company (Appling County), 54th Georgia; transferred to 1st SS Battalion, 30 July 1862; appears as Corporal, 28 Feb. 1863; appears as 3rd Corporal, 30 June 1863; wounded at Chickamauga, Sep. 1863; absent sick in Appling County, appears as 2nd Corporal, 31 Dec. 1863 and 29 Feb. 1864; wounded, Resaca or Calhoun, Ga., 14 or 16 May, 1864; does not appear on 31 Aug. 1864 MR; [file indicates existence of prisoner of war record but it is not copied]; 21-year-old laborer in the Wayne County 1860 census; born Appling County, 1839.

Thornton, Timothy, Sergeant, Private, C Company: enlisted 3 Oct. 1861 as 3rd Corporal, A Company, 1st Regiment, GST; mustered out Apr. 1862; enlisted for 3 years 21 Apr. 1862 in Savannah in B Company (Appling County), 54th Georgia; transferred to 1st SS Battalion as 5th Sergeant, 30 July 1862; appears as Private, 31 Oct. 1862; drew clothing at Macon by voucher, 23 Aug. 1864; absent in the hands of the enemy, 31 Aug. 1864; captured at Jonesboro, 1 Sep. 1864; exchanged at Rough and Ready, Ga., 19 or 23 Sep. 1864; 19-year-old laborer in the Wayne County 1860 census; born Appling County, 1841.

Thornton, William, Private, Corporal, C Company: enlisted 10 Oct. 1861 as Private, K Company, 2nd Regiment, GST; mustered out Apr. 1862; enlisted for 3 years 21 Apr. 1862 in Savannah in B Company (Appling County), 54th Georgia; transferred to 1st SS Battalion, 31 July 1862; present sick in hospital, 31 Dec. 1862; absent sick in Whitesville, 31 Dec. 1863; absent sick in Selma, Ala., 29 Feb. 1864; absent in the hands of the enemy, 31 Aug. 1864; captured at Jonesboro, 1 Sep. 1864; exchanged at Rough and Ready, Ga., 19 or 23 Sep. 1864; paroled as Corporal at Thomasville, 21 May 1865; 16 years old in the Appling County 1860 census.

Tidwell, Thomas J., Private, D Company: enlisted for 12 months 25 Sep. 1861 in Campbell County in F Company (Campbell Sharpshooters, Campbell County), 30th Georgia; transferred to 1st SS Battalion, 1 Aug. 1862; never reported; name appears on a descriptive list of transfers from 30th Georgia; appears as 2nd Corporal, 31 Dec. 1862; age 19, complexion fair, eyes fair, hair dark, height 5 ft. 10 in., born Meriwether County.

Touchstone, Stephen [M.], Private, D Company: enlisted for 12 months 25 Sep. 1861 at Stockton, Ga. in E Company (Alapaha Guards, Clinch County), 29th Georgia; transferred to 1st SS Battalion, 1 Aug. 1862; reenlisted for the war, 16 Feb. 1864; wounded, Kennesaw Mountain, 27 June 1864; absent wounded, 31 Aug. 1864; paroled at Thomasville, 10 May 1865; complexion dark, hair dark, eyes dark, height 5 ft. 9 in.; born Lowndes County, 3 Jan. 1840.

Triay, John, Private, A Company: enlisted for 1 year Aug. 6, 1861 at Savannah; transferred to 1st SS Battalion from D Company (City Light Guards), 1st (Olmstead's) Georgia; absent sick in Savannah, Aug. 31, 1862; present in confinement, Oct. 31, 1862; captured at Jackson or Clinton, Miss., July 7 or 10, 1863; received at Camp Morton, Ind., Aug. 8, 1863; enlisted in 7th Indiana Cavalry, Aug. 1863; absent without leave, Dec. 31, 1863; deserted, Feb. 29, 1864.

Turner, Henry, Private, B Company: conscripted for the war 9 Aug. 1862 at Camp Randolph in Gordon County; transferred to 1st SS Battalion Aug. 1862; absent on furlough, 29 Feb. 1864; present, 31 Aug. 1864.

Tuten, Hardy P., Private, B Company: enlisted for the war 27 Feb. 1862 at Fort McAllister in DeKalb Rifles (A Company, 1st (Olmstead's) Georgia); transferred to 1st SS Battalion, 23 July 1862; furnished Joseph M. Tuten as substitute, 30 Sep. 1862; born S.C., 37-year-old farmer in the Pierce County 1860 census; died in Appling County 5 Nov. 1863, age 40.

Tuten, Joseph M., Private, B Company: enlisted as a substitute for Hardy P. Tuten (MR, 31 Oct. 1862); discharged on certificate of disability, 10 May 1863; rejoined after being dropped from the roll in error, 29 Feb. 1864; captured at Marietta, 5 July 1864; received at Camp Douglas, Ill., 28 July 1864; absent sick (MR, 31 Aug. 1864); died of diarrhea, 1 May 1865; buried in Block 3, Chicago City Cemetery; 43-year-old farmer in the Ware County 1860 census.

Tuten, William S., Private, B Company: enlisted for the war 15 Sep. 1861 at Fort McAllister in DeKalb Rifles (A Company, 1st (Olmstead's) Georgia); transferred to 1st SS Battalion, 23 July 1862; died at Whitesville Hospital, 30 Oct. 1863; claim for final pay made by Anna Guest of Pierce County, mother by her former marriage, 9 May 1864; 26-year-old farmer in the Appling County 1860 census.

Twyman, H[orace].D., 1st Lieutenant, Captain, A Company: resigned from West Point, Apr. 1861; commissioned as Lieutenant in Virginia State Forces, 4 May 1861; applied from Richmond, Va., for C.S.A. position, 18 July 1861, age 21, resident of Madison County, Va.; appointed 2nd Lieutenant, C.S.A., 5 Sep. 1861 to rank from 16 Mar. 1861;

assigned as ordnance officer, advanced batteries, defenses of Savannah, Jan. 1862; transferred to Major Anderson's command, 19 July, joined 1 Aug. 1862; appointed 1st Lieutenant, 4 Oct. 1862 to rank from 12 July 1862; present sick in quarters, 31 Dec. 1862; assigned as Captain, 28 Apr. 1863; signs roll as 1st Lieutenant commanding, 30 Apr. 1863; granted leave by Spec. Order No. 5/18, Army of Tennessee, 29 July 1863; wounded at Chickamauga, Sep. 1863; appointed Captain, 3 Nov. 1863 to rank from 20 Jan. 1863; absent, detailed as inspector on Gen. Walker's staff, 31 Dec. 1863; granted 20 days leave as AAG, Walker's division by Spec. Order No. 27, Army of Tennessee, 27 Jan. 1864; signed voucher as company commander, 16 Apr. 1864; wounded, Calhoun, Ga., 16 May, 1864; paid at Fair Grounds Hospital, Atlanta, 2 July 1864; absent on sick leave to 1 Sep. 1864; appears on inspection report of 17 Sep. 1864 as absent wounded from 18 May; admitted to General Receiving Hospital (Charity Hospital), Gordonsville, Va., week of 7 Dec. 1864; surrendered at Greensboro, N.C. as Captain commanding E Company, 1st Confederate Georgia Battalion, 26 Apr. 1865; 19 years old in the Madison County, Va., 1860 census.

Underwood, G.C., Private, B Company: conscripted for the war 13 Aug. 1862 at Camp Randolph in Gordon County; transferred to 1st SS Battalion Aug. 1862; wounded at Chickamauga, Sep. 1863; absent sick in General Hospital, 31 Dec. 1863; present sick, 29 Feb. 1864; present, detailed as ambulance driver, 31 Aug. 1864.

Underwood, Gustavus A., Private: A Company, enlisted for 3 years 23 June 1862 in Glascock County in H Company, 54th Georgia; transferred to 1st SS Battalion; absent without leave, 31 Dec. 1863; deserted 8 July 1863 at Clinton, Miss. (MR, 29 Feb. 1864); not on muster roll for 31 Aug. 1864.

Underwood, James D., Private, B Company: enlisted for the war 14 Aug. 1861 at Fort McAllister in DeKalb Rifles (A Company, 1st (Olmstead's) Georgia); transferred to 1st SS Battalion, 23 July 1862; absent on detached service pursuing deserters, 31 Dec. 1862; wounded at Chickamauga, Sep. 1863; died at LaGrange Hospital, 31 Dec. 1863; born Camden County, 20-year-old railroad clerk in Chatham County 1860 census.

Vanzant, Daniel, Private, B Company: conscripted for the war 27 July 1862 at Camp Randolph in Gordon County; transferred to 1st SS Battalion Aug. 1862; died of typhoid fever in General Hospital in Savannah, 10 Sep. 1862.

Voluntine, Lewis (Valentine, William Lewis), Private, C Company: enlisted for 3 years 17 Aug. 1862 at Savannah; present sick in hospital in camp. 31 Oct. 1862; absent on sick furlough, 31 Dec. 1862; admitted 10 July 1863 to French's Division Hospital, Lauderdale, Miss.; captured in Atlanta, 22 or 23 July 1864; received at Camp Chase, Ohio, 2 Aug. 1864; absent in the hands of the enemy, 31 Aug. 1864; transferred to City Point, Va., for exchange, 4 Mar. 1865, died there before being exchanged; born New York; 14 years old in the Green County 1850 census.

Walker, Benjamin F., Sergeant, D Company: enlisted for 12 months 8 Oct. 1861 at Camp Black in A Company (Gordon County), 8th Georgia Battalion; transferred to 1st SS Battalion; appears as 4th Sergeant, 31 Aug. 1862; present sick, appears as 2nd Sergeant,

30 June 1863; absent in hospital in Atlanta, 31 Oct. 1863; reenlisted for the war, 16 Feb. 1864; received pay at Macon, 18 July 1864; absent in the hands of the enemy since 22 July at Decatur, appears as 1st Sergeant (MR, 31 Aug. 1864); received at Camp Chase, Ohio, 2 Aug. 1864; patient with variola at U.S. Army General Hospital, Camp Chase, vaccinated and returned to duty, 15 Oct. 1864; died of pneumonia, 15 Feb. 1865; transferred to City Point, Va., for exchange, 4 Mar. 1865.

Walker, M[arion] D., Private, D Company: enlisted for 3 years 5 Oct. 1861 at Camp Black in B Company (Littlefield Volunteers, Gordon County), 8th Georgia Battalion; transferred to 1st SS Battalion; present sick in hospital, 28 Feb. 1863; absent without leave, 31 Oct. 1863; absent sick, 31 Dec. 1863; deserted 27 Aug. 1863 on the march from Miss. (MR, 29 Feb. 1864); absent in the hands of the enemy since 25 or 27 Nov. 1863, captured at Missionary Ridge (MR, 31 Aug. 1864); received at Rock Island, Ill., 11 Dec. 1863; volunteered for frontier service in the U.S. Army, Oct. 1864; 18-year-old farm laborer in the Gordon County 1860 census.

Walker, Mitchell, Private, B Company: enlisted for the war 30 Apr. 1862 at Fort McAllister in DeKalb Rifles (A Company, 1st (Olmstead's) Georgia); transferred to 1st SS Battalion, 23 July 1862; absent, sent home on sick leave, 31 Aug. 1862; absent sick in Pierce County from 15 Aug. 1862; discharged on certificate of disability, 31 Dec. 1862; born Pierce County, age 21, complexion sallow, hair brown, eyes blue, occupation farmer; paralysis of the lower extremities, lost the use of his lower limbs.

Ward, James, Private, B Company: enlisted for the war 19 Aug. 1861 at Fort McAllister in DeKalb Rifles (A Company, 1st (Olmstead's) Georgia); transferred to 1st SS Battalion, 23 July 1862; absent without leave, 31 Aug. 1862; present, detailed as hospital orderly, 31 Aug. 1864.

Warren, Reuben, Private, C Company: enlisted 3 Oct. 1861 as Private in A Company, 1st Regiment, GST; mustered out Apr. 1862; enlisted for 3 years 18 Apr. 1862 at Savannah in K Company (Appling County), 54th Georgia; transferred to 1st SS Battalion 1 Aug. 1862; absent without leave, 31 Aug. 1862; absent sick at General Hospital in Savannah, 30 Sep. 1862; absent sick at home in Pierce County, 31 Oct. 1862; cook since 12 July at French's Division Hospital, Lauderdale, Miss., 31 July 1863; patient since 10 Aug. at French's Division Hospital, 31 Aug. 1863; admitted with dysentery to Floyd House and Ocmulgee Hospitals, Macon, 25 Sep. returned to duty, 30 Sep. 1863, post office, Patterson, Ga.; absent sick in Atlanta, 31 Dec. 1863; absent sick, 31 Aug. 1864; captured at Nashville, 16 Dec. 1864; took oath of allegiance at Camp Chase, Ohio, 15 May 1865; complexion dark, hair black, eyes black, height 6 ft. 2 1/2 in., age 22.
[other records, probably all the same man:
Rueben, W., Private, C Company: absent with leave since 25 Aug. on regimental return for 31 Aug. 1862; name appears on no muster roll.
Ward, Reuben A., Private, C Company: captured, 10 Dec. 1864; no other record.
Ward, Warren, Private, C Company: captured, 16 Dec. 1864; received at Camp Chase, Ohio, 6 Jan. 1865; no other record.]

Warren, W[illiam] D., Private, D Company: enlisted for 3 years 12 Nov. 1861 in Quitman County in H Company (Thomas County Volunteers), 29th Georgia; transferred to 1st SS Battalion, 1 Aug. 1862; absent sick in General Hospital, 28 Feb. 1863; transferred from General Hospital No. 1, Savannah, to Macon with fractured fibula, 28 Feb. 1863; absent sick at Jackson, Miss., since 30 June 1863; wounded at Chickamauga, Sep. 1863; patient at Frank Ramsey Hospital, Cassville, 31 Dec. 1863; absent sick, 31 Dec. 1863 and 29 Feb. 1864; wounded, Resaca or Calhoun, Ga., 14 or 16 May, 1864; absent wounded, 31 Aug. 1864.

Wasden [Wasdin], John, Private, B Company: enlisted for the war 15 Aug. 1861 at Fort McAllister in DeKalb Rifles (A Company, 1st (Olmstead's) Georgia); transferred to 1st SS Battalion, 23 July 1862; absent on sick furlough, 31 Oct. 1862; absent, wounded at Chickamauga, 31 Dec. 1863; absent wounded in Pierce County, 29 Feb. 1864; absent in the hands of the enemy, captured 1 Sep. 1864; exchanged at Rough and Ready, Ga., 19 or 22 Sep. 1864; paroled at Thomasville, 18 May 1865; complexion dark, hair dark, eyes gray, height 5 ft. 7 1/2 in.; 17 years old in Pierce County 1860 census; a farmer, died of Bright's disease, 13 Mar. 1903.

Waters, G.B., Private, D Company: enlisted for the war, 24 Apr. 1863 at Savannah; absent without leave, 30 Apr. 1863; deserted from Camp Jordan, 1 May 1863; dropped from the roll, 10 June 1863.

Waters [Watters], Jude [Judge] B., Private, Corporal, A Company: enlisted for 12 months 8 Aug. 1861 at Savannah in G Company (Brown Light Infantry, Screven County), 25th Georgia; transferred to 1st SS Battalion, 1 Aug. 1862; reenlisted for the war, 16 Feb. 1864; appears as 3rd Corporal, 29 Feb. 1864; appears as 1st Corporal, 31 Aug. 1864; captured at Nashville, 16 Dec. 1864; received at Camp Chase, 6 Jan. 1865; enlisted in U.S. Army; transferred to Chicago, 20 Mar. 1865.

Waters, O[swald] B., Sergeant, Private, A Company: enlisted for 1 year 17 Aug. 1861 at Savannah in D Company (Ogeechee Rifles, Screven County), 25th Georgia; transferred to 1st SS Battalion as 4th Sergeant, 1 Aug. 1862, reduced to Private, 31 Aug. 1862; provided James Comaskey as substitute and discharged, 6 Oct. 1862.
[another record, possibly the same man: Tanner, O.B., Private, A Company: absent without leave on regimental return for 30 Sep. 1862; name appears on no muster roll.]

Watts, Alfred M., Private, B Company: conscripted for the war 27 July 1862 at Camp Randolph in Gordon County; transferred to 1st SS Battalion, Aug. 1862; detailed to work at Fort Boggs, 28 Feb. 1863; died of debility at Gilmer Hospital, Marietta, 28 Feb. 1864.

Wayne, Robert [Pooler], 2nd Lieutenant, 1st Lieutenant, B Company, Field & Staff: enlisted for 1 year 12 May 1861 in Charleston, in K Company, 2nd South Carolina; 4th Sergeant; discharged 18 Nov. 1861; commissioned 2nd Lieutenant, 11 Nov. 1861 at Fort McAllister in DeKalb Rifles (A Company, 1st (Olmstead's) Georgia); transferred to 1st SS Battalion, 23 July 1862; reappointed 2nd Lieutenant, 4 Oct. 1862 to rank from 5 July 1862; detailed as adjutant, 31 Aug. 1862; promoted 1st Lieutenant and assigned as adjutant, 17 Nov. 1862 with rank from 18 Oct.; additional duty as acting assistant quartermaster by Battalion Spec. Order No. 22, 30 Apr. 1863; wounded at Chickamauga, Sep. 1863; received pay at General Hospital No. 1, Savannah, where receiving treatment for wound at Chickamauga, 31 Dec. 1863; received pay at General Hospital No. 1, Savannah, 12 Feb. 1864; detailed as acting assistant inspector general to General Stevens and signed battalion muster roll, 29 Feb. 1864; recommended for assignment as assistant inspector general with promotion to captain or major, 20 Mar., 15 July 1864; granted 60 days leave, 20 Aug. 1864; absent wounded, 31 Aug. 1864; absent wounded from 15 Aug. by inspection report of 17 Sep. 1864; leave request of 22 Oct. 1864 to go abroad for health approved; acting assistant inspector general to General Jackson, report of 7 Nov. 1864; assigned to temporary duty with Gen. Mercer at Savannah, 16 Dec. 1864; born 1 Mar. 1841, died 4 Feb. 1882 in Laurens County, age 41; 19-year-old clerk in the Chatham County 1860 census.

Wayne, Thomas S[mythe], [Jr.,], Sergeant, 2nd Lieutenant, A/B Company: enlisted 31 May 1861 at Savannah in D Company (1st Republican Blues), 1st (Olmstead's) Georgia; reenlisted for 3 years or the war 12 Apr. 1862 at Savannah in B Company, Savannah Volunteer Guards Battalion; transferred to 1st SS Battalion as 2nd Sergeant, 19 July 1862; present sick in quarters, 28 Feb. 1863; appointed 2nd Lieutenant, B Company, 30 May 1863 to rank from 3 May; absent sick, 31 Dec. 1863; patient at General Hospital No. 1, Savannah, 4 Jan. 1864; granted leave by Spec. Order No. 86/1, Army of Tennessee, 28 Mar. 1864; signed voucher as 2nd Lieutenant commanding company, 31 Mar. 1864; requested for duty at Rose Dew Post, Ga., by Major A.L. Hartridge, 1 Sep. 1864; recommended for promotion to 1st Lieutenant, 9 Sep. 1864; assigned to Rose Dew Post by Spec. Order No. 278/46, Adjutant and Inspector General's Office, 23 Nov. 1864; signed list of absentees and deserters from 27th Georgia Battalion, 14 Feb. 1865; surrendered with 27th Georgia Battalion at Greensboro, N.C., 26 Apr. 1865; born 29 June 1845, died 28 Jan. 1886 in Savannah, age 40; 15 years old in Chatham County 1860 census.

Werm, Lawrence, Private, A Company: enlisted for the war 12 Mar. 1862 at Fort McAllister in DeKalb Rifles (A Company, 1st (Olmstead's) Georgia); transferred to 1st SS Battalion, 23 July 1862; absent on furlough, 31 Dec. 1863; wounded at Jonesboro, 31 Aug. 1864; 35-year-old farmhand in the Chatham County 1860 census, born Saxony, Germany, died 23 May 1881 in Savannah, age 56.

Wetter, Augustus P[eter], Captain, Private, B Company: mustered in 5 June 1861 in Savannah as Captain, DeKalb Rifles; resigned 30 Oct. 1861; enlisted for the war 30 Aug. 1862 at Savannah in 1st SS Battalion; provided Henry Heine as substitute, discharged, 31 Aug. 1862; born Mainz, Germany, 1829; died Harrisburg, Pa., 1882; occupation, architect and merchant in 1860 Savannah city directory; 31-year-old planter in Chatham County 1860 census.

Wheeler, Benjamin [F.], Private, A Company: enlisted for the war 25 Nov. 1862 at Camp Anderson; deserted at Savannah, 4 May 1863; rejoined after 7 months absence without leave, 31 Dec. 1863; reenlisted for the war, 29 Feb. 1864; died of typhoid fever at Fair Grounds Hospital, Atlanta, 8 May 1864; absent sick in General Hospital, 31 Aug. 1864;

age 27, complexion light, eyes light, hair light, height 5 ft. 8 in.; 24 years old in the Appling County 1860 census.

Wheeler, Charles M. [W.], Private, A Company: enlisted for 3 years or the war 29 Apr. 1862 at Causten's Bluff, Ga. in F Company (Appling Rangers, Appling County), 11th Georgia Battalion; converted to 47th Georgia Regiment, 12 May 1862; transferred to 1st SS Battalion 1 Aug. 1862; present sick, 31 Oct. 1862; deserted 4 May 1863; rejoined after 7 months absence without leave, 31 Dec. 1863; reenlisted for the war, 29 Feb. 1864; deserted, 14 June 1864; age 19, complexion light, eyes light, hair light, height 5 ft. 8 in.; 21 years old in the Appling County 1860 census.

Wheeler, George M., Private, A Company: enlisted for 3 years 29 Apr. 1862 at Causten's Bluff, Ga. in F Company (Appling Rangers, Appling County), 11th Georgia Battalion; converted to 47th Georgia Regiment, 12 May 1862; transferred to 1st SS Battalion, 1 Aug. 1862; absent without leave, Aug. 31 and Sep. 30, 1862; no later record.

Wheeler, William, Private, A Company: enlisted for 3 years 22 or 29 Apr. 1862 at Causten's Bluff, Ga. in F Company (Appling Rangers, Appling County), 11th Georgia Battalion; converted to 47th Georgia Regiment, 12 May 1862; transferred to 1st SS Battalion 30 July 1862; absent without leave, 31 Aug. and 30 Sep. 1862; deserted at Savannah, 4 May 1863; rejoined after 7 months absence without leave, 31 Dec. 1863; reenlisted for the war, 29 Feb. 1864; detailed on brigade provost guard and hospital, 31 Aug. 1864; 16 years old in the Appling County 1860 census.

Wilcox, Washington, Private, Corporal, A Company: enlisted for 3 years 1 Apr. 1862 in Henry County, Ala., in E Company (Henry Light Infantry), 25th Georgia; transferred to 1st SS Battalion 30 July 1862; present sick in hospital, 31 Dec. 1862; wounded at Chickamauga, Sep. 1863; absent sick in Henry County, Ala., 31 Dec. 1863; reenlisted for the war, 16 Feb. 1864; absent wounded, 31 Aug. 1864; patient at Lee Hospital, Columbus, Ga., 31 Oct. 1864; petitioned for disability discharge, 16 Jan. 1865; 20-year-old farm laborer in the Henry County, Ala., 1860 census.

Wilkerson [Wilkinson], Thomas, Private, A Company: enlisted for 3 years or the war 14 May 1862 at Camp Deptford in A Company (Irish Jasper Greens), 1st (Olmstead's) Georgia; transferred to 1st SS Battalion; present in arrest, 31 Aug. 1862; transferred to C.S. Navy by special order of the District of Georgia, 30 June 1863; born North Carolina, 32-year-old tinsmith in Chatham County 1860 census.

William, Musician, A Company: enlisted, 1 Aug. 1862; present, 31 Aug. 1862; no later record.

Williams, John, Private, A Company: enlisted for 3 years or the war at Camp Anderson, 1 Oct. 1862; deserted from Camp Anderson, 29 Nov. 1862.

Williams, Luke B., Private, C Company: enlisted for the war 25 May [sic] 1864 at Dalton; wounded, north Georgia, 7-30 June 1864; absent without leave, 31 Aug. 1864;

captured at Nashville, 16 Dec. 1864; received at Camp Chase, Ohio, 6 Jan. 1865; died of pneumonia, 5 Feb. 1865; 14 years old in the Jasper County 1860 census.

Williams, Mathias, Private, B Company: enlisted for the war 14 Aug. 1861 at Fort McAllister in DeKalb Rifles (A Company, 1st (Olmstead's) Georgia); transferred to 1st SS Battalion, 23 July 1862; sent to General Hospital, Savannah, 27 Sep. 1862; detailed on special duty as hospital cook, 30 Apr. and 30 June 1863; captured at Chickamauga, 19 Sep. 1863; received at Camp Morton, Ind., 26 Oct. 1863; absent in the hands of the enemy, 31 Dec. 1863 through 31 Aug. 1864; transferred to Fort Delaware, Del., 19 Mar. 1864; released on oath of allegiance, 10 May 1865; complexion dark, hair black, eyes black, height 5 ft. 9 in.

Williams, Nathan M., Private, C Company: enlisted as Private in C Company, 6th Regiment, GST, 22 Oct. 1861; mustered out Apr. 1862; enlisted for 3 years 18 Apr. 1862 at Savannah in A Company (Jasper and Jones Counties), 32nd Georgia; transferred to 1st SS Battalion, 30 July 1862; present sick in quarters, 28 Feb. 1863; wounded, Resaca or Calhoun, Ga., 14 or 16 May, 1864; absent wounded, 31 Aug. 1864; admitted with gun shot wound to St. Mary's Hospital, West Point, Miss., 12 Jan. 1865; admitted wounded to Way Hospital, Meridian, Miss., 24 Jan. 1865.

Williams, William C., Private, B Company: conscripted for the war 9 Aug. 1862 at Camp Randolph in Gordon County; transferred to 1st SS Battalion Aug. 1862; absent at the convalescent camp in Springfield, 31 Aug. 1862; sent to General Hospital, Savannah, 30 Sep. 1862; absent, sent sick to Canton, Miss., 16 May 1863; admitted Breckinridge's Division Hospital No. 1, Lauderdale Springs, Miss., 4 July 1863; absent sick in General Hospital, 29 Feb. 1864; admitted with chronic diarrhea to Ocmulgee Hospital, Macon, 28 May 1864, granted 60 day furlough, 4 June, readmitted, 4 Aug. 1864, granted 30 day furlough, 13 Aug. 1864; absent sick, 31 Aug. 1864; readmitted, Ocmulgee Hospital, 12 Sep. 1864, transferred to Augusta, 25 Sep.; residence Americus, Sumter County; 30-year-old farmer in the Sumter County 1860 census.

Williams, William S., Corporal, C Company: enlisted as 4th Corporal in C Company, 6th Regiment, GST, 22 Oct. 1861; mustered out Apr. 1862; enlisted for 3 years 18 Apr. 1862 at Savannah in A Company (Jasper and Jones Counties), 32nd Georgia; transferred to 1st SS Battalion, 30 July 1862; 2nd Corporal, 17 Aug. 1862; appears as Private, 31 Oct. 1862; promoted 4th Corporal, 16 Feb. 1863; appears as 3rd Corporal, 31 Dec. 1863; absent sick in Newnan, 29 Feb. 1864; wounded, north Georgia, 16 May–6 June 1864; wounded at Jonesboro, appears as 1st Corporal, 31 Aug. 1864; captured at Nashville, 16 Dec. 1864; received at Camp Chase, Ohio, 4 Jan. 1865; released on oath of allegiance, 12 June 1865; residence Jasper County, complexion dark, hair dark, eyes brown, height 5 ft. 9 in., age 25.

Williamson, J[ohn] S. [or M.], Private, Corporal, D Company: enlisted for 3 years 29 Sep. 1861 in Thomasville in H Company (Thomas County Volunteers), 29th Georgia; transferred to 1st SS Battalion, 1 Aug. 1862; absent sick from 13 June 1863 at Yazoo City; absent without leave, 31 Oct. and 31 Dec. 1863; reenlisted for the war, 16 Feb. 1864; paroled, Talladega, Ala., 28 May, 1865; born N.C., 1828.

Willis, Robert M., Private, B Company: conscripted for the war 13 Aug. 1862 at Camp Randolph in Gordon County; transferred to 1st SS Battalion Aug. 1862; absent at the convalescent camp in Springfield, 31 Aug. 1862; detailed as company cook, 30 Apr. and 30 June 1863; died at Lauderdale Springs, Miss., 22 Aug. 1863.

Wilson, Alex, Private, A Company: enlisted for 3 years or the war 13 Aug. 1862 at Savannah as substitute for Pleasant M. Vickery; deserted from Camp Pemberton, 21 Aug. 1862.

Wilson, Robert, Private, B Company: enlisted for the war 7 June 1861 at Savannah in DeKalb Rifles (A Company, 1st (Olmstead's) Georgia); transferred to 1st SS Battalion, 23 July 1862; sent to General Hospital in Savannah, 3 Sep. 1862; transferred to C.S. Navy by order of Gen. Mercer, 1 May 1863.

Winn [Wince], A[llen] B., Private, D Company: enlisted for 12 months 25 Sep. 1861 in Campbell County in F Company (Campbell Sharpshooters, Campbell County), 30th Georgia; transferred to 1st SS Battalion, 2 Aug. 1862; furlough granted from 22 Sep. to 1 Oct. 1862; absent sick in Yazoo City since 13 June 1863; absent without leave, 31 Oct. and 31 Dec. 1863; deserted 26 Aug. on the march from Mississippi (MR, 29 Feb. 1864).

Winn, A[mos] H[amilton], Private, Corporal, D Company: enlisted for 12 months 25 Sep. 1861 in Campbell County in F Company (Campbell Sharpshooters, Campbell County), 30th Georgia; 4th Ccorporal, 1862; reduced to Private, 1 May 1862; transferred to 1st SS Battalion, 1 Aug. 1862; absent sick in Jackson, 30 June 1863; absent sick, 31 Dec. 1863 and 29 Feb. 1864; absent sick, appears as 2nd Corporal, 31 Aug. 1864; age 21, complexion dark, eyes black, hair black, height 5 ft. 8 in., occupation farmer; born Campbell County, 5 May 1841; died, Confederate Soldiers Home, Atlanta, 26 Dec. 1929.

Winn [Wince], J[ohn] C., Private, D Company: enlisted for 12 months 25 Sep. 1861 in Campbell County in F Company (Campbell Sharpshooters, Campbell County), 30th Georgia; transferred to 1st SS Battalion, 2 Aug. 1862; furlough granted from 22 Sep. to 1 Oct. 1862; absent sick in Canton, Miss., from 24 May 24 1863; attached to hospital as nurse, 1 June 1863; wounded, Jackson, Miss., July 1863; died of typhoid fever in hospital, Marietta, Ga., 19 or 20 Oct. 1863; age 27, complexion dark, eyes black, hair black, height 6 ft., occupation farmer, born Campbell County.

Withrow, John J., Private, A Company: enlisted for 3 years or the war 27 Feb. 1863 in Decatur; transferred from C.S. Navy by special order of the District of Georgia; first appears on muster roll for 30 June 1863; absent without leave, 31 Dec. 1863; deserted, 29 Feb. 1864; born N.C., 23-year-old farm hand in the Fannin County 1860 census.

Withrow, Joshua J., Private, A Company: enlisted for 3 years or the war 17 Feb. 1863 in Decatur; transferred from C.S. Navy by special order of the District of Georgia; first appears on muster roll for 30 June 1863; absent without leave, 31 Dec. 1863; deserted, 29 Feb. 1864; born N.C., 18-year-old farm hand in the Fannin County 1860 census.

Woodward, S[avoy] D., Private, A Company: enlisted for 3 years or the war 18 Aug. 1861 at Savannah in G Company (Brown Light Infantry, Screven County), 25th Georgia; transferred to 1st SS Battalion, 1 Aug. 1862; absent sick in Effingham County, 31 Dec. 1863; reenlisted for the war, 16 Feb. 1864; absent in General Hospital, 31 Aug. 1864; captured at Jonesboro, 1 Sep. 1864; received at Camp Douglas, Ill., 29 Oct. 1864; admitted to prison hospital with chronic diarrhea, 1 Jan. 1865; died, 20 Jan. 1865.

Wright [Right], Albert [W.], Private, A Company: enlisted for 3 years or the war 12 May 1862 at Fort Brown in B Company (Irish Jasper Greens), 1st (Olmstead's) Georgia; transferred to 1st SS Battalion, Aug. 1862; absent sick in Savannah, 31 Aug. and 30 Sep. 1862; present sick in quarters, 31 Dec. 1862; absent sick in hospital, 28 Feb. 1863; transferred to C.S. Navy, 30 June 1863.

DeKalb Rifles

These men were on the muster roll of the DeKalb Rifles when the company transferred from the 1st Georgia Volunteers into the sharpshooter battalion in August 1862 but never served with the sharpshooters.
Beier, Andrew, Private.
Bergner, Herman, Private.
Bird, Robert, Private.
Cammes or Cammis, Theodore, Private.
Cason, David, Private.
Franklin, John, Private.
Hoover, George, Private.
Krail, Fritz, Private.
Maier, William, Private.
McKenzie, Benjamin F., Private.
Morris, Wiley H., Private.
Nordheim, Charles, Private.
Pfeffer, Frederick W., Private.
Raudnitsky, Frederick, Private.
Riecke, Henry W., Private.
Rose _____, Private.
Schulz, William P., Private.
Selzer, Frederick, Private.
Tuten, Abram M., Private.
Walker, Richard, Private.
White, Patrick, Private.
Williams, John W., Private.
Wilson, Charlton L., Private.
Wolf, Morris, Private.

Incorrectly attributed to 1st Sharpshooter Battalion

Harper, J.N., Private, A Company: listed in a register of officers and soldiers killed in battle or died of wounds. John N. Harper was Private, D Company (Chatooga County), 34th Georgia; was captured in Tennessee and died a prisoner, 25 Oct. 1862. See Henderson, *Confederate Soldiers of Georgia*, 3: 789.

Johnsey, Hasting A., Private, F [sic] Company: captured 2 June 1864, at Etowah, Ga.; took oath of allegiance, 11 June 1864; confined at Rock Island, Ill., 16 June 1864; released 18 Oct. 1864, rejected by U.S. Army; residence Cass County, complexion light, hair brown, eyes blue, height 6 ft., age 33. H.A. Johnsy was Private, K Company (Murray and Gordon Counties), 1st Georgia State Line. See William Harris Bragg, *Joe Brown's Army, The Georgia State Line, 1862-1865*, 131.

Kimbrough, W.H., Private, B Company: died of disease at Lynchburg, Va., 9 Aug. 1862, residence Hains County, Ga.; reference Confederate Archives, Chapter 10, File 4, p. 142. William H. Kimbrough was Private, B Company (Muscogee County), 31st Georgia. He died of measles at General Hospital No. 2. See Henderson, *Confederate Soldiers of Georgia*, 3: 588.

King, John M., Private, B Company: died of wounds at Middleburg, [Va.?], residence Talbot County, Ga. John M. King was Private, I Company (Muscogee County), 20th Georgia, wounded at Malvern Hill, Va., 1 July 1862. See Henderson, *Confederate Soldiers of Georgia*, 2: 829.

Nix, William A., Corporal, A Company: captured Nickajack Creek or Ruff Mills, Ga., 5 July 1864; received at Camp Douglas, Ohio, 18 July 1864; released, 16 May 1865; residence Milton County. W.A. Nix was 4th Corporal, A Company (Catoosa County), 1st Georgia State Line. See Bragg, *Joe Brown's Army*, 131.

Taylor, Uel Ewell: captured Springfield, Ky., 27 Oct. 1862; died of variola or chronic diarrhoea in prison camp, Alton, Ill., 10 Feb. 1863; note in file indicates should be 1st Georgia Battery.

Uel E. Taylor was Private, B Company, 2nd Battalion Georgia Sharpshooters. See Dana M. Mangham, "Roster of the 2nd Georgia Battalion Sharpshooters, C.S.A.," *Georgia Genealogical Magazine*, 35 (No. 1-2): 73.

Turner, William M., Private: took oath of allegiance to United States at Chattanooga, 22 Aug. 1864; residence Campbell County, complexion light, hair sandy, eyes blue, height 5 ft. 9 in. Possibly William M. Turner of White County, who was Private, C Company, 65th Georgia, deserted in Tennessee, 25 July 1863, took the oath of allegiance at Chattanooga, 22 Mar. 1864. See Henderson, *Confederate Soldiers of Georgia*, 6: 610.

Waddill, Alfred, Private, I Company [sic]: captured at Etowah or Cassville, Ga., 20 May 1864; received at Rock Island, Ill., 1 June 1864; took oath of allegiance, 24 Oct. 1864; residence Resaca, complexion dark, hair light, eyes blue, height 5 ft. 8 in., age 40. Alford

Waddell was Private, I Company (Whitfield County), 1st Georgia State Line; born South Carolina, 36-year-old merchant in the Gordon County 1860 census. See Bragg, *Joe Brown's Army*, 131.

Unidentified

Bride, William T., Private, B Company: admitted with abcesses to CSA Post Hospital, Dalton, Ga., 28 Nov. 1862; no other record, not shown on any battalion muster roll.

Burnett, F.M., Private, G [sic] Company: captured Savannah, 21 Dec. 1864; admitted for debility to hospital in Savannah, 19 Jan. 1865; received at Ft. Delaware, Del., 12 Mar. 1865. No other record; not shown on any battalion muster roll.

[Possibly Barnett, Francis M.: enlisted 22 July 1861 in Capt. Jesse Burtz's company (Cherokee, Ga., Volunteers); 4th Corporal, 25 Sep. 1861; became Capt. Smith's company, Wise Legion ("Concord Rangers," Forsyth and Dawson counties), 26 Sep. 1861; became D Company, 2nd N.C. Battalion; became new Company E, 21st Georgia, 11 Apr. 1864; Barnett was last on MR for 31 Oct. 1862. See Henderson, *Confederate Soldiers of Georgia*, 2: 878.]

Edsall, D.A., Private, A Company: prisoner in jail, Macon, Ga., Nov. 1863; receipt for clothing, 8 Dec. 1863; no other record.

Harris, Benjamin F., Private, B Company: patient at the post hospital, Dalton, Ga., 28 Nov. to 24 Dec. 1862; not shown on any battalion muster roll.

Hoover, William, Private, D Company: captured Cassville, Ga., 20 May 1864; received at Rock Island, Ill., 1 June 1864; enlisted in U.S. Navy, 10 June 1864; name appears on no battalion muster roll.

Howard, Appleton W., Private: took oath of allegiance to U.S. at Chattanooga, 23 Aug. 1864; residence Henry County, Ala., complexion dark, hair light, eyes light, height 6 ft. 1 in.; name appears on no muster roll; no Confederate soldier of this name can be found in any NARA record.

Reddy, Richard, Private, C Company: enrolled May 1864 at Augusta, Ga.; reported as rebel deserter at Rowlesburg, W. Va., 15 Nov. 1864; took oath of allegiance and released, 16 Nov. 1864; born Ireland, residence Augusta, age 25, complexion fair, hair dark, eyes brown, height 5 ft. 6 in., occupation moulder; appears on no battalion muster roll.

INDEX